THE HARP IN THE MIDDLE AGES

Cover illustration: Munich, Bayerische Staatsbibliothek, Clm. 14523, f. 52r (detail), schematic drawing of a 'delta harp'. Freising (10th century).

THE HARP IN THE MIDDLE AGES

THE SYMBOLISM OF A MUSICAL INSTRUMENT

by

MARTIN VAN SCHAIK

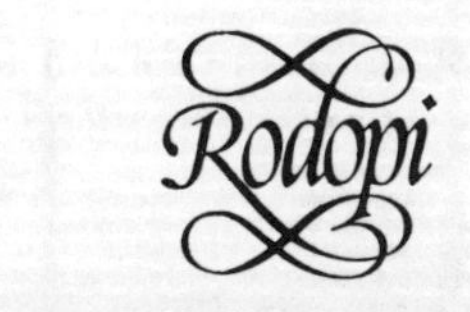

Amsterdam - Atlanta, GA 1992

The publication of this book has been made possible by financial contributions from:
— The Prins Bernhard Fonds
— The Janivo Stichting
— The Stichting Dr Hendrik Muller's Vaderlandsch Fonds

CIP-GEGEVENS KONINKLIJKE BIBLIOTHEEK, DEN HAAG

Schaik, Martin van

The harp in the Middle Ages : the symbolism of a musical instrument / Martin van Schaik. — Amsterdam - Atlanta, GA : Rodopi. — Ill.
Met lit. opg., reg.
ISBN 90-5183-367-9
Trefw.: harpen ; geschiedenis ; middeleeuwen / harpen ; iconografie.

Printed in The Netherlands

**TO MARIAN, EVELIEN
AND HELEEN**

CONTENTS

Introduction 9

Chapter 1 — Name and object
1.1. Introduction 16
1.2. Etymology 17
1.3. Name and object in medieval literature 19
1.3.1. Name and object in the glosses 23
1.4. Name and object in illuminations 32
1.5. Conclusion 36

Chapter 2 — The harp and David
2.1. Introduction 38
2.2. The harp: symbol and attribute 39
2.2.1. Ordering the microcosmos 39
2.2.2. Ordering the macrocosmos 44
2.3. Tuning as the reflection of reality 51
2.4. Conclusion 58

Chapter 3 — The delta harp
3.1. Introduction 62
3.2. Written evidence 63
3.2.1. Denomination 65
3.2.2. The delta form 70
3.3. Number of strings 76
3.4. Symbolic interpretations 77
3.4.1. Numerical symbolism 77
3.4.2. Symbolic contrasts 81
3.5. Symbol or actual instrument? 85
3.6. Conclusion 90

Chapter 4 — The harp in the Psalm initials
4.1. Introduction 91
4.2. Psalter plans 92
4.2.1. Illumination of initials 95
4.3. Harp illuminations in the Psalm initials 96
4.4. Conclusion 114

Chapter 5 — Ονος λύρας: The ass with the harp
5.1. Introduction 116
5.2. The written tradition of the lemma ὄνος λύρας 117
5.3. Paradox 126
5.4. The ass with the harp in illustrations 129
5.5. Conclusion 134

Excursion — The concept of *mensura* in the Psalm initials 136

Notes 143

Appendices — Overview of sources of pictorial material 170
I. The harp and David 170
II. The delta harp 176
A. Delta harps 176
B. Schematic representations of instruments resembling delta harps 177
III. The harp in the Psalm initials 178
IV. The ass with the harp 189

Abbreviations 192

Bibliography 193

List of illustrations 207

Illustrations 213

Index 241

INTRODUCTION

Swer die schrift verstên kan eben,
Der vindet künic Davîdes harpfen klanc.[1]

'He who can fully understand the Holy Scriptures,
will find the sound of King David's harp.'

The above quotation from the didactic poem *Der Renner* by the German author Hugh of Trimberg, which was probably written shortly before 1300,[2] refers to the subject-matter under investigation in the present study, which can be defined as the question of the interpretation of the medieval harp as a Christian symbol. The biblical figure of King David has a special relevance in relation to the significance of the harp. He is pictured with a harp innumerable times and in many different guises. Contemporary researchers of musical iconography assume that the various modes of appearance of the medieval harp — modes of appearance that strike us, here in the twentieth century, as stereotype — each had an individual meaning. These deeper meanings must be sought in the concepts represented by the various modes of appearance of the harp.

Although attributing symbolic significance to musical instruments in the Middle Ages was not in itself unusual, it was exceptional to treat a musical instrument then actually extant, as a symbol. In this respect the harp is unique among medieval musical instruments. The origin of the meanings which were attached to musical instruments in the Middle Ages was almost invariably religious with roots in the Bible exegesis of the Greek and Latin Church Fathers from the first centuries of our era.[3] Their purpose was to endow the musical instruments mentioned in the Old and New Testaments with a higher significance. The immediate motive for this was the moral opposition of the Church Fathers to the use of musical instruments in daily life and in the worship of gods.

In view of the religious context in which the harp was depicted in the Middle Ages, it is easy to imagine that its significance also was influenced — either directly or indirectly — by the biblical exegesis of the Church Fathers. The opinions of those who have conducted studies into the symbolism of the harp diverge. It is unclear whether the harp in the Holy Scriptures is an interpretation of one particular instrument (for example the *cithara, psalterium* or *lyra*), or of a group of instruments (for example, stringed instruments). This gap in our knowledge complicates research on the significance of the harp. It makes it very difficult to draw a boundary-line between the harp as symbol and as a real instrument in illustrations and written sources from the Middle Ages. Contemporary musical iconographical literature has not identified any basic criteria for such a division. This study aims to make a contribution to enlarging our understanding of the transmission and significance of the symbolism of the harp. I have attempted, as far as is feasible and necessary, to indicate a border-line between the harp as a symbol and as a real instrument.

This study has an interdisciplinary character — it involves theology, music studies and the history of art and literature — and has two major pillars. The first is iconographical research into the themes of the illustrations in which harps figure in medieval art, the second is an examination of the facts as they have been handed down and the significance of the harp in texts surviving from the Middle Ages. Many sorts of texts have been consulted, including the Holy Scriptures, biblical exegesis, glosses, theoretical writings on music and secular literature.

In order to distinguish between the harp as symbol and as a real instrument, it is necessary to study statements from secular poetry and treatises on musical theory. In poetry, especially, representations of the ideal give some indication of reality. For instance, poetic statements tell us how the harp was played and tuned.

By combining the study of texts with that of iconographical themes, we can gain an insight into the symbolic explanation; this dual approach is still lacking in many studies on instruments.

I do not wish to give excessive attention to the concepts of symbol and attribute in this introduction. Nevertheless, a slightly more detailed definition of their meanings would seem appropriate at the beginning of a study in which they occupy such a key position.

The following abstract description can be given of the concept of symbol: a symbol is a concentration of a concept or of a composite of concepts in a single representation.[4] In contemporary daily life the meaning of symbol is so diluted as to be synonymous with picture. But this is dangerous. We are not concerned with what a symbol is in a modern context but in a medieval one. The symbolism of the harp forms a part of the Christian allegory of instruments. The concealed meanings of the musical instruments reported in the Bible are the core of this allegory.[5]

In the *Studien zur Symbolik der Musikinstrumente im Schrifttum der alten und mittelalterlichen Kirche* by Helmut Giesel, which appeared in 1978, the concepts of allegory and symbolism are extensively discussed in connection with instruments. My descriptions of the concepts symbol and attribute are based on Giesel's study.

A symbol is a sign or an object which can be experienced through the senses and which represents something spiritual or abstract. The significance of symbols in medieval instrumental allegory is not clear-cut. Exegetes understood a musical instrument as a sign (*significatio*), a proof of one of the truths contained in the Holy Scriptures. This means that a sensually observable object (in other words, the form, the components or the sound which an object produces) is used to clarify a supernatural, spiritual idea. This applies particularly to the meaning of the harp in relation to David.

In medieval art the harp is the attribute of David. An attribute is an emblematic token which accompanies a depicted person. The harp ensures that David can be distinguished from others. Although at first glance an attribute does not seem to be a symbol in the real sense, and in fact it is not, the concepts of attribute and symbol are often very close.

I make a contrast between the harp as a symbol and the harp as a real instrument. I am aware that, due to the fact that there are virtually no extant harps dating from medieval times, every statement about the actual characteristics of this instrument is, in fact, hypothetical. Investigations into these characteristics imply an attempt to approximate reality, and sometimes non-medieval material has been used for comparison. However, despite this impediment, it is possible, on the grounds of the insight that has been gained into the symbolism of the harp, to adjust contemporary opinions on such matters as the form and placement of the tuning-pegs on the medieval harp.

An abundance of information on the medieval harp has come down to us via illustrations and writings. However, the amount of this material contrasts with the number of modern publications specifically devoted to this medieval instrument. We may even speak of a discrepancy between the extensive source material and the very few detailed studies on the subject. This can be partially explained by the inaccessibility of the source material. Studies based on quantitive data, like the present one, are possible only by virtue of large collections of photographs, such as that of the The Index of Christian Art of the Department of Art History of the Rijksuniversiteit of Utrecht. The iconographical source material used in this study is virtually all drawn from the above-mentioned Index, and would have remained largely out of reach without such a photographic collection.

If we make a chronological inventory of the most important studies in which the symbolic meaning of the harp in the Middle Ages has figured, then Hugo Steger's *David Rex et Propheta* of 1961 should be mentioned first. Steger carried out fundamental research into the iconographical representation of King David in medieval art. His broadly-based study covers a long period and touches many aspects of David. The fourth chapter gives an exposition on musical instruments; the harp of David is also discussed. Taking his own research as a starting point, Steger makes some assertions about the harp as an attribute of David and about the triangular shape of the harp.

The dissertation of Rosalyn Rensch which appeared in 1964 was the first study which took the medieval harp specifically as its subject. Her book, *Symbolism and form of the harp in western European manuscript illuminations of the ninth to the sixteenth century*, may be considered as the only publication completely devoted to the early harp. Using a large number of illustrations, Rensch sketches a picture of the development and transmission of the form of the harp. In doing so she pays much attention to the various hybrid forms of the harp from the ninth and tenth centuries. She makes a number of general statements on the symbolism of the harp.

In his study *König Davids Harfe in der abendländischen Kunst*, published in 1968, Hans Zingel gives a short description of the development, the designation and supposed symbolic interpretations of the harp of David. The book is a more complete version of his article, *Die Harfe als Symbol und allegorisches Attribut* which appeared in 1957.

Frederick Pickering is one of the few authors to attribute an entirely symbolic significance to the harp. In the chapter *Harp and bow*, in *Literature and art in the Middle Ages,* published in 1970, Pickering maintains that the harp is a symbol of the crucifixion. He supports this by reverting selectively to one particular explanation which is given in biblical exegesis.

The study of Tilman Seebass, *Musikdarstellung und Psalterillustration im früheren Mittelalter*, which, like that of Steger, appeared in 1973, is also broadly conceived. Seebass gives details of the symbolic significance of King David from different iconographical angles. A large number of musical instruments are discussed in this way, including the harp.

In his treatise *Harfen Westeuropas im Mittelalter* of 1977, the organologist Leopold Vorreiter adopts the approach of Rosalyn Rensch. He also tries to give a picture of the development of the form of the medieval harp. He links form and symbolic meaning. However, Vorreiter's conclusions show that he is not conversant with recent opinions, such as those of Steger and Seebass, concerning the symbolism of instruments.

In her article *Zum Problem der Klassifizierung von Harfendarstellungen in der Buchmalerei des frühen und hohen Mittelalters*, written in 1969, Dagmar Droysen presents her own classification system. The aim of this system is to make it possible to distinguish between the real and symbolic characteristics of harps found in illuminations. Her method makes it possible to formulate certain laws, but it does not explain them.

The excellent dissertation of Genette Foster, *The iconology of musical instruments and musical performance in thirteenth-century French manuscript illuminations*, which dates from 1977, is a major work. She handles the combinations of instruments pictured in French manuscripts fully. The appendix listing descriptions of combinations of instruments which appear in these manuscripts is very useful. Foster ascribes a symbolic meaning to the theme of David tuning the harp.

The unpublished thesis *Anglo-Saxon Hearpan: Their terminology, technique, tuning and repertory of verse 850-1066* of 1981 by Christopher Page, is entirely devoted to the harp in the Middle Ages. It follows the development of the harp in English-speaking regions before the Norman conquest.

In his article *The Trecento harp* published in 1983, Howard Mayer Brown gives an exposition of the iconographical representation of the harp in fourteenth-century Italy. Brown regards the theme of David with the harp in illuminations as a tradition adopted from France and quite unconnected with the Italian musical tradition.

The book, *Harfenbedeutungen*, by Bernd Kalusche dates from 1986. The subtitle, *Ideale, ästhetische und reale Funktionen eines Musikinstruments in der abendländischen Kunst — Eine Bedeutungsgeschichte,* indicates the wide scope of the study. Proceeding from a number of illustrations and artistic objects, the author treats the harp as a "Bedeutungsträger" in western art. As far as the significance of the harp in the Middle Ages is concerned, Kalusche refers principally to the often out-of-date opinions of Hans Zingel. He rarely quotes from important regenerative publications, such as those of Steger, Seebass and Foster. The main value of Kalusche's book with respect to the symbolism of the medieval harp is his inventory of existing opinions. His study does not make any significant contribution to pioneering research into the meaning of the harp.

It is essential to define the area of investigation in any study into the symbolic aspects of the medieval harp.

First, the boundaries in time. For a number of reasons my research has been chiefly directed to the harp in the period from c. 1000 to c. 1400. The prime one is that, from the eleventh century, there is steadily more evidence of a positive link between the name harp and the object harp. The number of surviving illustrations featuring harps increases notably in this period, to such an extent, in fact, that it is impossible to give a complete survey. Besides, this is not necessary. The conclusions are supported by a maximum number of sources with more or less the same themes. These are indicated in the pictorial material included in the appendices. A second reason for limiting research to this period is that it is possible to draw parallels between iconographical and written source materials in Latin and in the vernacular. A reliable picture of the significance of the harp can be gained by studying not only the surviving interpretations of the illustrations from the same period, but also the illustrations themselves.

The choice of the period 1000 to 1400 does not mean that no useful information on the harp survives from before the year 1000. On the contrary, it has been necessary to turn repeatedly to older, primarily written, sources. The reason is self-evident when we consider that the basis for the medieval interpretation was laid hundreds of years earlier.

A second limitation was the number of aspects of the harp in the Middle Ages which were researched. I have selected five subjects which may at first seem rather unconnected. Virtually nothing was known about some of these subjects until now ("Name and object", "The delta harp", "The harp in the initials of the Psalms"). Others have only been partially investigated and opinions on their significance are divided ("The harp and David", "Ονος λύρας: the ass with the harp"). Despite the various chapter headings, the harp in relation to David provides, to a greater or lesser extent, the connecting thread throughout the study. The current state of research into the subjects discussed is dealt with separately in the introduction to each chapter. The chapters end with a "conclusion" in which the most important conclusions are summarized. An excursion is added after the last chapter in which the *mensura* symbolism in the Psalm illuminations is considered.

The third limitation was geographical in nature, since the source material originated chiefly in France, England, Germany and Italy. The illustration centers in these countries were leaders in the art of illumination.

During the investigation it was continuously necessary to digress beyond the boundaries of music studies in the strict sense, making it possible to approach the problem areas in an interdisciplinary way. The result is a study with a rather unconventional set-up. However, in my opinion, the intertwining of iconographical, music historical, theological and literary aspects results in a better understanding of the symbolism of the harp.

Leaving the boundaries of one's own discipline is always a perilous undertaking. There are problems, especially practical ones, for example how to extract the required information from other disciplines, and dangers, such as misinterpreting the information, or not being able to interpret it at all. Fortunately, I received support in tackling these difficulties from many medievalists within the Faculteit der Letteren of the Rijksuniversiteit of Utrecht, and elsewhere. I would, therefore, like to conclude this introduction with a word of thanks.

Although it is impossible to thank all those who have personally contributed in the last years to the realization of this study, I would nevertheless like to mention a few names. First I would like to thank Dr. C. Vellekoop for his most expert and critical guidance in the area of musicology, and Prof. Dr. J.C.J.A. Klamt, who directed me along the right track through the history of art. I would like to thank the following persons especially: Dr. L. Okken, for his critical comments and philosophical attitude which has left its mark on the manner in which the source material has been digested; Prof. Dr.

A.P. Orbán, for his comments on my Latin translations; Prof. Dr. T. Seebass (Duke University, Durham, U.S.A.) and Prof. Dr. W. Zwanenburg for their valuable comments on Chapters 1 and 2; Prof. Dr. G.R. Dolezalek (Max Planck-Institut für europäische Rechtsgeschichte, Frankfurt am Main) for his help in solving a specific iconographic problem in Chapter 5; the harp builder R. Thurau (Wiesbaden, Germany) for the clarification given by his vision on a number of technical points concerning the construction of the medieval harp; Prof. Dr. H.W. Bodewitz and Drs. J. Bodewitz, Dr. E.S. Kooper and Dr. R.E.V. Stuip for their help with the translation of Greek, Middle English and Old French texts. I wish to express thanks to my wife Marian, for the many hours she spent looking up photographic material in The Index of Christian Art, for her repeated reading of the typescript and the way in which she has supported the enterprise during the last years.

Finally a word of special thanks to Penelope Baldwin, David Collyer and Nienke de Boer for their help during the various stages of the translation.

CHAPTER 1

NAME AND OBJECT

1.1. INTRODUCTION

The present state of research into the relationship between the denomination of the harp on the one hand and the object on the other, does not enable us to piece together a consistent idea of the developments which led to the designation of the instrumental denomination *harpa* and its etymological equivalents in the vernacular. In the present chapter we will see that, in principle, the Latin term *harpa* and its vernacular equivalents are used in the same way. Hereafter I shall, unless otherwise stated, use *harpa* to refer to the Latin term as well as its equivalents.

The term *harpa* was used as the name for a large number of very diverse objects ranging from a harrow, a corn sieve, an instrument of torture, a shelf for drying corn to musical instruments.[1] On the other hand the instrument, the harp, was indicated by the Latin terms *cithara*, *psalterium* or *lyra* in medieval religious writings.

Research into the relationship between *harpa* and the object harp is characterized by two basic problems. Firstly, the surviving data does not indicate what object was first designated by this name. Secondly, we do not know what criterion the name-giver took as the basis for the name. In other words, the etymology of the word *harpa* is hypothetical.

Western harps all belong to the same basic type, the frame harp. A representation of a stringed instrument must satisfy a number of criteria to merit the predicate of harp.[2] The instrument must have a framework which at least includes a sound box and a peg arm (neck). Freestanding (open) strings must be strung between the sound box and the pegs. Such a simple construction cannot, of course, support tight strings. Simple frame harps are pictured most frequently in ninth- and tenth-century illuminated Psalm manuscripts. From the first half of the eleventh century until the second half of the fourteenth century, we encounter a more sophisticated type of harp. The difference between this and the simple frame harp is that there is a curved forepillar (column) between the end of the neck and the lowest part of the sound box. The three separate parts of the framework can be clearly distinguished. This construction is capable of supporting tighter strings. Such a type of harp is sometimes referred to as the "Romanesque harp". The name "Romanesque" indicates the period in which this type of harp was used. The Romanesque harp is the most frequently portrayed of all medieval harps. Both the simple frame harp and the Romanesque harp are played by plucking the strings with the fingers.

In order to be able to distinguish a harp from a harp-psaltery in illuminations I would propose one further criterion, namely that the same background color must be visible between the harp strings as that which can be seen outside the framework of the instrument. Sometimes it is even possible to see the hand of the harpist on the back of the strings. In any case the color of the background must differ from that of the peg arm, the column and the sound box. This criterion makes it possible to prevent the harp-psaltery, which has a sound board behind the strings, from also being called a harp. However, this distinction does not hold true for sculptured harps, as will be seen in Chapter 5.4.

In this chapter I will examine the relationship between the use of the name and the mode of appearance of the musical instrument, the harp.

1.2. ETYMOLOGY

One of the oldest surveys on the etymology of *harpa* is the article *Wörter und Sachen*, written in 1904 by Rudolf Meringer.[3] Meringer, like many later scholars, proceeds from the Germanic root **harppō*.[4] Using the rule '*pp* comes from *pn, bn, bhn*', he reconstructs three pre-Germanic forms **korpnā* ('the calling one'; the Gothic *hropjan*), **korbnā* ('the murmuring one'; the Latin *crepare*) and **korbhnā* ('the plucker'; the pre-Germanic **korbā*). Meringer prefers the last form.

If investigation is limited to a reconstruction of the etymology of the word *harpa* in the sense of stringed instrument, this word origin would seem plausible. **Korbā* is the ablaut of the root **ker(b)*, "krümmen, sich zusammenkrümmen". **Ker(b)* can be regarded as a variant of the root **sker-* but without the *s*.[5] As I see it, the word *harpa* originally referred to the manner of playing the harp. The root **kerb* in its meaning of 'curving', 'drawing together', is suggestive of the manner in which the instrument is played: curved fingers pluck the strings.[6] The meaning of **korbhnā* fits in well with this idea. Moreover, the sound sequence of **ker(b)* corresponds well with that of the word *harpa*.[7] No etymological link can be shown between the word **kerb* and the Latin verb *carpere* ('to pluck'), in the sense of 'plucking strings'.[8]

Other possible origins of the name, such as the imitation of the sound of the harp or the shape of the instrument, are much more difficult to connect to the meanings that have been handed down.

The Germanic **harppōn* can also be placed alongside **harppō*. The Gothic **harpa* is formed from the Germanic **harppō/harppōn* and acted as a representative of Germanic at the time of the European migrations. This would mean that all late Latin and Romance forms are, therefore, derived from these two words.[9] These variants can be divided in two groups: one with an aspirate (beginning with **h**), the second group without (beginning with **a**). Schema 1 gives a schematic representation of the etymology sketched above.

Schema 1. Reconstruction of the etymology of the harp.

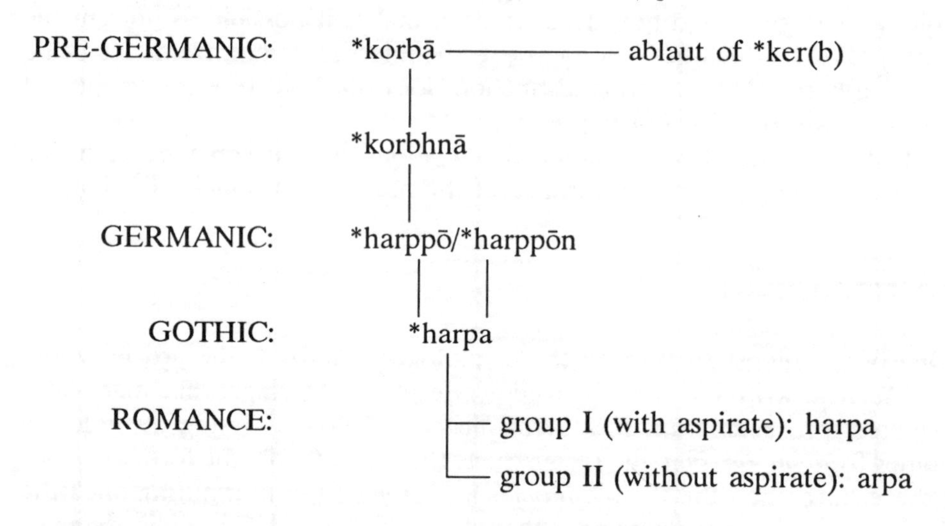

It is generally considered that the word *arpa*, which belongs to the second group, is borrowed from the Germanic.[10] It is difficult to defend the reasoning that the Gothic *harpa*, which is used to denote a musical instrument, is an old word borrowed from Greek. As far as I am aware, there is no single place in Greek literature where the word is used to indicate a musical instrument.[11]

We find an interesting derivative of the word *arpa* in the *Elementarium doctrinae rudimentum* by the Italian lexicographer Papias, dating from c. 1053. In it Papias explains: *Arpa dicta a gente Arporum, qui hoc instrumentum musicum invenerunt*, 'Arpa is named after the Arpi tribe, who first discovered this musical instrument.'[12] Papias' statement is based on the commentary that the scholar Remigius of Auxerre wrote around 900 on the fifth-century encyclopedia *De nuptiis Philologiae et Mercurii* of Martianus Capella. Remigius describes the relation of the personified Philology to the *Arpae* in the following words:

> DENIQUE PERTERRITA ipsa Philologia, ARPIS id est musicis instrumentis. Arpa autem dicta a gente Arporum qui primi hoc musicum instrumentum reppererunt.[13]

'Finally Philology herself was frightened by (h)arps, that is to say, musical instruments. Arpa, however, is named after the people of Arpi who first discovered this musical instrument.'

It is not clear on what information Remigius based his statement about the discovery of the harp. His explanation runs contrary to the surviving meanings of the word harp. It is possibly his own interpretation. In any case Martianus Capella made no reference to a musical instrument called the *(h)arpa* in his encyclopedia:

Denique *h*arpis bombisque perterrita tam intoleranda congressione virgo diffugit.[14]

'Finally, frightened by the Harpies and the growling noises, the maiden [=Philology] fled from such an unbearable meeting.'

By the term *(h)arpa* in the above quotation Martianus most probably means the Harpies, the storm demons of Greek mythology. According to Homer (*Odyssey*, Book XX, v. 76-8), they took on the guise of a bird of prey and the face of a girl. Obviously Remigius of Auxerre was not acquainted with this explanation.

1.3. NAME AND OBJECT IN MEDIEVAL LITERATURE

The problem of the relationship between name and object is felt most acutely when interpreting literary sources. In Chapters 1.3 to 1.5 we will see that, in addition to the term *harpa*, above all the biblical indication of *cithara* is used to denote the harp. Generally speaking it is not possible to deduce whether we are really concerned with a harp in the organological sense of the word from texts in which a *harpa* instrument is referred to.

The first evidence of the Latin indication of the instrument *harpa* can be taken to be a poem by Venantius Fortunatus (c. 530-601), Bishop of Poitiers. In his seventh book, *carmen* 8, lines 63-4 Venantius Fortunatus writes:

Romanusque lyra, plaudat tibi barbarus harpa,
Graecus Achilliaca, crotta Britanna canat.[15]

'And may the Roman bring you homage with the lyra, the German with the harpa, the Greek sing Achilles' songs, and the Briton sound the crotta.'

The term *barbarus* in the quotation above probably refers to the tribes of central Europe: the Germans. The relation between the instrument, the *harpa*, and the *barbari*, 'the Germans', has a remarkable literary parallel. In Lib. III, cap. 22,7 of his encyclopedic *Etymologiae*, Isidore of Seville (c. 560-636) used the words *cithara barbarica* to denote the musical instrument the *psalterium*. It is not clear whether the *harpa* and the *cithara barbarica* are two different terms for the same instrument. (The connection between the *cithara barbarica* and the *psalterium* will be discussed in Chapter 3.2.1.)

In the Old English poems *Beowulf* and *Widsith*, both dating from the end of the seventh century, *hearpe* is used as the name of an instrument.[16] Although this word exhibits an etymological similarity with the term *harpa*, we cannot be sure from the texts whether the stringed instrument indicated by *hearpe* really is a harp. The name is not used in these texts together with other instruments, so that no conclusions can be drawn from combinations of instruments. I find the assumption of Rensch that the instrument called *hearpe* in *Beowulf* refers to a *crwth*, a bowed asymmetrical lyre, extremely speculative.[17] The medieval *lira/lîre* is a relation of the ancient *lyra* and, moreover, the only type of lyre known in the Middle Ages.

From my own investigation into combinations of instruments in German literature in the period 800-1350, it can be concluded that terminologically the word *lîre* is used particularly to show a contrast with the instrument name *harfe*.[18] In more extensive combinations this is also the case with such indications as *rotte, videl/gîge* and *sambiût*. This observation is also supported by the harp glosses (see Chapter 1.3.1). The German account of the *Apollonius* story provides an exception with respect to the relationship between lyre and harp. In the story *Apollonius von Tyrland* (c. 1300-10), written by Heinrich of Neustadt, there is a detailed passage on the harp-playing of Apollonius in which the instrument is referred to by using the German *harpfe*.[19] The passage is based on the sixteenth chapter of the anonymous version of the *Historia Apollonii Regis Tyri*, which dates from the end of the fifth or the beginning of the sixth century. In this late Roman work, however, there is no single mention of a harp, only of a *lyra*.[20]

Another source in which there is a reference to the instrument *harpa* is the work of Milo (c. 809-c. 872), a monk in the monastery of St.-Amand near Tournay. In his poem *De sobrietate* he describes the excessive luxury and decadence displayed at a meal of Herod. This negative context also includes a list of musical instruments[21]:

Ebrietas luxus petulantia lusus inanis
Harpa lirae cytharae psalteria fistula musae
Cimbala sambucae simphonia timpana sistra.

'Dipsomania, luxury, licentiousness, senseless games, harpa, lyres, citharas, psalteria, flutes, muses, cymbala, sambucas, symphonia, drums, sistra.'

From the combination of instruments mentioned in the above quotation — *harpa, lira, cithara, psalterium* — we can only conclude that *harpa* probably refers to a (plucked) stringed instrument.

A clearer statement about the instrumental category to which the harp belongs can be found c. 900 in the *Epistola de harmonica institutione* by the German cleric Regino of Prüm. Regino includes a classification of musical instruments in this theoretical treatise on music. The musical instruments are divided into the three categories customary in the Middle Ages, that is stringed, wind and percussion instruments. He includes the *harpa* among the *tensibilia*, the 'stringed instruments'. In the words of Regino:

Tensibile fit intensione chordarum, ut puta in lyra, cithara, harpa, & huiusmodi.[22]

'Tension is achieved by stretching strings, as for example, in the case of a lyra, cithara, harpa and similar.'

The quotation from Regino's letter is the earliest evidence of a reference to the instrument name *harpa* in a theoretical text on music.

In the *Vita Sancti Dunstani*, a saintly life of St. Dunstan (c. 910-88) which was presumably written around the year 1000, there is a clear statement concerning the interpretation of the term cithara as 'harp'. The author says that Dunstan: [...] *sumpsit secum ex more cytharam suam quam lingua paterna hearpam vocamus*, 'as usual took up his *cithara* which we call *hearpa* in our language.'[23]

The translation of the term *psalterium,* indicating an instrument, with the word *harpa* only occurs in a religious context, for example in the commentary on the Psalms of Notker Teutonicus (c. 950-1022), a monk in the monastery at St.-Gall. Notker's writing, which dates from after 1000, gives an explanation of the concept *psalterium* in his discussion of Psalm 146:1.[24] *Psalterium* had several meanings in the Middle Ages and he translated it in different ways, including *harpfa*:

Vuaz ist daz? ane daz man an psalterio singet. Psalterium scillet also éin lîra. alde éin harpfa. alde éin organum.[25]

'What is it, except that it is sung from the psaltery? The psaltery sounds as a lyre, or a harp, or an organum.'

In view of the interpretation which Notker Teutonicus gives to the instrument described as *psalterium*, it is doubtful if he took the word to mean a harp-psaltery. In view of the literal meaning of the word, *psalterium* could refer to an instrument which served 'to praise God'. In that case *psalterium* could mean any stringed instrument used for this purpose.

A corresponding translation of the instrument name *psalterium* is found in the English Cambridge Psalter which dates from the twelfth century.[26] This manuscript includes Psalm texts in both Latin and Old English; the English text is a translation from the Latin. The instruments termed as *psalterium* and *cithara* are translated with *hearpan* as well as with *saltyre* and *citre*.

The anonymous *Ruodlieb* epic is the first literary source which includes a clear indication on how the harp was played. The *terminus a quo* ascribed to the poem is the year 1043, while the latest possible date is fixed at c. 1075.[27] The text of lines 38-9 of fragment XI is:

Pulsans mox leva] digitis geminis, modo dextra
tangendo chordas dulces reddit nimis odas.[28]

'He played the sweetest songs, now plucking the strings with two fingers of the left hand and then again with the right hand.'

The words *laeva* and *dextra* indicate the place where the hands are placed during playing, namely on the left and right hand of the harp respectively. This manner of playing agrees with other evidence from medieval illuminations and corresponds with present practice.

Another statement concerning the relationship between the name harp and the object harp is found in the *Tristan* story written c. 1210 by Gottfried of Strassburg.[29] In lines 8064-5, from the passage describing the great musicality of Princess Isolde, we can read that Isolde played the harp 'on both sides'. In the words of lines 8064-5:

Ir liren unde ir harpfenspil
sluoc si ze beiden wenden.[30]

Like the playing manner recounted in the *Ruodlieb* epic, this description in the *Tristan* story confirms what we know from medieval illuminations. In neither text can the instrument indicated by *harpa* and *harpfe* possibly have been a harp-psaltery.

From the beginning of the thirteenth century, the term harp seems to have been used consistently in poetry as the name for the musical instrument the harp.

1.3.1. NAME AND OBJECT IN THE GLOSSES

The problem of interpretation in connection with the relationship between name and object is also present in the glosses. The glossaries — lists of words or expressions with explanations — yield a scale of lemmata which are translated with *harpa*.

Medieval harp glosses have primarily come down to us in the form of compilations; this is especially true of glosses from the Old German linguistic area. One classic work is the *Glossarium Latino-Germanicum Mediae et Infimae Aetatis* of Lorenz Diefenbach from 1857. The five-volume publication, *Die althochdeutschen Glossen* of Elias Steinmeyer and Eduard Sievers (1879-1922), is slightly more recent. There is also the latest but only partially published *Althochdeutsches Glossenwörterbuch* edited by Taylor Starck and J. Wells (1972-.).

I have been able to check the texts originally used as source material for a number of harp glosses. First, there are the biblical passages, Daniel 3:5 and I Samuel 18:6. Further, the poems *Apotheosis*, *Cathemerinon* and *Peristefanon* by the Christian poet, Aurelius Prudentius Clemens (348-c. 410).

The manuscript collection of glosses *Summarium Heinrici* deserves a separate mention. This book, consisting of eleven glossaries, is regarded as a first attempt to present information in a scientifically systematic way in the German language. The books were compiled by a certain Heinricus, probably a schoolteacher from Lorsch, and are dated between c. 1021 and 1076.[31] The harp glosses in the *Summarium* are, as far as is known, based on the *Etymologiae* of Isidore of Seville.

The search for Latin names which are entered in the glosses as *harpa* resulted in the following inventory. The lemmata refer to the three categories into which instruments were classified: stringed, wind and percussion instruments. For the sake of completeness, a group of lemmata has been added which, although entered as *harpa*, does not refer to musical instruments. (In the inventory the indication Gl refers to the publication of Steinmeyer-Sievers. The indication of the respective section is followed after the comma by the page number and after the full stop by the line number where the gloss is found. The source reference is given after this in curved brackets.)

A. Stringed instruments

a) chelys	Gl II,	408.26:	*Chelis .i. musa vel harpha*
		485.43:	*harepha*
			(Prudentius, *Apotheosis*, v. 388).
		513. 8:	*hb̆phb* = *hárpha*; *hárffa*
			(Prudentius [*Apotheosis*, v. 388]).
		526. 1:	*hbrbphb* = *harapha*;
		537.27:	*Gelis harpha vel misa vel citara*;
		565.16:	*harfa*; *harfb*;
	Gl IV,	345.30:	*harpa*
			(Prudentius, *Apotheosis*, v. 388).[32]
b) testudo	Gl II,	457.40:	*Testudo haraffa vel cyt(h)arhus*;
		482 :	note 13: "Über chelis in demselben Verse scheint harpha gestanden zu haben (482.44: *testudo-cythara*);
		542.72:	*haraffa*
			(Prudentius, *Apotheosis*, v. 388).[33]

Although this is not explicitly stated in the glosses, both *chelys* and *testudo* can be counted as stringed instruments. The term *chelys* usually refers to a tortoise-shell lyre. *Testudo*, which can indicate any vaulted stringed instrument, is translated as *harpa* or *cythara* in Gl II 457.40. Verse 388 from the book *Apotheosis* of Prudentius is mentioned as source for both glosses. That verse is part of a passage about the use of musical instruments to praise Christ. The text of verse 388 gives no definite indication of the nature of the instruments:

Quidquid casta chelys, quidquid testudo resultat.[34]

'All the sounds from the chaste chelys and the testudo.'

I encountered only a few sporadic instances of the gloss which would have seemed most likely in this connection, namely that of *lyra-harpa*. Diefenbach mentions such a gloss twice. He names a *Glossarium Batavicum*, which he dates as being from the fourteenth century, as his source.[35]

A remarkable gloss is that of *chelys* with *musa* in a tenth-century Prudentius glossary. In Gl II, 408.26 and 537.27 *musa* and *harpa* are given as alternatives for *chelys*.
Musa is an indication of an instrument which we first meet in the *Epistola de harmonica institutione* of Regino of Prüm, where the instrument is grouped with the wind instruments.[36]

c) sambuca Gl II, 482. 38: *harephân*
(Prudentius, *Apotheosis*, v. 148).[37]

There is confusion about the nature of the instrument referred to as the *sambuca*. In the Book of Daniel the instrument is mentioned four times, the first instance being Daniel 3:5:

In hora qua audieritis sonitum tubae et fistulae et citharae / sambucae et psalterii et symphoniae et universi generis musicorum.

'As soon as you hear the sound of the horn, flute, cithara, sambuca, psalterium, symphonia and every sort of musical instruments.'

The term *sambuca* is repeated in lists of instruments in Daniel 3:7, 3:10 and 3:15. During the Middle Ages there was a lot of speculation about the nature and origins of this instrument in exegesis and in encyclopedic writings.[38] In his *Etymologiae* (Lib. III, cap. 21,7), Isidore counts it among the wind instruments. Papias in his *Elementarium doctrinae rudimentum* adopts Isidore's opinion and adds the alternative meaning of *Sambuca genus citharae rusticae*, 'a sort of peasant cithara'.[39] It is very doubtful if Papias was aware that the term *sambuca* was a Latin translation of the Greek *sambykē* — the name for a harp.
The text from the *Apotheosis* by Prudentius is probably an allusion to one of the passages from the biblical Book of Daniel. In the words of the *Apotheosis*, v. 147-8:

Haec ait et varios iubet obmutescere cantus, organa sambucas citharas calamosque tubasque.[40]

'He speaks thus and commands the songs, the organs, the sambucas, the citharas, the reed flutes and the trumpets to be still.'

d) cythara Gl III, 65. 1-2: *harpha; harpha; harfa; härpf* (*Summarium Heinrici*, Lib. II,18: De musicorum vasis = Hildebrandt 1974, p. 111): *Cithara harpha cuius forma inicio similis fuisse traditur pectori humano, quia uti vox e pectore, ita ex ipsa cantus ederetur, appellaturque eadem de causa. Nam pectus dorica lingua cithara dicitur.*

215.16: *harpfa* (*Summarium Heinrici*, Lib VI,10: De musicorum vasis = Hildebrandt 1982, p. 93).

231.27: *harpfa; herphe* (*Summarium Heinrici*, Lib. XI, [long alphabetic version] = Hildebrandt 1982, p. 221): *Cythara musicum instrumentum triangulum .xxiiii. cordarum.*

383. 4: *harfe* (glossary arranged in order of subject);

383.11: *cytharedus* = *harpfere* (glossary arranged in order of subject).[41]

Cythara-harpha is the most frequent of all harp glosses. The term *cithara*, derived from the Greek *kithara*, refers to a stringed instrument which was no longer extant in the Middle Ages. This instrument consisted of a wooden sound chest with two relatively long arms. Usually it had several strings of (roughly) equal length, strung vertically between the sound chest and a crossbar. The strings were stroked with a plectrum.[42]

The source, *De musicorum vasis*, mentioned in the *Summarium* is based on Chapters 21 and 22 of the third book of Isidore's *Etymologiae*. The passage referred to by Heinricus is based on Chapter 22.[43] In this chapter Isidore gives a resumé of various rhythmic instruments. Not only percussion instruments but also stringed instruments were counted as rhythmic instruments. Chapter 22 deals with 'strings and striking' (*pertinens ad nervos et pulsum*). The cithara is also mentioned in this connection:

Forma citharae initio similis fuisse traditur pectori humano, quo uti vox a pectore, ita ex ipsa cantus ederetur, appellatamque eadem de causa. Nam pectus Dorica lingua κιθάρα vocari.[44]

'The form of the cithara was originally, according to tradition, the same as the human chest, because as the voice came from the chest, so (also) did music. And this is the reason it is so termed. For in the Dorian language the chest is called *kithara*.'

The explanation in the *Summarium* is virtually the same as that of Isidore and can be translated as:

'The form of the cithara-harpha, was, according to surviving accounts, originally that of the human chest because music came out of it as the voice comes out of the chest. And for this reason it was named in this way. Since cithara is chest in the Doric language.'

The explanation of the form of the *cithara* given in the *Summarium Heinrici* (=Gl III, 231.27) will be discussed in Chapter 3.2.2. The source of the gloss is unknown. In his *Etymologiae*, Isidore mentions a delta-shaped *psalterium*, not a triangular *cithara*.
In the *Glossarium Latino-Germanicum*, Lorenz Diefenbach not only mentions the glosses which indicate instruments but also those which refer to the player. The terms *cith-arista, -rista, -areda, -aredus, -aridus, -arus* are glossed with *harpfer, harpfenspeler* or *harpfenslaher* and words with a related spelling.[45] In Gl III, 383.11 the term *harfere* is given as a synonym of the word *cytharedus*, the player of the *cithara*. The eleventh-century *Ruodlieb* epic is the oldest source in which the Latin indication *harpator* is used.[46] The words *cithari-zare, -sare, catharisare* indicate the playing of the harp; they are entered in the glosses as *harpffen, harpen*.[47]
In the Prudentius glosses Gl II, 537.27 (see section A.a.) and 457.40 (see section A.b.) *harpa* also is mentioned as an alternative translation for *cithara*.

e) exachordum Gl IV, 235. 9: *harpha* (Adespota).[48]

The term *exachordum* should probably be read as *hexa chordum*, which could indicate a 'six-stringed' musical instrument. It is not very probable that the number six was associated with the number of strings on the harp; in illustrations the medieval harp is almost always represented with more than six strings.
It is equally improbable that there is a relation between the term *exachordum* and the concept hexachord in medieval music theory. *Hexachordum* first appears in music theory as a term with a specific meaning in the eleventh century and is connected with Guido of Arezzo's treatise *Epistola de ignoto cantu* of c. 1028.

f) crotta Gl V, 47. 10: *crotta .i. harpa* (Adespota).[49]

Crotta is glossed only once with *harpa*. The word *crotta* must be classified with the group of French *rotta* names, which also includes *rota* and *rote*.[50] *Rotta* is the name for a harp-cither. The relationship between the *cithara* and the *rotte* is discussed in Chapter 3.2.1.

g) lyre Bischoff 1928, p. 167: *harph*.[51]

This gloss is mentioned by Bernhard Bischoff as a supplement to the Steinmeyer-Sievers edition.

B. Wind instruments

a) symphonia Gl I, 660.26: *harfpfa* (Daniel 3:5).[52]

It is not clear how the term *symphonia* should be interpreted. In the Middle Ages the word was often used as the name for a hurdy-gurdy or bagpipes. Medieval interpretations of Daniel 3:5 (see the quotation under A.c), where the term occurs, must be regarded with suspicion: both the hurdy-gurdy and the bagpipes are musical instruments which were developed during the Christian era.[53] In medieval music theory the term *symphonia* is used to indicate a consonant interval. The glossing of *symphonia* with harp could be connected with the fact that consonant intervals can be played on the harp.

C. Percussion instruments

a) tympanum Gl I, 401.66: *hbrphxn* = *harphun*;
405.43: *hbrphxn* = *harphun* (I Samuel 18:6).[54]

The percussion instruments *tympanum* and *sistrum* are glossed only once with *harpfa*. *Tympanum* is the name for a drum generally covered on one side only by a skin membrane. Sometimes it is provided with metal discs around the rim which produce a jingling sound. It is usually shown held in the left hand while being struck by the fingertips of the right. The passage in I Samuel mentioned as a source describes the joy of the people of Israel at David's victory over the Philistines. The celebrations were augmented 'by the sound of drums and rattles' (*in tympanis laetitiae et in sistris*).

b) sistrum Gl III, 258.54: *harpfa; harpfe*
(*Summarium Heinrici*, Bd. 2, Lib. XI/2 [long alphabetical version] = Hildebrandt 1982, p. 474): *Sistrum >harpfa vel< species organi >vel tubae<.*

Sistrum is the name for a metal rattle which was used in ancient Egypt and later in the region around the Mediterranean Sea. It is not known whether this gloss goes back to the encyclopedia of Isidore, or to the text in I Samuel.
Finally the gloss *harpa quoddam musicum instrumentum,* which is mentioned in the eleventh book of the long alphabetical version of the *Summarium Heinrici* (=Hildebrandt 1982, p. 327), is not very informative. In fact, this lemma can be placed in each of the three classes of instruments.

D. Other meanings

a) catasta Gl II, 389.30: *harfa;*
394.28: *catasta .i. harpha*
(Prudentius, *Peristefanon* X, v. 467).
434.61: *(Catasta) .i. genus poene, harapha vel ritipoume screiatum*
(Prudentius, *Peristefanon* II, v. 399).
492.62: *harfa;*
509.61: *hbrfb = harfa;*
563.23: *hbrphb = hárpha;*
573.54: *hbrphp;*
581.42: *hárpon*
(Prudentius, *Peristefanon* X, v. 467).
583 : footnote 12: Prudentius 55 — *Ad bipennem publicam*[?].[55]

Gl IV, 200.46: *harpa* [?].
241.20: *Catasta harepha genus pene .i. harapsa* with footnote 9: *Catasta eculeus; Catasta scala eculeo similis* [?].[56]

The Prudentius source mentioned under Gl II, 583 in footnote 12 is not specified. It probably refers to *Peristefanon* I, v. 56.[57] In this verse the word *catasta* is clearly meant as an instrument of torture, as is shown by the words of verse 55-6:

Seu foret praebenda cervix ad bipennem publicam
verberum post vim crepantum, post catastas igneas.[58]

'Or they must submit their neck to the executioner's axe, after being punished by strokes from the cracking whip or after the glowing hot hurdle.'

The other pieces of evidence concerning the glosses *catasta-harpa* support this interpretation. The passage in *Peristefanon* II (v. 397-400), which describes the execution of the Roman cleric Laurentius about the year 258, points clearly in the direction of a hurdle on which people were burnt:

Postquam vapor diutinus
decoxit exustum latus
ultro e catasta iudicem
conpellat adfatu brevi.[59]

'After the continuous heat had burnt his side Laurentius called to the judge and spoke to him for a short time from the hurdle.'

In Book 10 from the same source there is a detailed report of the torture of Romanus, a priest at Caesarea in c. 304. The term *catasta* is used in verses 466-7, although its meaning is not clear. Maybe it refers to a hurdle as in the previous quotation; in any case some sort of elevation is meant:

Audite cuncti, clamo longe ac praedico,
emitto vocem de catasta celsior.[60]

'Listen all: I call from afar and announce; I send my voice from the hurdle [the construction?] which raises me above you.'

In the Prudentius gloss Gl II, 451.13, *catasta* is first regarded as the same as *rostun*, 'hurdle'; the second half of the gloss *vel ritipoume screiatum* shows that the author was not sure of his ground because *catasta* can also mean *screiat*, 'whipping post'. The glossing in fact yields two alternative translations of the term *catasta*. It seems improbable that the expressions *screiat* and *rostun* are synonymous. The eleventh-century writers of glosses were apparently aware that the word *catasta* indicated an instrument of torture, but there was no unanimous agreement about its nature.[61]

b) puteal Gl III, 124.39: *harpha; herphe*
(*Summarium Heinrici*, Lib. VII,2: De edificiis publicis = Hildebrandt 1974, p. 257): *Puteal locus vel statua in foro harpha/herphe*.
209.49: *harpha*
(*Summarium Heinrici*, Lib. V,7: De edificiis publicis = Hildebrandt 1982, p. 81): *Puteal harpha locus vel statua in foro*.

From both entries of *puteal* in the *Summarium Heinrici* it is clear that a 'place' or 'pillar' at the market could be indicated with *harpa*. The term *puteal* cannot be traced back in the source of both glosses, the chapter *De edificiis publicis* (Lib. XV, cap. 2) in Isidore's *Etymologiae*.[62] The word may refer, in the first instance, to the place of execution, while in the second the instrument of torture itself, possibly a whipping post, is meant.[63]

c) plectrum Gl II, 488.36: *harfa*
(Prudentius, *Cathemerinon* IX, Hymnus omnis horae, v. 1).[64]

The classification of *plectrum* with *harpa* raises doubts also. *Plectrum* is usually the Latin indication of a plectrum in the form of a staff for plucking strings, but in Middle High German and Middle English literature it can also mean 'tuning key' in relation to the harp (see Chapters 2.2.2 and 2.3). In verse 1 of the poem *Hymnus omnis horae* of Prudentius, the word *plectrum* seems to be used in its original sense:

Da, puer, plectrum, choraeis ut canam fidelibus
dulce carmen et melodum, gesta Christi insignia.[65]

'Give me my plucking-staff, boy, so that I may sing a sweet and melodious song about the glorious deeds of Christ in heartfelt trochees.'

1.4. NAME AND OBJECT IN ILLUMINATIONS

In the discussion of the relationship between name and object, those sources which give the name of the instrument, and in addition show a graphic depiction of it, are particularly important. There are few such sources and none prior to the twelfth century. I will not deal here with the older illuminations of harps which illustrate specific passages in the text; these will be considered in the following chapters.

We find the first and also the earliest clue in an illumination in the *Hortus Deliciarum*, a large encyclopedia of religious texts and illuminations intended for the abbot Herrad of Hohenburg (called Herrad of Landsberg in earlier literature). The original version was probably written at Hohenburg between 1176 and c. 1196.[66] In 1870 the manuscript was lost in a fire. Fortunately, however, diverse copies still exist. In folio 32r a woman is pictured playing a harp (*fig. 1*). She personifies *musica* within the "Artes liberales". The instrument name *cithara* is written upside-down above the neck of the harp.

Another piece of evidence is to be found in the writing *De cantu et musica sacra* of Martin Gerbert, which dates from 1774. This is a three-volume history of church music.[67] The second volume includes a number of plates with drawings of musical instruments. These musical instruments were copied from a twelfth-century manuscript which was lost in a fire in 1768. On plate 32 (no. 19) there is a drawing of a harp under the heading *Cythara anglica* (*fig. 2*). In view of the form of the instrument, that of a Romanesque harp, the name can be translated as 'English harp' without too many reservations. In Gerbert's writing the *Cythara anglica* is represented next to the *Cythara teutonica*, an instrument with the form of a medieval *lira*. On the same plate there is a fiddle with the caption *Lyra* and a hurdy-gurdy (*organistrum*). The resemblance between the hurdy-gurdy, fiddle and harp of Gerbert and those pictured in the *Hortus Deliciarum* is striking. Did the illustration in the encyclopedia of Herrad of Hohenburg possibly serve as an example? The geographical distance between Strassburg and Molsheim (where the manuscript was found) is not great and it is known that Gerbert travelled through this region. It is possible that he saw the *Hortus Deliciarum* on one of his journeys and that he copied instruments from it.[68]

The instruments in the work of Gerbert are not exact copies of the twelfth-century source; eighteenth-century additions are visible in several places. The shading on the *Cythara teutonica* is probably meant to bring out the curved form of the sound box.[69] It is not clear why the harp is labelled as 'English'. The form of the harp in Gerbert's writing is not distinguishable in any way from the Romanesque harps which we find in other illustrations from the twelfth to fourteenth century in western Europe. There is insufficient evidence to support the hypothesis that the *Cythara anglica* is a specific name for the Romanesque harp, which would imply that this harp was developed in Britain.[70] It is improbable that the terms *Cythara anglica* and *Cythara teutonica* reflect a difference in the construction of the instruments connected with different geographic areas.[71] It seems to me more plausible that the name is based on the underlying idea of using traditional names (taken, for example from the Holy Scriptures) for native instruments.

The relationship between the harp and the area indicated as England, as in the writing of Gerbert, is not unique. A similar instance in also found in German poetry. In his epic *Parzival,* completed c. 1210, the poet Wolfram of Eschenbach explicitly uses the term *swalwe*, 'swallow' to indicate an 'English harp'. In the words of verses 663,15-8:

> Vrou Bêne ûz Gâwâns hende nam
> die êrsten gâbe ûz sînem rîchen krâm,
> swalwen, diu noch zEngellant
> zeiner tiuren harphen ist erkant.[72]
>
> 'The woman Bêne took the chief gift of his rich merchandise out of the hands of Gâwân, namely a swallow, which is regarded as an expensive harp in England even today.'

According to the above quotation the 'swallow' is the chief gift from among the merchandise from Gâwân; the instrument is described as 'expensive'. The name *swalwe* for harp is also used in verse 623,20 of the *Parzival* epic. This passage differs from that of verse 663,17, however, because there is no indication of any geographical area. In verse 623,19-24 it is proposed that the captive Duke of Gôwerzîn be exchanged for a *swalwe*, a *harpfe*:

> Welt ir ledegen den man,
> dar um sol ich swalwen hân.
> diu der künegîn Sekundillen was
> und die iu sande Anfortas,
> mac diu harphe wesen mîn,
> ledec ist duc de Gôwerzîn.
>
> 'If you wish to ransom the man, then I should get the swallow which belonged to Queen Sekundille and which Anfortas has sent you as barter object; if I am given this harp then the Duke of Gôwerzîn is a free man.'

The association between the *harpfe* and the *swalwe* is also found in the *Jüngere Titurel* by the German writer Albrecht. His work dates from between

1260 and c. 1273.[73] The first line of strophe 2997, positively a quotation from verse 663,16-8 of *Parzival*[74], is:

Ein herpfe heizet swalwe, diu ist der kram entrunnen.[75]

'A harp called a swallow, which has escaped from the merchandise.'

The word *swalwe* is quite unconnected with the traditional Latin name for the instrument. It is also unclear what criterion led to this term being used to denote the harp. The assumption of the German musicologist Herbert Riedel that *swalwe* could be a reference to the form of the instrument, for example the swallow-like form of the neck, is speculative.[76]

From the second half of the twelfth century the instrument known as the *cithara* in the Vulgate is increasingly often depicted as a harp in Christian iconography. This interpretation seems to be based primarily on the text in I Samuel 16:23, which recounts how King David freed King Saul from the 'evil spirit from God' by playing on the *cithara*. In the words of the Vulgate[77]:

Igitur quandocumque spiritus Dei arripiebat Saul / tollebat David citharam et percutiebat manu sua / et refocilabatur Saul et levius habebat / recedebat enim ab eo spiritus malus.

'And whenever a spirit of God gripped Saul, David took up the cithara and played it by hand; this gave Saul relief, he felt better and the evil spirit departed from him.'

The interpretation of the *cithara* as the harp of David became a recurring image in manuscripts of the Psalms.

The *cithara* interpretation of I Samuel 16:23 was known in medieval poetry as well as in Christian iconography. This is apparent, for example, from a passage in the *Weltchronik* of the German poet Rudolf of Ems (lines 24450-4) dated c. 1250:

Einis tags den kúnig begie
nah gewonheit sin unsin.
mit einir harpfen gie fúr in
David und woltim sinin mŭt
machin sempfter unde gŭt.[78]

'One day the king was overcome by his madness as usual; David appeared before him with a harp and willed his spirit to be calm.'

Although this is not explicitly stated in the biblical exegesis, the interpretation *cithara* = harp would certainly have influenced the underlying idea of applying the biblical name for the instrument to a native, and thus familiar, western European stringed instrument.

The relationship between *cithara* and *harpa* is also found in a number of treatises on the theory of music.

The precise connection is unclear in the theoretical treatise *Ars musica* (c. 1300) by the Spanish theoretician Johannes Aegidius of Zamora, who lived from c. 1240 until the early fourteenth century.[79] In the prologue Johannes announces that he intends to give an exposition on various musical instruments, including the *cithara* and the *harpa*, in chapter 17. Remarkably enough, the *cithara* and not the *harpa* is discussed in the seventeenth chapter, which clearly betrays the influence of Isidore's *Etymologiae*. An interesting passage has been added on the use of the tuning key at the end of the discussion of the *cithara*. Similar vernacular texts are usually concerned with the tuning of the harp (see Chapter 2.3). It is not clear whether Johannes regarded the *cithara* and the *harpa* as the same instrument or not.

We find further evidence in the fourth tract from the anonymous Berkeley Manuscript, University of California Music Libr., 744 (olim Phillipps 445). In the third chapter of this treatise on music theory, which was probably written in France c. 1350-75, there is a speculative exposition on the stringing of the *cithara* and the *lyra*.[80] The text is partially based on the theoretical treatise on music, *De institutione musica* (Lib. 1, cap. 20) of Boethius (c. 480-c. 525). The interesting thing about the explanation given in the Berkeley Manuscript is that, unlike *De institutione musica*, drawings of the instruments are added. However, these illustrations have little informational value in the investigation of the relationship between the name harp and the object harp. The author obviously intended the illustrations to actualize the way in which the strings were arranged and the pitch of the instruments referred to in the text. The instruments which accompany the text are thirteenth- and fourteenth-century instruments. The tuning of the *cithara* is thus illustrated by references to the strings of the fiddle and the mandola. A similar description is given for the lyre and the harp, and for the monochord and the psaltery. The harp is depicted in conjunction with a passage which tells how, at a dried-up river, a certain Linus (of Thebes) found the dried remains of an animal and stretched four strings over the cavity of its corpse (a tortoise shell?). Linus named this instrument the *lyra*.[81]

The discrepancy between the name and the depiction of the harp in the Berkeley Manuscript seems also to have struck one scribe, because a footnote to the fragment of text reports that in one manuscript of this treatise, *cythara* is given as the name of the instrument.

Another representation with a caption is to be found in an astrological treatise, written in the Netherlands in the beginning of the fourteenth century. The manuscript is now in London, BL., Sloane 3983. An armed man is depicted in folio 13r of this manuscript; to his left there are four musical instruments: a mandola, a fiddle, a hurdy-gurdy and a harp (*fig. 3*). Above the harp is the legend *giga et lira*. Both terms are unusual as names for the harp.

Finally we find information on the relationship between the name and the object in the treatise on music theory *Breviarium regulare musicae*. One copy of this treatise is in the Bodleian Libr. at Oxford, Bodley 842. The work must have been written about 1400 in England by a certain Willelmus. On folio 66v of the manuscript there is a description of how a five-stringed *cithara* (*fig. 4*) should be tuned using the tonal symbols from the Greek and western European tonal system. A schematic drawing of a harp is added to clarify the explanation of the tonal system. In the legend of this drawing the word *cythara* is used to indicate the instrument.[82]

1.5. CONCLUSION

From the sixth to the twelfth century the word *harpa* was used to designate a large number of very diverse objects. Proceeding from the generally accepted thinking in the field of contemporary organology on the subject of the harp in the Middle Ages, I have proposed a number of criteria in the introduction to this chapter on the basis of which we can distinguish between the harp and other stringed instruments.

Poetry and writings on the theory of music which date from before the eleventh century do not indicate with certainty which musical instrument is meant by the term *harpa*. It is sometimes possible to deduce that a stringed instrument is being referred to. This observation connects with the hypothesis that the name harp for a musical instrument goes back in etymological terms to the pre-Germanic root **kerb* and is associated with 'plucking with bent fingers'. Medieval ideas on the origin of the word *harpa*, such as the supposed discovery of the instrument by the Arpi tribe — expressed and documented in the *Elementarium doctrinae rudimentum* by the eleventh-century lexicographer Papias — are imaginative interpretations.

In the eleventh century the terms *cithara* and *harpa* are often used synonymously.

In glossaries dating from the tenth and thirteenth centuries the term *harpa* is used for a large number of diverse musical instruments. The glossing of *cithara* with *harpa* occurs more frequently than would normally be expected.

Data on the harp in medieval poetry from before the eleventh century is rare. A study of the texts reveals that the term *harpa* is used to indicate stringed instruments. The *cithara* is the stringed instrument that is most usually translated by 'harp'. The eleventh-century *Ruodlieb* epic contains the first passage from which it can be deduced with a large measure of probability that the instrument name *harpa* indeed refers to the instrument the harp.

From the middle of the twelfth century onward a clear connection can be shown between the *cithara* mentioned in I Samuel 16:23 (Vulgate) which was played before King Saul by David, and the harp of David, both in Christian iconography as well as in poetry. It may also have penetrated outside the religious context under the influence of the widespread distribution of Psalm iconography. Several fourteenth-century texts on music theory also include the interpretation *cithara*=harp.

CHAPTER 2

THE HARP AND DAVID

2.1. INTRODUCTION

The various ways in which (King) David was depicted with a harp in the Middle Ages suggest that this instrument was significant as an Old Testament attribute, but not exclusively so. The German musicologist and art historian Reinhold Hammerstein noted in his article, *Die Musik am Freiburger Münster*, published in 1952, that "verschiedene musikalische Sinngehalte" are united in the person of David.[1] This view is rightly shared by many contemporary researchers of harp iconography.[2] However, many of them see David, and not the harp of David, as the object of study. The opinions of researchers on the symbolism of David's harp are often incomplete and mutually contradictory — if they are given at all. Even in the study, *König Davids Harfe in der abendländischen Kunst* by Hans Zingel, who has a particular interest in the subject, the various appearances of David-with-the-harp are not correlated with any variations in significance. According to Zingel: "Ob David sein Instrument spielt oder nur stimmt, ob er es neben oder vor sich hält, ohne die Saiten zu berühren, ob der Psalmist im Gebet kniend oder gegen Goliath kämpfend das Saitenspiel auf den Boden gelegt hat, ist im ganzen gesehen unwesentlich."[3] Many researchers, therefore, regard the harp as an attribute of David[4]; an attribute which they see as a symbol of Christian praise.

On the basis of iconographical research I distinguish three general ways in which the harp is depicted in relation to (King) David:
— the harp is held by David without being played, or is depicted together with David as a separate object;
— the harp is tuned by David;
— the harp is played by David.

In this chapter I will investigate whether a specific symbolic significance can be linked to the above-mentioned iconographical types. The extent to which the iconographical representation of the harp is a true reflection of the harp in the Middle Ages will also be discussed.

2.2. THE HARP: SYMBOL AND ATTRIBUTE

The thesis that the harp in David's hands has a symbolic value is primarily based on the many illustrations in which David is seen holding the harp after the manner of a ruler. The argument in favor of this proposition is the supposed similarity between the insignia of power of medieval rulers (orb and scepter) and the harp of David.[5] In the initial D of Psalm 26 in the Psalter London, BL., Additional 44874, f. 37v (*fig. 5*), we see King David holding the scepter in his right hand and the harp in his left hand. This scene recurs in some frontispieces of Psalm manuscripts, as for example in folio 12v of the tenth-century Psalter, Bibl. Vaticana, lat. 83 in Rome (*fig. 6*). Such frontispieces are intended as introductory illustrations to the Psalm text. Usually, however, the insignia or the harp are pictured separately in relation to David.

It is undeniable that the above-mentioned insignia are actually carried by King David. Moreover, in the Middle Ages he was regarded as a real king, as *David rex*.[6] In this guise David embodies the medieval idea of a just, wise Christian king. His kingship is, therefore, indicated with the same insignia as those which pertain to the ruler-status of the worldly monarch: among other things by the orb and scepter. The reproduction of these insignia in the hands of David is not evidence for the thesis that the harp too should be seen as a symbol of power.[7] The harp is never pictured as a symbol of power in the hands of any other rulers — there are no parallels which can serve as evidence. Steger's comparison of the harp with the insignia of power of a worldly king, then, says nothing about the significance which was attributed to the harp.

2.2.1. ORDERING THE MICROCOSMOS

I have researched the above-mentioned problem of interpretation further by examining illuminations depicting scenes from the period after David had been anointed king but did not actually fulfil this function. The representations based on the biblical text in I Samuel 16:23 especially are relevant to this point. We can deduce from this pictorial evidence that the harp was played, or that it was held, by David as an attribute.[8] However, it is difficult to imagine that the harp in the illuminations based on the text in Samuel — for example, in the initial D of Psalm 52 in the manuscript Oxford, Bodleian Libr., Liturgical 407, f. 77v (beginning of the thirteenth century) (*fig. 7*) — would have the same significance as the insignia of power. Nevertheless, there is a clear similarity between the manner in which the insignia are presented and the way in which the harp is held, as in the

Psalm manuscript in London (*fig. 5*). The assumption that a hidden significance could be attached to the harp would seem to be justified. A study into this specific significance is called for.

In medieval illuminations depicting David playing the harp for Saul, the harp is actually an interpretation of the biblical *cithara*. The relationship between the two instruments has already been discussed in the previous chapter. The influence of David's music on Saul's spirit — its power to drive away the evil spirit — is unique! Its inspiration does not lie with David but is sent by God, as we can read in I Samuel 16:18: *Dominus est cum eo*, 'the Lord is with him'. This idea was also familiar in the Middle Ages. Guido of Arezzo, for example, in his treatise on the theory of music, *Micrologus* (c. 1027), confirmed the importance of godly wisdom as a means of obtaining an understanding of the power of music. Guido's statement is based on the explanation described in I Corinthians 2:10-6 regarding the wisdom revealed to man by the Spirit of God. In Guido's own words:

> Item et David Saul(is) daemonium cithara mitigabat et daemoniacam feritatem huius artis potenti vi ac suavitate frangebat. Quae tamen vis solum divinae sapientiae ad plenum patet, nos vero quae in aenigmate ab inde percepimus.[9]

> 'Likewise David also calmed Saul's angry spirit with the cithara and broke the wildness of the evil spirit with the mighty power and sweetness of this art. However, this power is only fully accessible for godly wisdom; thanks to it, moreover, we have understood matters which are veiled in mystery.'

In the Middle Ages an important symbolic explanation was given to the *historia* of I Samuel 16:23; it was seen as a reference to the imposition of order on the microcosmos by David. This explanation has its roots in Greek philosophy. According to Pythagorean teaching, numbers are the basic principles of all things. Things relate to each other in certain ways which can be expressed in numbers. The Greeks saw numerical relationships in the movement of the stars, in the elements, the seasons and music as well as in other things. In the philosophy of Plato (c. 428-347 B.C.), a healthy human soul is also made up of musically consonant intervals which can be expressed by simple numerical relationships.[10]

Undoubtedly the interpretation of David's harp-playing before King Saul would have played a role analogous to the Greek idea of the harmony of the soul.[11]

The Hellenistically educated Jewish philosopher Philo of Alexandria (c. 25 B.C.-c. 50 A.D.) was also familiar with the relationship between the harmonious order of the soul and the cosmos. Philo was the first to describe the image of God as a musician who plays the human soul like a well-tuned lyre.[12] About a century later, in his theological tract, *Protreptikos* ('The exhortation of the Greeks'), the Greek Church Father Clement of Alexandria (c. 150-c. 215) connected the organization of the macro- and microcosmos with David. To translate Clement's words:

> 'He [=David] arranged this great world, harmoniously through the power of the Holy Spirit; yes, and also the small world, that of body and soul. And he makes music for God on this many-voiced instrument of the cosmos, and he sings together with the human instrument.'[13]

In the theory of music it was primarily Boethius who passed on to the Latin writers of the Middle Ages the Greek idea of harmony. In his treatise, *De musica institutione* (Lib. I, cap. 2), Boethius distinguishes between the *musica mundana*, 'harmony of the cosmos', and the *musica humana*, 'the harmony of body and soul'.

It was the theoreticians of music who seized the verses cited above from the book of Samuel to emphasize the healing influence of music on the human spirit.[14] In the words of Isidore's *Etymologiae*:

> Musica movet affectus, provocat in diversum habitum sensus. [...] Excitos quoque animos musica sedat, sicut de David legitur, qui ab spiritu inmundo Saulem arte modulationis eripuit.[15]

> 'Music moves the feelings and changes the emotions. [...] Music also soothes troubled spirits, as we can read of David, who freed Saul from the unclean spirit by the art of ordered melody.'

Although such passages are usually a broad reiteration of the text in Samuel, there are a few writers who stress the significance of playing the harp. The text about David's string-playing before Saul is coupled with other 'historical' examples, partly taken from Greek mythology, whose purpose is to serve as evidence of the beneficial influence of music on the human spirit. Several music theoreticians seized this as an opportunity — supported by biblical data — for resisting the church's prohibition on the playing of musical instruments. One such example is the *Institutiones*, a didactic book on spiritual and worldly knowledge by the Roman writer Cassiodorus (c. 490-583). Besides the influence of the lyra-playing of Orpheus, Cassiodorus stresses the effect which emanated from the Sirens' singing; he reports further how the Greek doctor Asclepiades cured a madman by playing a melody.[16] In the first chapter of his treatise on music theory, *Musica disciplina* (c. 850), Aurelianus, a monk at the St. Jean monastery in Réôme, emphasized the taming effect of Orpheus' lyra-playing on wild animals. In his *Ars musica* (c. 1300), the Spanish author Johannes Aegidius of Zamora points out the manipulative influence which music can have on those in power. He also ascribes the power of healing to harmonious music:

> Item per dulces voces, et cantilenas et harmonias musicas, infirmi et maniaci et frenetici ad sensum mentis et sanitatem corporis saepius revocantur.[17]
>
> 'Likewise the sick, the mad and possessed are very often cured in spirit and body by sweet voices, songs and musical consonances.'

In the case of David's harp-playing before King Saul, the spiritual significance is drawn from the effect of music on the spirit. Through his harp-playing David is able to exercise influence on Saul's spirit and so restore the harmony between body and soul. The disturbed microcosmos is, as it were, set in order anew.

According to the instrumental exegesis the power required to expel the evil spirit emanates from the *cithara* itself and, in particular, from the cross form of the instrument. Niceta (who died after 414), Bishop of Remesiana, present-day Bela Palanka, was the first to associate the form of the cross of Christ with the supposed mystical cross form of the *cithara*.[18] The cross form, it is argued, is revealed in the wood and the tension of the strings. The strings, made of gut, are in turn explained as the death of the flesh. This explanation, which was widespread in the Middle Ages[19], would certainly have contributed to the *cithara* being regarded from the eleventh century onward as the forerunner of the harp, especially in relation to the text from Samuel.[20]

The influence of the passage from I Samuel is also present in the written vernacular. In the didactic poem, *Der Renner*, written between c. 1290 and 1300, Hugh of Trimberg explains that harp-playing always triumphs over devil possession. The example of David and Saul serves to prove this. In the words of lines 5848-56:

> Bî sûren herzen ist harpfen unwert:
> Swer sûren herzen süezen sanc
> Singet, der dient in ân allen danc.
> Mit der schrift ich wol bewêre:
> Ob ein mensche beheftet wêre,
> Daz der vînt ez nimmer betrüebte
> Die wîle man seitenspil vor im üebte:
> Davîd und Saul sint des geziuge
> In der schrift, daz ich niht liuge.[21]

> 'Harp-playing is not worth anything to those with bitterness in their hearts [=wicked people]: those who sing a sweet song to those with bitterness in their hearts do them an unwelcome service. With the Holy Scriptures I can make a strong case to show that, if a human being is possessed, the enemy [=the devil] will never upset him as long as he practises string-playing before him: David and Saul are the biblical witnesses that I speak the truth.'

From the eleventh century on there is a proportionally large amount of illuminations whose subject is David playing the harp. It is unclear how far this theme is a concise iconographical representation of the text from I Samuel. There is often no single clear meaning that can be linked with the playing of the harp. The crucial factor when deciding whether or not harp-playing has a deeper meaning, is the context. The motif of King David playing his harp, which can be seen in the frontispieces of the Book of Psalms or in the B initials of Psalm 1, symbolizes the Christian idea of David as poet and singer of Psalms. The same theme in the illuminations of other Psalm initials, however, need not have the same significance. (Examples of this are given in Chapters 4.2.1 and 4.3.)

In the initial E of Psalm 80 in folio 84r in the manuscript New York, Pierpont Morgan Libr., 102, which dates from the second half of the thirteenth century, the harp is depicted behind the back of King David (*fig. 8*). David himself is playing the *cymbala* with two hammers. *Cymbala* are small bells which, the illuminations suggest, were suspended from a horizontal rod and were struck with one or two hammers. The harp is presented as an unused attribute in David's hands or is shown in relation to him primarily as an identification sign.[22] As such the harp can be compared with other personal attributes, like the sword of Solomon (I Kings 3:24) or Christ's scroll with the seven seals (Revelation of St. John 5:1 and 5:5).[23]

Very occasionally the harp of David is pictured together with the attributes of other figures. One example is the initial B of Psalm 1 in the Huntingfield Psalter, dated c. 1200, in New York, Pierpont Morgan Libr., 43, f. 27v (*fig. 9*). The subject of the illustration is the *Stirps Jesse*, 'The tree of Jesse', based on Isaiah 11:1. According to Christian exegesis, this text announces the coming of Christ. In the exegesis of the Psalms, it is stressed that David not only points forward to the coming of Christ as a *propheta*, but is also himself regarded as the *praefiguratio Christi*, the 'figure that foreshadowed Christ'.[24] The illumination in the Huntingfield Psalter shows the genealogical relation between David and Christ. Twigs grow out of the head of the sleeping Jesse and lead to four elliptical medallions which picture respectively from bottom to top, David with a harp, Solomon with a sword, Mary and finally Christ with the book with seven seals.[25]

2.2.2. ORDERING THE MACROCOSMOS

In present-day musical iconography David tuning the harp is ascribed a symbolic meaning. Researchers are unanimous that the act of tuning is related to the phenomenon of imposing order. The question of what sort of order is imposed is not, however, answered with the same unanimity.[26]

The thematic precedent to David tuning his harp with a tuning key in medieval illustrations is often sought in classical Greece and then in the person of Pythagoras. According to the legend, this Greek theoretician was the discoverer of the consonant interval relationships. This legend survived into the Middle Ages thanks to the *Harmonikon encheiridion* (Lib. I, cap. 6) by the Greek music theoretician Nicomachus of Gerasa, who lived around the year 100 A.D. The content of the legend can be summarized as follows: as he was passing by a smithy, Pythagoras noticed that the hammers striking the iron two at a time formed certain consonant intervals. He recognized the octave, the fifth, the fourth and the whole tone. When he looked at the phenomenon more closely, it turned out that the difference in sound was not caused by the force of the hammer blow or the form of the hammers, but by their weight. Pythagoras weighed the hammers, then returned home, where he took four strings of equal length and thickness, and weighted these down with weights corresponding to the weights of the hammers. When he struck the strings he found the following relationships: 12:6 (the octave), 12:8 (the fifth), 12:9 (the fourth), 9:8 (the whole tone).

The conclusions of Pythagoras' experiments, however, are at odds with physical reality. The proportions mentioned for the hammers are indeed valid for the proportional lengths of the strings, but not for the proportions of the weights. In order to obtain the right ratios for the weights, not the double but the quadruple value must be taken. In order to increase the vibration number 2, 3 and 4 times, as the legend requires, the weights used for tightening the strings must be increased 4, 9 and 16 times.[27]

Three different versions of the legend survived in the Middle Ages.[28] The most frequently quoted version goes back to *De institutione musica* (Lib. I, cap. 10) of Boethius. A second group of writings is based on Macrobius' commentary on the *Somnium Scipionis* (Lib. II, cap. 1) of Cicero. This commentary, which consists of a series of unconnected statements from neoplatonic teaching concerning, among other things, music and cosmology, dates from around 400. The third and least common version is first found around 900 in the *Epistola de harmonica institutione* of Regino of Prüm.[29] Although the wording is different in the different versions, the essence is the same: it was Pythagoras who discovered the relationships of consonant intervals.

In addition to the Greek, non-Christian interpretation of the origin of music, medieval writers also knew of a version given in the Bible. This is based on Genesis 4:21-2, in which Jubal is described as 'the father of the cithara and organ players' and Tubal-cain as a competent smith. Tubal-cain is also regarded as the father of all smiths.

> Et nomen fratris eius Iubal ipse fuit pater canentium cithara et organo / Sella quoque genuit Thubalcain / qui fuit malleator et faber in cuncta opera aeris et ferri / soror vero Thubalcain Noemma.
>
> 'And his brother's name was Jubal; he was the father of those who play the cithara and the organ. Sella also bore Tubal-cain who was a smith and skillful in all copper and iron work. And Tubal-cain's sister was Naamah.'

In medieval commentaries on this passage from the Bible, Jubal and Tubal-cain are often mistaken for each other.[30] The idea of Tubal(-cain) and not Jubal as the *inventor musicae* in the Bible, is first manifest in the *Etymologiae* of Isidore of Seville:

> DE INVENTORIBUS EIUS [=de musica]. Moyses dicit repertorem musicae artis fuisse Tubal, qui fuit de stirpe Cain ante diluvium. Graeci vero Pythagoram dicunt huius artis invenisse primordia ex malleorum sonitu et cordarum extensione percussa.[31]
>
> 'On her [=music's] discoverers. Moses says that Tubal, who [originally] was of the family of Cain before the flood, was the discoverer of the art of music. However, the Greeks say that Pythagoras discovered the principles of this art in the sound of the hammers and the plucking of stretched strings.'

Besides the Old Testament discoverer, Isidore also mentions the Greek 'discoverer' of music. The relation between Tubal(-cain) and Pythagoras is based on these two contradictory versions of Isidore. Both figures are often regarded as the *inventores musicae*, although chronologically speaking Tubal has the older claim. The universal occurrence of the legend of the smithy — a sign of the authority of Pythagoras — was responsible for the fact that he was not superceded as the 'discoverer' by Tubal.[32] In the *Historia Scholastica* of Peter Comestor (died 1179 or 1189), even aspects from the legend of the smithy are linked with Tubal(-cain).[33]

From the eleventh century on we find the name of David in texts which deal with the origins of music, in addition to the names Tubal(-cain) and Pythagoras. A passage in the theoretical treatise on music, *Musica disciplina* (cap. 2), by Aurelianus of Réôme, is often quoted in evidence.[34] The title of the chapter is *De nomine et inventoribus* [*musicae*], and it purports to be a treatment of the nomenclature and the discoverers of music. From the text it is clear that the discovery is ascribed to Pythagoras and Jubal. David is known as the most important musician in the Bible, but is not regarded as the discoverer of music or consonant interval proportions. However, the invention of certain musical instruments is ascribed to him. It is difficult to say in how far this interpretation is influenced by the apocryphal Psalm 151. In verse 2 of this Psalm, which refers to David, we read: *Manus meae fecerunt organum et digiti mei aptaverunt psalterium*, 'my hands have made the organ and my fingers have restored the psaltery.' There is an illustration of this text in folium 91v of the Utrecht Psalter, which must have been written about 830 in the neighbourhood of Reims.[35] The illustration shows, among other things, a person (David?) seated behind an organ. According to Seebass this organ could stand as a "Symbol für den harmonischen Zusammenklang der im Lobpreis vereinigten Gläubigen".[36] In the Utrecht Psalter the *psalterium*, is represented as a harp-like instrument in keeping with the Greek signification.[37]

Moreover, medieval authors were not completely consistent in their ideas on who invented music. The anonymous eleventh-century author of the *Ruodlieb* epigrams was of the opinion that not only David but also Tubal-cain, Pythagoras and Boethius had invented musical instruments. In the words of epigram 11:

> Tubalcain invenit cytharam et organa,
> Pithagoras testudinem, id est harpam,
> David psalterium triangulum, id est rottam,
> Boetius monochordum.[38]

> 'Tubal-cain discovered the cithara and the organa, Pythagoras the lyre that is the harp, David the triangular psaltery that is the rotte, Boethius the monochord.'

The numerical arrangement which Pythagoras discovered in the musical intervals was not exclusively limited to music. It turned out to be universally present. This originally Greek way of thinking also acquired a Christian interpretation in the Middle Ages. Medieval authors often pointed to the words *sed omnia in mensura et numero et pondere disposuisti* from the *Sapientia Salomonis* (11:21) to stress that the arrangement of the cosmos according to size, numbers and weight was the will of God. In the mind of Boethius, who set the tone for medieval thinking on numerical proportions in relation to music, *arithmetica* prevailed over *musica* and the other branches of knowledge. Numerical arrangements, he maintained, were at the foundation of the whole cosmos. The question of which discipline should be regarded as the most important, was answered by Boethius in a complicated fashion in his *Institutio arithmetica*, probably written in the sixth century:

> Haec est autem arithmetica. Haec enim cunctis prior est, non modo quod hanc ille huius mundanae molis conditor deus primam [*sic*!] suae habuit ratiocinationis exemplar et ad hanc cuncta constituit, quaecunque fabricante ratione per numeros adsignati ordinis invenere concordiam, sed hoc quoque prior arithmetica declaratur. [...] Musica vero quam prior sit numerorum vis, hinc maxime probari potest, quod non modo illa natura priora sunt, quae per se constant, quam illa, quae ad aliquid referuntur. Sed etiam ea ipsa musica modulatio numerorum nominibus adnotatur, et idem in hac evenire potest, quod in geometria praedictum est.[39]

> 'This one is indeed arithmetic, since it is prior to all others. Not only because God the Creator of this great universe took arithmetic first as the model for his reasoning and created everything according to it, having rationally forged all things through numbers of assigned order to find concordance, but also because arithmetic is prior in this. [...] The extent to which the power of numbers is prior to music can best be explained in this way, that not only those things which exist naturally in themselves are prior to things which are perceived in relation to something [else] but also the musical 'form' itself is expressed using the names of numbers, and the same that is already discussed in geometry can be expressed in the case of music.'

David is allotted an important role in cosmology. He is regarded as the Old Testament foreshadowing of Christ-Logos: Christ who as part of the Trinity (=God the Son), the Logos, is the incarnation of the creative concept of God.[40] The Logos embraces the order which is the precondition of the creation.[41] Christ is the symbol of this orderly arrangement and maintains it by his coming. The reason why David is linked to the imposition of this cosmological arrangement cannot be conclusively ascertained. It may possibly be sought in the Bible itself. The efforts of David to organize the song of the Jewish liturgy are described in diverse places, for example in I Chronicles 6:31, where we read that: 'These were they who appointed David to lead the singing in the house of the Lord.'

Similar wording can be found in I Chronicles 15:16, 16:4-7 and in Jesus Sirach 47:11. It is then not surprising that theological dissertations contain many instances showing David's ordering role. This is the case in the *Questiones in Vetus Testamentum* of Isidore of Seville, in which the harmonious arrangement of music by David is spoken of in relation to the Church:

> Erat autem David in canticis musicus eruditus. Diversorum enim sonorum rationabilis moderatusque concentus concordi varietate compactam ordinate Ecclesiae insinuat unitatem.[42]

'But David was a skillful musician [in the performance] of songs. For a logical and moderate harmony of different sounds indicates the unity of the Church brought about in an orderly fashion through concordance in diversity.'

Other terms which emphasize David's ordering role are also found on the frontispieces of some Psalters. We find an early example in the Vivian Bible dating from c. 850 in the Bibliothèque Nationale in Paris.[43] A distichon in folio 215v above the frontispiece of the Book of Psalms reads:

Psalmificus David resplendet et ordo peritus.
Eius opus canere musica ad arte bene.

'The psalmist David shines and [there is] skilful order. His work can be well sung if one is skilled in music.'

On the illustration under the distichon (*fig. 10*) we see King David surrounded by four co-psalmists (Asaph, Ethan, Heman and Jeduthan), one in each of the four corners. To the left and right of David are two armed soldiers: Cerethi and Phelethi. In the four corners outside the inner frame are personifications of the four cardinal virtues: Prudentia, Justitia, Fortitudo and Temperantia. The four co-psalmists who surround David are not founded on any biblical reality. The number four is taken from an introduction to the Book of Psalms of pseudo-Bede, known under the name of *Origo Psalmorum* and probably dating from the eighth century.[44] In this *Origo* text, data from the Books of Chronicles giving information on the creation of the Psalms and the arrangement of liturgical song by David intertwine with medieval elements.[45] The *Origo* text tells how David selected the four men mentioned by name to 'make' (*facere*) the Psalms with him, that is to say, to create the words and the composition. These four prominent persons from the tribe of Levi each gave David seventy men. Each of the co-psalmists plays an instrument, while David, positioned in their midst, holds a *psalterium*. According to pseudo-Bede the passage in the *Origo* text is as follows[46]:

Et unus quidem eorum feriebat cymbala, alius cynira, alius cithara; alius vero tuba cornea exaltans. In medio autem illorum stabat David tenens ipse Psalterium.

'And one of them struck the cymbala, another the kinnor, another celebrated on the cithara, another with a trumpet which resembles a horn. In their midst stood David holding the psalterium himself.'

In the Vivian Bible a triangular harp and not a psaltery is represented.

The *Origo* text which has survived via pseudo-Bede is of Greek origin. One of the oldest sources is a moral sermon of Hippolytus (c. 170-c. 236).[47] From the eighth century on we find a large number of manuscript illuminations inspired by the *Origo* text. However, they are not based on the text of pseudo-Bede, but on the Carolingian version. The name *cynira* (=*kinnyra*) for a lyre-like instrument, does not occur in the latter written tradition[48] — its meaning was possibly forgotten. In illustrations the missing instrument is sometimes replaced by a *crwth*, but mostly by a fiddle. The influence of the Carolingian version is not equally evident in all illustrations. Although folium 12v of the Ambrose manuscript Rome, Bibl. Vaticana, lat. 83 (*fig. 6*), is clearly influenced by the *Origo* text, the four co-psalmists are not shown playing music but writing. King David is indicated by the right hand of God (*dextera Domini*) at the top right of the illumination. David himself is holding a scepter and a delta harp.

The number of four co-psalmists was not chosen at random. Four is an important number in the Bible and in Biblical exegesis. It is often attributed with a symbolic meaning: it can symbolize the creation, the written revelation and the redemption.[49] This is shown in various ways in the illustrations. For example, in the Vivian Bible David is placed in a numerical relationship to the macrocosmos through the number four. The four co-psalmists and the four virtues symbolize the perfection of the creation. A striking similarity between the *Majestas Domini* illuminations and the Psalter illuminations which are based on the *Origo* text again reflects the medieval attempt to establish a relationship between David and Christ.[50] In *Majestas Domini* illuminations Christ is seated on a throne in the middle of the illumination, surrounded by four evangelists or their four symbols. When used in connection with the four evangelists of the New Testament, the number four is primarily the number of the Revelation. The symbols of the evangelists are the man, the bull, the lion and the eagle (Revelation of St. John 4:7). These four figures were often depicted in *Majestas Domini* illustrations in the Middle Ages.[51]

Another example of a Psalm illumination in which David's role in imposing order is stressed is found in the manuscript Coblenz, Staatsarchiv, Abt. 710, Nr. 110, which dates from the eleventh or twelfth century. In folio 153v (*fig. 11*) there is a legend and an illustration which indicate David's ordering role with respect to religion:

David psalmografus in tactu(s) spiritus almi
Christo psalterio psallebat et in monocordo
Efera dulcisonis demulcens pectora verbis.

'The psalmist David, touched by the blessing of the Spirit, sang for Christ with the psaltery and on the monochord, soothing the disturbed heart with sweet-sounding words.'

The illumination shows David with a lyra in his left hand and a monochord in his right. The Pythagorean proportions of musical intervals can be demonstrated by using a monochord. This instrument of music theory was often attributed with a symbolic meaning in the Middle Ages: the monochord symbolized perfection, the unity of God and the reality which surrounds us. This surrounding reality is sometimes represented in illustrations by the planetary symbols, with God denoted by a single string.[52] The proportions of the musical intervals point to the orderly arrangement of the cosmos, but in this case not from the point of view of Greek philosophy, but from a Christian outlook. It is particularly appropriate from this perspective that the monochord should be in David's hands.[53] The words *efera dulcisonis demulcens pectora verbis* from the legend on the manuscript evoke an association with David playing the harp for Saul.

A similar symbolic meaning is attached to David tuning the harp: David is the reflection of the Christ-Logos who maintains the order of the macrocosmos. In ninth- and tenth-century illustrations the sort of stringed instrument used to represent the symbolism of the tuning process seems to have been a subordinate matter. This changed in the eleventh century. Under the influence of the 'historic' setting in which David was placed, tuning the monochord was replaced by tuning the harp. This is manifest chiefly in the illumination of the initials in the Psalms (see Chapter 4.3). To judge by medieval illuminations, the illustrators regarded first the harp (*cithara*) and, to a lesser extent, the psaltery, the lyra and the monochord — instruments mentioned in relation to David in the biblical exegesis — as suitable objects for David to tune.

My investigation into harp-tuning shows that the theme of the tuning key often occurred in identical places in illustrations. The results of that study are processed in Table 1. It can be deduced from the table that tuning the harp occurs as an illustration theme especially in the initial B of Psalm 1, as well as on the frontispieces of Psalm manuscripts. The presence of David with a tuning key at these two places in the Psalm manuscripts underlines the great importance which illustrators attached to the placement of this theme. Apart from the initial B of Psalm 1, we also find the tuning theme — though to a lesser extent — in the initial Q of Psalm 51, the initial E of Psalm 80 and the initial C of Psalm 97.

The imposition of order on the macrocosmos is expressed in different ways according to the context. While King David is shown to be connected with this process by the depiction of a stringed instrument in the initial B of Psalm 1, the symbolism of the imposition of order is present in a much broader way throughout the Psalm illuminations. Both the classification of medieval musical instruments as well as the *mensurae* based on it determined what instruments were depicted in the initials of Psalms 1, 80 and 97. The tuning of the harp, thc striking of the *cymbala* and the playing of the organ (or the singing of a cleric) are signs of the divine *ordo* (see the Excursion.)

The arrangement of world harmony is also expressed by explaining the *corpus Christi* as a harmonious stringed instrument, an explanation which often relates to the *psalterium* but is closely intertwined with the instrument exegesis of the *cithara*.[54] According to this explanation, the body of Christ symbolizes the Church whose members are referred to as the strings of a single instrument. In this connection, man is regarded as the microcosmic reflection of this world-instrument.

2.3. TUNING AS THE REFLECTION OF REALITY

The tuning of the harp is depicted most frequently in Psalm illuminations from the twelfth to the fourteenth century. It is almost always David who does the tuning. His posture while tuning can be described as follows: (King) David is seated on a throne, usually with his body slightly skew so that his right shoulder is visible. The foot of the harp rests between his thighs or in a harp bag on his lap. This can be clearly seen in folio 6r of an English Psalter in Schloss Herdringen dating from c. 1290 (*fig. 12*).[55] The instrument appears to be pressed against David's chest or left shoulder at the place where the sound box joins the neck. The shoulder is then mostly not visible. The tuning key is held in the left hand and placed vertically on the upperside of the peg arm, with the result that the lower part of the tuning key grips a tuning peg or tuning pin. By depicting some of the fingers of the right hand — usually the thumb and index finger, although occasionally also the middle finger — near to the strings, the illustrator seems intentionally to create the impression that certain strings are being plucked.

David's tuning posture, decribed above, is so frequently reproduced that it is fair to regard it as stereotype. From the sum total of tuning key illustrations, I know of only three examples where his posture deviates from this norm. In those cases the deviation is such that the customary attitude is shown as though reflected by a mirror.[56]

To judge from the illustrations, the key can be placed on every tuning peg in the fashion described above. The tuning pegs are secured in holes which seem to be bored vertically through the neck (*fig. 13*). In the initial B of the Psalter in Schloss Herdringen (*fig. 12*) tuning pegs are clearly visible on the upper side of the neck! The illustrator has worked very inaccurately in this case. Three tuning pegs are placed on the column of the instrument, the middle one appearing without a string. The placement of tuning pegs on the upperside of the neck virtually only occurs in the case of David's harp and then mostly when he is shown tuning the instrument. This manner of tuning presupposes a different way of attaching strings from that found on present-day harps. The vertical placement of the tuning pegs, nonetheless, deviates from the placement of the tuning pegs on illustrations of medieval harps which are not being tuned: these usually have tuning pegs bored horizontally through the neck of the harp (*fig. 14*).

As was shown in Chapter 2.2.2 the tuning key illustrations in the Psalm manuscripts have a symbolic meaning. Consequently the frequency with which the tuning process is pictured is not a yardstick for the actual frequency with which medieval harps were tuned. It only says something about the popularity and the distribution of the illustration theme.

I feel that the illustrators chose the vertical position for the tuning key because of the symbolic significance of tuning. The illustrators wished to express this significance as clearly as possible. Turning tuning pegs which are placed horizontally in the peg arm with a tuning key makes a much less striking picture: the reader only sees the back of the hand clasping the tuning key, but not the tuning key itself.

The illumination on folio 21v in the twelfth-century Hunterian Psalter in Glasgow (*fig. 15*) provides some support for my proposition regarding the interpretation of the vertical placement of tuning pegs. Here David is tuning the harp holding the tuning key in the usual way. It is interesting to see the way in which the tuning pegs are depicted. Although we are looking at the left side of the harp, the tuning pegs on the front side of the neck seem to be oriented diagonally upwards. On the back side of the neck the parts of the tuning pegs around which the strings are strung point down. In this connection we should consider an illustration in the fourteenth-century Psalter London, BL., Egerton 3277. On folio 46v King David is depicted on the left next to the initial S of Psalm 68 (*fig. 38*). The tuning pegs on the harp which David is holding in his left hand seem to be positioned diagonally. On this occasion the harp is not being tuned but held as an attribute. Harp illustrations in which tuning pegs are represented in a diagonal position only occur sporadically. It seems to me out of the question that such a diagonal placement of tuning pegs should truly reflect the customary manner of instrument construction in the Middle Ages. The vertical position of tuning pegs is an even further abstraction for the sole purpose of clarifying the symbolism of the tuning. The same is true of the exceptional size of many tuning keys in relation to the harp.

Technical constructional objections can also be made concerning the vertical placement of tuning pegs. The neck of a harp with horizontally placed tuning pegs is weighted on one side and can therefore only bend slightly with the pressure from the strings. This is not the case when the tuning pegs are placed vertically: the massive solidity of the neck is interrupted repeatedly for each string, resulting in a situation in which downward tension can easily crack the neck of the harp. A very deep thick neck construction would be required to prevent this. Such a construction does not correspond with that found in harps in medieval illustrations; these have a slightly curved narrow neck.

In addition to illustrations, texts also provide us with information on the tuning of the harp. One important question is to what extent these descriptions tally with the above-mentioned statements on the significance of the act of tuning as carried out by King David.

In medieval literature, the tuning key of the harp is usually referred to by the Latin name *plectrum*. This is not, however, the original meaning of *plectrum*. The older and — as far as western European languages are concerned — original meaning of the Greek-Latin word *plectrum* was 'plucking stick'. The borrowed word has survived in western European linguistic usage with this meaning.

Written evidence on the use of the *plectrum* in the specific sense of tuning key dates from the thirteenth century. The tuning of the harp with the help of a tuning key is first described in the *Tristan* story of the German writer Gottfried of Strassburg in c. 1210. In lines 3547-61 he explains how Tristan, after playing some *ursuoche*, 'experimental melodies', tunes his harp in front of his audience. He uses a tuning key which is referred to in line 3558 with the word *plectrûn*:

> Sus nam er sinen plectrun:
> nagel unde seiten zoher,
> dise niderer, jene hoher,
> rehte als er si wolte han.[57]

> 'Taking his tuning key, therefore, he turned the tuning pegs/pins, loosening this one, tightening that one, precisely as he wished to have them.'

Gottfried refers to the tuning pegs by the Middle High German term *nagel*. *Nagel* is a translation of the Latin word *clavus*. Diefenbach gives "luten oder harpffen nagel" for the gloss of *clauus, clamis* and cites several examples as evidence.[58]

If the harpist turns the *nagel* slightly around the longitudinal axis with the *plectrûn*, he can tighten or loosen the strings depending on the direction in which he turns the tuning key. In the *Tristan* passage the verb *ziehen* has the word *nagel* as its object, so that the expression *nagel unde seiten* must be regarded as a hendiadys construction meaning 'tuning pegs/pins'. It should be noted that pulling on the strings can only tighten but not loosen them. In the above passage, however, a combination of both, now tightening, now loosening, is brought about by the 'pulls' of the tuning key. When the tuning key is placed on the *nagel* it can be turned [*ziehen*] in both directions around the longitudinal axis. In this respect it can be compared to a screw-driver ("Schraubenzieher" in German).

Tristan turns these pegs/pins *niderer* or *hôher*. The slight turn which the harpist gives the pegs/pins which protrude sideways from the harp neck, can be closely watched by Tristan's audience because they are shown the hand of the player as it turns and the side of the player as he moves *niderer* (down) and *hôher* (up). The 'up' and 'down' can also imply the variable tension and pitch of the strings.

Tuning the harp is also a subject which is touched on in the *Apokalypse* of the German author Heinrich of Hesler.[59] This poem, based on the Revelation of St. John, probably dates from c. 1300.[60] In lines 9732-8 tying martyrs to the cross is compared with tightening the strings of a harp:

> Sie worden an daz holz gedenet
> mit herten seilen und widen,
> dar sie die martere liden,
> als man die schafseiten tuet,
> die man an der harfe zuet
> mit wirbelen uf und wider,
> dise ho, jene nider.

> 'They were stretched on the wood [of the cross] with rough cord and ropes of plaited willow twigs, where they underwent a martyr's death, as sheep's strings are tightened which are pulled up and down on the harp with the tuning pegs [=turned with the tuning pegs], this one up, that one down.'

The word *schafseiten* probably indicates strings which are made of sheep gut. Harp strings are mentioned earlier in line 9713; there they are called *schefinen seiten*. The strings are tuned using *wirbelen*. The Middle High German substantive *wirbel* has two meanings; it can indicate both a 'tuning peg' and a 'tuning key'.[61] In Heinrich's *Apokalypse* the plural *wirbelen* is used, and for this reason I favor the meaning 'tuning pegs'.

During tuning the strings are moved *uf und wider* by means of the tuning pegs. In this way the tension of the strings and, thus, the pitch can be varied. The words *hôh(er)* and *nider(er)* seem to be borrowed from the turning motion of the hand of the person tuning the harp, as in the *Tristan* story.

The acts of tuning described in the *Tristan* story and the *Apokalypse* presuppose a harp construction in which the tuning pegs are attached horizontally through the neck. In this respect the act of tuning in both poems contrasts with that depicted in relation to David.

Besides expositions on tuning the harp, a number of medieval texts have survived in which the tuning of the *cithara* is described. These are also included in this study because of the close relationship between the *cithara* and the harp.

The French theologian Michael (born 1199), dean of Meaux, gives a detailed allegorical exposition about the component parts of the *cithara* in his commentary on Psalm 97:5.[62] The text deals, among other things, with both the tuning and the way in which the strings are attached. Disregarding the allegorical element, the passage includes the following particulars on the construction of the instrument and the manner of tuning:

> In cithara duo sunt ligna, superius et inferius; inferius concavum, superius solidum. Inter hec tenduntur corde, quibusdam clavis deorsum tendentibus, quibusdam sursum trahentibus. Superiores clavos plectrum torquet, ad inferiores cordas. Corde digitis percusse sonant. [...] Corda siccatur et tenditur ut sonum reddat [...]. Inferiores clavi rotundi sunt, superiores solidi.

> 'The cithara consists of two wooden parts, an upper and a lower part; the lower part is hollow and the upper part is solid. The strings are stretched between these. In this process some tuning pegs turn downward and others upwards. The tuning key twists the upper tuning pegs towards the lower strings. The strings sound when they are plucked with the fingers [...] The string is dried and taut in order to make it sound. [...] The pins are round at the bottom and square on top.'[63]

In the quotation the word *clavus* has the meaning of 'tuning peg' or 'pin'; the tuning key itself is indicated by the term *plectrum*. Christopher Page, who has made a detailed study of this text, concludes from the description given by Michael of Meaux that this must be a "triangular harp without pillar". Page has tried to make a drawing of the instrument based on the description of Michael of Meaux. In this drawing the tuning pegs are positioned vertically on the 'neck' of the instrument. There is no justification for this in the text. Page's note, "the tuning key tightens the upper pegs", written next to the tuning key, suggests that the reason for the vertical placement of the tuning pegs lies in the interpretation of the words *superiores clavi* and *inferiores clavi*. If we take *superiores* to mean "upper pegs" and *inferiores* the "lower pegs", one may wonder where the *inferiores* were placed and what their function was (difference in pitch or double stringing?). Page neither asks nor answers these questions. In his drawing he only shows where the "upper pegs" are placed. I know no iconographical evidence for the existence of a harp with two rows of tuning pegs on its neck.[64]

As far as I can ascertain, Michael of Meaux only wishes to inform the reader that the strings can be tuned differently using a tuning key. He uses the verb 'tighten' (*tendere, trahere* respectively) to indicate the tuning of the strings. The term *trahere* is equivalent to Gottfried's term *ziehen*: they both mean 'turning (with the tuning peg)'.

The final sentence in this quotation describes the various points at which the strings are attached. The round pins ("Stegstifte") are on the resonance board of the sound box; the ends of the strings are attached to them. The square parts of the 'tuning pegs' stick horizontally out of the peg arm; during tuning the somewhat larger square opening of the tuning key is placed over this square part of the peg. The Brian Boru-harp in Trinity College in Dublin, which presumably dates from the end of the fourteenth century, provides evidence for the existence of such tuning pegs.[65]

The word *plectrum* is also discussed in connection with the tuning key of the *cithara* in the treatise on music *De proprietatibus rerum* by Bartholomaeus Anglicus, dating from the first half of the thirteenth century.[66] In the words of Chapter 141:

> Plectrum autem dicitur instrumentum, quo temperantur chordae et tenduntur.[67]
>
> 'The plectrum is an instrument with which the strings are loosened and tightened.'

Johannes Aegidius of Zamora expressed himself in more or less the same words in his treatise on music *Ars musica* (c. 1300).[68] Instead of the verb *tendere* ('tighten'), however, Johannes uses *extendere* ('stretch out') which stresses the tightening of the strings even more.

The oldest illustration of a tuning key which includes the name *plectrum* is found in the treatise *Breviarium regulare musicae* of Willelmus, dating from around 1400.[69] The tuning key, depicted in the third chapter, is shaped like a bar (of metal?) with a somewhat rounded handgrip and a conical end (*fig. 4*). The tuning key is pictured next to a schematic drawing of a harp bearing the legend *cithara*. The tuning pegs are positioned horizontally on the peg arm. The plaiting on the upperside of the tuning key is very probably a sketchy representation of a wire or cord with which the tuning key is attached to the instrument or the player. The harp depicted on the frontispiece of an eleventh-century copy of Augustine's Psalm commentary in the Bibl. de la Ville in Avranches (*fig. 16*) provides evidence for the existence of such a cord.[70]

A variant on the word *plectrum*, the Middle High German *wreistel*, dates from the thirteenth century.[71] *Wreistel* means 'tuning key', which tallies with the etymology of the word. According to Pokorny the root is the Indo-Germanic *u̯er* ("drehen", "biegen"). A rich vocabulary is derived from this root.[72] Thus the substantive *wrest/wrast* ('tuning key') is found in Middle English literature as well as the verb *wresten/wrasten* ('to tune'). These words, too, are frequently used in connection with tuning the harp.[73] In the fourteenth and fifteenth centuries we also find that the term *plectrum* is used to indicate a tuning key.

Ten different types of tuning key can be distinguished in the harp illustrations (see Schema 2).

Schema 2. Types of tuning key (arranged according to frequency).

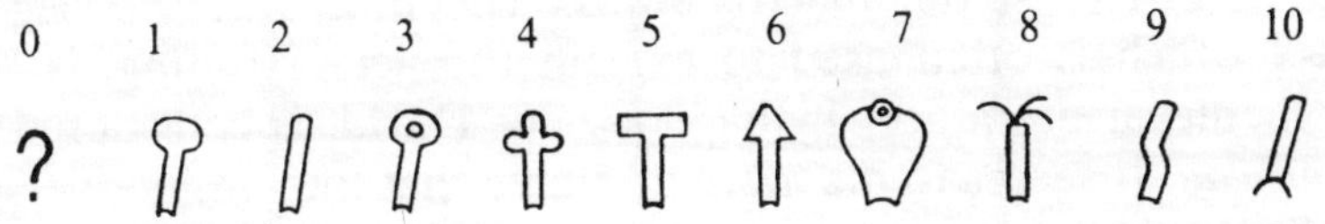

In the case of type 0 tuning key, the form of the tuning key cannot be determined either because of blurring or the poor quality of the illustration. However, it is clear from David's posture that he must be tuning an instrument.

Some illustrations show a bar-like handgrip instead of a rounded handgrip, giving the tuning key a T form (Table 1: type 5 with type 4 as variant). Despite the variation in the design of the handgrip, we can assume that all types of tuning key have a circular opening on the underside, where the square protrusion which can grip round the tuning peg/pin is found.[74] It is impossible to say to what extent these types of tuning key are realistic. Types 1, 3 and 5 very much resemble the form of the tuning keys we know today. The cross form of type 4 was possibly inspired by information contained in the New Testament.

2.4. CONCLUSION

A study of the various forms in which David appears with the harp reveals three motifs, each with its own significance.

The first motif concerns the harp as an attribute of David. The harp is little more than a means of identification.

The second motif, David playing the harp, has a definite symbolic meaning. In general, David playing the harp is a means of referring to his role as poet and composer of Psalms. In addition the motif can be specifically chosen on the basis of the text in I Samuel 16:23, which is linked with a particular symbolic meaning. His harp-playing before King Saul can be explained as the imposition of order on the microcosmos. The roots of this interpretation lie in Greek philosophy. The motif shows a close affinity with the idea of the 'harmony of the soul', as put forward by Plato, Philo of Alexandria and other writers.

The text in I Samuel 16:23 was seized upon by a number of music theorists to advocate the playing of musical instruments on theological grounds.

The third motif, the tuning of the harp by David, symbolizes the imposition of order on the macrocosmos. The link with the 'legend of Pythagoras', which is often used to explain the act of tuning, is hard to justify. In medieval literature, Pythagoras, not David, is considered as the *inventor musicae*. It seems to me more probable that the familiar verse from the Bible, *Sapientia Salomonis* 11:21, which announces that God has ordered all things by size, number and weight, gave rise to the illustration theme. The *mensura* symbolism which is concealed in the illustration themes of the initials of Psalms 1, 80 and 97 gives an important clue in this direction. In illustrations which have the tuning of the harp as their subject, reality is almost always subordinate to symbolism: the tuning pegs are not represented at the side but on the top of the neck. From the point of view of constructional technique, the form of the harp neck, as shown on medieval illustrations, would not allow tuning pegs to be positioned vertically. The downward pull of the strings would crack the relatively thin neck. Vertical placement of the tuning pegs, therefore, serves exclusively to clarify the tuning symbolism.

In the Middle Ages David was regarded as the prefiguration of Christ. By linking David with the imposition of order on both the micro- and the macrocosmos, it was possible to represent him in Christian iconography as the *figura* of the Christ-Logos who maintains this same order.

Table 1. The tuning key in harp illustrations.

The manuscripts in this table are ordered chronologically according to the type of tuning key (Schema 2). The complete library references are given in Appendix I. The place where the tuning key is depicted in the source is indicated in the middle column left under the heading 'illustration theme'; in the middle column right the figure relating to the tuning key is noted.

place source	illustration theme	key type	date
Paris, Bibl. Ste.-Genev., 8-10, f. 194r	Init. B - K. David	0	12th
Oxford, Bodl. Libr., Can.P. lat. 217, f. 3r	Init. B - K. David	0	late 12th
Hereford, Cath. Libr., O.3.XV, f. 43r	Init. B - K. David	0	12th/13th
Florence, Bibl. Laur., Plut. XV.11, f. 275r	Init. B - K. David	0	early 13th
Kassel, Landesbibl., quart. 8, f. 251r	Init. B - K. David?	0	early 13th
Cambridge, Fitzwill. Mus., 330, no. 6	Stirps - K. David	0	1st h.13th
Dresden, Arnhold Coll., Psal., n.s.m., f.12v	Init. B - K. David	0	c. 1250
London, BL., Egert. 2867, f. 244v	Init. B - K. David	0	13th
New York, Pier. Mor, Libr., 97, f. 24v	Init. B - K. David	0	13th
Paris, BN., lat. 40, f. 199v	Init. B - K. David	0	13th
Rouen, Bibl. Municipale, 3106, f. 22r	Init. B - K. David	0	13th
London, BL., Yates Thom. 18, f. 9r	Init. B - K. David	0	c. 1300
Paris, BN., lat. 1029A, f. 10r	Init. B - K. David	0	13th/14th
Arras, Bibl. de la Ville, 88, f. 1r	Init. B - David	0	14th
London, BL., Roy. 2.A.XXII, f. 15r	Init. B - K. David	1	late 12th
New York, Pier. Mor. Libr., 43, f. 27v	Init. B - K. David	1	c. 1200
Munich, BayS.-bibl., Clm. 835, f. 31r	Init. B - K. David	1	12th/13th
Oxford, Bodl. Libr., Bodley 284, f. 1r	Init. B - K. David	1	1210-20?
London, Lambeth Pal. Libr., 563, f. 20r	Init. B - K. David	1	c. 1220
Berlin, S.-bibl., theol. lat. 379, f. 232v	Init. B - K. David	1	c. 1240
London, Soane Mus., 9, f. 132r	Init. B - K. David	1	1st h.13th
London, BL., Roy. 1.B.XII, f. 178r	Init. B - K. David	1	1254
The Hague, KB., 76.E.11, f. 2r	Init. B - K. David	1	13th
London, BL., Add. 44874, f. 115r	Init. E - K. David	1	13th
London, BL., Add. 54179, f. 76v	Init. E - K. David	1	13th
Princeton, Univ. Libr., Garrett 28, f. 209r	Init. B - K. David	1	13th
St.-Paul im Lavanttal, Kathedral-Archiv, XXV.2.19, f. 18r	MargI, Ps. 1 - K. David	1	13th
Vienna, Ös. Nationalbibl., 1139, f. 166r	Init. B - K. David	1	2nd h.13th
London, BL., Add. 21926, f. 26r	Init. B - K. David	1	late 13th
London, BL., Add. 21926, f. 115v	Init. E - musician	1	late 13th
Cambridge, CC. Col., 53, f. 19r	Init. B - K. David	1	early 14th

London, BL., Roy. 2.B.VII, f. 85r	Init. B - K. David	1	early 14th
Mancetter, Church, stained glass	Stirps - K. David	1	14th
Oxford, Bodl. Libr., Laud. M. 752, f. 236v	Init. B - musician	2	12th
Oxford, Bodl. Libr., Auct. E.in. 1-2, f. 2r	Init. B - K. David	2	1180-90
London, BL., Harley 5102, f. 77v	Init. E - David?	2	c. 1220
Copenhagen, Kongelige Bibl., 2, f. 120r	Init. B - K. David	2?	1st h.13th
Frankfurt, Kunstgew.-Mus., L.M. 20, f. 74r	Init. B - K. David	2	c. 1265
Oxford, Bodl. Libr., Douce 50, p. 265	Init. E - David?	2	13th
Oxford, Bodl. Libr., Laud. Lat. 87, f. 215r	Init. B - K. David	2	13th
London, BL., Harley 2839-40, f. 285v	Init. B - K. David	2	13th
London, Beatty Coll., 50, f. 144r	Init. B - K. David	2	13th
New York, Pier. Mor. Libr., Gl. 42, f. 167v	Init Q - David	2	13th
Philadelphia, Free Libr., Lew. 185, f. 77v	Init. Q - David	2	13th
Amiens, Bibl. de la Ville, 124, f. 7v	Init. B - K. David	2	late 13th
Cambrai, Bibl. Mun., 102-3, f. 232r	Init. B - K. David	2	1295-6
Oxford, Bodl. Libr., Auct. D.4.2, f. 15v	Init. B - K. David	2	13th/14th
Brussels, KB., 9391, f. 4r	M.Ps.1 - K. David	2	14th
London, BL., Add. 44949, f. 39r	Init. B - K. David	2	14th
Lyons, Gillet Coll., Psal., n.s.m., f. 7r	Init. B - K. David	2	14th
Lyons, Mus. Hist. des Tissus, embroidery	Stirps - K. David	2	14th
Merevale, church, stained glass	Stirps - K. David	2	14th
London, BL., Egert. 1139, f. 23v	Init. B - K. David	3	12th
Belvoir Castle, Psalter, n.s.m., f. 98r	Init. C - K. David	3	c. 1250
Boulogne-s-M., Bibl. de la V., 5, f. 177r	Init. B - K. David	3	2nd h.13th
Manchester, Rylands Libr., 117, f. 9r	Init. B - K. David	3	13th
Munich, BayS.-bibl., Clm. 2599, f. 96v	- David?	3	13th
London, BL., Add. 38116, f. 14v	Init. B - K. David	3	late 13th
London, BL., Add. 42130, f. 13r	Init. B - K. David	3	c. 1340
Herdringen, S.-bibl., Psalter, n.s.m., f. 6r	Init. B - K. David	4	c. 1290
Avranches, Bibl. de la Ville, 3, f. 3r	Init. B - K. David	4	13th
Oxford, Bodl. Libr., Auct. D.3.2, f. 195r	Init. B - K. David	4	13th
Oxford, Bodl. Libr., Lyell empt. 4, f. 8v	Init. B - K. David	4	early 14th
London, BL., Arundel 83, f. 55v	MargI - David?	4	1st h.14th
Oxford, Bodl. Libr., Auct. D.2.2, f. 8r	Init. B - K. David	4	14th
Glasgow, Univ. Libr., Hunter 229, f. 21v	frontP - K. David	5	12th
Cambridge, Gonv. and Caius Col., 350/567, f. 159r	Init. B - K. David	5	c. 1235
Cambridge, Fitzwilliam Mus., 13, f. 7r	Init. B - K. David	5	13th
Bourges, Bibl. Municip., 3, f. 255v	Init. B - K. David	6	12th
Evreux, Bibl. Municip., 4, f. 135r	Init. E - K. David	6	13th
New York, Publ. Libr., Spencer 2, f. 15r	Init. B - David	6	1st h.14th

Avranches, Bibl. de la Ville, 76, f. 1v	frontP - K. David	7	c. 1050
Turin, Bibl. Naz. Univ., D.V.19, f. 50r	Tlaw - 2 donkeys	7	early 13th
Oxford, Bodl. Libr., Bodley 842, f. 66v	MusT. -	7	c. 1372
Oxford, All Souls Col., 7, f. 7r	Init. B - K. David	8	early 14th
London, BL., Add. 47674, f. 1r	Init. B - K. David	9	12th/13th
London, BL., Add. 49622, f. 8r	Init. B - K. David	10	early 14th

Explanation of abbreviations in Table 1, columns 2 and 3:

frontP	frontispiece Psalter
Init.	Initial
K.	King
M.	Miniature
MargI	Margin illustration
MusT.	Theoretical treatise on music
Ps.	Psalm
Stirps	Stirps Jesse
Tlaw	Treatise on law

CHAPTER 3

THE DELTA HARP

3.1. INTRODUCTION

When we classify medieval harps according to their morphological characteristics, we find one category which deviates significantly from the others. This deviant group is referred to as the delta harp in contemporary literature on music because of its physical resemblance to the form of the Greek capital letter delta (Δ).[1] Opinions of researchers on this type of instrument vary considerably. For some the delta harp was never anything more than a symbol, while others feel that the instrument actually did exist.

The considerable differences in the way in which we see delta harps being held in illustrations caused Steger to doubt if such an instrument ever really existed.[2] However, there is little evidence to support his hypothesis that medieval illuminators wished to use the delta harp to illustrate statements of the Church Fathers about the triangular psaltery of, for example, the ancient Egyptians.[3] The Church Fathers not only described the *psalterium* but also the *cithara*, the *laudatorium* and the Hebrew instrument the *nebel* as delta-shaped. In addition to admitting the possibility that an instrument with this form may actually have existed, Steger also proposes an alternative idea, namely that the form symbolizes the Trinity.[4] Rensch does not distinguish any separate type of delta harp. She regards the instrument as a "triangular-shaped frame harp" and is interested in it from the point of view of morphological development.[5] Pickering, in contrast, suspects that drawings of delta harps are an attempt to comply with an instrument description originating with Jerome.[6] Vorreiter, like Rensch, studied the surviving evidence on forms extensively and has many reservations about suggestions that the delta form symbolizes the Trinity.[7] He gives two arguments for his scepticism. First, he points out the lack of a written tradition relating to this symbolic concept in religious writers, scholars of the theory of music and harp builders. Secondly, Vorreiter says that he does not know of any mystical or magical concepts in the symbolism of numbers which would justify such an explanation. Neither argument shows an acquaintance with the latest thinking on the symbolism of instruments. Esmeijer, who in contrast to the two previous researchers, is primarily concerned with research into visual exegesis, interprets the delta form as pure symbolism.[8] Like Steger, she regards the delta form as a symbol of the Trinity. Finally, Giesel thinks that the delta form may possibly have been transmitted from the Hebrew angled harp to the *psalterium* and the *cithara*.[9] Giesel and Steger, therefore, both take the position that this form is derived from an real instrument which once existed.

The phenomenon of the delta harp is, in view of the present state of research, still unsatisfactorily explained. The extent to which the delta harp is the distillation of symbolic interpretations remains unclear, as also the nature of these interpretations. The question of how far the comparison with the capital letter delta indeed rests on an association with Egyptian or Hebrew instruments has also not been satisfactorily resolved. We must again ask the most essential question about the phenomenon of the delta harp — that concerning its reality. In order to be able to answer this question it is necessary to investigate in depth the exegetic background which led to this instrumental form.

3.2. WRITTEN EVIDENCE

A large number of medieval writings include descriptions which emphasize the delta form as a characteristic form for instruments.[10] These often consist of exegetic interpretations of objects from the Holy Scriptures accompanied by an allegorical commentary. In the introduction, I already pointed out the development of instrumental allegory by the Greek and Latin Church Fathers in the first centuries A.D. In explaining the Holy Scriptures, the Church Fathers, who rejected musical instruments for moral reasons, discovered passages which referred to instruments in the Jewish culture. The books of the Old Testament especially are full of references to music and musical instruments. The exegetist scholars began to wonder how God could allow his chosen people to honor him with these, in their eyes, profane instruments.[11] This awakening awareness made a theological explanation of the phenomenon of musical instruments imperative.

Most statements on delta-shaped musical instruments are found in commentaries on and introductions to the Book of Psalms.[12] Musical instruments are mentioned in no less than sixteen Psalms (32, 42, 46, 48, 56, 67, 70, 80, 91, 97, 107, 136, 143, 146, 149 and 150). Because the exhortation to praise God with music is central to this biblical book, it very often provides the occasion for an exegetic exposition on music. Even if the statements on a delta-shaped instrument are not part of a Psalm commentary or Psalm introduction, the delta form is still often brought into connection with particular Psalm texts or at least with the person of David.[13] Not only theological writings but also secular medieval literature speaks about the relationship between David and a delta-shaped stringed instrument. One of the anonymous *Ruodlieb* epigrams from the eleventh century makes this link. In epigram 11 we read: *David* [*invenit*] *psalterium triangulum, id est rottam*, 'David has invented the triangular psaltery, namely the rotta.'[14]

Medieval authors point particularly to Psalms 42:4 and 143:9 when discussing the relationship between Psalm texts and instrumental form. When the delta-shaped *cithara* is mentioned in the exegesis, the words: *Confitebor tibi in cithara Deus Deus meus*, 'I praise you with the cithara, o God, my God' (Psalm 42:4) are usually quoted.[15] The delta-shaped *psalterium* is usually brought into connection with Psalm 143:9, *In psalterio decacordo psallam tibi*, 'I will sing you Psalms on the ten-stringed psalterium.'[16] This line from the verse, as also the words *exsurge psalterium et cithara*, 'awake psalterium and cithara' (Psalms 56:9 and 107:3) are quoted when a 'square-shaped' *psalterium* is mentioned in the explanation.[17] The 'square-shaped' psaltery — sporadically depicted as a quadrangular harp — contrasts with the form and description given of the delta-shaped *cithara* in the exegesis. Both the *cithara* and the *psalterium* serve to praise God in the Holy Scriptures.

The Dardanus passages occupy a unique place in the surviving accounts. By Dardanus passages I mean textual fragments which are based on the pseudo-Jerome letter *De diversis generibus musicorum*.[18] This letter is addressed to a certain Dardanus, probably the well-known magician of Greek and Roman antiquity.[19]

The pseudo-Jerome letter was widely distributed in the Middle Ages. Large chunks of text from the letter occur in the chapter entitled *De musica et partibus ejus* in the encyclopedia *De universo* by Raban Maurus (c. 776/784-856), which is from about 843.[20] The text of *De musica et partibus ejus* is not, however, written in the form of a letter. It is not known if the text of Raban or an even older piece of writing served as the source for the Dardanus letter. According to Hammerstein, the 'original text' probably does not predate the Carolingian period, that is to say about 800.[21]

The passages based on the Dardanus letter provide vital evidence on the delta harp. The Dardanus passages also have an explanatory character, like the previously mentioned exegetical texts which speak of delta-shaped instruments. The Dardanus passages differ from the first group of texts in that schematic drawings are added to illustrate or clarify what is written.

Illuminations depicting delta-shaped instruments are found in the following manuscripts dating from the tenth to twelfth centuries:
— Munich, Bayerische Staatsbibl., Clm. 14523, f. 51v, 52r (10th century);
— London, BL., Cotton Tiberius C.VI, f. 16v (1041-66);
— Paris, BN., lat. 7211, f. 150v (11th-12th century);
— Oxford, Balliol College, 173a, f. 76r and 76v (early 12th century);
— St.-Blasien, *De cantu et musica sacra*, II, of Martin Gerbert (1774), Pl. 24, Fig. 9; Pl. 25, Fig. 10; Pl. 29, Fig. 9; Pl. 30, Fig. 10. (Drawings from a codex from the second half of the 12th century; lost in a fire in 1768).

3.2.1. DENOMINATION

The instruments denoted with the Latin denominations *cithara* and *psalterium* — actually Greek borrowings — are described as delta-shaped in medieval exegesis. When explaining musical instruments in the Holy Scriptures, the Church Fathers tried to furnish both these instrumental names with a word history. These were not etymologies in the modern sense but rather a summary of terms which they regarded as being equivalent. I will refer to these terms as etymological equivalents.

The latinized denominations *nablum* and *psalterium* and the Latin term *laudatorium* were used for the *psalterium*. Variants on *nablum* are *nablat(h)* and *nablon*. Remigius of Auxerre also used the latinized instrumental indication *organum* as an etymological equivalent.[22]

Although, in fact, the Latin word *cithara* should go back to the Hebrew *kinnor* (various spellings) from the Old Testament, this term is not present in the biblical exegesis. The etymological connection between the Hebrew *kinnor* and Greek *kithara*, however, has not been accepted.[23] Only the Latin *cithara barbarica* is mentioned as an etymological equivalent for the instrumental denomination *cithara*.

From the study of the two groups of literary sources (exegetical works and the Dardanus passages) it appears that the 'etymology' used with respect to the *cithara* and the *psalterium* is very consistent (Table 2). There must have been a written tradition behind the etymological equivalents. We should, therefore, investigate whether the indication *delta* for a form is connected with surviving ideas on the form of the biblical instruments the *cithara* and *psalterium* and their etymological equivalents.

Table 2. Comparative table. Etymological equivalents of the instruments *cithara* and *psalterium*.

author or manuscript	source			name of instrument cithara	psalterium
Cassiodorus	CCL	97,	11		nablum
Isidore of Seville	III,	22,	7	barbarica	
Pseudo-Bede	PL	93,	481B		nablat
			1099		nablum
Raban Maurus	PL	109,	346A		nablum
			346B		laudatorium
	PL	111,	498A		nablum
			498A		laudatorium
			498B	barbarica	
Pseudo-Jerome	PL	30,	215A		nablon
			215A		laudatorium
Walafrid Strabo?	PL	113,	651D		nablum
			651D		laudatorium
Remigius of Auxerre	PL	131,	138C		organum
			138C		laudatorium
			138C		nablum
			147C		nablath
			147C		organum
Notker Teutonicus	III,	3,	1117		(rotta)
Bruno of Würzburg	PL	142,	44C		nablum
Summarium Heinrici		VI,	10	(nablum)	nablum
Bartholomaeus Anglicus		cap.	142	barbarica	
Johannes of Zamora	CSM	20,	118	barbarica	
London, BL., Cot. C.VI		f.	16v		nabulum
Paris, BN., lat. 7211		f.	150v		nablum
		f.	150v		laudatorium

(See notes 12 and 13, and Appendix II for an extensive list of sources.)

The Septuagint and the Vulgate show a remarkable diversity in the names given to musical instruments. I will examine how these fluctuations correlate with each other in both biblical translations as far as the instruments *nebel* and *kinnor* are concerned; in doing so I will proceed from the numbers of instruments reported in the original Hebrew (and Aramaic) text.

In the Hebrew Old Testament we come across *nebel* 27 times. The Septuagint gives four different translations for *nebel*: *kithara, nabla, organon* and *psaltērion* (Table 3). The Vulgate also gives four translations. The difference with the Greek translation is that the *organon* indications are dropped. Moreover, in four cases *nebel* is translated with *lyra*, and there is a noticeable shift in favor of *psalterium* in the translation of *nebel*.

In the Septuagint the instrumental name from II Ezra 12:27 is missing. Moreover in both the Septuagint and the Vulgate the term *nebel* is translated wrongly in Isaiah 14:11, and as a result is dropped as an indication for an instrument.[24] This is also the case in Psalm 70:22 of the Vulgate where the term *nebel* is translated with *vasum psalmi*.

Table 3. Fluctuations in the denomination given for the biblical instrumental indication *nebel* in absolute numbers.

Hebrew			nebel			
Greek	kithara		nabla	organon	psaltērion	
Latin	cithara	lyra	nablum		psalterium	
Hebrew O.T.			27			
Septuagint	1		14	2	8	/-2
Vulgate	1	4	3		17	/-2

In the Hebrew text of the Old Testament we find the indication *kinnor* 42 times. In the Septuagint this indication is translated in four different ways: *kinnyra, kithara, organon* and *psaltērion* (Table 4). In the Vulgate the term *kinnyra* no longer occurs; it is replaced by *lyra* and by *cithara*.
The instrumental name from II Ezra 12:27 also does not occur in the Septuagint.

Table 4. Fluctuations in the denomination given for the biblical instrumental indication *kinnor* in absolute numbers.

Hebrew	kinnor						
Greek		kinnyra	kithara		organon	psaltērion	
Latin			cithara	lyra	organum	psalterium	
Hebrew O.T.	42						
Septuagint		18	20		1	2	/-1
Vulgate			37	2	1	2	

Despite the fact that in the exegesis the delta form of the *cithara* and of the *psalterium* (as also their etymological equivalents *cithara barbarica, laudatorium, nablum, organum*) relate to particular biblical passages, in neither the Septuagint nor the Vulgate are there any indications to make us think that the instruments were delta-shaped. It is, therefore, important to investigate the formal characteristics attributed to these instruments in present-day organology.

The term *cithara*, being the latinized form of the Greek *kithara*, is important as a translation of the Hebrew *kinnor* in the Septuagint and the Vulgate. There are major differences of opinions concerning this instrument. As far as is known, no authentic representations of the *kinnor* have survived.[25] In the eleventh century, the German school master Heinricus glossed the Greek *kinnyra* with the Latin term *cynerum* in his *Summarium* (Lib. VI, cap. 10). Contemporary organology presumes that the Hebrew *kinnor* must have been a lyre-like instrument comparable to the ancient Greek *kithara* in construction and in the manner in which it was played.[26] The *kithara* was a stringed instrument consisting of a wooden sound chest with two relatively large arms. The instrument usually had seven strings which were stretched vertically between the sound chest and the yoke-crossing between the two arms. The strings were sounded with the help of a *plectron*, a small plucking tool.

Isidore of Seville, and later Raban Maurus, Johannes Aegidius of Zamora and Jerome of Moravia, report the instrumental indication *cithara barbarica* as a synonym for *kithara*. In his *Etymologiae*, Isidore formulates this as follows: *Psalterium* [...] *est autem similitudo citharae barbaricae in modum* Δ *litterae*, 'the psalterium is formed like the letter delta, as the cithara of the Germans.'[27] A formal similarity between the *cithara barbarica* and the Greek *kithara* is not probable. The definition *barbarus harpa* of Venantius Fortunatus mentioned in Chapter 1.3 should be borne in mind in this connection. It is presumed that the indication *cithara barbarica* is a middle-Latin name for the *rot(t)a* or *rotte*, a native instrument of the Franks or West Goths.[28] The *rotte* has a triangular form with one right angle and belongs to the same instrumental family as the board cithers. It may possibly be the instrument referred to by the German author Notker Teutonicus when he wrote that the *rotta* is derived from the delta-shaped *psalterium decachordum* although the form and the number of strings differ:

> Sed postquam illud symphoniaci quidem et ludicratores ut quidam ait ad suum opus traxerant formam utique eius et figuram . commoditati suae habilem fecerant et plures chordas annectentes . et nomine barbarico Rottam appellantes mysticam illam trinitatis formam transmutando.[29]

> 'But after this the musicians and actors — as a certain spokesman reports — with an eye to their work, had adapted the form [of the psalterium decachordum] to make it suitable for their use, by both setting several strings on it as well as giving it the barbarian [=German] name rotta. In this way they have changed the triangular form, which has a 'mystical' significance.'

The *rotte* illustrations on the capitals in the church of the Abbey of Saint-Pierre in Moissac (capital of the cloister, c. 1100) and in the Musée des Augustins in Toulouse (no. 473, capital of the convent Ste.-Marie-la-Daurade, late eleventh century) also have the form of a right-angled triangle (*figs. 17* and *18*). Both illustrations can be called interpretations of instruments from the Holy Scriptures. An important indication in this direction is the inscription chiseled in stone on the capital in Moissac. It reads: *NAME* [=EMAN] *CUM ROTA*. Eman is, together with David, one of the co-authors of the Psalms who is also mentioned in the introduction to the Psalms, *Origo Psalmorum*. The theme on the capital from Toulouse resembles that from Moissac, although the scene in Toulouse is not accompanied by an inscription.

The comparison between the *psalterium* and the *cithara barbarica* in the *Etymologiae* of Isidore could, therefore, have been used deliberately to emphasize the contrast with the *kithara*.

Nablum is a latinized form of the Hebrew instrumental indication *nebel* or the Greek *nabl(i)a*.[30] Apart from *nablum* we also find the word written as *nablat(h)* and *nablon* in Psalm commentaries. The fact that the instrument *nebel* is first mentioned in the Old Testament in I Samuel 10:5 is, according to biblical historians, an indication of Assyrian rather than Egyptian influence.[31] Therefore Sendrey presumes that the form is related to the Assyrian types of harp. The majority of researchers is inclined to regard the instrument as a triangular Hebrew angular harp. Also the manner in which the *nebel* is played — plucked with the fingers — indicates an analogy with the way in which the harp is played.[32]

Organum is the latinized form of the Greek *organon*. The word has a very broad meaning; it can generally indicate any appliance or tool. In the Middle Ages it often signified *instrumentum musicum*.[33]

The Book of Psalms is often referred to in Hebrew by the words *Sefer Tehillim*, which mean 'The Book of Songs of Praise'.[34] This significance is expressed in Greek by the term *psaltērion* and in Latin by *psalterium*. The word *psalterium* had a double meaning in the Middle Ages. It could indicate both the Book of Psalms and the stringed instrument used for giving praise to God.[35] Because of the analogy in name with the Book of Psalms, which in the Middle Ages was regarded primarily as the work of David, this instrument is often mentioned in connection with David.

As McKinnon has been able to make clear, it can be established with certainty that the term *psaltērion* indicates a stringed instrument with the form of a right-angled triangle. In this respect the *psaltērion* is comparable with the Greek angular harp *trigōnon*.[36] Also the relationship with the Greek verb ψάλλειν, 'to pluck', points in the direction of a stringed instrument.[37] The majority of researchers, therefore, considers the instrument indicated by the term *psaltērion* to be a harp.[38] However, the medieval *psalterium*, like the *rotta*, is not categorized as a harp but as a harp-psaltery. This latter group of instruments is characterized by a sounding board placed behind the strings. In this respect the medieval instrument *psalterium* differs from the Greek *psaltērion*.

Laudatorium is the literal Latin translation of *psaltērion*. The eulogistic character expressed by *psaltērion* is also incorporated in the term *laudatorium*. The meaning of this word is described as *est idem quod laus*, 'that is the same as "laus"' — an explanation which is found in the *Epistola* 429 of Jerome.[39] Only in exegetical texts have I found the word *laudatorium* used as an indication of an instrument.

From the summary given above, it can be deduced that the formal description of the Hebrew instrument *nablum* points in particular in the direction of the delta form. Lack of evidence makes it impossible to prove conclusively that the *nebel* in fact had the shape of a regular triangle.

It is improbable that the instrument the *psaltērion* had a regular triangular shape. Probably it had the shape of an angular harp with a right angle between the two parts of the wooden frame. Strings were strung diagonally over this frame.

3.2.2. THE DELTA FORM

There is a remarkable similarity in the words used by medieval authors when they mention a delta-shaped musical instrument.

The most common phrasing is: *Psalterium est* [...] *in modum* Δ *deltae litterae (formatum)*, 'the psalterium is formed as the letter delta.'[40] The connection between instrument and form is represented in this statement by means of a comparison in which the outward appearance, in this case that of the *psalterium*, is compared with the Greek (capital-)letter delta. The Psalm commentary of the Church Father Cassiodorus is the first evidence of this description of the form. An identical description is found in a number of Dardanus passages.[41]

Apart from the phrase just mentioned, three authors use the formulation in *modum deltae (compositum)*, '(made up) in the manner of a delta'.[42] Here the comparison between the form of the musical instrument and the (capital-)letter delta is not explicit. This formulation is an abbreviated form of the previous one, and apparently through the use of the word *delta*, sufficient in itself to suggest an association with the form of the Greek (capital-)letter in the minds of the authors. Gerhoh (1093-1169), provost of the Augustinerchorherrenstift in Reichersberg, is the only exegete who uses both phrases in his Psalm commentary.[43]

Honorius of Autun (c. 1080-c. 1156) chose completely different words in his exposition on the Psalms. Here we read: *Delta, ad cujus formam Psalterium fit, quarta littera in ordine alphabeti notatur*, 'the psalterium is made in resemblance to the delta, the letter which is noted fourth in the alphabet.'[44] The content of Honorius' words expresses the same kinship in form between instrument and letter as the two expressions cited earlier.

Apart from the explicit mention of the term *delta*, Remigius of Auxerre, Gerhoh of Reichersberg and Heinricus also use *triangulum*, 'triangular', to refer to the form (see Table 5). The strong resemblance with the textual passages in which a delta-shaped instrument is spoken of show that *triangulum* can be regarded as a synonym.

In some Psalm commentaries and Dardanus passages, the text in which the *psalterium* is linked with the delta form is attributed to the Church Father Jerome (c. 342-420), who was much respected in the Middle Ages. But the wording chosen in the two groups of texts differs. The attribution in the Psalm commentary of Cassiodorus, which is the first source in which it occurs, reads: *Ut Hieronymus ait*, 'as Jerome says'. In view of the identical formulation in pseudo-Bede, Remigius of Auxerre and Bruno of Würzburg (?-1045), it is plausible that this is based on Cassiodorus.[45] The Dardanus passages in Munich, Bayerische Staatsbibl., Clm. 14523, f. 52r (*fig. 19*), Oxford, Balliol College, 173a, f. 76v, St.-Blasien, Pl. 25, Fig. 10 (*fig. 21*) and Pl. 29, Fig. 9 (*fig. 22*) include a similar formulation. In contrast to the non-Dardanus texts, only the phrases *ut Hieronymus dicit* ('as Jerome says') and *ut Hieronymo dicitur* ('as is said by Jerome') are used. However, there is no basis for such attributions: no text can be found in the oeuvre of Jerome which could have served as Cassiodorus' source. Cassiodorus is the first to mention the attribution to Jerome.[46]

The oldest manuscript which is based on the Dardanus letter and includes an attribution to Jerome is the Psalter of Angers, Bibl. Municipale, 18, which is dated about the year 845.[47] In folio 13r of the manuscript, the following is reported concerning the illuminations and the captions of musical instruments: *Haec dictas a sancto Hieronymo legis interpretatione beatissimo*, 'these things are said by the holy Jerome who is most blessed because he explained (translated) the law [=the Old Testament].' In the text there is no reference to a delta-shaped instrument.

Two hypotheses can be proposed with respect to the attribution of the delta-shaped instruments to Jerome: the attribution is based on a lost text of Jerome, or was added by Cassiodorus because of Jerome's authority.

The delta form is, if the etymological equivalents are left out of consideration, applicable to both the *cithara* and the *psalterium*. I have investigated both instruments regarding the frequency with which the form and number of strings are indicated. The results are correlated and summarized in Table 5. Texts, illustrations and captions were once again used in the comparison.

Medieval authors were divided in their opinion about the instrument which was regarded as delta-shaped. Although the delta form was originally only linked to the *psalterium*, this changed in the chapter entitled *De musica et partibus ejus* in *De universo* by Raban Maurus.[48] Raban's text deviates in several respects from older texts which discussed the delta form, such as those of Cassiodorus, Isidore and pseudo-Bede.[49]

The prime difference is that not only the *psalterium* but also the *cithara* is indicated as having a delta form. The indication of the form 'delta' in relation to the *cithara* is found twice in the *Summarium Heinrici* from the middle of the twelfth century. In the chapter *De musicorum vasis*, the delta form is noted as a common feature of the instruments *cithara, nebel* and *psalterium*; in the words of Lib. VI, cap. 10: *Cynerum vel nablum vel psalterium unum sunt in modum delte literae*, 'the kinnor, the nebel or the psalterium are one in the manner of the letter delta.' In this gloss a compilation is made of various data on instruments taken from Isidore's *Etymologiae* (Lib. III, cap. 22). The second source of evidence is found in the long alphabetical version of the eleventh book of the *Summarium Heinrici*, where *Cythara musicum instrumentum triangulum .XXIIII. cordarum* is reported as a gloss for *harpfa/herphe*.[50] This translates as: 'The cithara is a triangular musical instrument with 24 strings.' The source is unknown.

The *cithara barbarica* is also reported as delta-shaped in two thirteenth-century theoretical writings on music, namely *De proprietatibus rerum* of Bartholomaeus Anglicus and *Ars musica* of Johannes Aegidius of Zamora.

Table 5. Comparative table. Form and number of strings of the delta-shaped instruments, the *cithara* and *psalterium*.

author/manuscript	sources (Appendix II.)	formal indication cith.	formal indication psalt.	number of strings cith. T.	cith. ill.	psalt. T.	psalt. ill.
Cassiodorus	CCL 97, 11		delta				
Isidore of Seville	III, 22, 7		delta			10	
Pseudo-Bede	PL 93, 481B		delta			10	
	PL 93, 1099		delta				
Raban Maurus	PL 109, 346B					10	
	346C	delta		24			
	PL 111, 498A	delta		24			
	498B	delta				10	
Pseudo-Jerome	PL 30, 214C	delta		24			
	PL 30, 215A					10	
Walafrid Strabo?	PL 113, 652A	delta		24		10	
Remigius of Auxerre	PL 131, 138D		delta				
	PL 131, 147C		triangulum			10	
Notker Teutonicus	III, 3, 1117		delta			10	
Bruno of Würzburg	PL 142, 44A		delta				
Summarium Heinrici	VI, 10	delta	delta				
Summarium Heinrici	XI	triangulum		24			
Rupert of Deutz	PL 167, 1096C		delta			10	
	PL 167, 1180D		delta			10	
Honorius of Autun	PL 172, 271D		delta			10	
Gerhoh of Reichersberg	PL 193, 629		delta			10	
			triangulum				
Herrad of Hohenburg	97, 202		delta				
Bartholomaeus Anglicus	cap. 142	delta				10	
Johannes of Zamora	CSM20, 118	delta	delta			10	
Jerome of Moravia	GS I, 9b		delta			10	
Munich, BStb., Clm. 14523	f. 52r	delta		24	24		
	f. 51v		delta			10	
Turin, BNU., D.III.19	f. 34r		delta				10
London, BL., Cot. C.VI	f. 16v	delta	delta				10
Paris, BN., lat. 7211	f. 150v	delta	delta	24		10	10
Oxford, Ball. Coll. 173a	f. 76r	delta		24	12		
	f. 76v		delta?			10	10
London, coll. Ches., 32	f. 1r		delta			10	10
Gerbert 1774	Pl. 24, Fig. 9		delta			10	
	Pl. 25, Fig. 10	delta		24	24		
	Pl. 29, Fig. 9	delta			12		
	Pl. 30, Fig. 10		delta		31		

T. = text, ill. = illustration

Because the authors not only use the name *cithara barbarica* but also the same wording as Raban, it seems likely that these are taken from *De musica et partibus ejus*. This does not apply to the entry in the *Glossa Ordinaria* which was formerly attributed exclusively to Walafrid Strabo (c. 808-49).[51] Although the *cithara* is described there as delta-shaped, the word-usage deviates considerably from that in *De musica et partibus ejus*.

A second point on which Raban's text differs from previous texts is that the delta form is not attributed to Jerome. Nor is it attributed to him in the *Glossa Ordinaria* or in the cited writings of Bartholomaeus Anglicus or Johannes Aegidius of Zamora.

Regarding the form of the instrument, the description in the Dardanus passages does not correspond with that of Raban Maurus. The principal difference is that, with the exception of the manuscript Paris, BN., lat. 7211, f. 150v, all other Dardanus passages include an attribution to Jerome. It seems that the delta form is attributed at random in the Dardanus passages, as also in the Raban text; now the formal indication applies to the *cithara*, now to the *psalterium*.[52]

The origin of the disagreement about which instrument should be regarded as delta-shaped can partly be explained by the nature of Raban's writing. Raban's aim was to compile an encyclopedic work. He used material from all sorts of sources.[53] Parts of the Dardanus letter apparently provided material for Raban's exposition on music. Due to the difference in starting-point with respect to the Psalm commentaries, Raban's organological exposition deviated from that of traditional instrumental exegesis. On the other hand, it remains possible that the authors of the Dardanus passages in their turn used the work of Raban and the exegetes as source material.

Another change took place when exegetes no longer limited themselves to the traditional description of the forms of instruments, but also came to include schematic drawings of these instruments in which both the form and the construction appear to be unrealistic. The delta-shaped *cithara*, as reproduced in some Dardanus passages (*figs. 21* and *22*), does not agree in any respect with the construction of the Greek *kithara*, as described in Chapter 3.2.1. The delta-shaped *psalterium* depicted in folio 34r of the tenth-century *Etymologiae* manuscript Turin, Bibl. Nazionale Universitaria, D.III.19 (*fig. 20*) also has a strange construction. The delta form is reproduced in this case as a regular triangle with the point pointing downward. Moreover, the tuning pegs stand vertically on the upper side of the peg arm.

The manner in which the strings are attached to the delta-shaped instruments in the Dardanus passages is also very surprising. The strings seem to disappear into thin air on the underside of the instrument, and despite there being ten or more strings, sometimes only one, two or three tuning pegs are drawn at the triangular top of the delta. The reversed tuning peg at the top of the instrument on Pl. 25, ill. 10 in Gerbert's writing (*fig. 21*) is organologically inexplicable. Such reversed tuning pegs can also be seen in illustrations to the Dardanus passages in the manuscripts Oxford, Balliol College, 173a, f. 76r and Munich, Bayerische Staatsbibl., Clm. 14523, f. 51v (*fig. 19*). Gerbert's delta-shaped *cithara* (*fig. 21*) shows a remarkable resemblance to the instrument in the Dardanus letter in Munich.

A twofold argumentation can be offered to explain these unusual illustrations. First it is possible that the instrumental depictions are representations of the symbolic interpretations of musical instruments from the Holy Scriptures. Musical instruments of the Jewish culture were only known to medieval theologians from written accounts. The only real information which these authors had about Jewish instruments was the name of the instrument and the instrumental category to which it belonged.[54] Ideas on construction, playing and sound character were the result of centuries of instrumental allegory. It was impossible for medieval writers and illustrators to form any kind of real picture of biblical instruments on the basis of such explanations. The author of the Dardanus letter was aware of this when he wrote:

> Cogor a te, ut tibi, Dardane, de aliquibus generibus musicorum, sicut res docet, vel visione, vel auditu brevi sermone respondeam. Alia enim ad lucidum proferre non possum: quia unaquaeque res secundum ingenium ejus est: quae autem possunt enarrari libenter explicabuntur.[55]

> 'I see myself, Dardanus, impelled by you to inform you briefly and concisely about some sorts of musical instruments, according to the way reality teaches either by means of personal observation or from hearsay [from those who saw the real thing]. Now, I cannot clarify everything, however, because each matter [=instrument] has its own nature. But the things about which something can be said will be willingly explained.'

Moreover, the authors added new interpretations to the existing instrumental exegesis in order to be able to explain the musical instruments as unreal objects. In this way, the *cithara* and *psalterium*, instruments with a pagan origin, were explained in Christian terms.

The biblical context, especially the Book of Psalms in which the instruments the *psalterium* and *cithara* are often mentioned together (Psalm 32:2, 56:9, 80:3, 91:4, 107:3 and 150:3), and the person of David — who, according to surviving accounts, played both instruments — accounted for the fact that the exegesis attributed a single symbolic form to both instruments: the delta form. The symbolic character of the triangular form of the *psalterium* is emphasized by Notker Teutonicus:

> Sciendum est . quod antiquum psalterium instrumentum dechachordum utique erat . in hac videlicet deltae literae figura multipliciter mistica.[56]
>
> 'One should know that the old psalterium was in any case a ten-stringed instrument; through its form, which was moreover the form of the letter delta, it had in many ways a mystical significance.'

Notker rightly notes here that there were several symbolic interpretations of the delta form. The form can, for example, be explained as the correlation of particular numbers. Research shows that, apart from the form, also the number of strings and the sound box of the delta-shaped instrument were interpreted in a symbolic way. Under the heading *De mystica compositione psalterii decachordi* in his *De trinitate et operibus ejus*, Rupert of Deutz (c. 1070-1129) calls the *psalterium* completely symbolic.[57] It is a symbolism which, according to Peter Lombard (c. 1100-60), can only be understood by the initiated:

> Quidquid in hoc psalterio ligneo instrumento reperitur. totum habet mysticum sensum. et ab imperitis non intellegitur.[58]
>
> 'All that is found in this wooden instrument, the psalterium, has an entirely symbolic meaning, which, however, is not understood by laymen.'

3.3. NUMBER OF STRINGS

A particular number of strings is often mentioned in connection with the *cithara* and the *psalterium*. These numbers are not chosen at random. From Table 5 we can deduce that the number of strings is very constant in both groups of texts, both for the *cithara* and the *psalterium*. For the *cithara* the number is 24 and for the *psalterium*, 10. The 12 and 31 strings on some *cithara* illuminations in Dardanus passages form the exception. Probably the 31 strings is the result of inaccurate drawing; it is not certain if this is also the case with the 12 strings.

The number of strings per instrument seems to be more constant than the etymological equivalents, this irrespective of whether the instrument is described as delta-shaped or as 'square-shaped'. I have not found any direct link between the delta form and the number of strings. The consistency regarding the number of strings can be explained from the expositions of the early medieval Church Fathers on the musical instruments which are mentioned in the Holy Scriptures. However, they attributed the number of strings also with a symbolic meaning. The numbers 10 and 24 should, therefore, definitely not be understood as a reflection of the real number of strings of the instruments *cithara* and *psalterium*.

3.4. SYMBOLIC INTERPRETATIONS

3.4.1. NUMERICAL SYMBOLISM

Although in our time numerical symbols are often determined by convention, in the Ancient World and the Middle Ages symbolism was part of the nature of numbers. Medieval numerical symbolism was strongly influenced by the Greek theory of numbers and the gnostic way of thinking.[59]

For the Greeks the archetypal numbers (1,2,3,4) played a particularly important role. In the Pythagorean theory of numbers they were combined together in the *tetraktys*, 'the system of four numbers', which includes the characteristics of the first four numbers and their correlations. In the eyes of the Greeks, the sum of every number of subsequent arithmetic numbers up to and including 4, beginning with 1, was perfect: 3 (1+2), 6 (1+2+3), 10 (1+2+3+4).[60]

In contrast to the present day, when numbers are abstract arithmetic units, the *tetraktys* consisted of figurative numbers. In this case figurative numbers are understood to be the geometrical depiction of numbers by means of points. When broken down into abstract units, figurative numbers in a level plane are represented as geometrical planes and in space as geometrical bodies in space. The *dekas*, the 'tens' can be obtained (see Schema 3) by adding up the component parts of the *tetraktys*. The 10 forms the first boundary in the decimal system.

Schema 3. The tetraktys.

```
      1           .
     2 3         . .
    4 5 6       . . .
   7 8 9 10    . . . .
```

The geometric illustrations which can be derived from figurative numbers were especially important for the Greeks: one point forms a geometric definition of space; linking two points forms a line; three points delimit an area and so form a surface (the triangle), and four points form a body (the pyramid). For this reason archetypal numbers were regarded as the building blocks of the cosmos which surrounds us.[61]

The use of figurative numbers was also known in the Middle Ages.[62] The significance then attributed to numbers differed from that attributed to them by the ancient Greeks. For the medieval exegetical writers, *aritmetica* was a means to explain the numbers in the Old Testament, and, to a lesser extent, the numbers in the New Testament.

The exegetes themselves found one biblical indication of the use of *aritmetica* for conceiving and explaining biblical data using numerical symbolism, namely the well-known verse in *Sapientia Salomonis* 11:21. Here they could read that God 'has ordered all things through measure, number and weight'. The presumed numerical ordering of the cosmos also made it necessary to explain reality by means of numerical exegesis. The importance of numerical symbolism as a means to explaining 'all known forms' was underlined by Isidore of Seville in his *Etymologiae*:

> Sic et alii in scripturis sacris numeri existunt, quorum figuras nonnisi noti huius artis scientiae solvere possunt.[63]

> 'Thus there are also other numbers in the Holy Scriptures, whose figures can only be unravelled by those who have knowledge of this art.'

A study of exegesis reveals that especially the numbers 3 and 4 are associated with delta-shaped musical instruments. The symbolic relationship between the number 10 and the delta form is hypothetical. In addition, symbolic interpretations are linked to the 10 and 24 strings of the *cithara* and the *psalterium*.

The number 3

Since the Pythagorean theory of numbers was first formulated, the number 3 has counted as the first complete number.[64] It consists of a combination of the numbers 1 and 2 (unity and separation), and represents the perfect unity, a perfection which is also represented by a regular triangle.

Medieval writers of exegesis were also aware of the perfect character of the number 3. In his *De scripturis et scriptoribus sacris*, Hugh of St. Victor (1097-1141) classified the number 3 under the category *secundum qualitatem compositionis* — 'according to the nature of the composition' — as *indissolubilia et incorruptibilia*, 'indivisible and incorruptible'.[65]

Its perfect character made it an excellent symbol of the Trinity in medieval biblical exegesis[66], and this explanation was also given in relation to the delta shape of musical instruments. In his Dardanus letter pseudo-Jerome explains the delta form of the *cithara* as a figure of the Trinity:

> Cithara [...] trinam formam habens, quasi in modum Deltae litterae, per fidem sanctae Trinitatis manifestissime sine dubio significat.[67]
>
> 'The cithara, which has a triangular form, as in the fashion of the letter Delta, most clearly and indubitably indicates the faithfulness of the Holy Trinity.'

The author of the *Glossa Ordinaria* and Raban Maurus use virtually the same words.[68] They too apply the explanation to the *cithara*. Notker Teutonicus also connects the delta form with the Trinity, but this time it is the *psalterium* to which the symbolism of form relates.[69]

The number 4

In the Hebrew and Greek languages numbers were written using letters (A=1, B=2, etc.). These conventions led to the development of gematria: the explanation of numbers through corresponding letters, and the other way around, the explanation of letters through corresponding numbers.[70] Gematria was used by the Jews and the gnostics to interpret words from the Holy Scriptures.

In terms of gematria, the number 4 corresponds with the Greek capital letter delta (Δ). The gematric explanation is used in the Psalm exegesis of Honorius of Autun. It shows a correlation between the delta form of the *psalterium* and the fourth letter of the alphabet: *Delta, ad cujus formam Psalterium fit, quarta littera in ordine alphabeti notatur*, 'the delta, according to whose form the psalterium is made, is noted as the fourth letter in the alphabetical order.'[71] Also in the symbolic explanation which follows the Honorius passage, the instrument is brought into connection with the number 4. In this way the number symbolizes the body of Christ and the four gospels. In the words of the *Selectorum Psalmorum expositio* of Honorius:

> [...] et corpus Christi quatuor elementis compaginatur: sive Ecclesia, quae est corpus ejus, quatuor Evangeliis aedificatur.
>
> 'And the body of Christ is composed of four elements: or rather, the Church, which is His body, is edified by the four gospels.'

In the study of Giesel the *cithara* is linked with the four gospels but not with the body of Christ or the Church.[72] The explanation of Honorius may then also be regarded as 'innovative'. I know of no gematric relationship between the Greek capital letter delta Δ and the first letter of the name David — however obvious this may seem — in the biblical exegesis.[73]

The number 10

In the Psalm translation of the Septuagint the number 10 is represented by the Hebrew word *asor*. In three Psalms (32:2, 91:4 and 143:9) this indication is named in connection with the Old Testament instrument *nebel*. The query then arises whether the word *asor* should be considered as an adjective or as a substantive. In other words, is it a question of a *psalterium decem chordarum* ('a ten-stringed psalterium'), or — as Jerome phrased it in Psalm 91:4 in connection with the *Psalterium iuxta Hebraeos — in decacordo et in psalterio* ('with the ten stringed and with the psalterium'), which could be a hendiadys. In the exegetical treatises of Jerome the word is used as an adjective so that, partly on his authority, the *psalterium* is attributed with having ten strings. This opinion was taken over by all Psalm commentators after him.[74]

As has already been mentioned, the number 10 was regarded in medieval exegesis as a number which expressed perfection. Two hypotheses can be offered which could justify a symbolic relationship between the number 10 and the delta form. Both are strongly influenced by the Greek way of thinking and can only be understood fully in this context.

The geometric congruence between the delta shape and the number 10 can be given as the first supposition. I have already pointed out that the *dekas* can be obtained by adding up the *tetraktys* numbers. The *dekas* forms the boundary of the decimal system and, in geometric terms, results in a regular triangle (Schema 3). In addition the *tetraktys* numbers influenced the medieval theory of music. Their relationships are those of the consonant musical intervals: 1:2 (octave), 2:3 (fifth) and 3:4 (fourth). The perfect character of the triangular stringed instrument and the consonant character of the intervals can be interrelated.

A second hypothesis is the correlation between the number 10 and the sign Δ. The connection is based on the derivation of the first capital letter (Δ) of the Greek word *deka*, 'ten'.[75] However, there is no surviving explanation from the Middle Ages which shows a relationship between the triangular shape of instruments and the number 10. Nevertheless, the number 10, when used in connection with the number of strings, is attributed with a symbolic meaning. The consistent opinion of theologians concerning the attribution of this number of strings to the *cithara* and the *psalterium* is connected with this. The *psalterium* has a fixed number of ten strings. This number was chosen on the grounds of Psalm verses 32:2, 91:4 and 143:9 in which the *psalterium decachordum* was referred to. In the exegesis the ten-stringed, delta-shaped instruments are almost unanimously linked to the ten Commandments: *Psalterium cum decem chordis Ecclesia est cum Decalogo legis*, 'the psalterium with the ten strings is the Church with the ten Commandments.'[76] Only the explanation of pseudo-Bede deviates in this respect:

> Docet etiam decem principalia praecepta per decem chordas musici instrumenti significata, in quibus omne Novum et Vetus Testamentum comprehenditur.[77]

> 'It also teaches the ten principal Commandments, which are indicated by means of the ten strings of a musical instrument; the entire Old and New Testaments are comprehended in this.'

The number 24

The number of 24 strings is reported in all texts on the delta-shaped *cithara*. Some *cithara* illuminations in Dardanus passages show a different number of strings. One such case is the illumination in the manuscript Oxford, Balliol College, 173a, f. 76r. The delta-shaped *cithara* depicted there has 12 strings, while the text refers to 24 strings. Whether the halving is due to inaccurate drawing or to other considerations (for example, reduction so that the number of strings can be clearly distinguished) is uncertain. The *cithara* on Pl. 29, Fig. 9 in *De cantu et musica sacra* also has 12 strings (*fig. 22*).

In the *Glossa Ordinaria* the number of 24 strings is connected to the *viginti quatuor seniores*, 'the twenty-four Elders' of the Revelation of St. John.[78]

3.4.2. SYMBOLIC CONTRASTS

Not only are numbers symbolically associated with delta-shaped instruments; also the construction of the instruments is interpreted in a symbolic way by the exegetes.

It is especially the place where resonance occurs that is most often chosen in the instrument exegesis to express the distinction between *cithara* and *psalterium*. Hippolytus, in his Psalm commentary, is the first who links the construction of the *cithara* and the *psalterium* with a symbolic explanation. Because the *psalterium*, according to Hippolytus, is the only instrument which does not have any curved lines and because the sound chest is not situated underneath as with the *cithara* but at the top of the instrument, he attributes the instrument with the highest degree of perfection. Hippolytus compares the *psalterium* with the *corpus Christi* whose structure is 'without any bend or curves'.[79] As far as the position of the sound chest is concerned, the distinction between the two instruments may be based on the real organological characteristics of the Greek instruments *psaltērion* and *kithara*. Hippolytus' idea of a *psalterium* without curved lines may have given rise to the later interpretation of the delta-shaped *psalterium*. This instrument does indeed have three straight sides.

The exegesis of Hippolytus was taken further by Eusebius, Bishop of Caesarea.[80] The explanation was passed on to the West through the writings of Hilary of Poitiers (c. 315-367).[81] Cassiodorus was the first western Church Father who applied the exposition on resonance to the delta-shaped *psalterium*. In the introduction to his *Expositio Psalmorum* we read:

> Psalterium [...] obesum ventrem in superioribus habens, ubi chordarum fila religata disciplinabiliter plectro percussa, suavissimam dicuntur reddere cantilenam. Hinc citharae positio videtur esse contraria, dum quod ista in imo continet, illud conversa vice gestat in capite.[82]

> 'The psalterium has a vaulting bulge in the upper parts where the strings are attached and struck with the plectrum according to the rules of the art; it is now said that these strings make a very pleasant sound. On the other hand the construction of the cithara seems to be the opposite, while [the psalterium] in turn carries what the other [the cithara] has beneath, on top.'

The attachment of the strings of the *psalterium* mentioned by Cassiodorus can be seen in the manuscript Munich, Bayerische Staatsbibl., Clm. 14523, f. 51v (*fig. 19*). The supposedly contrasting construction of the *cithara* is not, however, clear from the illustrations. On *citharae* in *De cantu et musica sacra* (*fig. 21*), and in the manuscripts in Munich (*fig. 19*: f. 52r) and Oxford, Balliol College, 173a, f. 76r, the strings are also drawn more or less vertically under the tuning pegs.

Isidore of Seville, who also describes the difference in resonance between the *cithara* and the *psalterium* in his exposition on the delta-shaped *cithara* in his *Etymologiae*, leaves out the passage on the attachment of the strings:

Sed psalterii et citharae haec differentia est, quod psalterium lignum illud concavum, unde sonus redditur, superius habet et deorsum feriuntur chordae, et desuper sonant. Cithara vero concavitatem ligni inferius habet.[83]

'But the psalterium differs in this from the cithara, namely that the psalterium has that curved wood where the sound is produced at its top; the strings are plucked below, and they sound from above. The cithara, however, has the wooden vaulting below.'

Notably enough, the statements of Cassiodorus and Isidore on form and resonance are at odds with the absolutely straight lines of the delta form as described by Hippolytus. According to Cassiodorus and Isidore there is namely a curved or vaulted sound chest on either the upper or lower side of the instruments. Apparently in this case traditional characteristics of form and instrumental symbolism overlap. This assumption is supported by the varying attribution of the delta form to, first, the *cithara* and then to the *psalterium* (see Table 5), without the statements on resonance and the related significance being essentially altered.

Two musical instruments are depicted (*fig. 20*) in the tenth-century *Etymologiae* manuscript Turin, Bibl. Nazionale Universitaria, D.III.19, folio 34r, in between the exposition on the *psalterium* and that on the *cithara*. The delta-shaped *psalterium* discussed in the text is reproduced in the right column on the right side. In order to demonstrate clearly the contrast with the form and the place of resonance of the *cithara*, a drawing of this latter instrument is also made immediately below the *psalterium*. The drawing shows an uniquely personal idea of the construction of the instrument.

The Psalm exegesis of Honorius of Autun and Remigius of Auxerre do not include any such contradictions. Although we can conclude from their words that the resonance of the *psalterium* came from the upper part of the instrument, they do not make any direct statements on the form of the sound chest. In the words of Honorius:

Dum enim inferius percutitur, [psalterium] superius resonat.[84]

'While the psalterium is plucked at the bottom, it sounds from the top.'

As a result of the idea that there was a difference in the place where resonance occurred — from the lower part in the case of the *cithara* and from the upper part of the instrument in the case of the *psalterium* — the *psalterium* was seen by the exegetes as an instrument eminently suitable for the praise of God. Moreover, this explanation offered the opportunity for the formation of diverse theological dualisms. The polarity of the place of resonance with respect to the place where the strings were struck was often explained as the contrast between heaven and earth, an explanation which we already met in the Psalm commentary of Cassiodorus. Cassiodorus supports his explanation with a passage based on the Gospel according to St. John (St. John 3:31-32):

> Qui est de terra, de terra est, et de terra loquitur; qui autem de caelo venit, quae vidit et audivit testatur.[85]
>
> 'He who is of the earth, is from the earth and speaks from the earth. But whoever comes from heaven, bears witness to what He has seen and heard.'

A different explanation is that the *cithara* and the *psalterium* are the *consonantia* of the Old and New Testament, which bring about a harmony of *nova cum veteribus*.[86]

It is important to remember that these above-mentioned interpretations are only given when both instruments are compared with each other.

The *psalterium* was preferred as the most noble instrument, undoubtedly because of the association which its name suggests with the word Psalm. The relationship between King David and the *psalterium*, as writer of the Psalms and performer on the delta-shaped musical instrument, is expressed both in writing and in the illustrations. A clear example is found in a twelfth-century Psalm commentary of Peter Lombard, Ms. 32 in the collection of A. Chester Beatty in London. On folio 1r, the frontispiece shows a visual exegetical scheme of the *psalterium decachordum* (*fig. 23*). Various symbolic interpretations are incorporated in the drawing.[87] David is in the center as a Christ figure in the posture of the crucifixion (*syndesmos* posture). We know that this figure really is both David and Christ from the captions *David* and *Christ caput ecclesiae* next to the head. David is represented as the *figura* of Christ. The *syndesmos* posture symbolizes a division in four parts which is formed by the David/Christ figure and the horizontal bar to which the strings are attached. The particular symbolic explanation for this is that of the *concordia discors*, the 'harmony of opposites'. The harmony of opposites is expressed, among other things, in the crucifix posture and the cross itself; together they refer to future salvation. In addition, the left and right sides of the cross are denoted respectively as the favorable and unfavorable sides.[88]

The accentuation of the division in three is interesting for research into the delta harp. It is relevant to the form of the *psalterium*, as the text beneath the frame of the illustration shows:

> In modum etiam delte littere formatus est. que figuram habet sancte Crucis. Nos enim gloriari oportet in cruce domini nostri Iesu Christi.

'The [psalterium] is formed in the manner of the letter delta, which has the form of the holy cross. We ought, moreover, to glory in the cross of our Lord Jesus Christ.'

It is certain that the word *figura* refers to the *psalterium* as a foreshadowing of the holy cross. Moreover, that particular instrument from the Old Testament is explained as the cross in the New Testament. There are exegetical texts on both sides of the body of David/Christ, between the frame of the illustration and the two converging lines which run from the ends of the horizontal crossbeam of the cross to the feet of the body. The two converging lines, together with the horizontal crossbeam, delimit an inverted triangular shape. In this way a division in four and a division in three are both realized in the one figure.

The *psalterium* depicted is explained as the *corpus Christi*, 'the body of Christ', which is completely in keeping with the exegesis. According to the text at the top of the illustration, Christ is the head of the Church.

Pickering, among contemporary scholars, goes so far that he regards not only the delta harp, but the harp of David in general as a symbol of the crucifixion.[89] In his argumentation Pickering uses one particular explanation from the medieval instrumental exegesis, but ignores the fact that the *cithara* was attributed with many other meanings.

If we sum up and classify a list of delta-shaped instruments, a number of interesting points emerge (see Table 6: types of form). In the delta-shaped instruments depicted in the Dardanus passages, the point of the triangle is constantly directed upwards and the position of the strings is vertical (form type R.1). This is not so in the case of delta harps, where the delta form seems to have been applied more freely (Table 6: types of form differing from R.1). The reason for this greater freedom is not known. Possibly certain symbolic interpretations of the Trinity were more important than an accurate reproduction of the delta form.

3.5. SYMBOL OR ACTUAL INSTRUMENT?

Although all the illustrations of delta harps have survived without exegetical inscriptions, the phenomenon of the delta harp can, I believe, be explained as a visual representation of the delta-shaped instruments mentioned in the exegesis. There is no reason to suppose that such instruments ever really existed. The following arguments are given to support this proposition:

— The places where the delta-shaped instruments are depicted or described. Delta-shaped instruments are referred to especially in commentaries on, or in introductions to the Book of Psalms. Depictions of delta harps are chiefly found in title illustrations, especially in Psalm manuscripts (see Table 6: context).

— King David as delta-harp player. In the Middle Ages it was thought that David was the discoverer of the *psalterium triangulum*.[90] This was expressed by representing him together with the delta harp. This musical instrument is found almost exclusively in relation to King David, who is either playing the instrument or holding it as an attribute (see Table 6: context). Only in the manuscripts Piacenza, Bibl. Capitolare, 65, f. 262v and Turin, Bibl. Nazionale Universitaria, D.III.19, f. 34r, is the relationship with the Bible or with David lacking.
In medieval manuscripts David is depicted with the triangular psaltery, as well as with the delta harp. One example can be seen in folio 59r in the *Hortus Deliciarum* (*fig. 24*). The triangular form of the instrument reveals similarities with the drawings of delta-shaped instruments which are provided with inscriptions in the Dardanus passages. Next to the instrument are the words *Psalterium dicitur decacordum* and the name of the performer, *David rex*. The connection between the illustration and the delta form is again emphasized in the accompanying text in which aspects from I Chronicles and the *Origo*-text are taken up. In the words of the *Hortus Deliciarum*:

[...] postquam Psalterium (musicum instrumentum in modum Δ) composuit, quatuor milia juvenum eligit, quibus omni musico instrumento cantare Psalterium precipit, et nunc solum melos (id est melodiam), nunc ipsa verba cantare instituit, quibus etiam centum quinquaginta psalmos instituit, et his quatuor precentores prefecit, scilicet Eman, Ethan, Asaph, Ydithun.[91]

'After he [=David] had composed (built) the musical instrument the psalterium after the manner of a delta, he selected four thousand young boys. He taught them to sing the psalterium with every musical instrument. On occasions he instructed them only in the melos, that is the melody, at other times he taught them to sing the words. He also taught them the hundred and fifty Psalms and appointed four lead singers over them [=the young men], namely Heman, Ethan, Asaph and Jeduthan.'

The text stresses the role of David as the discoverer of the delta-shaped *psalterium* and as the teacher and cantor of the Psalms. We read further that he was assisted in his teaching of the Psalms by four co-psalmists.

— The relationship between the harp and the triangular *cithara*. In the *Summarium Heinrici* the delta-shaped *cithara* with twenty-four strings is glossed with the words *harpfa/herphe*.[92] This gloss forms a synthesis between the delta-shaped *cithara* in the exegesis and the general characteristics of the form of the harp. Apparently in this case, the author is not thinking of a real harp but of a delta harp.

— The dates of the illustrations. As a final argument, it can be said that the time of the origin of the delta harp illustrations and that of the Dardanus illustrations coincide to a large extent. The manuscripts in which delta harps are depicted all date from the ninth to the fourteenth century. Dardanus illustrations are found in manuscripts from the tenth to the twelfth century.

Table 6. Delta-shaped stringed instruments arranged according to type of form.

sculpture or manuscript	types of form	context
St.-Blasien, Pl. 24, Fig. 9	R.1.	Dardanus passage
St.-Blasien, Pl. 25, Fig. 10	R.1.	Dardanus passage
St.-Blasien, Pl. 29, Fig. 9	R.1.	Dardanus passage
St.-Blasien, Pl. 30, Fig. 10	R.1.	Dardanus passage
Dresden, SLand.-bibl., Oc. 50, f. 11v	R.1.	24 Elders (Rev. 5:6)
Munich, BayS.-bibl., Clm. 14523, f. 51v	R.1.	Dardanus passage
Munich, BayS.-bibl., Clm. 14523, f. 52r	R.1.	Dardanus passage
Oxford, Balliol College, 173a, f. 76r	R.1.	Dardanus passage
Oxford, Balliol College, 173a, f. 76v	R.1.	Dardanus passage
Paris, BN., lat. 7211, f.150v	R.1.	Dardanus passage
Rome, Bibl. San Paolo, n.s.m., f. 147v	R.1.1.	Frontispiece Psalter: David plucking the strings of the harp
Bamberg, Staatsbibl., lit. 5, f. 2v	R.3.	Frontispiece Troper: musician passes harp to David?
London, Beatty coll., 32, f. 1r	R.3.	Frontispiece Psalter: David/Christ as a *psalterium decachordum*
Paris, BN., lat. 1, f. 215v	R.3.	Frontispiece Psalter: David plucking the strings of the harp
St.-Gall, Stiftsbibl., 21, p. 5	R.5.1.	Psalter ill.: musician accompanying David plucks the harp
St.-Gall, Stiftsbibl., 23, p. 12	R.5.1.	Psalter ill.: David holding the harp as an attribute
Turin, Bibl. Naz. U., D.III.19, f. 34r	R.5.1.	Isidore, *Etymologiae*: psalterium explanation
Piacenza, Bibl. Cap., 65, f.262v	R.6.1.	Boethius, *De institutione musica*: musician plucking the strings of the harp
Paris, BN., lat. 1, f. 216r	R.7.1.	Psalter ill.: initial P
Poitiers, cathedral, console south side	R.8.	Sculpture: David playing the harp
Rome, Bibl. Vat., 83, f. 12v	R.8.1.	Frontispiece Psalter: David holding the harp as an attribute

(For an extensive reference on sources, see Appendix II.)

Notes to Table 6, column 2 (types of form).

The codes in column 2 correspond to the types of form from the diagram below. In this diagram the delta forms are presented according to the rotation principle (R). The formal indications in the table correspond approximately to those of the instruments in the illustrations; this is also true for the placement of the strings.

Rotation of the R.1 form type (vertical strings) occurs through 90, 180 and 270 degrees and is indicated respectively as R.2, R.3 and R.4. (The form types R.2 and R.4 do not occur on the illuminations studied.)

Rotation of the form type R.5 (horizontal strings) also occurs according to the rotational principle R.1-R.4 and is indicated as R.6, R.7 and R.8. respectively. Intermediary form types, whereby rotation occurs over 45, 135, 225 and 315 degrees are indicated by a subnumbering: R.1.1, R.2.1, R.3.1, etc.

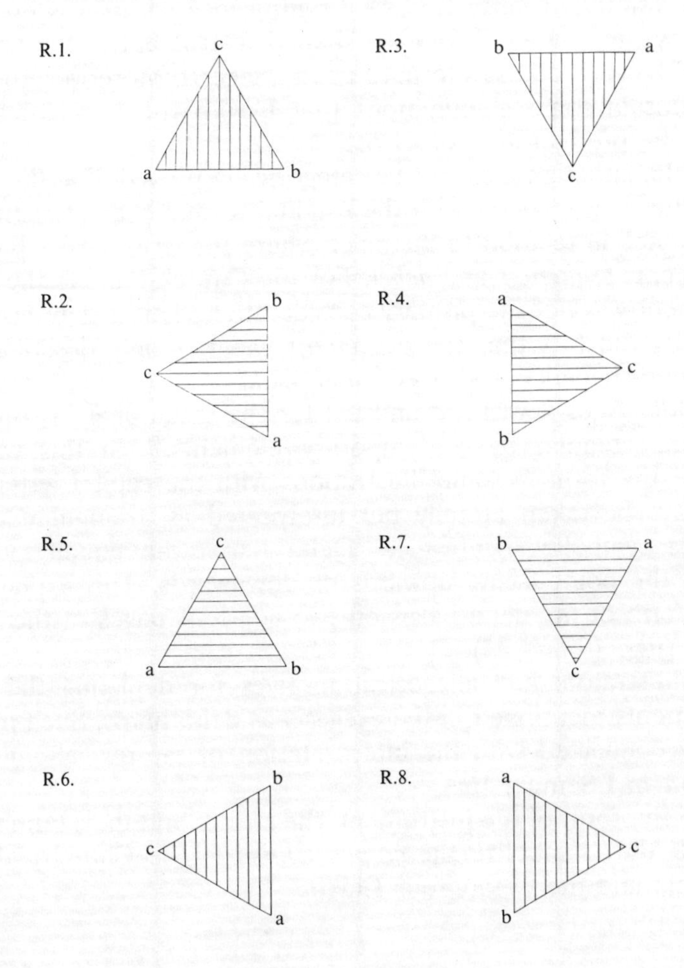

3.6. CONCLUSION

The delta harps which we find in illustrations from the ninth to the fourteenth century are a product of centuries-long instrumental exegesis which originated with Cassiodorus. In the exegesis, the significance of the delta harp is chiefly coupled to the *psalterium*, which, because of its double meaning was considered as the most suitable instrument for praising God. The form, the regular triangle directed upwards (towards heaven?) and the number of strings supposedly reflected this function.

The formal symbolism which is attributed to the biblical instrument the *psalterium*, although without written explanation, is also expressed in illustrations of the delta harp. The triangular form can be explained as a symbol of the Trinity, of perfection — a significance which was presumed to be known by the 'initiated'. A delta-shaped instrument in the hands of David can also be regarded as a form of visual exegesis. Moreover, there are clear indications in some illuminations that David with his delta-shaped instrument is the prefiguration of Christ.

It is plausible, although it cannot be categorically proved, that the formal indication 'delta' is associated with the original formal characteristics (the place of resonance in relation to the place where the strings were plucked) of the instruments *psaltērion* and *nebel*. For the Church Fathers the reality of the instrument was not the primary consideration. This is demonstrated, for example, by the fact that the *psalterium* was not only described and depicted as delta-shaped but also as 'square-shaped'.

In the Middle Ages it was not unusual for the traditional instrumental exegesis to be extended by contemporary elements.[93] In this way the relationship of the form in some illustrations with the capital letter delta need not always be taken literally but interpreted as 'triangular' on the grounds of its symbolic significance. Delta harps can equally well be depicted with the point facing upwards or downwards. This explains the difference in form of the delta harps on two adjacent pages of the Vivian Bible in Paris (*figs. 10* and *25*).

Medieval illustrators had allegorical motives for depicting the delta-shaped instruments mentioned in the exegesis as delta harps. Such motives were probably connected with the interpretation of the text about David with the *cithara* in I Samuel 16.

Apart from the form of the instrument, the strings and their number are also explained; they symbolize the *corpus Christi* (=the Church), the ten Commandments and the twenty-four Elders.

CHAPTER 4

THE HARP IN THE PSALM INITIALS

4.1. INTRODUCTION

The Book of Psalms provides a rich reference source on musical instruments. In the previous chapter I pointed out that one or more instruments are mentioned in sixteen of the Psalms. These allusions to musical instruments had repercussions on the illustration of Psalms in the Middle Ages and manuscripts were often adorned with a large number of depictions of musical instruments. The harp occupies an important place among these, not only with respect to the number of times it appears in illustrations, but also regarding its positioning. Harps are found regularly at certain places in the manuscripts: on the frontispiece(s), in the initials of certain Psalms and in the margins.

The point of departure of the present chapter is the quest for the considerations which played a role in the minds of medieval illustrators when depicting the harp in illuminations. This starting point has been chosen for two reasons.

The first concerns the choice of area of investigation. Despite the large amount of surviving iconographic material, the musical instruments depicted in Psalm initials have been superficially and only partially studied. The second concerns the content. A monothematic study, such as a study into the iconography of the harp in the Psalm initials, makes it possible to gain an insight into instrument allegory, particularly harp symbolism.

In the past attempts have been made to answer the question which we have taken as our starting point by looking for resemblances between the motif in illuminations and the related Psalm texts. The German art historian Günther Haseloff has conducted fundamental work in this area in his study *Die Psalterillustration im 13. Jahrhundert*.[1] Nevertheless, the result of his research, especially in connection with the explanation of musical instruments, is unsatisfactory. It turns out that many aspects of the depictions cannot, or can only be partially explained because there is no apparent direct link between Psalm text and illustration theme. This is particularly true as regards the harp.

Contemporary musical iconographic research is chiefly directed towards the study of musical instruments on the frontispieces of Psalm manuscripts and towards illustrations made for Psalm 150.[2] The sources on which this study is based come from a wide geographic area and cover a long time span. The harp is only one of the musical instruments investigated.

There is as yet no quantitive study of the harp in Psalm illuminations. In his study on David, Steger only mentions Psalm illuminations of David with the harp as an example. His statements are based on Haseloff's book.[3] Rensch deals with the various harp forms which occur in the *Beatus* illuminations of Psalm 1. She does not deal with the symbolic significance of the harp theme in illuminations.[4] Foster is the only scholar who devotes any attention to the meaning of the musical instruments in the initials of Psalms 1, 80 and 97.[5] (I have already referred to most of her ideas in Chapter 2; others will be discussed in the Excursion which follows Chapter 5.)

First the size and scope of the research area will be delimited by sketching a picture of the various schemes of arrangement applied in Psalters and Psalter illustrations. Then I will proceed to a detailed study of Psalm illustrations figuring the harp.

4.2. PSALTER PLANS

The term Psalter, derived from the Latin *psalterium*, is usually used to denote medieval Psalm manuscripts. The Book of Psalms is the only book from the Holy Scriptures that was used not only by clerics but also by laymen in the twelfth and thirteenth centuries as a prayer book. Since reading the Psalms formed the chief ingredient of the canonical Hours, the Psalter was one of the most important and most frequently copied liturgical books. In addition to a number of so-called biblical Psalters — separate Psalm manuscripts destined for the purpose of philological study — there were a large number of Psalters exclusively intended for use as part of the liturgy.[6] Hereafter I will use the word "Psalter" to indicate the Book of Psalms, irrespective of whether the text is bound together with other books from the Bible or not.

The choice of which Psalm initials should be illuminated was closely connected with the ideas on Psalter arrangement which were accepted at that time. These varied both according to geographic area and period. Two factors had a strong influence on this plan:

- Due to the high costs of illumination, the commissioning party could only very exceptionally afford the luxury of illuminating all one-hundred and fifty Psalm initials.[7] More usually only a few Psalm initials were accentuated.

— The liturgical application for which the Psalter was intended played an important role in the division and illustration of the Psalters. This determined differences in content and internal arrangement of the Psalters.[8] More than one planning system was used in most Psalm manuscripts.

Generally speaking, four planning schemes for Psalters are distinguished at present: the Hebrew, the Byzantine, the Roman and the formal plan. In keeping with the Hebrew division of the Psalter into five books, Psalms 1, 41, 72, 89 and 106 (according to another counting system 1, 42, 73, 90 and 107) are accentuated. The Byzantine Psalters are generally divided into two chief *kathismata*. The beginnings of Psalms 1 and 77 are particular focal points. Furthermore, every primary division is divided into ten *kathismata* which are chosen on liturgical grounds. Neither the Hebrew nor the Byzantine plan, however, had much influence on the western European scheme of arrangement.[9]

However, the Roman or liturgical Psalter plan found in Psalters for the Roman or Gallican liturgy was of real importance for western European countries.[10] This Psalm plan, dating from the sixth century — or earlier — was based on the use of the Psalter in the Office, in which all 150 Psalms were read or sung within the period of one week (*psalterium per hebdomadam*).[11] The Psalter plan is, therefore, related to the scheme of Hours. Counting proceeded according to a total of 150 Psalms, excluding the apocryphal Psalm 151. The division in eight parts, made on liturgical grounds, is most frequent in French and Italian Psalm manuscripts.

The opening Psalms of Matins and Sunday Vespers were attributed more significance than others. Eight Psalms (1, 26, 38, 52, 68, 80, 97 and 109) formed the beginning of the portions for daily reading. The Roman Psalter plan is characterized by a split which followed the course of the week: the first series (Psalms 1-108) apparently connected with the Morning Office, the second series (109-47) in connection with Vespers. Recent theological research is of the opinion that the division was not made on the grounds of content, but for practical reasons connected with the actual number of Psalms available.[12] The remaining Psalms (148-50) were intended for Sunday Complines or were sung daily during Lauds. This plan in eight parts is represented in Schema 4. Horizontal lines indicate Psalms which were often decorated with figurative illuminations in thirteenth- and fourteenth-century western European Psalters.

Schema 4. Three types of plan found in western European Psalms.[13]

Office		Psalm
Dies dominica. Ad matutinum:	Ps.	1
		20
Dies dominica. Ad primam:	Ps.	21
		25
Feria II. Ad matutinum:	Ps.	26
		37
Feria III. Ad matutinum:	Ps.	38
		51
Feria IV. Ad matutinum:	Ps.	52
		67
Feria V. Ad matutinum:	Ps.	68
		79
Feria VI. Ad matutinum:	Ps.	80
		96
Sabbatum. Ad matutinum:	Ps.	97
		101
		108
Dies dominica. Ad vesperas:	Ps.	109
		113
Feria II. Ad vesperas:	Ps.	114
		120
Feria III. Ad vesperas:	Ps.	121
		125
Feria IV. Ad vesperas:	Ps.	126
		130
Feria V. Ad vesperas:	Ps.	131
		136
Feria VI. Ad vesperas:	Ps.	137
		142
Sabbatum. Ad vesperas:	Ps.	143
		147
Sabbatum. Ad completorium:	Ps.	148
		150

subdivisions: 3, 8, 10

Besides the Roman division in eight parts, in western Europe there was a division in three parts based on purely formal grounds — beginning with Psalms 1, 51 and 101. This plan originated in Ireland and spread via England to the mainland of Europe. Elements from it can be found in manuscripts from Belgium, the Netherlands, Germany, Switzerland and northern Italy.

In the period between 1066 — the Norman conquest — and 1200 the two planning systems merged together in France and England, resulting in a division in ten parts (Schema 4). The initials which are the basis of this merged system of arrangement were extra accentuated by color and size.[14]

4.2.1. ILLUMINATION OF INITIALS

There was no uniformity in the scheme of arrangement of west European Psalters before the twelfth century. From the second half of that century a transition took place in the illumination of Psalters from partly ornamental, partly figurative illustration to completely figurative illustration of all initials from the eight parts. This new development is first seen in a number of English manuscripts whose precise geographic location is uncertain.[15] In the second half of the twelfth century the development, which took place in England, was adopted by the Benedictine monasteries in Anchin, St.-Bertin, St.-Amand and Marchienne in the provinces along the border of northern France. In the beginning of the thirteenth century the developments in the art of illustration moved their location as a result of increasing centralization around Paris and its region.

The figurative illustration of initials flourished in the thirteenth and the first half of the fourteenth century. Thereafter, in the second half of the fourteenth century, the illustration themes were often replaced by a miniature above or next to the initial.

Initials with a figurative depiction are indicated as historicized initials. The basis of such initials is formed by a letter with a painted representation in or around it, either narrative or symbolic. In general it can be stated that illustrators found inspiration for the themes of figurative initials in the texts of the Psalms. The themes were very much dependent on the principles of illustration which were adopted. Two principles of illustration were used for motifs of musical instruments:

a. the historic principle of illustration,
b. the principle of word illustration.

When the historic principle of illustration was applied, a characteristic event from the Holy Scriptures was chosen in relation to the first words of the Psalm text to serve as starting point for the illustration of the initial.[16] The historic principle of illustration was chiefly applied in English manuscripts in the period between c. 1150 and c. 1250. However, the practice of this principle of initial illustration was limited because the abstract contents of the Psalms offered few opportunities for historic illustrations. Only in the case of Psalms with titles with an historic content, or when the illustration could be symbolically linked to an historic incident on the grounds of the first lines of the text, could such an illustration principle be applied. An example of this is the harp-playing of David before King Saul in the initial Q of Psalm 51. Representations of historic illustration themes are also found in the initials of Psalms 26, 38 and 80.

The principle of word illustration was primarily practiced in France, but from c. 1240 it gradually found its way to England.[17] Word illustration made a direct link with the text possible. The title, the actual first words and the first verse(s) of the Psalm could all provide the motif for a figurative representation. Such words, as for example *Beatus vir* from Psalm 1, could be explained in various ways in relation to David.

Such a link between the first words and the depiction can also be shown for the illustration themes in the initials of Psalms 38, 80 and 97.

In exceptional cases, illustration themes could be based on verses which were not part of the beginning of a Psalm. Verses 3 and 4 of Psalm 80 provide such an example. The musical instruments are depicted in a number of illuminated capitals E. Such exceptions are also found in the initials of Psalms 38, 68 and 97.

It is primarily the principle of word illustration which was used for the development of fixed illustration themes. The themes from the initials taken together often form what is known as the David cycle. David cycles are series of representations of certain episodes from David's life. The themes are often chosen on the grounds of the typological exegesis.[18]

From c. 1250 onward the historic principle of illustration was almost completely replaced in both France and England by that of word illustration.

As research material I chose the Psalm initials in manuscripts from England and France because the illustration principles developed most notably into fixed themes in these countries. The influence of these themes is apparent from the fact that they were taken over by other illustration centers in western Europe. For the purposes of a quantitive study, it was important to have as large a number of illustrations as possible to draw on. For this reason Psalm initials in manuscripts from other bordering areas — Belgium, Germany, Italy and the Netherlands — have been involved in the study. (The source references for all the illuminations of initials which I studied have been listed in Appendix III.)

4.3. HARP ILLUMINATIONS IN THE PSALM INITIALS

In order to answer the question which served as the starting point of this chapter, the criteria for the selection of initials which were illustrated with harps must be investigated.

I have found that harps occur in the illuminations of initials from all ten divisions, although there are considerable quantitive differences for each initial. Moreover, in many cases the harp is depicted in relation to David. The application of David cycles must undoubtedly have played a role in this.

Most of the illuminations picturing harps are found in the initials of Psalms 1, 38, 80 and 97. The preference of the illustrators for these initials shows that the addition of the harp as an attribute of David was apparently not viewed as necessary in all cases. By applying David cycles, the initials of Psalms 26, 51, 52, 68, 101 and 109 were also often provided with illustration themes centred around David, although the harp is usually missing in those initials illustrated by fixed themes. The selectivity of the illustrators when depicting the harp in the Psalm initials suggests that the harp as an attribute of David cannot have been the sole criterion on which their choice depended. Other factors must also have played a role.

My research supports this hypothesis. It emerges that the choice of a harp illustration was primarily determined by the place of the initial in the arrangement scheme, by references to instruments in the Psalm text, by the Psalm exegesis and by ideas on the symbolism of David and the harp.

In the following exposition, I will examine every Psalm resulting from the tenfold division with regard to the relationship between the depiction of the harp in the initial and the contents of the Psalm text or the exegesis, as the case may be. Because in most cases it is a question of a word illustration, the title (in capital letters) and first line(s) of the ten Psalms are given.

Psalm 1 B-eatus vir qui non abiit in consilio impiorum
et in via peccatorum non stetit

The first Psalm occupied a special place in the theological ideas of the Middle Ages. The Psalm was regarded as the introduction to the whole Psalter. In his commentary on the Psalms, Peter Lombard stressed the special place of Psalm 1 with the words:

> Hinc primo psalmo, ideo titulus non apponitur, quia psalmus iste principium est et praefatio, et caput libri. [...] iste psalmus, quasi titulus et prologus est sequentis operis.[19]
>
> 'For this reason, therefore, no title is added to the first Psalm because that Psalm is the beginning, introduction and head of the book. The Psalm is, as it were, the title and the prologue of the work that follows.'

Christ himself, in the personification of the *Beatus vir*, is the subject of the Psalms. According to the medieval exegesis, the contents were made known to David through God. In this context David is indicated as *propheta*. Human beings, according to this explanation, can only understand the contents of the Psalms through the coming of Christ, that is by the fulfillment of the prophecies. For this reason, a deliberate decision was taken not to add a title to the first Psalm. Honorius of Autun clarified this interpretation in his explanation of the Psalms with the words: *Quia proprie est de Christo qui nullum habet initium*, 'because the Psalm is, in its literal sense, about Christ, who has no beginning.'[20]

The content of the text of Psalm 1 consists of two opposing themes: good and bad. This polarity, which occurs so often in medieval thinking, is explained by Honorius in relation to Psalm 1 as follows:

> Psalmus hic habet duas partes: unam Beatus vir, in qua Christi incarnatio et corpus ejus Ecclesia notatur; alteram non sic impii, in qua corpus diaboli demonstratur.[21]
>
> 'This Psalm has two parts: one is "Beatus vir", with which the incarnation of Christ and his body the Church are indicated; the other is "non sic impii", with which the body of the devil is represented.'

Thus the words *Beatus vir* in verse 1 refer to the birth of Christ, while the phrase *non sic impii* (v. 5) indicates the devil and his followers.

In the Psalm exegesis the idea of David as the *figura* of Christ is often explained as the personification of good. This is especially the case in the *Enarrationes in Psalmos* of Augustine:

> In figura Christi David, sicut Golias in figura diaboli; et quod David prostravit Goliam, Christus est, qui occidit diabolum.[22]
>
> 'David represents Christ, as Goliath represents the devil; and because it is David who killed Goliath, it is Christ who has killed the devil.'

The initial illuminations of Psalm 1 often present this interpretation. Illustrators regarded the illustration theme of the figure of David — the poet and composer of the Psalms — as a particularly suitable one.

The origin of his presence in Psalm illustration goes back a long way before the beginning of the figurative illumination of initials. As early as the ninth century, we find David on the frontispieces of western European Psalm manuscripts.[23] David, with or without a musical instrument, occupies a central position in these illustrations and his figure is accentuated, especially by its size (*fig. 11*). In the corners of the illuminations there are often representations of the four co-psalmists from the *Origo* text (*fig. 10*); this theme, as has already been mentioned, originated in the eastern Roman empire.

By following the development of figurative illustration of the initial B from c. 1150, an impression can be gained of the reduction of the thematic material of earlier frontispieces. A number of chronologically overlapping stages can be distinguished in this process.

The thematic material in the initial B was still largely identical with that of the frontispieces during the second half of the twelfth century. However, there was a shift in the placement and size of the illumination. The theme was increasingly transferred from the frontispiece to the initial B. The illustration could occupy a whole page as in the Huntingfield Psalter (*fig. 9*), or take the form of a smaller illuminated B.[24]

From the second half of the thirteenth century the initial B became smaller. The cause of this is not certain, but cost will undoubtedly have played a role in the production of illuminations. This was certainly the case with Psalters which were not meant as decorative pieces but were made for utilitarian purposes. The reduction in the size of the B initials entailed a reduction in the number of the accompanying musicians. King David is sometimes shown in the company of a single fiddler, as in the thirteenth-century Psalter in Berlin, Kupferstichkabinett, 78.A.8, f. 14v (*fig. 26*).[25] The musician has even disappeared in a Bible in Boulogne-sur-Mer, Bibl. de la Ville, 5, f. 177r, also dating from the thirteenth century. An unplayed fiddle is depicted next to King David tuning the harp (*fig. 27*).[26]

Due to the reduction in the size of the initial B in the course of the thirteenth century, King David increasingly became the sole subject of illuminations. The representation of his figure, therefore, grew in both relative size and importance.[27] Despite the reduction of the original theme, the symbolism of David as the *princeps musicus* remained intact.

The form of the initial B offered an excellent opportunity for the presentation of a double illustration theme. In many cases this resulted in illustrations with a polarizing character. In the upper half of the initial the personification of the good and the perfect is depicted, in the lower half evil or the fight against evil, in accordance with the exegesis of Augustine. Two historical themes were preferred: the motif of King David playing the harp in the upper half of the illumination, and the theme of David's victory over Goliath in the lower part. On the basis of the illustrations the latter theme, which is based on I Samuel 17:48-51, can be summarized as follows: little David stands facing the giant Goliath. Goliath has a sword or a spear in his right hand and a shield in his left. David holds a sling with a stone in his right hand. He girates the sling (aiming at Goliath). The stone hits Goliath, who falls to the ground. He lies backwards, half on his back, or bent forward, half on his side. His shield, which he is holding with his left arm, seems to prevent him from falling full length. Little David climbs onto the giant and thrusts the long sword into his neck, or cuts off his head with a sword. An illustration which largely tallies with this description can be seen in the thirteenth-century Paris Psalter in the BN., lat. 1073A, f. 17r (*fig. 28*).[28]

In two Psalters, one in Paris, Bibl. Mazarine, 36, f. 214r, and one in Florence, Bibl. Laurenziana, Plut. XV.11, f. 275r, the placement of the polarizing illustrations has been interchanged.

Instead of David's victory over Goliath, illustrators sometimes pictured another motif in the lower half of the initial: the evil spirit being driven out of King Saul by David's harp-playing.[29] This subject symbolizes David as the foreshadowing of the Christ-Logos who maintains the order of the microcosmos. In general terms the illustration indicates Christ's victory over Satan. This was a very popular theme, especially in French illustrative art.

Finally, the tuning of the harp by David can also be regarded as a common motif. This illustration, which we find almost exclusively in the initial B of Psalm 1, likewise symbolizes David as the *figura* of the Christ-Logos, although now in the sense of He who maintains the order of the macrocosmos.[30]

In addition to the polarizing themes, the initial B is also sometimes illuminated in a non-polarizing way, although this is less frequent. It is noticeable that there is a greater variety of non-polarizing themes than of polarizing ones.

In some B-initials, including the one in the Psalter Munich, Bayerische Staatsbibl., Clm. 16137, f. 7r (thirteenth century), King David is depicted as the poet and composer of the Psalms (*fig. 29*).[31]

Another illustration theme is the relationship between King David and Christ. Christ is the subject in the upper half of the initial, and in the lower half, David with the harp. This reveals the close connection that there was presumed to be between Christ and David in the Middle Ages: David, the *Beatus vir*, carries the *figura Christi*. This relationship between David and Christ is depicted in a thirteenth-century Psalter, probably of English origin, in London, BL., Additional 44874, f. 7v (*fig. 30*).[32] The *Stirps Jesse*-theme, in which David is placed in a genealogical relationship to Christ, also has the same significance.

The depiction of David in relationship to the Holy Ghost can be regarded as the third non-polarizing theme. The Holy Ghost is symbolized by a dove with its beak pointing towards David. The representation of the Holy Ghost as a dove derives from the story of the baptism of Christ in the river Jordan (Matthew 3:16).[33] Again as in the previous theme, David is depicted in the bottom half of the initial, as can be seen in a thirteenth-century Psalter in Munich, Bayerische Staatsbibl., Clm. 15909, f. 8r (*fig. 31*).[34] The origin of this theme should probably be sought in I Samuel

16:13 where it is written: *Et directus est spiritus Domini in David a die illa et in reliquum*, 'from that day on the Holy Ghost took hold of David.'

In addition to the more usual themes reported above, there are a few which only occur sporadically. The representation of King David with the harp in relation to an angel is one of these.[35] It is Gabriel who announces the birth of Christ to Mary in Luke 1:26-38. The angel which appears now and again in the upper half of the B could be a representation of the angel Gabriel. This theme is a variation on that of David as the *figura Christi*.

A less controversial representation of King David as the *figura Christi* is to be found in folio 1r in the Oxford manuscript, Bodleian Libr., Bodley 284, which dates from the beginning of the thirteenth century (*fig. 32*). Here David with the harp is placed in relation to Mary and the Christ-child. A comparable illustration is to be seen in a thirteenth-century Psalter in Florence, Bibl. Riccardiana, 323, f. 14v, although in this case the illustration of King David is not pictured inside one of the B-medallions but in the back of the letter B.

Psalm 26 DAVID PRIUSQUAM LINIRETUR
D-ominus inluminatio mea et salus mea quem timebo

In the initial D of Psalm 26, David is only occasionally depicted with a harp. A thirteenth-century illustration in the manuscript London, BL., Additional 44874, f. 37v (*fig. 5*) has the coronation and anointment of King David as its subject. David's anointment as king by Samuel (I Samuel 16:13) is the general illustration theme of this illumination. The figure on the right side of David performs the anointment. David is seated on a throne, holding a harp in his left hand and a staff in his right. Both attributes have a specific significance. The harp is David's personal attribute; the staff indicates his status as a worldly ruler. David's kingship is emphasized by his coronation, this being a medieval interpretation. On some initial illuminations the anointment is completely supplanted by the coronation of David.

The choice of theme seems to depend on the Psalm title. The Psalm commentary of Gerhoh van Reichersberg gives an indication in this matter: *Hic titulus mittit nos ad historiam. Legitur in libris Regum David ter fuisse unctum*, 'this title leads us to the history [=The Books of Samuel]. In the Books of Samuel one reads that David was anointed three times.'[36] In the Middle Ages Books I and II Samuel were sometimes referred to as I and II *Regum*, in conformity with the divisions of the Greek translators of the Old Testament.

Three initials, dating from the twelfth to the fourteenth century have illustration themes based on I Samuel 16:23. They show David playing the harp before King Saul.[37] Although Psalm commentaries do not furnish a justification for this, the medieval illustrators apparently made a connection between the Psalm text and the illustration theme. The initial of Psalm 26, dating from c. 1210 in the Psalter of Queen Ingeborg of Chantilly, Musée Condé 9 (1695), f. 58v, provides written evidence of this. Here King Saul is depicted standing; he is holding an inscription in both hands. On it is written: *Provide mi aliquem bene psallentem et aduc eum ad me*. The text is an abbreviated version of the one in I Samuel 16:17: *Et ait Saul ad servos suos / providete mihi aliquem bene psallentem at adducite eum ad me*, 'Saul said to his servants: Provide me with someone who can play well and bring him to me.' With this request Saul is following up the recommendation of his entourage; and David, who is still under his father's authority, is sent.

The D-initial on f. 28r in the thirteenth-century manuscript Oxford, New College, 322, is important in this context (*fig. 33*). It is one of the few illuminations based on I Samuel 16:23 in which harp-playing David and Saul are both depicted as monarchs. From an Old Testament point of view this representation seems wrong. However, the following hypothesis provides a possible explanation: taking the usual illustration theme of this initial — the anointment of David — a step further, the medieval illustrator has portrayed the idea of 'being crowned'. Psalm exegesis which emphasize that David has precedence over King Saul, such as that of Gerhoh of Reichersberg, could have been the reason for this.[38] In the illumination in Oxford an attempt has been made to represent this by placing the crowned (=anointed) King David — who, in contrast to Saul, is not only a temporal ruler but also a prophet — opposite to King Saul.

Psalm 38 IN FINEM IDITHUN CANTICUM DAVID
D-ixi custodiam vias meas
ut non delinquam in lingua mea

The initial of Psalm 38 was first provided with a figurative illustration c. 1200. As with the initial of Psalm 26, the theme was positioned within the contour of the letter D.

From the beginning of the thirteenth century, an historic illustration theme is used in English Psalm manuscripts for the initial of Psalm 38. This is based on the words from verse 2: *Dixi custodiam vias meas / ut non delinquam in lingua mea*, 'I have spoken [with myself]: I wish to keep to my ways, so that I do not sin with my tongue.' These words were placed in Solomon's mouth and referred to his judgement (I Kings 3:16-28). The judgement of Solomon can be regarded as the general illustration theme for this initial.

About the middle of the thirteenth century the historic illustration theme was replaced by another based on the principle of word illustration. Now the words *ut non delinquam in lingua mea*, 'so that I shall not sin with my tongue', are chosen as the starting-point for the illustrations.[39] This verse provided one of the fixed illustration themes of French illustrative art from the first decades of the thirteenth century: David pointing to his mouth with his finger.

The explanation of this verse which is given by the exegetes connects closely with the Psalm text. The words *ut non delinquam in lingua mea* are interpreted by pseudo-Bede, for example, as *ut nec etiam peccem in lingua*, 'so that I do not even sin with my tongue'.[40] Such authors as Cassiodorus and Gerhoh of Reichersberg point to verses 3:2 and 3:8 in The Letter of James in which 'sins of the tongue' are discussed.[41]

Only a few thirteenth-century manuscripts have illuminations in which David is depicted with a harp. The presence of this instrument cannot be explained directly from the content of the Psalm text and the revealed illustration themes.

The initial illumination on folio 257r in the thirteenth-century biblical manuscript Kassel, Landesbibl., theologica in quarto 8 (*fig. 34*), shows King David sitting on a throne with his left hand pointing to his mouth and holding a harp in his right hand. In this case, the instrument functions as a symbolic attribute emphasizing his status as the poet and singer of the Psalms.

An unusual motif, David playing the harp before King Saul, is depicted in the initials D of Psalm 38 in two thirteenth-century Psalters.[42] The Psalter Cambridge, University Libr., Ee.IV.24, belongs to a group of manuscripts in which each Psalm is supplied with a title with a figuratively illustrated initial. The titles are firstly meant as instructions for the illustrator although they also elucidate the meaning of the illustration for the reader. They are placed together on the pages preceding Psalm 1. The title to Psalm 38 on folio 4r reads:

> Un latre [=altre?] sera comment saul li rois se siet en sa chaiere. E desous sera david harpant et saul li getera I glaive por li ocire et david s'aclinera por echuer le cop.

> 'Another [initial] will show how King Saul is seated in his chair. And under him David playing on the harp will be shown, and Saul will hurl a sword at him to kill him and David will lean forward to avoid the blow.'

As I see it, the thematic material of both illustrations could be connected with an interpretation of the words *amove a me plagas tuas*, 'take your plagues away from me', in Psalm 38:11. This verse from the Psalm brings to mind the text in which King Saul is plagued by the *spiritus Dei malus*, 'the evil spirit of God', which is described in I Samuel 16:15. David tries to drive out the demon by his harp-playing. In both passages the theme is God being beseeched to bring deliverance from plagues. The illustration theme of David who succeeds in expelling the evil spirit from Saul, is most suitable for embodying this thought.

Psalm 51 IN FINEM INTELLECTUS DAVID CUM VENIT DOEC IDUMEUS ET ADNUNTIAVIT SAUL ET DIXIT VENIT DAVID IN DOMO ACHIMELECH
Q-uid gloriatur in malitia qui potens est iniquitate

Only a few initials of Psalm 51 have David's harp-playing before Saul as their subject. In the initial Q in the thirteenth-century biblical manuscript New York, Pierpont Morgan Libr., Glazier 42, f. 167v, David is tuning his harp (*fig. 35*). On the left of the illustration King Saul is depicted, seated on his throne. Although there are no indications in the Psalm text which give rise to this motif, I think the illustration can be explained from the Psalm exegesis. As in Psalm 1, the textual content of Psalm 51 is characterized by polarity: good versus evil, life opposed to death. This contrast is expressed by means of personifications based on biblical themes, such as David's struggle against Goliath, or Doeg killing the priest Ahimelech (I Samuel 22:6-23). The relationship between David and Saul is also polarizing. Honorius of Autun put this into words in his commentary on Psalm 51: *Per Saul significatur mors; per David vita Christi* [...], 'Saul stands for death; David for the life of Christ.'[43] The act of tuning carried out by David shows his superiority to Saul; it emphasizes David's foreshadowing of the Christ-Logos.

In the initial Q of a thirteenth-century Psalter in Philadelphia, Free Libr., Lewis 185, f. 77v, the polarity is expressed even more strongly. The illustration shows David playing the harp before King Saul, while Saul wants to kill him with a spear, as described in I Samuel 18:10-1 (or 19:9-10). Like some initials D to Psalm 26, both David and Saul are depicted as crowned in the illustration in Philadelphia.

In a Psalter in London, BL., Additional 50000, folio 83r, dating from the second half of the thirteenth century, David is shown playing the harp while King Saul clutches a drawn sword (*fig. 36*). Behind Saul a second figure draws a sword. This is almost certainly Doeg, the Edomite, mentioned in the heading. In the story in I Samuel 22, Doeg was the one who told Saul, when David was fleeing before him, that the priest Ahimelech and his family had provided David with lodgings, food and a weapon. On Saul's order, Doeg killed the priest Ahimelech and his family with a sword. Attempts have been made to express this aspect in the illustration by placing Doeg as the accomplice of Saul opposite David. This motif must not be confused with the attempt of Saul himself to kill David with a spear. The Old Testament account, moreover, does not give any report of Saul threatening David with a sword. The representation in the London manuscript is probably only based on the idea of the polarity in the relationship between David and Saul. By placing the harp-playing of David opposite to Saul's drawn sword, the triumph of Christ over the devil is represented symbolically.

The theme of Saul's suicide is depicted in four Psalm manuscripts from the second half of the thirteenth century and the fourteenth century, without David and his harp being included.[44]

Psalm 52 IN FINEM PRO MELECH INTELLEGENTIAE DAVID
D-ixit insipiens in corde suo non est Deus

A thirteenth-century manuscript in Cambridge, St. John's College, D.6, f. 75r, shows King David holding up a remarkably small harp or harp-psaltery as an attribute in his raised left hand (*fig. 37*). Opposite him a second figure holds up a fiddle in his right hand in the same way. There is, as I see it, insufficient evidence for Haseloff's conclusion that this latter figure is Amalek, an enemy of the people of Israel (Exodus 17:8-16).[45] The initial D in the Psalter Oxford, Bodleian Libr., Liturgical 407, f. 77v, which presumably originated in France about the beginning of the thirteenth century, has David's harp-playing before King Saul as its subject.

Although normally speaking the harp has a symbolic meaning in both illustrations, there are insufficient indications both in the Psalm text as well as in the relevant exegesis which could justify such a conclusion in this case. I am inclined to regard both illustrations as editorial mistakes.

The temptation of Christ by the devil can be regarded more or less as a fixed theme for the initial of Psalm 52. The subject is based on Matthew 4:1-11 (Mark 1:12-3 and Luke 4:1-13). This scene is found in D-initials since the end of the twelfth century. Proceeding from the words *Dixit insipiens*, 'the fool has said', the theme of the temptation is replaced in the thirteenth century by that of David and a fool.[46]

Psalm 68 IN FINEM PRO HIS QUI COMMUTABUNTUR DAVID
S-alvum me fac Deus quoniam intraverunt aquae usque ad animam meam

In the S-initials in Psalters of English origin a link is made from c. 1150 onwards between the opening words of the Psalm and Jonah's prayer of thanks to God (Jonah 2:6): *Circumdederunt me aquae usque ad animam*, 'waters surrounded me, they threatened my life.' Manuscripts originating in France deviate from this theme. In the upper loop of the S they usually depict the figure of Christ, while in the lower one King David is shown up to his waist in water with outstretched arms reaching up toward Christ. The latter theme was also introduced into English initials from the second half of the thirteenth century.[47]

The initial S in the fourteenth-century Psalter London, BL., Egerton 3277, f. 46v, does not conform to the usual themes. The illumination comprises four scenes from the life of David (*fig. 38*). In one of them King David is shown playing a harp in front of the Ark of the Covenant. He is accompanied by two trumpet players. To the left of the initial S King David is again depicted with a harp. However, the instrument is now held as an attribute. The first theme mentioned is an historical illustration, based on information from I Chronicles 15:25-9; the second symbolizes David as chief psalmist and king.

The illustration theme of King David with the harp could be based on the words of verse 31: *Laudabo nomen Dei cum cantico / magnificabo eum in laude*, 'I shall praise the name of God with a song, I will magnify him in a song of praise.' The theologian Gerhoh of Reichersberg made a link in his Psalm commentary between Psalm 68:31 and Psalm 80:3 in which the praise of God by means of the psaltery and the cithara is also mentioned.[48] This deviatory initial illustration for Psalm 68 seems to derive from the line of thought that musical instruments should serve in praising God.

Psalm 80 IN FINEM PRO TORCULARIBUS ASAPH
E-xultate Deo adiutori nostro
iubilate Deo Iacob

The initials of Psalm 80 underwent the switch from ornamental to figurative illustration at a relatively late date (at the end of the twelfth century in England and the beginning of the thirteenth century in France). The lack of an incentive for an historical illustration theme can be given as the reason for this delay.[49]

The mention of Jacob in the first line of the Psalm text gave rise in England to an historical illustration theme in which certain facets of the life of Jacob, such as his dream of the heavenly ladder (Genesis 28:10-22) or his fight with the angel (Genesis 32:24), were depicted.

However, by far the majority of E initials are decorated with a word illustration. Proceeding from the words *Exultate Deo*, 'Sing out in praise of God', most of these initials have illuminations showing a few persons playing music and a number of musical instruments. A mixture of the historical and word illustration principles can be seen in a thirteenth-century Psalter in London, BL., Additional 54179, f. 76v. In the initial, Jacob's dream of the heavenly ladder is depicted in addition to a harp and *cymbala*. Such combined themes within one initial form a very small minority of the surviving E initials.

Interpretations of the instruments mentioned in Psalm 80:3-4 are depicted in a larger group of initials. In these verses we read:

> Sumite psalmum et date tympanum / psalterium iucundum cum cithara / bucinate in neomenia tuba / in insigni die sollemnitatis nostrae.
>
> 'Raise a song, let the tympanum sound, the sweet psaltery with the cithara. Blow the tuba on the new moon, on the special day of our solemnity.'

In the initial E (*fig. 39*) in a Psalter in Heiligenkreuz, Stiftsbibl., 66, f. 65r, dating from the thirteenth century, a harplike instrument, a psaltery, a drum and a trumpet are depicted. These are the instruments *cithara, psalterium, tympanum* and *tuba* mentioned in the Psalm text. None of the musicians in this illustration can be identified as King David. A similar identification problem occurs in two English manuscripts from the end of the twelfth and the first half of the thirteenth century.[50] The absence of David can be explained as a difference in word illustration between verses 3 and 4 on the one hand, and the opening words of Psalm 80 on the other.

In some manuscripts the group of musical instruments from verses 3 and 4 is only partially depicted.[51] In one interesting group of illustrations cymbala are shown, as well as a number of instruments mentioned in the text. I have researched the cymbala illustrations in depth.[52] By *cymbala* I understand a row of small bells which, at least according to the illustrations, were suspended from a horizontal bar. The bells were struck using one or two hammers, as can be seen in the fourteenth-century Psalter Oxford, Bodleian Libr., Douce, 131, f. 68v (*fig. 40*). The arrangement of elements within such illuminated initials E is strongly reminiscent of the initial B of Psalm 1. King David and the cymbala are placed in the upper part of the letter E, while other musicians, such as the fiddler and trumpet player, are depicted in the lower half.[53] In the Oxford manuscript the cymbala are again reproduced in the upper half of the initial E. The bells are struck with hammers by two crowned figures. In the lower half of the initial two crowned figures can also be seen; they are playing a harp and a psaltery. The four musicians are all in a seated position. It is possible that the four crowned persons were meant to depict four versions of the figure of King David. The musical instruments can easily be traced to those mentioned in the Psalm text as far as the harp and the psaltery are concerned. It is otherwise with the cymbala. The instrument name *cymbala* is not found in the text of Psalm 80! The introduction of the cymbala is even more remarkable because it is precisely King David, striking the bells with one or two hammers, who provides the central theme in the large majority of illuminated letters E, especially in French Psalters from the thirteenth century. From the total of illustrations of cymbala in initials E of Psalm 80 which I have studied, there are only a few in which the bells are not struck by King David but by other figures.[54]

In this connection it is interesting to note a miniature on folio 48v in a fourteenth-century northern French Book of Hours in Brussels, KB., 9391 (*fig. 41*). The miniature above the initial E not only shows four instruments; the text also includes the Latin names of the instruments and gives a French translation. These names are: *tympanum-timpan, psalterium-psaltere, cytara-harpe, tuba-buisines*. Linguistically these instrumental denominations connect closely with those mentioned in verses 3 and 4 of Psalm 80. The instruments depicted, at least as far as the harp, the psaltery and the trumpet are concerned, can be traced back to the instruments in the text. The choice of the cymbala theme, however, seems not to be directly connected with the Psalm text. Neither the opening words of the Psalm nor the other verses would justify the presentation of King David as bell ringer. Moreover, etymological and symbolic considerations make the interpretation of *tympanum* as *cymbalum* improbable. The choice of cymbala as illustration theme for the initial E is probably connected with the presentation of this particular group of instruments in writings on musical theory in which the tuning of the bells is also explained. The cymbala thus represent a certain order which had been brought about by calculation. There are very strong indications that the explanation must be sought in the relationship between the cymbala theme and two other illustration themes: the harp tuned by David in the illuminated B of Psalm 1 and the organ played by David or the singing cleric(s) in the initial C of Psalm 97. The method of sound production of the 'instruments' mentioned and the *mensurae* on which their tuning was grounded can be regarded as representative for all musical instruments in the Middle Ages. David's tuning of these instruments emphasizes his status as the *figura* of the Christ-Logos who maintains the order of the macrocosmos. (The *mensura* concept in the Psalm initials is extensively discussed in the Excursion.)

In the illumination of Psalm 80 the harp is only present as symbol or attribute to a moderate extent. In a number of manuscripts the harp is depicted in the vicinity of David as a free-standing attribute, while he himself is playing the cymbala.[55]

Very occasionally David's status as chief Psalmist is stressed, as in the thirteenth-century Psalter London, BL., Additional 44874, f. 115r. There, Christ is depicted in the upper half of the initial, and in the lower half King David with his harp is shown. This theme, which expresses the prefiguration, is generally found in the initial B of Psalm 1.

In the initial E in a Book of Hours of Philip the Fair in Paris, BN., lat. 1023, f. 36v, dating from the end of the thirteenth century, we see a number of singing monks behind King David who plays the harp. This seems to be a combination of illustration themes from Psalm 1 (David's harp-playing) and Psalm 97 (singing cleric(s)).

In their explanation of verse 3, the Psalm commentators emphasize the relationship between the *psalterium* and the *cithara*. This connection consists of the traditional polarity between the two instruments in which the presumed external formal characteristics — *psalterium sonat de superiori, cithara vero de inferiori* — form the basis for dualisms in the theological area.[56] Cassiodorus interprets the *psalterium* as the word of God (*verbum Dei*) and the *cithara* as human behavior (*humanus actus*).[57] However, it does not strike me as very likely that this explanation formed the point of departure for the harp illustrations: the relationship between King David and the *psalterium* in the exegesis conflicts with that depicted in the harp illustrations. As the names on folio 48v of manuscript 9391 in Brussels (*fig. 41*) confirm, the harp in the hands of David is an interpretation of the *cithara* from verse 3 of Psalm 80. Moreover, the exegetes do not apply the dualistic explanation consistently. Despite the outward differences between the two instruments, Peter Lombard and Gerhoh of Reichersberg also explained the *cithara* in a positive sense: it had a 'good effect' (*bona operatio*).[58]

The familiar motif of David playing the harp before King Saul is reproduced in two thirteenth-century manuscripts, one in Evreux, Bibl. Municipale, 4, f. 135r and another in London, BL., Additional 16975, f. 86r. I am not quite clear about the connection between this illustration theme and the textual content of Psalm 80. Possibly the illustrators were influenced by the Psalm exegesis. The source could have been a passage in the *Expositio in Psalmos* of Cassiodorus. In his commentary on verse 3 Cassiodorus examines the importance of music and musical instruments in the Holy Scriptures. In doing so he refers to a number of miracles from the Bible which were brought about by means of music. As an example he names David playing the *cithara* before Saul: [...] *per citharam canoram David legimus a Saule fugasse daemonium*, 'we read that David chased the angry spirit from Saul with harmonious melody from the cithara.'[59]

Psalm 97 PSALMUS DAVID
C-antate Domino canticum novum
quoniam mirabilia fecit

From the beginning of the thirteenth century the initial of Psalm 97 came to include a figurative illustration within the semicircular opening of the letter C. Most of the themes are of the word illustration type and are based on the words of verse 1: *Cantate Domino canticum novum*, 'Sing the Lord a new song'. In initial illustration this resulted in the depiction of one or more singing clerics.[60] In northern French illuminated manuscripts David is mostly pictured as an organist.[61] Both these themes, together with that of the harp-tuning in the initial B of Psalm 1 and the cymbala-playing in the E of Psalm 80, constitute part of a macrocosmic concept of order. (See the Excursion.)

The initial in a thirteenth-century Bible in Paris, BN., lat. 11560, has the harp-playing of King David as its subject. This manuscript is known as a "Bible moralisée". The characteristic feature of such a Bible is that its biblical sections alternate with the related moral commentaries. The commentaries usually conform with the biblical interpretation of the twelfth and thirteenth century; sometimes they are concerned with the state of affairs or events at that time. Both the text and the commentaries in a "Bible moralisée" can be illustrated. In the Paris manuscript, the illustrations to Psalm 97 are found on folio 26r. The representation based on the Psalm text shows God separating heaven from earth. The illustration of the moral commentary shows King David playing his harp. On the left next to him two men are standing pointing to the right where Mary and the Christ-child are depicted. The Old Testament *historia* serves as prefiguration of the corresponding situation in the New Testament. The text to this illustration reads:

> Psalmus iste hortatur nos ad laudem et exultationem quia christus natus est quem nichil fuit mirabilius quam quod virgo pareret.
>
> 'This Psalm exhorts us to praise and celebration because Christ is born, who was in nothing more wonderful than that a Virgin brought [Him] into the world.'

The quotation has the announcement of the birth of Christ as its subject. The accompanying illustration, which shows David as the foreshadowing of Christ, is typological in nature and pictures the New Testament fulfillment of the prophecy from the Old Testament. The theme of the annunciation also occurs in the illuminated C of an early thirteenth-century Bible in Kassel as well as in the Biblical manuscript in Paris.[62] In both illustrations the harp is an attribute which serves to identify David.

It turns out that the exegetes attached a prophetic meaning especially to the words *canticum novum* from the first verse. Bruno of Würzburg explains these words of the Psalm in the following way: *Novum canticum est de Domini incarnatione narrare vel cantare*, 'a new song is (means) telling or singing about the Lord who became man.'[63] In contrast to Haseloff, I am of the opinion that the last phrase *quoniam mirabilia fecit* refers to the deeds of Christ on earth and, therefore, was not the point of departure for the annunciation theme.[64] Both the illustration of the singing cleric(s) and that of King David playing the harp are relevant to the *canticum novum*: the first subject as the literal illustration of the *historia*, connected with the words *Cantate Domino*; the second as a representation of the prefigured event celebrated by Christianity.

The less widespread illustration theme of the announcement of the birth of Christ to the shepherds also has a typological character. This is based on Luke 2:10-20. It is frequently depicted in English Psalters from the first half of the thirteenth century.[65]

Nevertheless, it is not only the words from the first verse which point forward to Christ; the title of Psalm 97 is also explained in this way. Pseudo-Bede interprets the words *Psalmus David* as an indication of the twofold coming of Christ: the incarnation and the second coming at the Last Judgement.[66]

All the same, the presence of David with the harp in this initial is apparently not based on the words in the title. The text of Psalm 97:5-6 forms the basis for the choice of musical instruments in the illuminations. The text of these verses reads:

> Psallite Domino in cithara / in cithara et voce psalmi / in tubis ductilibus et voce tubae corneae.
>
> 'Sing Psalms in the Lord's honour with the cithara, with the cithara and with Psalm singing, with (bronze) trumpets and the sound of the horn.'

The Psalter of the Duke of Rutland in Belvoir Castle written in c. 1250 provides evidence for this view. In the illuminated C in folio 98r, the entire group musical instruments from Psalm 97:5-6 is reproduced. In this case, also, the depicted instruments are medieval interpretations of those mentioned in the Bible. David plays the harp (*cithara*), a second figure is singing (*cantate et exultate et psallite*), and a third is blowing a trumpet (*in tubis ductilibus et voce tubae corneae*). The *cithara* in verse 5 is explained in various ways in the Psalm exegesis. The playing of this instrument is often interpreted as the performance of good works (*opera bona*) through which the believer works towards his sanctification.[67] According to the Psalm commentary of Cassiodorus, the words *psallite Domino in cithara* indicate the fulfillment of the godly commandments.[68] Seen from this perspective, the harp — the medieval interpretation of the *cithara* — belongs eminently in the hands of King David. The illumination in the Iona Psalter in Edinburgh, National Libr. of Scotland, 10000, f. 85v, dated c. 1210, could be an illustration which explains such a perspective (*fig. 42*).

According to Bishop Bruno of Segni (1045/9-1123), the two *citharae* mentioned in verse 5 represent the Old and the New Testament.[69] This explanation concurs with medieval ideas of David as the *figura* of Christ. The harp in David's hands is seen as symbolizing the Holy Scriptures; in a number of ways (genealogically and typologically) David himself forms a link between both Testaments.

In the thirteenth-century Psalter of Queen Ingeborg in Chantilly, Musée Condé, 9 (1695), f. 127r, we find a variant of the prefiguration theme. The illumination shows David playing the harp before King Saul.

Psalm 101 ORATIO PAUPERIS CUM ANXIUS FUERIT ET CORAM DOMINO EFFUDERIT PRECEM SUAM
D-omine exaudi orationem meam

From the second half of the twelfth century a word illustration was often applied in the D initials of Psalm 101. This is especially the case in English Psalters. The theme is based on the words of the Psalm *Oratio pauperis*, 'a prayer of the distressed' and *Domino exaudi orationem meam*, 'Lord, hear my prayer'. In these illuminations a figure kneeling at prayer before Christ is depicted. Sometimes the kneeling figure can be identified as David. The theme was also used in thirteenth-century French manuscripts and may be regarded as usual for the initial of Psalm 101. Around the year 1200 we again come across a variant of the above-mentioned illustration theme: Ecclesia kneeling before Christ.[70] However, this theme was not very widespread.

I know of only one illumination of Psalm 101 in which the harp is played by King David. This is found in the English Psalter Cambridge, St. John's College, K. 30, f. 86r, from the end of the twelfth century (*fig. 43*). Apart from King David, there are three other musicians in this initial: one double-flute player and two fiddlers. The musicians are placed in four ellipse-shaped medallions within a circular frame surrounding the capital D. Neither the Psalm text nor the relevant exegesis contain any indication to justify such an illustration theme. The illustration is possibly inspired by the *Origo* theme.

Psalm 109 DAVID PSALMUS
D-ixit Dominus Domino meo sede a dextris meis

The first verse of this Psalm usually provides an opportunity for the representation of the Trinity: God the Father, Christ and the Holy Spirit. The Holy Spirit is also symbolized by a dove in the illuminated B of Psalm 1.

Musical instruments are not mentioned in the text of the Psalm; they rarely appear in illuminations of Psalm 109. In only one of the two examples with which I am familiar is a harplike instrument depicted, namely in a Bible in Dijon, Bibl. Communale, 2, f. 278v, which dates from the eleventh or twelfth century. In the initial a harp or harp-psaltery is being tuned by King David. The relationship between the Psalm text and the depiction is unclear. However, we can say something about the presence of King David without a harp in some initials of Psalm 109. His presence seems to be connected with the interpretation of the words *Dominus Domino* in verse 1. In the commentary of Cassiodorus on Psalm 109, these words are explained as follows: Christ in his human form is a descendant of David, but in his godly form is the Lord of David.[71] The theme of the illustration in Dijon can be explained in this way: the tuning of the harp by David points forward to the Christ-Logos who maintains the order of the microcosmos.

The other initial illumination is found in the manuscript Paris, BN., lat. 1987, f. 217v, a copy of Augustine's *Enarrationes in Psalmos*, and dating from the eleventh or twelfth century. The illumination shows three figures playing various musical instruments (*fig. 44*). The crowned figure in the middle is King David; he holds a fiddle. To his right there is a figure playing a flute and to his left someone is standing and plucking the strings of a triangular psaltery. Both are inspired by the heavenly fire which, like the dove, symbolizes the Holy Ghost. The right hand of God is shown above David's head. This illustration is probably drawn from an illustration theme based on the *Origo* text but with a reduced number of accompanying musicians. The illustrator may have chosen just three musicians because of the association with the Trinity. No symbolic meaning can be attributed to the musical instruments in this illustration.

4.4. CONCLUSION

The theme of David-with-the-harp occupies an important place in historicized Psalm initials from the twelfth to approximately the middle of the fourteenth century. Quantitatively speaking we find the theme most frequently in the initial B of Psalm 1; the initial B also exhibits the greatest variety of themes. The forms in which David appears with the harp are, I think, to a great extent determined by the prefigurative significance attributed to the combination of David with the harp. The importance attached to the theme of prefiguration is especially reflected in the initial illustration of Psalm 1: this initial was considered as the frontispiece of the Book of Psalms.

After Psalm 1, we find the majority of harp depictions in the initials of Psalms 38, 80 and 97. These illumination themes developed relatively late compared to those of Psalms 26, 51, 52, 68, 101 and 109, that is to say c. 1200, under the influence of a freer textual interpretation: the word illustration. In the initials of Psalms 26, 51, 52, 68, 101 (and 109) the theme of David with the harp has an incidental character. The themes of the illustrations of these initials developed, with the rise of figurative initial illustration, from the second half of the twelfth century. Towards the end of this century the subjects represented in these initials had more or less taken on the form of fixed illustration themes.

David with the harp is depicted in three symbolic ways in the Psalm initials:

- As composer/poet of the Psalms. This theme can be found especially in the illuminated B of Psalm 1, in addition occasionally in the initials of Psalms 26, 38 and 68. Closely linked to this is the idea that the Psalms are a prophetic pointer to the coming of Christ — a theme which is especially expressed in the initial C of Psalm 97.
- As the one who imposes order on the macrocosmos. The tuning of the harp in the initial B of Psalm 1 forms part of a macrocosmic connection in which King David acts as the representative of the godly *ordo*: as the foreshadowing of the Christ-Logos who maintains the order of the macrocosmos. This symbolism of the order is expressed by the illustration themes of Psalms 1, 80 and 97. (See the Excursion.) Apart from Psalm 1, the tuning of the harp is also sporadically depicted in the initials of Psalms 51, 80, 97 (and 109).
- As the one who imposes order on the microcosmos. This explanation is reflected in the depiction of David's harp-playing before King Saul. This biblical motif does not appear to be linked to a particular initial. We find it in Psalms 1, 26, 38, 51, 52, 80 and 97. The motif indicates the triumph of good over evil, or the triumph of Christ over the devil — an explanation which applied to the whole Psalter. In a specific sense the motif em-

phasizes David as the prefiguration of the Christ-Logos who maintains the order of the microcosmos. The presence of the motif in the initials of Psalms 26, 38, 51 and 80 can be quite satisfactorily explained. This is not true for the initial of Psalm 52, where there seems to be an incidental deviation from the usual illustration theme.

CHAPTER 5

ΟΝΟΣ ΛΥΡΑΣ: THE ASS WITH THE HARP

5.1. INTRODUCTION

From the beginning of the tenth century we find miniatures, and later also church fronts and capitals on which animals performing music are depicted. As a role these animal figures symbolize a Christian message: they represent good and evil, reflecting the fundamental dualism which is also basic to the animal world.[1] Such representations declined in numbers during the twelfth and first half of the thirteenth century. Depictions of animals no longer necessarily had a symbolic meaning during this period; they increasingly gained a decorative function.[2] The illustrations of harp-playing asses occupy a special place among the pictures of music-making animals. Although most depictions of the ass with the harp stem from this transition period, they nevertheless belong to the category of animal illustrations with a symbolic meaning.

According to the art historian Francis Klingender, animal figures may be interpreted as symbolic if the following criterion applies: "[...] only those images might legitimately be interpreted as symbolic with which some contemporary document supporting the claim can be incontestably associated."[3] The interpretation of the ass-with-the-harp illustrations satisfies this criterion.

We find these illustrations especially in France during the twelfth century. (Appendix IV lists the places where they are found.) From the twelfth to the fourteenth century they are also found outside France, namely in England, Italy and Spain, although with less frequency. The source of the illustration theme of the ass with the harp has been extensively discussed in scholarly literature.[4] The interpretation of the German scholar Reinhold Hammerstein has found widest support. In his study *Diabolus in musica* Hammerstein considers the theme of the harp-playing ass as the iconografic counter-image of King David with his harp.[5] On closer scrutiny, this proposition, which will be discussed in the following chapter, turns out to be only partially true. In fact the symbolic meanings which were connected with both the harp and the ass in the Middle Ages have been almost completely neglected until now. Only Adolf and Rensch, the latter in imitation of Randall, report in passing about an interpretation of the ass as a symbol of the 'pagan mind' — i.e. those who only listen to the Word of God but do not behave according to it.[6] Research reveals that the illustrations of the ass with the harp can be explained quite precisely by this symbolic significance.

5.2. THE WRITTEN TRADITION OF THE LEMMA ΟΝΟΣ ΛΥΡΑΣ

The medieval illustration theme of the ass with the harp is based on the written tradition of the words ὄνος λύρας, 'the ass with the lyre'. In this chapter I will trace the history of this tradition and show how it connects with the illustration theme.

The theme of the ass playing the harp is an ancient one. Such images appear in illustrations surviving from Sumerian (c. 3000 B.C.) and Egyptian culture (c. 1200 B.C.). Although there is probably no direct iconographic link between the Sumerian and Egyptian illustrations and the twelfth-century illustration theme, it is possible that imagery from these cultures was preserved and passed on through Greek texts. Egyptian scroll seals with depictions of both lyre- and harp-playing asses especially spring to mind.[7] In this sense we can speak of a certain continuity from pre-Christian cultures through to the Middle Ages.

The fable, *Asinus ad lyram*, recounted by the Greek-Roman poet Phaedrus (c. 15 B.C.-c. 50 A.D.) is often cited as inspiration for the illustration.[8] The fable has the title *Quomodo ingenia saepe calamitate intercidant*, 'how talents are often lost through misfortune', and deals with the ass's incapability of performing on the lyre:

> Asinus iacentem vidit in prato lyram; accessit et temptavit chordas ungula. sonuere tactae. "Bella res mehercules male cessit" inquit "artis quia sum nescius. si reperisset aliquis hanc prudentior, divinis aures oblectasset cantibus." Sic saepe ingenia calamitate intercidunt.[9]

> 'The ass saw a lyre lying in the meadow; he walked up to it and felt the strings with his hoof; they sounded as soon as he touched them. He said: "Truly a beautiful thing, but what a pity that I do not master the art of playing it. If someone more skillful had found the lyre, he would have pleased the ears with divine melodies." And so talents are often lost through misfortune.'

It seems improbable that the medieval illustrations are directly related to this fable, although this is, theoretically speaking, possible. The fable probably did not survive in more than one manuscript in the Middle Ages and this was lost after Niccolo Perotti (1430-80) had copied the text.[10] It is more plausible to presume that the illustrations spring from the words ὄνος λύρας, which refer to a fable. The fable from ancient Greece survived as a lemma in abbreviated phrases. In Greek the lemma is ὄνος λύρας, in Latin *asinus ad lyram* and refers to the concept of 'foolishness', 'lack of understanding'.[11]

Greek writers before the time of Phaedrus used ὄνος λύρας as a lemma. The lemma, together with its explanation, is translated as: 'The ass that listens to the lyre: the people without understanding.' Although this can be taken to mean 'those insensitive to art', the general interpretation of 'people who are not cultivated' is the predominant one.[12]

We find an extended version of this lemma in the Greek encyclopedic lexicon *Suidas* which dates from c. 1000 but whose author is no longer known to us. Its substance — 'the ass listens to the lyre, the swine to the salpinx' — which occurs in the works of several other writers, is used in this instance to indicate people without a musical education.[13] Both formulations betray a denigrating attitude to the musical sensitivity of the ass: the way in which the ass passively listens to music symbolizes an intellectual incapacity for understanding.

Lambertus Okken has studied the philology of the Greek lemma and its reception in western literature.[14] I quote two passages from his exposition in their entirety in the following pages. These are pertinent to the understanding of the transmission of the words ὄνος λύρας. Where necessary I have supplied the Latin quotations with a translation; sometimes the footnotes have been abbreviated or amplified with extra information.

"Der früheste Zeuge für den Gebrauch der griechischen Redensart im römischen Schrifttum ist Marcus Terentius Varro (116-27 v. Chr.). Ob er als Zeuge auch im Mittelalter seine Wirkung tat, ist freilich sehr zweifelhaft. Seine Satiren [*Satirae Menippeae*], in deren Kontext die griechische Redensart erschien, haben das Römische Reich ja bloss zitatweise überlebt; das Zitat mit jener griechischen Redensart ist nur durch das Wörterbuch des Nonius Marcellus aufbewahrt worden[15]; und der Archetypus der mittelalterlichen Nonius-überlieferung hat das bewusste Zitat noch verderbt dargeboten, so dass die Gelehrten im Mittelalter bestenfalls diesen Wortlaut zu lesen bekamen:

> Si quis melodinist ὄνος λύρας
> praesepibus se retineat forensibus[16]
>
> ['He who happens to play like the ass on the lyre, let him hang around in houses of ill repute at the markets.']

Der zitierende Wörterbuch-Autor hatte den Varro-Text als Beleg für einen übertragenen Gebrauch des Wortes *praesepia* angeführt; die griechischen Wörter hatte er nicht erklärt. Das aus seinem Zusammenhang gerissene und obendrein verderbt überlieferte Zitat dürfte den mittelalterlichen Nonius-Lesern wohl kaum zum Verständnis der griechischen Redensart verholfen haben."[17]

The Church Father Jerome (c. 347-c. 420) is probably responsible for handing on the words ὄνος λύρας with their explanation to Latin western Europe of the Middle Ages through two of his letters. In the twenty-seventh letter they are translated into Latin: *Asino quippe lyra superflue canit*, 'for the ass sounds the lyre to no effect.' This letter has survived in 120 manuscripts. The formulation *asino lira superflue canit* also survived in two other cases in the form of an excerpt. These summaries, however, date from the fourteenth and the second quarter of the fifteenth century.[18] Jerome reports the lemma a second time in the fourth chapter of letter no. 61. This time the author uses the Greek words to indicate lazy stupid people:

> Verum est illud apud Graecos proverbium: ὄνῳ λύρα.[19]
>
> 'There is truth in the familiar Greek figure of speech: the ass with the lyre.'

The use of the term *proverbium* — literally 'substitute for an expression' — indicates that Jerome was of the opinion that the words ὄνος λύρας functioned as a proverb in Greek.

The tradition of the Greek lemma in the encyclopedia *De nuptiis Philologiae et Mercurii* of Martianus Capella, which was much used in the Middle Ages, is of particular relevance. The philological exposition on this point is, in the words of Okken: "Die Redensart ὄνος λύρας steht ferner in einem Satz der wunderlichen Enzyklopädie, die gegen Ende des 4. Jahrhunderts von Martianus Capella verfasst wurde und die dem mittelalterlichen Gelehrtentum unentbehrlich geworden ist:

> Saltem Prieneiae ausculta nihilum gravate sententiae et ni ὄνος λύρας, καιρὸν γνῶθι.[20]
>
> ['But listen willingly to the opinion of [the man from] Priene; and unless ὄνος λύρας [applies to you], gain understanding!']

— so hatte der Autor seinen preziösen Satz formuliert. Die Kopisten haben den Wortlaut mal intakt und mal korrupt überliefert, so dass statt KAIPON auch KAIΛYPON in den Handschriften zu lesen war.[21]

Dem erzählenden Zusammenhang eingefügt, war die zitierte griechische Redensart verständlich genug, falls sie verständig oder doch wenigstens glücklich kommentiert wurde.

Der Sachverstand mag den frühesten mittelalterlichen Kommentatoren weitgehend gefehlt haben, aber das Glück war ihnen hold. Man lese die Erklärung aus der Feder des Johannes Scottus Eriugena (ca 810-nach 877):

> ET NI subaudi ausculta. NI pro nisi. ONOΣ id est asinus. ΛΥΡΑΣ ludis ac si dixisset: Ne turpiter more asini ludas. KAI KAIPON ludentem te. ΓΝΩΘΙ id est cognosce ludentem te nisi ludas ut asinus.[22]

> ['ET NI, understand: 'listen'. NI, for 'unless'. ONOΣ, that means: 'the ass'. ΛΥΡΑΣ 'you play'; as if he [=the author] had said: 'do not play in the graceless way of the ass'. KAI KAIPON, 'you as player'. ΓΝΩΘΙ, means: 'get to know yourself as a performer, unless you play like an ass.']

Man lese auch, wie des Johannes geistiger Erbe, nämlich Remigius von Auxerre, um 900 den Text erläutert hat:

> ET NI scilicet ausculta, NI pro nisi. ONOC asinus, ΛΥΡΑC ludas, ac si dixisset: Ne turpiter more asini ludas, KAI et ΛΥΡΟΝ ludentem, ΓΝΩΘΙ, id est scito, scilicet te, id est cognosce ludentem te ni ludas ut asinus. Sive ita: Et nisi ut asinus ludis, ludentem scito scilicet te. Aliter: Et nisi es asinus, lyrae ludentem scito te; asinus enim non attendit ad lyram.[23]

> ['ET NI, and of course: 'listen', NI, for 'unless'. ONOC, 'the ass', ΛΥΡΑC, 'that you play'; as if he had said: 'do not play in the graceless way an ass plays'. KAI, 'and', ΛΥΡΟΝ 'playing', ΓΝΩΘΙ, that is: 'understand', and of course: 'yourself', that is: 'get to know yourself as a performer, unless you play like an ass '. Or in this way: 'but if you do not play as an ass, know yourself as a performer' (thus: 'know yourself'). Otherwise: 'And if you are not an ass, know that you are a lyre-player. For an ass does not concentrate its attention on a lyre.']

Es ist ein Bündel abenteuerlicher Ansätze zu einem Gedankengang, der auf falscher Bahn mit mehr Glück als Weisheit immerhin das Ziel eines brauchbaren Textverständnisses erreicht. Wer immer sich dieses Textverständnis zu eigen machte, hat die Redensart in richtiger Weise anwenden können. Und die Chance, dass gelehrte Leute sich den rechten Gebrauch der Redensart aneigneten, war nicht ganz gering: Martianus Capella gehörte ja das ganze Mittelalter hindurch zum Grundstock einer ordentlichen Bibliothek; er wurde viel benutzt, und der Martianus-Capella-Kommentar des Remigius von Auxerre begleitete im 10., 11. und 12. Jahrhundert autoritativ die Martianus-Capella-Lektüre.[24]

Das abgekürzte griechische Sprichwort ὄνος λύρας aber wurde den westeuropäischen Literaten geradezu aufgenötigt durch Boethius (ca 480-524). Erscheint der ursprüngliche griechische Wortlaut nicht in seiner 'Consolatio Philosophiae', dem Buch, das seit etwa 900 allgemein als Schulbuch diente und in weit mehr als 400 Handschriften überliefert ist? Man lese dazu:

> (Die personifizierte Philosophie hat dem Gefangenen ihre trostbringenden Verse vorgetragen und fragt ihn sodann:)
>
> Sentisne, inquit, haec atque animo illabuntur tuo, an ὄνος λύρας? Quid fles [...]?[25]
>
> ['Do you understand this, she said, and does it penetrate into your mind? Or [is the same thing happening to you] maybe [as happens to] the ass with the lyre? Why do you weep?']

Der Schulmeister Notker III. von St. Gallen (um 950-1022) wusste freilich nichts Rechtes mit dem griechischen Wortlaut anzufangen. Verständnislosigkeit bekundet sich in Notkers kommentierendem Vorlesungsmanuskript:

> Sentisne inquit haec . s. carmina . atque illabuntur animo tuo?
> Ferstâst tu díh tísses îeht chád si . álde gât iz tíh îeht ín? Táz íh tír liudôn . bechúmet tíh táz îeht? Ananos liras . i. expers lirae . quid fles? Léidego . únde lîrûn spíles ergázto . uuáz ríuzest tu?[26]

Unser Schulmeister hat den Schulklassiker offenbar noch um 1000 ohne rechtes Verständnis erklären müssen:

> "Verstehst Du dies einigermassen, so sprach sie, oder geht es Dir einigermassen ein? Was ich Dir gesungen habe, erreicht Dich das einigermassen? *Ananos liras* — das heisst: Leierloser — *quid fles?* Der Du gekränkt bist, weil Dir die Leier aus der Hand gewunden worden ist, warum weinst Du?"

Notker von St. Gallen vermochte seinen Schülern die Stelle nicht recht zu erläutern, weil der zuständige Kommentator — es war kein anderer als Remigius von Auxerre — ihm die Stelle falsch erklärte.[27]

Remigius, der den ὄνος λύρας-Beleg im Martianus Capella recht glücklich zu erklären wusste, weil sein Gewährsmann Johannes Scottus ihm glückbringend vorgearbeitet hatte — derselbe Remigius versagte vor dem ὄνος λύρας-Beleg in der 'Consolatio Philosophiae', weil diesmal sein einer Gewährsmann — ein anonymer St. Galler Consolatio-Kommentator — ihm die Erklärung schuldig geblieben war und sein anderer Gewährsmann, von dem gleich noch die Rede sein wird, ihm das Richtige vergeblich an die Hand gab. Ein Jahrhundert später konnte Notkers heller Verstand deshalb nicht weiterkommen! Zwei Jahrhunderte lang hat ja der Consolatio-Kommentar des Remigius von Auxerre die Consolatio-Lektüre überall beherrscht. Wie hätte Notker sich der herrschenden Tradition entziehen sollen? Ihn trifft kein Vorwurf.

Der Vorwurf fällt auf Remigius zurück. Remigius hätte die ὄνος λύρας-Stelle richtig kommentieren können, denn neben dem unzulänglichen Kommentar des St. Galler Anonymus lag ihm ein zweiter Kommentar vor, der ihm für die fragliche Stelle eine gute Erläuterung bot. Remigius aber hat diese Erläuterung in verballhornter Wiedergabe seinem Kommentar einverleibt! So entging den vielen Lesern des von Remigius verfassten Consolatio-Kommentars diese gute alte Auslegung:

> SENTISNE, INQUIT, quia putabat eum adhuc esse in stupore, ut superius dixerat. Ideo dicit ei Philosophia: Intelligis quae dico ATQUE ANIMO INLABUNTUR TUO, AN es ΟΝΟΣΛΥΡΑΣ? id est asinus ad lyram expers sapientiae sicut asinus, qui nihil scit lyrae, id est iucunditatis.[28]

> ['Understand this, she said, because she thought that he was still in a stupor, as he had said above. Therefore Philosophia said to him: do you understand what I am saying, and does it penetrate into your mind, or are you perhaps the ὄνος λύρας? That is: the ass with the lyre, cut off from understanding as the ass that understands nothing about the lyre, that is: the attraction [of music].']

Während Remigius mit seinem neuen Kommentar langfristig die Consolatio-Kommentierung beherrschte, geriet der von ihm missbrauchte gute alte Consolatio-Kommentar in ein Schattendasein", according to the explanation of Okken.[29]

Alessandro Vitale-Brovarone, who claims to have studied all the medieval commentaries on the cited works of Martianus Capella and Boethius, concludes on the grounds of the number of surviving glosses that the lemmata in Boethius received more attention from readers than those in Martianus Capella.[30] This picture agrees partly with that given by the transmission of the proverb in poetry and scholastic literature. Only since the twelfth century did the inaccurate interpretation *expers lyrae* ('deprived of the lyre') become replaced by the correct reading *asinus ad lyram*. In the anonymous *Consolatio* treatise Erfurtensis Q.5, dated in the twelfth century, we read:

> An ΟΝΟΣ ΛΥΡΑΣ: idest liras; an es asinus ad liram, idest an tu es auscultator mei sermonis sicut asinus lirae, qui non sentit quia stultus est.[31]

> 'Maybe ΟΝΟΣ ΛΥΡΑΣ: that is [in Latin letters:] 'lyras'; are you perhaps the donkey at the lyre; that is: are you perhaps listener to my speech as the ass is to the lyre, who has no understanding because he is stupid.'

It is not known at what point in time scholars became able to explain the Greek words in Boethius' text. Okken considers that some clarification on this matter may have come from Byzantium.[32] The Greek words are completely translated into Latin in a Boethius commentary of pseudo-Thomas Aquinas, dating from the fourteenth or fifteenth century:

> Et subiungit Graecum: Esne asinus ad lyram? [...] Nota quod proverbium erat apud Graecos cum aliquis audivit verba alicuius et non avertit nec curavit; qui audit sonum lyre sed non percipit melodiam nec proportionem sonorum intelligit, nec delectatur in ea; sic aliquis audiens verba et non curans intellectum eorum dicitur esse asinus ad lyram.[33]

> 'And he added in Greek: "Are you like the ass to the lyre?" Note that this was a proverb with the Greeks whenever someone heard another's words and did not register or pay attention to them. Whoever hears the sound of the lyre but does not notice the melody, nor is familiar with the proportions of the sounds and does not enjoy them; of him it is said that he is someone who hears words and does not care about understanding them [as] an ass to the lyre.'

The translation of the expression in the *Consolatio* vernacular texts is remarkable. Here the term *lyra* is translated in what seems to be a random way. In the Old French translation of the *Consolatio* which probably dates from the first half of the fourteenth century, there is no mention of an ass with the harp, but of an ass with a fiddle (Lib. I, Prosa 4): *U es tu l'asne a le viele?*[34] In one of the sources of the Old French translation, the *Consolatio* commentary of William of Aragon, from the last quarter of the thirteenth century, all the Greek words are translated into Latin:

> An es asinus ad lyras, istud fuit proverbium inter grecos quotiens aliquis audit verba et sententias non intendit sicut asinus ad liram.[35]

> '"Are you maybe as the ass to the lyre?", that was a proverb with the Greeks, as often as someone hears things being said without understanding their meaning, as an ass to the lyre.'

In Book I, prosa 4, of Geoffrey Chaucer's English *Consolatio* translation from c. 1380 the formulation: *Artow like an asse to the harpe?* is given.[36] The words ὄνος λύρας are translated here as 'an ass to the harp'.

The fact that, as a proverb, the lemma radiated out from the *Consolatio* study is apparent in view of the references which contain the words *an* ὄνος λύρας (thus the interrogatory form, with *an*). From the eleventh century on the proverb seems to have become common property among learned authors. As the dean of the Prague cathedral, Cosmas of Prague (1045-1125), puts the words into the mouth of a soldier on the battlefield:

Quid stas? An onos lyras? Quare non adiuvas fratrem tuum?[37]

'What are you doing standing there? Maybe [as] an ass before a lyre? Why don't you help your comrade in arms?'

At the beginning of the thirteenth century an anonymous writer derided the decoration of churches with animal figures, including the *onos liras Boetii*, in a scornful speech.[38]

The formulation *asinus lyrae* or *asinus ad lyram* is used elsewhere. In the tract on music theory *Epistola de harmonica institutione* Regino of Prüm says: *frustra enim lyra asino canitur*, 'moreover, the lyre is played for the ass to no avail', very probably after Jerome.[39]

As has been said, from the eleventh century on there was an important increase in the number of references which contain the proverb. The words have a clear import in the seventh letter of the French theologian Peter Abelard (1079-1142) to his mistress Heloise. The letter is his reply to Heloise's request for an adaptation of the Rule of St. Benedict. Abelard uses the expression to express criticism of clerics who, although they pretend to make an effort to read the Holy Scriptures, either do not understand or do not wish to understand their content:

Qui autem scripturam conspicit quam non intelligit quasi caecus ante oculos (speculum) tenet in quo qualis sit cognoscere non valet, nec doctrinam quaerit in scriptura ad quam ipsa est tantummodo facta et tamquam asinus applicetur ad lyram, sic otiosus sedet ad scripturam [...].[40]

'But whoever looks into the Holy Scriptures without understanding it, is like a blind person who holds up a mirror in front of himself in which he cannot see how he is and does not attempt to get to know the teaching in the Holy Scriptures, for which sole purpose it was composed; thus he sits like a good-for-nothing in front of the Holy Scriptures, as the ass at the lyre.'

The figure of speech is discussed again in connection with Chapters 48 and 55 from the *Regula* of Benedict. This time Abelard does not use the formulation *asinus ad lyram*, but the words of Boethius. Here again *ignorantia*, 'ignorance' is meant:

Notum quippe est illud Sapientis proverbium: Legere et non intelligere, negligere est. Tali quippe lectori merito illud philosophi: Anonos lyras improperandum est. Quasi enim asinus est ad lyram lector librum tenens, id ad quod liber est factus agere non valens.[41]

'There is a well-known saying of the wise man: 'To read without understanding is to neglect.' The statement of the philosopher about the ass and the lyre must be apt for such a reader. For a reader who holds a book and cannot do that for which the book is made, is as the ass at the lyra.'

From the twelfth century onward the proverb of the ass at the harp also occurs in vernacular literature. The signification of 'ignorance' is maintained in these texts. In poetry the term *lyra* is sometimes translated with the word harp, as in the *Consolatio* translations. This is the case in the poem *Le Comput* of the Anglo-Norman writer Philippe de Thaon (Thaun) from the beginning of the twelfth century. In lines 68-70 we read:

Se li envius est tant de putes murs,
Que il ne l' voillet oir, alt sei de luinz gesir,
Si i pot esculter cum li asnes à harper.[42]

'If the envious man has such profane manners, that he will not listen to criticism, keep him at a distance; there he can listen, as an ass to the harp-playing.'

In the introductory verses of the French *Roman de Thèbes*, which dates from c. 1160, the author warns about immature people who have as little understanding of what he has to say as the ass of the harp. In the words of lines 13-6:

Or s'en voisent de tot mestier,
Se ne sont clerc o chevalier,
Car aussi pueent escouter
Come li asnes al harper.[43]

'Let the people of all sorts and conditions go away, if they are neither 'cleric' or 'knight', because they can listen just as well as the ass to the playing of the harp.'

We first come across the figure of speech in English poetry at the end of the fourteenth century. In the poem *Troilus and Criseyde* of Geoffrey Chaucer, written c. 1380, Pandarus, Criseyde's cousin, compares the Trojan prince Troilus to a stupid ass. The words of line 731, which are used in a proverbial sense, are a literal quotation from Chaucer's translation of Boethius' *Consolatio*. In the words of lines 731-5:

Or artow lik an asse to the harpe,
That hereth sown whan men the strynges plye,
But in his mynde of that no melodie
May sinken hym to gladen, for that he
So dul ys of his bestialite?[44]

'Or are you like an ass to the harp, which hears sound when the strings are played, but from which no melody penetrates his mind to give him pleasure, because he is so dull through his animal ignorance.'

In *The Churl and the Bird* from c. 1410, the English poet John Lydgate uses the ass listening to the harp as a simile for someone who will not listen to good advice. In the words of lines 274-6:

To heeryn a wisdam thyn eris ben half deeff,
Lik an asse that listeth on a harpe,
Thou maist go pypen in a ivy leeff.[45]

'When it comes to listening to wisdom your ears are half deaf, like an ass listening to a harp: you might as well go whistling in an ivy leaf [you can whistle after it [=the wisdom]!]'

In the vernacular texts mentioned above we are dealing with comparisons with the ass who listens passively to the harp but is insensitive to music. After 1400 the words *asinus ad lyram* and *asinus lyrae* are regularly used in western European literature to signify ignorance.[46] This completes the reception of the Greek lemma.

5.3. PARADOX

In almost all cases the ass with the harp is depicted in connection with Christian religious objects: sculptures on or in church buildings, and illustrations in liturgical books. (Source references for the illustrations are found in Appendix IV.) We should therefore ask whether these visual images had the same significance as the figure of speech in literature. In order to answer this question, we must examine how medieval theologians thought about the ass.

In the Bible the ass is described as a humble beast of burden and its gentle character is often emphasized. Owning an ass was a mark of status in Jewish culture: the animal served primarily as a means of transporting persons or burdens.

It is clear from iconographical sources that medieval illustrators were aware of this function. The ass figures in illustrations of the flight of Joseph, Mary and Jesus to Egypt although it is not mentioned in so many words in the text from Matthew 2:13-5, on which the illustration is based.

Another important event involving an ass is Jesus's entrance into Jerusalem (Zech. 9:9; Matt. 21:5-7; Luke 19:29 and John 12:15). This event was celebrated and re-enacted in medieval times. It is known that on 14 January, after the octave of Epiphany, a procession with an ass was held in Beauvais to commemorate the flight of Joseph, Mary and Jesus into Egypt. The ass was used here as a means of transport. In the mass following the procession, the conductus of the ass, *Orientis partibus*, was sung.[47] Similar paraliturgical celebrations are known to have taken place in Bourges and Sens. Apparently in some cities an ass was ridden into the church during the Palm ass processions and taken right up to the altar.[48]

On the other hand the ass has also had negative associations from of old. The Greek author Aelian (c. 170-c. 230) already wrote that various Mediterranean peoples experienced the braying of the ass as frightening.[49] In the *Vita Sancti Antonii*, written by Athanasius of Alexandria in the fourth century after Christ, it is pointed out that the devil has ass's feet.[50] In his commentary on the Letter of Paul to the Galatians, Jerome compares the braying of the ass to the singing of the devil.[51]

Western theologians especially placed the ass in a bad light by considering the animal as a symbol of Jewry.[52]

We find iconographic elaboration of this idea in the *Hortus Deliciarum* of Herrad of Hohenburg, from the second half of the twelfth century. The crucifixion of Christ is depicted in a copy of the manuscript in folio 150r (*Fig. 45*).[53] On the right side of Christ we see the tetramorph, a symbol for the *Ecclesia* — the Church of Christ; on his left an ass carries the Jewish Synagogue. The ass carries the inscription: *Animal synagogae asinus stultus et laxus*, 'the ass, the animal of the synagogue, ignorant and lazy.'[54] Such legends as *Synagoga excecata*, 'the Synagogue is struck with blindness' and *ibi corrupta est genitrix tua*, 'where your mother is destroyed' — indicating the disinherited synagogue — characterize the Jewish people in a negative way.

Western theologians linked the idea of the ass as a symbol of the Jewish people and of sinful man with Genesis 22:5. Here we read that Abraham left his servants waiting at the bottom of the mountain while he climbed it with his son Isaac in order to sacrifice him to God: 'And he [Abraham] said to his servants: wait here with the ass; I and the boy will go thither and will return to you when we have prayed.' Raban Maurus interprets the ass in this text as 'the unwisdom of the Jewish people': *Asinus, Judaeorum stultitia, ut in Genesi: "Exspectate hic cum asino, postquam adoraverimus, revertemur ad vos"*.[55]

In thirteenth- and fourteenth-century vernacular religious literature, the ass from Genesis no longer explicitly indicates the Jewish people but sinful man in general. The fourteenth-century sermon of the German cleric Johannes Tauler explains this clearly. In the words of Tauler:

> Und mit aller kraft erhebe er sich dar úber in sin obersten, als Abraham: der lies den knecht und den esel do nidenan an dem berge, do er Gotte opheren solte; er gieng allein uf die hȏhin des berges mit sim sune. Also las den esel, den vihelichen menschen der wol ein esel ist, und den knecht, das ist dine natúrliche vernunft, die ist hie wol ein kneht; wan si hant her zů gedienet, wan si leitent den menschen an den berg dis ufganges; aber do sol si bliben.[56]

The *viheliche mensch*, 'man controlled by his animal instincts', is symbolized by the ass. The animal side of man and *der natúrlichen vernunft*, 'natural reason', must be made subordinate to the *gotformiger*, *got gebildeter mensch*.[57] The striving after sensual lust and wisdom is contrasted with the believing Christian man.

We find a similar explanation in an anonymous German sermon from the beginning of the thirteenth century, this time in connection with the figure of speech of 'the ass with the harp':

> Der esel horet die harfe lůsticlichen die er doch zutrete, ob er sie vunde in dem wege.[58]

> 'The ass listens to the harp with pleasure, yet he would simply tread on it if it lay in his path.'

After this the author of the sermon explains:

> Der ist ouch wol ein esel zu der harfen der da vroliche unphet [=receives] daz gotes wort un daz dar nach betrietet [=tramples; or fouls] mit suntlichen werken. hastu nu wol gemerket daz hie vor gesprochen ist, so ist bi dem esele rechte der sůndere bedůtet.

The German schoolmaster Hugh of Trimberg must also have been thinking of such an interpretation when he used the theme of the ass-with-the-harp for the purpose of comparison in his didactic poem *Der Renner,* which was completed c. 1300. In the words of lines 23592-600:

> Ein man mac sich wol selben touben,
> Der einen esel wil harpfen lêren
> Und sôgetâne liute wil bekêren:
> Wenne sant Paulus geschriben hât
> In sînen briefen an einer stat:

"Ein vihelich mensche verstêt des niht,
Daz von gotes geiste geschiht:
Gein süezer andâht ist ez laz,
Sîn fleischlich tumpheit füeget daz."[59]

'A human being is very capable of making a fool of himself, when he tries to teach an ass to play the harp and wishes to convert such people. For St. Paul has written at one place in his letters: "A carnal person understands nothing which emanates from God's Spirit; [he] is lazy when it comes to pondering gentle heavenly things, his fleshly ignorance sees to that".'

The figure of speech in line 23593 is also used here in the sense of 'absence of understanding'. Similarly to the two sermons already cited, Hugh of Trimberg uses the expression with the same specific theological significance: the theme of the ass-with-the-harp is applied to the *viheliche mensch* (line 23597). He reinforces this explanation with a passage based on one of Paul's letters, presumably to the Romans. The text of Romans 1:20-1 has the same purport as the words in *Der Renner*. The comparison between the ass with the harp and sinful humanity in these texts does not apply to people with a lack of knowledge of the 'free arts', as the ancient Greeks understood it, but is used to disqualify a certain group of people in a religious sense. It refers to those who have shown themselves to be obstinate and unbelieving: those who are deaf to Christ's message of redemption and do not consciously open themselves to it, exhibit *ignorantia*. From this time on the medieval interpretation of the figure of speech differs from that of classical Greece: the significance of the theme of the ass-with-the-harp must no longer be sought in the tradition of a *fabula* but in the theological ideas of the twelfth and thirteenth century.

The apparently contradictory opinions in medieval theology concerning the ass are bound up with the dualistic division of the cosmos into a positive half (directed towards God) and a negative half (directed towards the devil). Both the type and the antitype are formed in accordance with the same laws of existence. These laws allowed one and the same animal to be explained in a positive or a negative way, depending on the context.[60]

5.4. THE ASS WITH THE HARP IN ILLUSTRATIONS

The proposition of Hammerstein that the ass with the harp is the counter-image of King David, is based on the similar use of the harp in illustrations of David from the twelfth and thirteenth century.[61] The evidence for this thesis is, however, superficial and one-sided. Until now research has only tried to explain the theme within the framework of the dualistic division between good and evil, the godly world and the underworld. The question of whether or not the parallel between David's harp and that of the ass also extends to the symbolism of the instruments is not asked. Moreover, up to the present, research has proceeded from the classical Greek meaning of the figure of speech ὄνος λύρας. It is too facile to answer the question of exactly why the ass forms the counter-image of David by pointing to the 'absence of understanding' which is attributed to the animal. But is it not remarkable that, from the end of the eleventh century, the ass is always depicted with a harp instead of with a *lyra*, an instrumental term which was only very occasionally glossed with the word harp in the Middle Ages? This also prompts Hammerstein to ask some questions. Referring to these illustrations he rightly remarks: "Merkwürdigerweise sind die der Lyra ähnlichen und im frühen Mittelalter sehr verbreiteten Leierformen nie verwendet."[62] Twelfth-century illustrations of the ass with the harp seem, in this respect, to be at odds with the tradition of the figure of speech in Latin literature and with the way the word harp was glossed.

As regards the depiction of the subject in sculptures, very little certainty can be obtained about whether the instrument which is depicted with the ass is indeed a harp. Sculptors faced the technical problem of chiseling the strings of the harp out of stone. In many sculptures a wall is visible behind the strings. One good example, from the second half of the twelfth century, is the 'harp' on the south portal of the church of Saint-Pierre-de-la-Tour in the French Alnay-de-Saintonge (*Fig. 46*). The wall at the back could be a sounding board. In that case the sculpture would not represent a harp, but a harp-psaltery.[63]

The sculptor has supplied the 'harp' on the southern side of the bell tower of Chartres (13th century) with a sound board with strings on both sides. The sound board functions as a partition (*Fig. 47*). A similarly shaped instrument is found on a capital dating from the eleventh or twelfth century in La Plaisance-sur-Gartempe. The criterion which I formulated in Chapter 1.1, which makes it possible to distinguish between a harp and a harp-psaltery, cannot be applied to sculptures. It is quite possible that in the twelfth century it was technically impossible for sculptors to reproduce the strings of a harp without a wall behind them. Sculptured strings without a wall behind are vulnerable, more so since they often form part of sculptures on the exterior of church buildings, exposed to wind and weather. The following may explain why the sculptor depicted a two-sided harp-psaltery: the columns of all harps with two-sided stringing are directed forward; the plane in which the strings stand is at right angles to the wall behind. A capital or a figure on a ledge can be approached from two sides. In order to show the representation clearly on both sides, the instrument depicted had to resemble a harp from both sides. In this situation the intervening wall has the same function as the wall at the back, namely that of reinforcing the strings. The question of whether the respective instrument is a harp or a harp-psaltery must remain unanswered. But it can be deduced with certainty from the illustrations that the stringed instrument represented is not a medieval lyre!

The ass is not only depicted with a harp, it is sometimes depicted playing the organ, bagpipes, psaltery, fiddle and various wind instruments.[64] On the other hand, asses are again not the only harp-playing animals; also demons, sirens, even apes, dogs and wild boars are shown in connection with this instrument.[65] Such figures are, in contrast to the ass with the harp, only incidentally depicted with the instrument and then in very different contexts. Such depictions are mostly decorative illustrations in the margins of manuscripts. The theme of the harp-playing ass seems, on the other hand, to have a specific meaning.

Animals and the devil were closely interconnected in the medieval imagination, as were animal and satanic noises.[66] In medieval society — a society in which only a few mastered the art of reading — the Church used the art of figurative illustration, especially illustrations of the ass with the harp, to make the connection between the devil and instrumental music clear. We often find sculptures of the ass and the harp in church buildings, on the exterior, on fronts and on church portals, where an attempt is made to represent the devil and the demonic atmosphere. They occur on capitals and in cloisters. The relationship with the powers of darkness is doubly reinforced if the depiction is placed on or in the vicinity of the west portal, as in the case of the church of Saint-Julien (12th century) in the French Meillers. Darkness and demons come from the west, according to medieval beliefs. Here the ass is also shown with the harp on the church in Fleury-la-Montagne and on the Collegiata cathedral in the Spanish Tudela.[67]

Hammerstein's exposition on the ass on the Beatus page in the Psalter of Queen Isabella of England (Munich, Bayerische Staatsbibl., gall. 16) demonstrates how a superficial study of an illustration can easily lead to misinterpretation. The manuscript dates from after 1308. At the bottom of folio 8r there is an illustration in the margin (*Fig. 48*). On the left we see King Saul; opposite him is David playing his harp. Behind David's back we see an ass on a leash, with a little white goat bound to its back. The ass is resting its right forehoof on a stone. According to Hammerstein, who seems to want to find a link with the theme of the ass-with-the-harp at all costs, the illustration must be interpreted as follows: "Dieser Zug entspricht der antiken Fabel, auch wenn aus dem Musikinstrument möglicherweise ein Stein geworden ist. Am Sattel ist ausserdem ein zur Schlachtbank bereites, gefesseltes Lamm befestigt, möglicherweise eine Anspielung auf Christus. [...] David mit der Harfe vor Saul, das ist biblisch und bedeutet Heilung der Melancholie durch die Musik. Das Stimmen der Harfe weist auf deren vorgängige Ordnung. Der Esel aber steht, wie seit alters, für Unwissenheit und Unfähigkeit. In allem ist er der Gegenspieler Davids und damit aller wahren Musik. Nimmt man hinzu, dass auf derselben Seite der Handschrift der französische Psaltertext mit dem ersten Psalm beginnt, der das Gegensatzpaar von *Beatus vir* und *consilium impiorum* exponiert, dann erweitert sich der Beziehungsreichtum der auf den ersten Blick nur als elegant-humorvolle Marginalie erscheinenden Miniatur um eine weitere Dimension."[68]

As I see it, the above mentioned illustration is concerned with an historic illustration of two different passages from the biblical book of I Samuel. David and the ass are depicted in connection with the passage which follows Saul's request to Jesse, David's father, to send David to him. Jesse grants this request. In I Samuel 16:20 we read that Jesse gave David presents to take to King Saul: 'Then Jesse took an ass, bread, and a bag of wine and a little goat and let his son David bring them to Saul.' I do not consider the presumed meaning of 'ignorance' and 'incompetence', which Hammerstein maintains were symbolized by the ass, to be present in this illustration. According to the biblical *historia*, the ass is carrying out a practical transportation duty. The suggestion that the lyre was changed into a stone raises the question of what the reason for this might have been — a question which Hammerstein neither asks nor answers. Finally the lamb turns out to be nothing other than the goat which David was given by his father as a present for Saul; it was probably meant for slaughter.[69] The second illustration theme, that of David playing the harp before Saul, is based on I Samuel 16:23. Saul's demon is represented in the form of a fantastical bird placed on his right. The theme is used to symbolize David's prefigurative role in relation to He who brings order to the microcosmos. The "Beziehungsreichtum" which is linked to the illustration according to Hammerstein is then only applicable to the last mentioned aspect and is, as already mentioned in Chapter 4.4., a normal illustration theme for Psalm 1.

We must, I think, seek to explain the association of the ass with David in the symbolic antithesis of David as the prefiguration of Christ. The ass represents disbelief in the coming of Christ as being the fulfillment of prophecy. In particular, the Jews are accused of disbelief. The Jewish people are, therefore, symbolized by the ass: *stultus* and *laxus*. The author of the *Hortus Deliciarum* was aware of this, witness the fact that a plate with the words *et ego nesciebam* was added to the Synagogue in the illustration in folio 150r discussed earlier. These words, based on Genesis 28:16, were spoken by Jacob when he became aware of God's presence after a dream.

In the illustration in the *Hortus Deliciarum* the words express conscious disbelief in Christ.[70]

The harp depicted with two figures also has another important association. The strings of the harp, in fact the *cithara*, are explained in the biblical exegesis as the members of the *Ecclesia* — the Church of Christ. This concept lies behind depictions of the ass with a harp; the strings of its instrument indicate accordingly the community of unbelievers. Such an idea enabled medieval artists to express the dualism between David and the ass by means of the instrument which they had in common.

The contrast between good and evil, respectively between Christ and the devil, is represented in a general sense by the contrast between the God-fearing world and the demonic animals. This is apparent from an illustration in an English Psalter, London, BL., Lansdowne 420, f. 12v, dating from the first half of the thirteenth century. The ass is part of a group of eight music-making animals placed in medallions encircling the initial B of Psalm 1 (*Fig. 49*). The animals contrast with six religious figures portrayed in the medallions on an outer frame. The illustrator emphasizes the contradiction even further by depicting David and the ass with a harp(-psaltery?). David and the ass are not accentuated in size compared to the other figures in the illumination. However, the positioning of the depictions is meaningful: King David is placed in the half medallion left in the middle behind the 'back' of the letter B; the ass is in the uppermost medallion of the inner surround. We usually find depictions of King David at these places in B initials. The polarizing theme of the illustration echoes the text of Psalm 1 in which the concepts *Beatus vir* and *consilium impiorum* are contrasted.

Another instance of an association with the harp of King David is found on the capital of the west portal of the church of Saint-Julien (12th century) in Meillers, where an ass is tuning the harp (*Fig. 50*). It is possible that the depiction alludes to David tuning the strings of the *cithara*, which among other things is explained as the harmony of the *Ecclesia*. By way of contrast, the tuning of the harp strings by the ass could point to the community of unbelievers of which the ass is itself a symbol, the Jewish Synagogue.

Depictions of the ass with the harp in two other manuscripts also suggest an association with the tuning of the harp. This is the case in the initial D of Psalm 17 in a thirteenth-century Psalter in London, BL., Harley 5102, f. 13v. In this Psalm initial, which did not usually carry a figurative illustration in the Middle Ages, an ass is shown tuning a harp with the help of a tuning key. The other illustration is found in the legal treatise *Petri Exceptiones legum Romanorum* in Turin, Bibl. Nazionale Universitaria, D.V.19. The manuscript dates from the beginning of the thirteenth century.[71] In folio 50r two asses are pictured on both sides of an *arbor consanguinitatis* (*Fig. 51*). They carry chains or cords round their necks to which tuning keys are attached. The illustration probably reflects the original meaning of the figure of speech ὄνος λύρας. The *Petri Exceptiones* is a textbook for students embarking on a legal study. Those reading the first folios of this book are like the ass with the harp; they have no understanding of jurisprudence. Later, when the student is competent in reading the most complicated legal texts, the ass changes into a scholarly devout person. He can comprehend the order in apparent chaos.

The twelfth-century representation on the capital of the Palacio de los Reyes in Estella also deserves attention. It depicts a scene in hell. The ass is seated on a throne playing the harp; in front of him is a dog (possibly a listener). The fact that the ass is shown seated does not necessarily point to an association with David. Harpists are often pictured seated in medieval manuscripts; this position reflects the real performing posture. It is unusual to picture the dog as the audience of the ass in conjunction with the theme of King David, but it does emphasize the negative character of the illustration.

A large number of illustrations suggest that the ass is plucking the harp strings with its hoof.[72] The figure of speech makes it possible to construct a *fabula* with a harp-playing ass, although this image would not be in conformity with the medieval interpretation, in which the ass only listens to the instrument! The illustrations also do not tally with the fable of Phaedrus. Phaedrus' ass touches the strings with its hoof, but then ascertains that it is not able to play the lyre, a modesty which is missing in medieval illustrative art. The depictions suggest that the ass does indeed master the harp. Again we find an association with David's harp-playing: the plucking of the strings point to the playing of the *cithara*. This denotes, among other things, the praise of God by Christian humanity in accordance with the medieval biblical exegesis. The harp-playing of the ass forms the antithesis of this.

5.5. CONCLUSION

The ass with the harp occupies a special place in medieval harp illustrations. The representation is most probably based on the Greek lemma ὄνος λύρας, 'the ass with the lyre'. The words ὄνος λύρας, which refer to an ancient Greek fable, relate to people who have deficient understanding, people who are not able to comprehend 'wisdom'.

We find the theme of the ass-with-the-harp especially on French church fronts and capitals from the twelfth century. It is difficult to reproduce the free-standing strings of the harp in sculpture; strictly speaking, we should then refer to a psaltery instead of a harp. We know from manuscript illuminations and written accounts that these psalteries were intended to represent harps.

In present-day scholarly literature it is assumed that the ass with the harp is a symbol for David with his harp — albeit with a contrasting meaning. I find this idea lacking in nuance. From the eleventh century on, therefore, the depiction of the ass with the lyre was presumably associated with the Greek figure of speech by all men of letters. But was this within the possibilities of the religious illustrators? The meaning of the Greek figure of speech is interpreted in a specific way in medieval exegeses: the ass contrasts with David because it symbolizes the unbeliever who deliberately wishes to remain ignorant. An association with the Jews' lack of faith in Christ is obvious.

Vernacular poets sometimes use the word 'harp' for *lyra*. An explanation for this is only possible in the form of a hypothesis. There are virtually no vernacular texts from prior to the second half of the twelfth century. By this time the idea of the ass with the harp as the antithesis of David was already fully present in the iconography of the plastic arts. It is quite conceivable that the figure of speech ὄνος λύρας and the religious visual presentation of 'the ass with the harp' became merged in the representational world of many authors.

EXCURSION

THE CONCEPT OF *MENSURA* IN THE PSALM INITIALS

Since late antiquity musical instruments have been classified according to the principle of the *divisio instrumentorum*. As far as the West is concerned, this classification system goes back to Boethius' *De institutione musica* (Lib. I, cap. 10-1). Boethius links the concept *mensura* — meaning 'measure' and 'measurement' — with the correspondence between interval size and Pythagorean numerical proportions. The theoretical explanation of this phenomenon is referred to as the *mensura* theory which elucidates how musical intervals and the tonal system connected with them are determined by numbers and proportions.[1] The evidence that fundamental musical data, such as tones and interval relationships, are dependent on a higher *ordo* is a primary element of this theory, which was developed by Boethius for all three classes of instruments: stringed, wind and percussion.

The *divisio instrumentorum* has not only been described frequently in musical theoretical treatises from the Middle Ages; it is also found repeatedly in many Psalm commentaries. One such example is the twelfth-century *Commentarium in Psalmos* of Gerhoh of Reichersberg. At the end of an exposition on the musical instruments mentioned in Psalm 80, Gerhoh adds an interesting passage which seems to be intended to justify the use of musical instruments from a religious point of view:

> Notandum quod musicis instrumentis jubemur Deum laudare. Antiqui enim solebant in sacrificiis his uti artibus: unde et nos in divinis officiis utimur organis. [...] Musica enim ars est coelestis disciplina, cujus prima partitio est harmoniaca [*sic!*], rhythmica, metrica; secunda partitio percussibilis ut cymbala; intensibilis, ut cithara; inflatilis, ut organa. Tertia partitio in septem symphoniis. Quarta in quindecim tonis.[2]

> 'It must be noted that we are commanded to praise God by means of musical instruments. The ancients [the Greeks and Romans] used to use these arts [or: instruments] at their sacrifices: that is why we too use the organ in religious ceremonies. [...] The art of music is, after all, a heavenly science of which the first part consists of the harmonic, the rhythmic, and the metric divisions. The second part is divided into percussion instruments, such as the cymbala; stringed instruments, such as the cithara; and wind instruments, such as the organ. The third part consists of the seven symphoniae [=musical intervals]; and the fourth part is that of the fifteen tones.'

Gerhoh of Reichersberg divides the field of the science of music into four parts. What is also striking is the division into percussion, stringed and wind instruments: the tripartite grouping of the medieval musical-instrument classification system.

Gerhoh continues his argument by mentioning that God is praised with the sound of the organ, the cymbala and the bells:

> Ideo hac arte instructi divina verba in hac laude modulamur ut hymnos et caetera, et instrumentis hujus artis ut organis, cymbalis et campanis Deo servimus, quia et psalmos per musica instrumenta prolatos scimus.[3]

> 'That is why, having been instructed in this art [=music], we accompany sacred words like hymns etcetera with this praise and serve God with instruments of this art, such as the organ, the cymbala and the bells; because we know that also the Psalms were performed by means of musical instruments.'

The canon Bruno of Cologne (c. 1030-1101) describes a similar classification of instruments, not however while expounding on Psalm 80, but in his commentary on Psalm 150. In this passage the theme is again that of praise by means of musical instruments:

> Non solum, o fideles, laudetis Deum in chordis et organo et cymbalis [...].[4]

> 'That, o ye faithful, you do not merely praise God with stringed music and the organ and cymbala.'

Gerhoh of Reichersberg and Bruno of Cologne did not make an arbitrary choice of instruments to use as examples. They not only represent all instrument classes recognized in the Middle Ages, but also all the known forms of tone production, these being tone production by 'tension' (*intentione*), by 'air current' (*spiritu* or *flatu*) and by 'stroke' (*percussio* or *pulsu*).

In medieval Psalm initials we encounter instruments from all three classes as well. In the Psalters they are depicted at three stereotyped places and they are nearly always played by King David (see Schema 5).

Schema 5. Fixed illustration themes depicting musical instruments in the initials of Psalm 1, 80 and 97.

Initial B Psalm 1 David with a harp	Initial E Psalm 80 David with cymbala	Initial C Psalm 97 David with organ or singing monk(s)

The tripartition into stringed, wind and percussion instruments is depicted in the Psalm initials not only from a systematic viewpoint, but represents a symbolical line of thought. It symbolizes perfection. This tripartition is portrayed in various ways in relation to the three instruments mentioned. King David is the person who is considered, at least by common medieval consent, to be the poet of the Psalms, the purpose of which is to praise God. Accordingly, in Psalm illuminations David is depicted in the role of author of the Psalms and as supreme Psalmodist. In my opinion it is not a coincidence that it is precisely David who is depicted in relation to these three instruments: the instruments represent the threefold exaltation of God.

The choice of instruments presented in Psalm initials seems to be based on the biblical exegesis. Since the time of the Church Fathers the *cithara*, *cymbala* and *organum* are repeatedly named as instruments of praise. In texts on musical theory from the eleventh century onwards the concepts *mensura* (measure), *numerus* (number) and *pondus* (weight) are often related to the monochord, the organ and the cymbala.[5] These instruments are used to demonstrate Pythagorean numerical proportions.

In Chapter 2.2.2 the role of David as the *figura* of the Christ-Logos, who maintains the order of the macrocosmos, is discussed. The words of *Sapientia Salomonis* 11:21: 'God has ordered everything according to measure, number and weight' had considerable influence in this connection. The initial illuminations in twelfth- and thirteenth-century Psalters give further evidence of the importance of this passage, in which the concept of ordination is expressed through the depiction of these three musical instruments in relation to David. The instruments represent the arithmetic principle of ordination:

— The initial of Psalm 1 shows King David tuning the strings of the harp with the help of a tuning key; the strings have different lengths (*mensurae*).

— In the initial illumination to Psalm 80 David is depicted striking bells of different thickness and, occasionally, size with one or two hammers. In medieval treatises the concept *pondus* was used to indicate measurement in connection with bells. The word virtually always refers to the wax weights (*pondera cerae*) of the false bells which served as models for bronze bells. These false bells or wax models were encased in loam. When the loam had hardened, the wax was melted out and the remaining space was filled with molten bronze.[6]

— The initial of Psalm 97 shows King David playing the organ. From the *mensura* texts on organ pipes it is clear that there is a close relationship between the concepts *mensura* and *numerus*. Since the tenth century, however, the theoretical view that the relative proportion of pipes and their corresponding intervals depend on only one variable, namely the *mensura* (the length of the pipe), ran up against practical problems. The idea, supposedly universal and based on one variable, of a correspondence between proportion and interval — as suggested by the Pythagoras legend — turned out to be a physical impossibility due to the discrepancy between the theoretical and actual length of a pipe. Nevertheless, authors writing on the organ *mensura* took account of the experience of medieval organ builders that in cylindrical pipes the pitch also depends on diameter (*mensura diametri*). In the calculation of the *mensura* an extra factor was added as a complementary value to the proportional variation of length; naturally this occurred within a *mensura* based on pipes of identical diameter.[7]

The trinity of *mensura*, *numerus* and *pondus* in combination with the harp, the organ and the cymbala symbolizes, in relation to David, the divine *ordo* of musical instruments: the *musica mundana*. This explains why Gerhoh of Reichersberg viewed the art of music as 'a heavenly science' in his Psalm commentary!

Apart from the three classes of instruments, the Psalms in which the instruments are depicted are also closely connected with the praise of God. As noted above, illuminations in the initial E of Psalm 80 and the initial C of Psalm 97 are both based on the opening words, which are full of jubilation: *Exultate Deo* ('Sing out in praise of God') and *Cantate Domino* ('Sing to the Lord'). The theme of David-with-the-harp in the initial B of Psalm 1 is based on the words *Beatus vir* and serves as a frontispiece for the whole Psalter. Although illuminations in which King David is shown with a monochord have survived, especially in tenth- and eleventh-century Psalters, it seems that this instrument — partly through the 'historical' context in which King David was placed from the very beginning of the initial illumination of Psalm 1 — was replaced by the harp (=*cithara*).

Not only the theme in the initial B of Psalm 1 but also that in the initial of Psalm 97 underwent change. The organ, found particularly in the initial C in northern French Psalm manuscripts in the period between about 1230 and 1250, was replaced in the second half of the thirteenth century in both French and English Psalters by the theme of 'the singing cleric(s)'. Foster sought an explanation for this change of theme in the desire to avoid ambiguity between sacred and profane music: it can be clearly seen that it is a cleric who is singing the *canticum novum*.[8] However, this conclusion is open to question because, as in the initials of Psalms 1 and 80, the presence of the person of David would nullify such an ambivalence in Psalm 97. It seems to me more plausible that there was an attempt to link the initial illumination more closely to the opening words of Psalm 97.

The theme change within the initial of Psalm 97 does not conflict with the concept of *ordo*. We know from theoretical treatises that the *mensura* and *numerus* of the human voice had already been incorporated in the musical *ordo* in the eleventh century. In *Musicae artis disciplina*, written by Pseudo-Odo about the year 1000, we read:

> Qua in re divinam sapientiam admirans glorificare poteris, quia sicut omnia reliqua, ita et voces hominum, ut se laudarent in numero et mensura, constituit.[9]

> 'In this thou shalt be able to praise, full of admiration, the divine wisdom because this wisdom has created, like all else, also the human voices to praise Him through number and measure.'

The instrumental trinity, which serves in praising God, underwent no substantial change through the shift in theme. However, the prefigurative role of David in the initial illumination of Psalm 97 became unclear; we only encounter this again in the initials of Psalms 1 and 80.

It seems doubtful whether the symbolism is also reflected in the initial illuminations in which, apart from bells being played, figures with a stringed or wind instrument are also depicted. Although these instruments represent the three classes, they might, for example in the case of Psalm 80, just as well be a partial interpretation of instruments mentioned in the Psalm text. Usually only one of the three instruments is depicted in direct relationship to David. The symbolism of order is only partially presented in such initials. Moreover there is only a small number of illustrations with such a theme.

It is possible to see an allusion to the symbolism of order in the initial E in a thirteenth-century English Psalter in Oxford, Bodleian Libr., Douce 50, p. 265. Here King David is depicted twice, both with the harp as well as with bells (*ill. 52*).

It is improbable that instrumental combinations occurring in initial illuminations should be seen as actual ensembles.[10] The exegesis on which such combinations are based cannot be counted as evidence, because it was written as the result of an allegorical thought-process and therefore does not attempt to describe reality.

The question of why the illustrators selected the initials of Psalms 1, 80 and 97 for the portrayal of the *mensura* symbolism now presents itself.

The use of the illustration theme of David-with-the-harp in the initial B of Psalm 1, and the significance associated with it, have been discussed in detail in Chapter 4. The answer to the above question with respect to the other two initials is, as I see it, closely connected with the rise of the principle of word illustration which was employed in Psalm illustrations. The initials of Psalms 80 and 97 switched over from an ornamental to a figurative illumination at a relatively late stage, in England at the end of the twelfth and in France at the beginning of the thirteenth century. The initials of Psalms 80 and 97 were not subject to the relatively prolonged thematic development which, for example, Psalms 26, 68, 101 and 109 underwent, whereby certain historical events from the Old Testament were selected as fixed illustration themes. The themes of these Psalms came into being at a time when the development of fixed illustration themes for most of the other initials had already taken place.[11]

We can only speculate on why the illustrators adopted the cymbala depiction in the initial of Psalm 80 and not in that of Psalm 97. Due to the relatively late stage at which the principle of word illustration came into being, the choice of Psalm initials without a strongly historical illustration theme was limited. That the choice for the depiction of the cymbala fell on the E of Psalm 80 and not on the C of Psalm 97, may be related to the interpretation of the opening words of both Psalms. The illustrators apparently considered the words *Exultate Deo* more suitable for association with the cymbala than with an organ or a singing cleric. The meaning of the word *cantare* may have played a role in this connection. The depiction of the cymbala in the initial E of Psalm 80 was an even more obvious choice, because the opening words of the other Psalms which were generally provided with illuminated initials, were not concerned with the expression of praise. In this way it was possible for the medieval illustrators to portray the symbolical conception of the musical *ordo* willed by God in the illumination of the Psalm initials.

NOTES

INTRODUCTION

1 Lines 5816-7 (ed. Ehrismann, I, p. 242).
2 Dating according to Schweikle 1983, 268-71 [=column].
3 Vellekoop-Van Schaik 1988, pp. 79-83.
4 See Van Dale 1984a, 3, p. 2830; Van Dale 1984b, p. 1225.
5 See for example Rietschel 1965, pp. 13-21; LW [1], 95-6; LW [2], 2609-21; LdM 1, pp. 420-7.

CHAPTER 1

1 Zupitza 1896, p. 52, No. 7; Sperber 1912, pp. 70-1; Holthausen 1930, p. 258 and Steger 1971, p. 105: footnote 81.
2 See Rensch 1964, p. 3, Pl. I; Sachs 1964, p. 177b.
3 Meringer 1904, pp. 128-33.
4 Kluge 1967, p. 289; Onions 1967, p. 428.
5 See the large number of references in Persson 1912, 2, pp. 864-5. There is also a large number of references to the root **(s)ker-*, used in the sense of 'to draw together' (Pokorny 1959, p. 948) . Cf.: Torp 1909, p. 78; Pokorny 1959, p. 935; Klein 1966, p. 704; Kluge 1967, p. 289b and De Vries 1977, p. 212b.
The variation between the roots **kerb* and **kerp*, "pflücken" makes Meringer (1904, p. 130) and Persson (1912, 1, p. 57) strongly sceptical. Pokorny (1959, p. 944) regards **kerb* and **kerp* as two separate "Labialerweiterungen" with distinct meanings.
6 Sperber 1912, p. 68 and Kluge 1967, p. 289b.
7 See Meringer 1904, 129. Words related to **ker(b)* are: in Old Norwegian *herpask*, 'to retreat into oneself convulsively'; in Russian *koróbit*, 'to draw together', 'to curve'; in Greek *krambos*, 'shrivelled'.
8 The Latin *carpere* is derived from the root **(s)kerp-* and has a different meaning from **kerb* (see note 5).
9 *Harpa* in Old Swedish and Old Norwegian; also *harpha* in Old High German, *harp* in Middle Dutch, *harpfe* in Middle High German, *harpe* in Old French and *hearpe* in Old English. See Sperber 1912, p. 70; Holthausen 1934, p. 43; Onions 1967, p. 428.
10 *Arpa* in Italian, Spanish, Portuguese, Old Provençais. See Klein 1966, p. 704.
11 Körting 1907, pp. 508-9.
12 Angelis 1980, No. 216. Dating according to Angelis 1977, pp. I-VI.

13 Angelis 1980, footnote to No. 216: Rem. ad. Mart. Cap., II, 75.22 (ed. Lutz 1962, p. 202, l. 20-2).

14 Ed. Dick 1969, II, p. 75, l. 22-3. Lenaz (1975, p. 222) renders the word *harpis* as 'crooked swords' or 'sabres'. I do not consider this interpretation very convincing in relation to the passage of Martianus Capella.
De nuptiis Philologiae et Mercurii was written, according to Herzog (1969, 1054-5), at the end of Martianus' life, in the second half of the fifth century. Herzog challenges a fourth-century dating for Martianus: "Ihn bereits auf 300 anzusetzen, verbietet seine weit entwickelte neuplatonische Lehre."

15 MGH, Auctores Antiquissimi, IV/1, p. 163.

16 *Beowulf*, ll. 89, 2107, 2262, 2459, 3023 (ed. Nickel 1976). *Widsith* ll. 105 (ed. Malone 1962).

17 Rensch 1964, p. 47.

18 Van Schaik 1983, pp. 104-6; Steger 1971, p. 37.

19 Ed. Singer 1906, v. 1747 e.v. Dating follows Ochsenbein 1981, 839-40.

20 Ed. Kortekaas 1984, pp. 311-3; dating according to p. 116.

21 Lib. II, ll. 161-3 (MGH, Poetae Latini Aevi Carolini, III/2, p. 650); dating of Milo follows p. 557 of the edition.

22 GS I, p. 236b. See Van Schaik 1990, pp. 153-4 and 156.

23 Stubbs 1965, p. 21; dating according to p. x-xi.

24 Dating follows Karg-Gasterstädt 1955, 775-6; see also column 779-82 in connection with the quoted work.

25 Ed. Sehrt-Starck 1955, III, 3, p. 1038, l. 9-11.

26 Cambridge, University Libr., Ff. 1. 23 (ed. Wildhagen 1964). See respectively Psalms 32, 42, 150 (*cithara-hearpan*) and Psalms 56, 80, 91, 107, 143, 149, 150 (*psalterium-hearpan*). Dating follows Wildhagen 1964, p. XIII.

27 Knapp 1977, p. 228: "Datierung ins letzte Drittel des Jahrhunderts vorzuziehen." Crocock (1985, p. 8) and Vollmann (1985, p. 27) share this opinion. Cf. Zeydel 1959b, p. 9.

28 Ed. Crocock 1985, p. 146. The words *pulsans mox laeva* are a reconstruction by Seiler 1882. The critical edition of Vollmann (1985, p. 143) notes "<Pulsans mox leva> *digitis geminis, m*<odo> *d*extra" in verse 38 of fragment XI. The following comment is given in a footnote to verse 38 (p. 143): "Vers 38 ist heute auch unter der Quarzlampe mehr zu ahnen als zu lesen."

29 Dating follows Kuhn 1981, p. 155.

30 Ed. Ranke 1969, p. 101.

31 Dating after Hildebrandt 1986, p. 125.

32 Gl II, 408.26: Rome, Bibl. Vaticana, Pal. lat. 1715 (Gl IV, 609: Prudentius' glosses, 10th century); Gl II, 485.43: St.-Gall, Stiftsbibl., 136 (CCL 126, p. XVII: mid-11th century; Gl IV, 443: Prudentius' glosses); Gl II, 513.8: Cod. monasterii heremitarum [?] 316 (Prudentius' glosses) and Zürich, Zentralbibl., C 164 (Gl IV, 669-70: Prudentius' glosses, 11th century); Gl II, 526.1: Bern, Stadt- und Universitätsbibl., 264 (CCL 126, p. XVII and Gl IV, 387: Prudentius' glosses, 11th century); Gl II, 537.27: Florence, Bibl. Medicea-Laurenziana, XVI, 5 (Gl IV, 430-2: Prudentius' glosses, 13th century); Gl II,

565.16: Brussels, KB., 9968 (Gl IV, 396-7: Prudentius' glosses, 11th century); Gl IV, 345.30: Berlin, Staatsbibl. Preussischer Kulturbesitz, Hamilton 231 (Gl IV, 348: Prudentius' glosses, 11th century).

33 Gl II, 457.40: Paris, BN., nouv. acq. lat. 241 (Gl IV, 600: Prudentius' glosses, 11th century) and Munich, Bayerische Staatsbibl., Clm. 14395 (Gl IV, 538: Prudentius' glosses, 11th century); Gl II, 482 opm. 13: Kiel, Universitätsbibl., 145 (Gl IV, 472: Prudentius' glosses, 11th century); Gl II, 542.72: Cod. comitum de Apponyi [?] (Prudentius' glosses).

34 CCL 126, p. 90. Maas-Snyder 1989, pp. 79-112.

35 The source named by Diefenbach (1968, p. 333a), a *Glossarium Batavicum*, is not to be found on p. XIX under nos. 99 and 108 in the publication he mentions, "Horae Belgicae VII, nr. 1-4" (ed. Hoffmann von Fallersleben 1968 =Horae Belgicae 5-8). Horae Belgicae VII does include a *Glossarium Belgicum*, although this does not include the gloss referred to by Diefenbach. The source of the second gloss, also referred to as *Glossarium Batavicum*, is in Part II of *Diutiska* (ed. Graff 1827, p. 222). There is an extract from a thirteenth-century Latin-Low German dictionary (Codex 641, in Bern) on pp. 195-239 of this edition.
On p. 333a Diefenbach (1968) further glosses *lyricen* with *harper, herper* and *herpere*. The sources of these glosses date from the fourteenth and fifteenth century — in so far as they are mentioned at all. A gloss proposed by Hugo Steger (1971, p. 88) cannot be checked due to his imprecise reference system.

36 GS I, p. 236b. The source for the passage in the letter of Regino of Prüm is Lib. I, cap. 2 from *De institutione musica* of Boethius (see Bernhard 1979, p. 40); however, the instrument name is not given.

37 Gl II, 482.38: Kiel, Universitätsbibl., 145 (see note 33).

38 Van Schaik 1985, pp. 189-93.

39 Papias 1966, p. 302b.

40 CCL 126, p. 81.

41 Gl III, 383.4 and 383.11: Oxford, Bodleian Libr., Junius 83 (Gl IV, 590-1: *Libellus diversarum glosarum*, 13th century).

42 Maas-Snyder 1989, pp. 53-78, 139-164.

43 Hildebrandt 1974, p. 111; also p. XXVII.

44 Ed. Lindsay 1966, I: Lib. III, cap. 22,2-3.

45 Diefenbach 1968, p. 124a-b. It is difficult to date Diefenbach's sources; some are to be found in late medieval glossaries. The terms *cithara* and *citharista* are first seen in English literature in the eleventh century and are glossed as *hearpe* and *hearpere*. The number of references increases in the fourteenth century (Latham, Fascicule II, p. 348a).

46 Fragment XI, v. 26 (ed. Vollmann 1985, p. 143).

47 Diefenbach 1968, p. 124b.

48 Munich, Bayerische Staatsbibl., Clm. 17142 (Gl IV, 555: Book of Excerpts, 12th century).

49 Trier, Stadtbibl., 40 (Gl V, 79-83: 10th century).

50 See Steger 1971, pp. 91-135, especially pp. 100-9.

51 Bischoff 1928, p. 167: "Aratorfragmente". The gloss is found in the pieces from Tegernsee marked with a *b* in the Ms. Munich, Bayerische Staatsbibl., Clm. 29035 (Gl IV, 584: 11th century).
52 Munich, Bayerische Staatsbibl., Clm. 19440 (Gl IV, 570-2: Bible glosses, 10th-11th century).
53 Van Schaik 1983, pp. 185-6; Sendrey 1970, p. 24: "die Sackpfeife lässt sich nicht vor dem 1. Jahrhundert u. Z. nachweisen"; Sachs 1940, p. 84 and p. 141.
54 Gl I, 401.66: Munich, Bayerische Staatsbibl., Clm. 18140 (Gl IV, 561-2: Bible glosses, 11th century); Gl I, 405.43: Munich, Bayerische Staatsbibl., Clm. 19440 (see note 51).
55 Gl II, 389.30: London, BL., Add. 16894 (Gl IV, 490: Prudentius' glosses, 11th century); Gl II, 394.28: Vienna, Österreichische Nationalbibl., 247 (Gl IV, 632-3: Prudentius' glosses, 11th century); Gl II, 434.61-2: Paris, BN., nouv. acq. lat. 241 (Gl IV, 600: Prudentius' glosses, 11th century) and Munich, Bayerische Staatsbibl., Clm. 14395 (see note 32); Gl II, 492.62: Stuttgart, Württembergische Landesbibl., poet. 6 (Gl IV, 620: Prudentius' glosses, 12th century); Gl II, 509.61 Cod. monasterii heremitarum 316 [?] and Zürich, Zentralbibl., C 164 (see note 32); Gl II, 563.23: Cologne, Diözesan- und Dombibl., LXXXI (Gl IV, 416: Prudentius' glosses, 11th century); Gl II, 573.54: Brussels, KB., 9968 (see note 32); Gl II, 581.42 and 583: Düsseldorf, Landesbibl., F.1 (CCL 126, p. XIV: 11th century; Gl IV, 419: Prudentius' glosses).
56 Gl IV, 200.46: Trier, Bibl. des Priesterseminars, R.III.13 (Gl IV, pp. 620-1: Prudentius' glosses, 11th-12th century); Gl IV 241.20: Vienna, Österreichische Nationalbibl., 223 (Gl IV, 630-1: Bible glosses, 11th century) and St.-Gall, Stiftsbibl., 299 (Gl IV, 449-50: Bible glosses, 10th-11th century).
57 See Deferrari-Campbell 1932, p. 217.
58 CCL 126, p. 253.
59 Ibid., p. 271. Dating follows ODCC, p. 804.
60 CCL 126, p. 346. Dating follows ODCC, pp. 1197-8.
61 Sperber 1912, p. 74 points to a passage from *De gubernatione Dei* of Salvianus (c. 400-c. 480) as the reason for the conflicting meanings of Gl IV, 241.20; dating follows ODCC, p. 1231. In Lib. III,22 (MGH, Auctores Antiquissimi, I, 1, p. 28, l. 14-7) it is reported that the *catastae* and *eculei* on which the Christian martyrs were tortured were 'as it were' (*quodammodo*) the ladders on which they rose to heaven. The glossator seems to have intepreted the instrument of torture literally as a ladder. A similar description is found in the very early martyrs' death document *Passio Sanctarum Perpetuae et Felicitatis*. Lorenz Diefenbach (1968, p. 106c) places the term *catasta* among the *genus tormenti*.
62 Ed. Lindsay 1966, II.
63 Graff 1963, IV, 1031-2; Grimm (1984, X, 475) gives the undocumented explanation "es ist wohl ein Pfahl zum Staupenschlag"; Sperber 1912, pp. 72-4; The publication of Starck-Wells (1978, p. 257) notes as the meaning of *catasta*: "Folterbank".
64 St.-Gall, Stiftsbibl., 136 (See note 32).

65 CCL 126, p. 47.
66 Green 1979, Commentary, pp. 104-6 and Reconstruction Pl. 18. In connection with the designation, see Herrad of Hohenburg: Green 1979, Commentary, pp. 9-12; dating according to pp. 12-5.
67 Gerbert 1774. See Kneif 1963, pp. 100-3.
68 Page 1983, p. 82.
69 Ibid.
70 Steger 1961, pp. 52-3.
71 Cf. Steger 1971, p. 98.
72 Ed. Leitzmann 1965. Dating follows Okken 1983, p. 70.
73 Dating follows Huschenbett 1978, 161.
74 Borchling 1897, p. 179.
75 Ed. Wolf 1964, p. 261.
76 Riedel 1959, p. 160.
77 All ensuing biblical quotations come from the Vulgate translation (Vulgate 1969) unless otherwise stated.
78 Ed. Ehrismann 1915. Dating follows Ehrismann 1943, lines 1121-6. Similar references are found in lines 23922-35 and 24307-25. See also Priebsch 1909, p. 40, l. 15.
79 Ed. Robert-Tissot 1974, p. 34; dating according to p. 13.
80 Ed. Ellsworth 1984, pp. 191-212.
81 Ibid., p. 196.
82 Ed. Reaney 1966, p. 21; dating according to p. 5.

CHAPTER 2

1 Hammerstein 1952, p. 212.
2 Steger 1961, p. 71 and 73; Seebass 1973b, pp. 96-8; Foster 1977, p. 16; Kalusche 1986, p. 49.
3 Zingel 1968, p. 17.
4 Watson 1934, p. 109; Zingel 1957, pp. 39-48; Forstner 1961, p. 583; Wimmer 1966, p. 37; Heinz-Mohr 1971, p. 70. Foster 1977, pp. 30-1 mentions a distinction between the harp used as an identifying attribute for David and the harp whose music symbolizes cosmic harmony.
5 Steger 1961, p. 73. His opinion is followed by Zingel 1968, p. 20. Examples of illustrations in which the sceptre and the harp are held by David are found in the Mss. London, BL., Cotton Tiberius C.VI, f. 10r; London, BL., Add. 38116, f. 14v; London, BL., Add. 44874, f. 37v.
The harp is depicted as attribute in the Mss. Bamberg, Staatsbibl., Lit. 5 (olim Ed.V,9), f. 2v; Cambridge, Magdalena College, 7, f. 8v; Dijon, Bibl. Municipale, 14, f. 13v; Geneva, Bibl. Universitaire, fr. 2, f. 213r; Heiligenkreuz, Stiftsbibl., 8, f. 3r; Kassel, Landesbibl., theologica in quarto 8, f. 251r; London, BL., Cotton Tiberius C.VI, f. 30v; New York, Pierpont Morgan Libr., 43, f. 27v; Rome, Bibl. Vaticana, lat. 83, f. 12v.

6 Kahsnitz 1979, p. 170 and 172.
7 Steger 1961, p. 73.
8 For example in the Mss. Arras, Bibl. de la Ville, 561, f. 122v; Cambridge, Univ. Libr., Ee.IV.24, f. 13r; Chantilly, Musée Condé, 9 (1695), f. 72r; Evreux, Bibl. Municipale, 4, f. 135r; London, BL., Add. 16975, f. 86r; Oxford, Bodleian Libr., Liturgical 407, f. 77v; Oxford, New College, 322, f. 28r; Paris, Bibl. Ste.-Geneviève, 56, f. 2v; Philadelphia, Free Libr., Lewis 185, f. 77v; Verdun, Bibl. Municipale, 107, f. 1r; Zagreb, 'National and University Libr.', MR 159, f. 232r.
9 *Micrologus*, cap. 14,16-9 (ed. Smits van Waesberghe 1955, p. 161). Palisca 1978, p. 51 dates the text between 1026 and 1028.
10 Bower 1967, p. 46, footnote 19.
11 Ibid., pp. 44-8, footnotes 16, 17 and 20; Esmeijer 1978, p. 116.
12 *Quod Deus immutabilis sit*, VI (LCL 247=Philo III, p. 22, 24-5); dating of Philo follows Barker 1984, p. 124.
13 *Protreptikos*, cap. 1, l. 13-7; the translation is based on the text edition LCL 92, p. 13.
14 Cassiodorus, *Institutiones*, Lib. II, cap. 5,9 (ed. Mynors 1963, pp. 148-9); Nicetius of Trier, *De laude et utilitate spiritualium canticorum*, cap. 3 (GS I, p. 10a/b); Isidore of Seville, *Etymologiae*, Lib. III, cap. 17,1-3 (ed. Lindsay 1966, I); Raban Maurus, *De Rerum Naturis*, XVIII, 4 (PL 111, 495D); Guido of Arezzo, *Micrologus*, cap. 14,7-20 (ed. Smits van Waesberghe 1955); Johannes Aegidius of Zamora, *Ars Musica*, prologue,7; cap. 2, 16 and cap. 17,99 (ed. Robert-Tissot 1974). Aribo, *De Musica*, (ed. Smits van Waesberghe 1951a, p. 47); Aurelianus of Réôme, *Musica Disciplina*, cap. 1 (ed. Gushee 1975, pp. 58-9).
15 Lib. III, cap. 17,1-3 (ed. Lindsay 1966, I).
16 Lib. II, cap. 5,9 (ed. Mynors 1963, pp. 148-9).
17 Cap. 17,94 (ed. Robert-Tissot 1974, p. 122).
18 *De utilitate hymnorum* 4 (PL 68, 371C-D). According to McKinnon (1987, p. 134), this text was formerly attributed to Nicetius, bishop of Trier (c. 522-66). Cf. Pickering 1970.
19 Giesel 1978, p. 130; Daniélou 1957, 599.
20 The shift from *cithara* symbolism to the *psalterium* is depicted in the twelfth-century Ms. London, Beatty coll., 32, f. 1r. This Ms. includes a Psalter and the Psalm commentary of Peter Lombard (see Chapter 3.4.2).
21 Ed. Ehrismann, I, pp. 243-4.
22 Also in the Mss. London, BL., Lansdowne 431, f. 64v; Zagreb, 'National and University Libr.', MR 159, f. 246r.
23 The identification of the symbols is based on Watson 1934, p. 109.
24 Steger 1961, p. 116 and 124. According to medieval interpretations David is closely related to Christ. David stands at the beginning of a genealogical line which ends with Christ (Matthew 1:1-17). The relationship between David and Christ is sometimes carried so far that David is equated with Christ. This is the case in the *Prolegomena* of Bruno of Würzburg: *Psalmi vero omnes, qui*

inscribuntur ipsi David ad Christi pertinent sacramentum, quia David dictus est Christus (PL 142, 47C-48A).

25 Thematically related illustrations are found in the Mss. London, BL., Add. 38116, f. 14v; London, BL., Add. 49622, f. 8r, and London, BL., Yates Thompson 14, f. 7r.

26 Hammerstein 1952, p. 211: "Ordnung des Tonsystems"; Zingel 1957, p. 41: "ein geordnetes Tonsystem"; Zingel 1968, p. 28: "die Ordnung im Tonsystem"; Steger 1961, p. 120: "Lenker des geordneten Weltensystems"; Foster 1977, p. 31: "cosmic harmony".

27 Münxelhaus 1976, pp. 37-9.

28 Ibid., pp. 39-41.

29 GS I, p. 239b.

30 Sometimes there is a change of name: *I*ubal=*T*ubal; at other times there is a change of person: Iubal=Tubal(-Cain). For hypotheses on these changes I refer to the explanations in Vogel (1973, I, p. 11) and Münxelhaus (1976, pp. 47-50).

31 *Etymologiae*, Lib. III, cap. 16,1 (ed. Lindsay 1966, I). Münxelhaus 1976, p. 48 considers that, when used in connection with personal names, the letters *I* and *T* were possibly mistaken for each other in Isidore.

32 Münxelhaus 1976, pp. 46-7; Foster 1977, p. 23.

33 PL 198, 1079A-B. Dating follows ODCC, p. 1071.

34 Ed. Gushee 1975. Cf. Seebass 1973b, p. 97.

35 Utrecht, Bibl. der Rijksuniversiteit, 32, f. 91v. See Vellekoop 1984, p. 194 and Seebass 1973a, pp. 35-48.

36 Seebass 1973a, pp. 45-6.

37 Ibid., pp. 46-7.

38 Vollmann 1985, p. 181.

39 *De institutione arithmetica*, Lib. I, cap. 1 (ed. Friedlein 1966, pp. 10-1).

40 ODCC, p. 833; Zahlten 1979, p. 105; Timmers 1985, p. 23,5.

41 Zahlten 1979, p. 106.

42 *Questiones in Regum* I (PL 83, 399A-B).

43 An extensive explanation of the illustration in the Ms. Paris, BN., lat. 1, f. 215v is given by Steger 1961, pp. 166-8: Denkmal 11, Pl. 5.

44 The title *Origo Psalmorum* is based on Kessler 1977, p. 98. Stegmüller, 2, No. 1665 classifies the text under the works of pseudo-Bede (PL 93, 477D-480A). Migne (PL 93, 477D and 478D) reports *Enarratio, qualiter spiritus sanctus psalterium dictaverit* as caption. Steger 1961, p. 152 adds to this caption the title *Origo Prophetiae David Regis Psalmorum.*

45 Asaph: I Chronicles 15:19, 16:5-7, 25:6 and Psalm 49. Heman: I Chronicles 15:19, 16:42, 25:6. Ethan: I Chronicles 15:19. Jeduthun: I Chronicles 16:42, 25:6 and Psalm 38.

46 Pseudo-Bede (PL 93, 478D).

47 Kessler 1977, p. 104: "Because the *Origo Psalmorum* was, itself, derived from the homily of Hippolytus, the Carolingian artists found the Byzantine compositions well suited to serve as illustrations for their Latin preface. The

conformity of the borrowed images to the *Origo* text was, however, imperfect. The Greek frontispieces include as many as nine companions to David and sometimes four large groups; and the musicians play a variety of instruments in addition to the cymbals, cythara, and horn that are described in the Carolingian variant of the prologue." Other sources are given in Seebass (1973b, p. 133). He remarks: "[...] der Text findet sich wenig anders gegliedert und ähnlich im Wortlaut auch in Byzanz, und zwar schon seit frühchristlicher Zeit, zum Beispiel in dem schon herangezogenen Vorwort des Theodoret." Seebass refers to PG 84, 24 in footnote 55 on p. 133.

48 The Carolingian version is first found in the Dagulf Psalter in Vienna, Österreichische Nationalbibl., 1861, f. 11r (Köhler 1958, pp. 42-3) written c. 783 and c. 795. The *Origo* text with an illustration is in the Mss. Paris, BN., lat. 1, f. 215v (illustration), f. 216r (text); Paris, BN., lat. 1152, f. 1v (ill.), f. 2r-2v (text); Rome, Bibl. San Paolo, Bible of Callisto, f. 147v (illustration), f. 169r (text). More illustrations are described by Kessler 1977, pp. 99-110. The *Origo* text in Kessler 1977, pp. 98-9 is based on the manuscript Paris, BN., lat. 1152; and agrees more or less with the one reproduced by Migne in footnote 118 of the *Prolegomena* of Bruno of Würzburg (PL 142, 17C).

49 Meyer 1975, pp. 123-7.

50 Many examples are found in Kessler 1977, ills. 49, 50, 51, 52, 53 and 61.

51 The parallels between the *Majestas Domini* illustrations and the Psalter illuminations based on the *Origo* text are discussed at length by Steger 1961, pp. 113-21, Seebass 1973b, pp. 134-5 and Kahsnitz 1979, pp. 168-215. The influence of the *Origo* theme on the illustrations in the initial B of Psalm 1 is discussed in Chapter 4.3.

52 The monochord acquired a symbolic dimension under the influence of the Pythagorean symbolism of numbers relating to the "harmony of the spheres" (Steger 1961, p. 71). Harmonious circles, indicating the orbits of the planets, are expressed visually on the monochord (Adkins 1963, pp. 423-43).

53 For example the Werdener Psalter in Berlin, Staatsbibl. Preussischer Kulturbesitz, theol. lat. fol. 358, f. 1v.

54 Bandmann 1960, pp. 20-1; Esmeijer 1978, p. 117; Giesel 1978, pp. 140-1.

55 The harp bag probably served to protect the harp during transportation. Moreover it provides extra support for the harp when it is held on or between the thighs during performance. Harp bags only occur in illustrations and sculptures in England and in northern French manuscripts in which the influence of English illustrative art is clearly traceable.

56 London, BL., Add. 21926, f. 26r; Oxford, Bodleian Libr., Douce 50, p. 265; Sankt Paul im Lavanttal, Kathedral-Archiv, XXV.2.19, f. 18r.

57 Ed. Ranke 1969, ll. 3558-61. On the subject of musical terminology in the *Tristan* story, see Van Schaik 1985, pp. 181-4.

58 Diefenbach 1968, p. 126b.

59 Ed. Helm 1907, p. 143.

60 Dating follows Masser 1981, 750-1: "gegen und nach 1300".

61 See for *wirbel* in the sense of 'tuning pin' Lexer 1970, p. 925 and Kluge 1967, p. 826. When used in the sense of 'tuning key' Diefenbach 1968, p. 442b gives the spellings *werbel* and *wirbel*. In the *Summarium Heinrici*, Lib. II, cap. 18 (ed. Hildebrandt 1974, p. 112) and Lib. VI, cap. 10 (ed. Hildebrandt 1982, p. 93) the Latin *pliroma* is glossed with the German *wirbel*. In both cases the glosses are based on Isidore's *Etymologiae* (Lib. III, cap. 22). *Pliroma*, derived from the Greek, indicates 'by which something is perfected'. Blaise 1975, p. 679 also notes that "pliroma"="plénitude". *Pliroma* can mean 'tuning key' in relation to a stringed instrument.

62 Page 1987, p. 233.

63 *In Psalmos*. There is no critical text edition. The quotation is based on the text in the fourteenth-century manuscript Oxford, New College, 36, f. 54r-v which is printed in Page (1987, pp. 231-2). Other sources of the work are mentioned by Stegmüller, 3, No. 5638.

64 One illustration exists of a harp-psaltery with two rows of tuning pins being tuned by David. It is found in an eleventh-century Bible in Pommersfelden, Graf von Schönbornsche Schlossbibl., 334 (olim 2777), f. 148v. Steger, who has studied the illustration in detail (1961, pp. 198-9, Denkmal 29a, Pl. 14), suggests on p. 199: "Die zwei Reihen von Wirbeln könnten darauf hinweisen, dass das Instrument doppelseitig bespannt ist." It may also simply be a mistaken representation.

65 Steger 1961, Pl. 33, No. 3.

66 Dating follows Müller 1909, p. 243.

67 Ibid., p. 252.

68 Ed. Robert-Tissot 1974, p. 118.

69 Oxford, Bodleian Libr., Bodley 842, f. 66v (ed. Reaney 1966, p. 21).

70 In the legal manuscript Turin, Bibl. Nazionale Universitaria, D.V.19, f. 50r two harp-playing donkeys are depicted; both donkeys carry a tuning key on a cord around their necks (ill. 51).

71 Dating follows Graff 1827, II, p. 195.

72 Pokorny 1959, p. 1152, paragraph 3.

73 See the sources mentioned in Carter 1980, p. 557-9.

74 Cf. also Steger 1961, p. 72 and Textabbildung V.

CHAPTER 3

1 Steger 1961, pp. 51-2; Pickering 1970, p. 291; Seebass 1973b, p. 114.

2 Steger 1961, p. 52.

3 Ibid., p. 52: "Es ist ganz klar, dass die Miniatoren diese authentischen deltaförmigen Instrumente nachbilden wollen." Steger refers to the study of Hickman 1953 in a footnote.

4 Steger 1961, p. 70, No. 2.

5 Rensch 1964.

6 Pickering 1970, p. 291: footnote 1.

7 Vorreiter 1977, p. 46.
8 Esmeijer 1978, p. 120.
9 Giesel 1978, p. 131.
10 See the references to the sources in notes 12 and 13.
11 McKinnon 1965a, 1965b and 1968; Giesel 1978, pp. 46-99.
12 Cassiodorus, *Expositio Psalmorum*, Praefatio, cap. 4 (CCL 97, p. 11); pseudo-Bede, *De Psalmorum libro exegesis*, Praefatio altera (PL 93, 481B). On the attribution to pseudo-Bede, see Dekkers 1961, p. 311, No. 1384 and Stegmüller, 2, p. 189, No. 1665. Likewise in pseudo-Bede, *Interpretatio psalterii artis cantilenae, vel specierum singularum, vel nominum quae commemorantur in Psalmis* (PL 93, 1099); Remigius of Auxerre, *Enarrationes in Psalmos*, Praeambula (PL 131, 138B and PL 131, 147C); Bruno of Würzburg, *Expositio Psalmorum, canticorum, orationis Dominicae et symbolorum*, Prolegomena, cap. 4 (PL 142, 44A); Rupert of Deutz, *De trinitate et operibus ejus libri XLII*, Prologus Ruperti in librum Psalmorum, cap. 3 (PL 167, 1180D); Gerhoh of Reichersberg, *Commentarius aureus in Psalmos*, Ps. 1 (PL 193, 629); Honorius of Autun, *Selectorum Psalmorum expositio* (PL 172, 269B and PL 172, 271D); the *Commentarium in Psalmos* of Peter Lombard in the Ms. London, Beatty coll., 32, f. 1r.
The passages in the following are not directly connected with the Psalms: Isidore of Seville, *Etymologiae*, Lib. III, cap. 22,7 (ed. Lindsay 1966, I); Notker Teutonicus, postscript to *Fides Sancti Athanasii Episcopi* (ed. Sehrt-Starck 1955, III, 3, p. 1117, l. 8-10); Bartholomaeus Anglicus, *De proprietatibus rerum*, cap. 142 (Müller 1909, pp. 252-3); *Summarium Heinrici*, Lib. VI, cap. 10 (ed. Hildebrandt 1982, p. 93) and Lib. XI (long alphabetical version): *cythara* (ed. Hildebrandt 1982, p. 221); Johannes Aegidius of Zamora, *Ars musica*, cap. 17 (ed. Robert-Tissot 1974, p. 118); Jerome of Moravia, *Tractatus de musica*, cap. 4 (GS I, p. 9b).
13 Raban Maurus, *Commentarium in librum I Paralipomenon*, cap. 15: Psalm 42:4 (PL 109, 346C); Raban Maurus, *De universo*, Lib. XVIII, cap. 4: Psalms 42:4 and 143:9 (PL 111, 498A and B); pseudo-Jerome, *Epistola* 23: Psalm 42:4 and Ps. 143:9 (PL 30, 214C and 215A); Walafrid Strabo?, *Glossa Ordinaria*, Lib. I Paralipomenon, cap. 15 (PL 113, 652A); Rupert of Deutz, *De trinitate et operibus ejus libri XLII*, In libros Regum, Lib. I: David (PL 167, 1096C); Herrad of Hohenburg, *Hortus Deliciarum*: *Paralipomenon. Verba dierum* (ed. Green 1979, Reconstruction No. 202; based on the manuscript Paris, BN., nouv. acq. fr. 6045). In this text the discovery of the delta-shaped *psaltery* is attributed to David.
14 Ed. Vollmann 1985, p. 181. In Zeydel's edition of the text (1959a, p. 261) the word *triangulum* is missing; the translation does report "das Triangulum" (p. 262). Probably a mistake was made in the edition as well as in the translation of the missing word.

15 Pseudo-Jerome, *Epistola* 23 (PL 30, 214C); Raban Maurus, *Commentarium in librum I Paralipomenon*, cap. 15 (PL 109, 346C) and *De universo*, Lib. XVIII, cap. 4 (PL 111, 498A).
16 Raban Maurus, *Commentarium in librum I Paralipomenon*, cap. 15 (PL 109, 346B) and *De universo*, Lib. XVIII, cap. 4 (PL 111, 498B).
17 See note 16. The 'four-cornered' form can be both a square and a rectangle. An example of a rectangular psaltery is found in the eleventh-century Psalm manuscript London, BL., Cotton Tiberius C.VI, f. 17r (Seebass 1973b, Bildband Pl. 118).
18 PL 30, 213B-215C: *Epistola* 23. Frede 1981, p. 372.
19 Hermann 1957, 593-4.
20 Lambert 1970, pp. 108-11, No. 323. *De universo*, Lib. XVIII, cap. 4 (PL 111, 495B-500B). Dating of *De universo* follows Pietzsch 1929, p. 22 and dating of Raban Maurus follows ODCC, p. 1154.
21 Hammerstein 1959, p. 118.
22 *Enarrationes in Psalmos*, Praeambula (PL 131, 138C and PL 131, 147C). Dating follows ODCC, p. 1152.
23 Maas-Snyder 1989, p. 53-4: "Although the etymology of the instrument's name must remain a mystery, it seems a safe guess that the Greeks borrowed the word from one of the languages of Asia Minor."
24 Sendrey 1970, p. 261.
25 Giesel 1978, p. 123.
26 Sendrey 1970, pp. 250-1.
27 Lib. III, cap. 22,7 (ed. Lindsay 1966, I). Raban Maurus follows Isidore with an almost identical formulation in *De universo*, Lib. XVIII, cap. 4: *Est autem similitudo citharae barbaricae (ut alii volunt) in modum deltae litterae* (PL 111, 498B); Johannes Aegidius of Zamora, *Ars musica*, cap. 17: Δ=*deltae* (ed. Robert-Tissot 1974, p. 118) and Jerome of Moravia, *Tractatus de musica*, cap. 4: *Est autem similitudo cithare barbarice in modum Delte littere* (GS I, 9b).
28 Steger 1971, p. 130.
29 Ed. Sehrt-Starck 1955, III, 3, p. 1117, l. 10-5. Steger 1971, p. 109: footnote 97.
30 Lexicon Aegidii Forcellini IV, p. 221; Gressmann 1905, pp. 23-4.
31 Sendrey 1970, p. 260 and 267.
32 Ovid, *Ars amatoria*, Lib. III, v. 327-8 (LCL 232, p. 140).
33 E.g. Augustine, *Enarrationes in Psalmos* (PL 36, 671): *Organa dicuntur omnia instrumenta musicorum*. See Giesel 1978, p. 168.
34 Sendrey 1970, p. 70.
35 Blaise 1975, p. 749; Migne 1890, p. 1820; Niermeyer 1976, p. 869.
36 McKinnon 1984, pp. 626-7; McKinnon-Remnant 1984b, pp. 151-5.
37 GEW II, p. 1129.
38 Sendrey 1970, pp. 287-9; Lexicon Aegidii Forcellini IV, p. 972.
39 Lexicon Aegidii Forcellini III, p. 712.
40 Cassiodorus, *Expositio Psalmorum*, Praefatio, cap. 4 (CCL 97, p. 11). Isidore of Seville, *Etymologiae*, Lib. III, cap. 22,7 (ed. Lindsay 1966, I) uses similar

wording; pseudo-Bede, *De Psalmorum libro exegesis*, Praefatio altera (PL 93, 481B): *in=ad*, and *Interpretatio psalterii artis cantilenae, vel specierum singularum, vel nominum quae commemorantur in Psalmis* (PL 93, 1099); Raban Maurus, *Commentarium in librum I Paralipomenon*, cap. 15 (PL 109, 346C) and *De universo*, Lib. XVIII, cap. 4 (PL 111, 498A and B); pseudo-Jerome, *Epistola* 23 (PL 30, 214C); Walafrid Strabo?, *Glossa Ordinaria*, Lib. I Paralipomenon, cap. 15 (PL 113, 652A); Remigius of Auxerre, *Enarrationes in Psalmos*, Praeambula (PL 131, 138B); Notker Teutonicus, postscript to *Fides Sancti Athanasii Episcopi*: *modum=figura* (ed. Sehrt-Starck 1955, III, 3, p. 1117, l. 10); Bruno of Würzburg, *Expositio Psalmorum, canticorum, orationis Dominicae et symbolorum*, Prolegomena, cap. 4 (PL 142, 44A); Gerhoh of Reichersberg, *Commentarius aureus in Psalmos*, Ps. 1: *deltae Graecae litterae* (PL 193, 629C); Johannes Aegidius of Zamora, *Ars musica*, cap. 17 (ed. Robert-Tissot 1974, p. 118); Jerome of Moravia, *Tractatus de musica*, cap. 4 (GS I, p. 9b).

41 The Mss. London, BL., Cott. Tib. C.VI, f. 16v; Munich, Bayerische Staatsbibl., Clm. 14523, f. 51v; Oxford, Balliol College, 173a, f. 76r, 76v; Paris, BN., lat. 7211, f. 150v; Gerbert 1774, II, Pl. 24, Fig. 9; Pl. 25, Fig. 10; Pl. 29, Fig. 9 and Pl. 30, Fig. 10.

42 Rupert of Deutz, *De trinitate et operibus ejus*: *In libros Regum*, Lib. I (PL 167, 1096C) and *Prologus Ruperti in librum Psalmorum*, cap. 3 (PL 167, 1180D); Gerhoh of Reichersberg, *Commentarium aureus in Psalmos*, Ps. 1 (PL 193, 629B); Herrad of Hohenburg, *Hortus Deliciarum*: *Paralipomenon. Verba dierum* (ed. Green, 1979, p. 97, No. 202).

43 *Commentarium aureum in Psalmos*, Ps. 1 (PL 193, 629B and C). Dating according to ODCC, pp. 559-60.

44 *Selectorum Psalmorum expositio* (PL 172, 271D). Dating follows Giesel 1978, p. 88.

45 Only one manuscript by Cassiodorus (CCL 97, p. 11 footnote cap. 4: Ms. D) mentions *dicit* instead of *ait*. See further pseudo-Bede, *Interpretatio psalterii artis cantilenae, vel specierum singularum, vel nominum quae commemorantur in Psalmis* (PL 93, 1099); Remigius of Auxerre, *Enarrationes in psalmos*, Praeambula: *Hieronymus=Jeremias* (PL 131, 138B); Bruno of Würzburg, *Expositio Psalmorum, canticorum, orationis Dominicae et symbolorum*, Prolegomena, cap. 4 (PL 142, 44A).

46 Cassiodorus, *Expositio Psalmorum*, Praefatio, cap. 4 (CCL 97, p. 11) footnote to cap. 4: "2/5 Hieronymus?". In footnote 118 on p. 180 Esmeijer (1978) concludes rather too presumptuously: "The description of the cithara and the psaltery [...] as delta-shaped goes back to Jerome's commentary on the Psalms."

47 Dating follows Steger 1961, pp. 159-60: Denkmal 6 and 7; Seebass 1973b, p. 175.

48 *De universo*, Lib. XVIII, cap. 4 (PL 111, 495B-500B).

49 Cassiodorus, *Expositio Psalmorum*, Praefatio, cap. 4 (CCL 97, p. 11); Isidore, *Etymologiae*, Lib. III, cap. 22,7 (ed. Lindsay 1966, I) and pseudo-Bede, *De Psalmorum libro exegesis*, Praefatio altera (PL 93, 481B).
50 Ed. Hildebrandt 1982, p. 93 and 221.
51 See ODCC, p. 1454. Cf. Stegmüller, 5, No. 8324.
52 Hammerstein 1959, pp. 126-7 (followed by Giesel 1978, p. 131) assumes that the medieval *cithara* inherited the formal characteristics of the Hebrew angular harp *nevel* (=*nebel*) via the Greek *psalterion.* However the *psalterion* has the form not of a regular triangle but of a right-angled triangle. This latter form resembles that of a medieval harp-psaltery more than that of the harp.
53 In connection with the origin of the passages from the chapter *De musica et partibus ejus*, see Heyse 1969, p. 32 and Seebass 1973b, p. 143.
54 Steger 1961, p. 42.
55 *Epistola* 23 (PL 30, 214B).
56 See note 29.
57 Rupert of Deutz, *De trinitate et operibus ejus*: In libros Regum, Lib. I (PL 167, 1095D) and *Prologus Ruperti in librum Psalmorum*, cap. 3 (PL 167, 1180B-C). Dating follows ODCC, pp. 1208-9.
58 Psalter and commentary (London, Beatty coll., 32, f. 1r). I was not able to trace the quotation in the *Commentarius in Psalmos Davidicos* in the Migne edition (PL 191, 55 ff.). Dating of Peter Lombard follows ODCC, p. 1073.
59 Von Naredi-Rainer 1986, p. 34; Meyer 1975, pp. 59-64; Hopper 1938, p. 51 and 70.
60 Von Naredi-Rainer 1986, pp. 34-6; Meyer 1975, p. 59.
61 Meyer 1975, p. 60.
62 See e.g. Augustine, De musica, Lib. I, cap. 12,26 (PL 82, 1098). Von Naredi-Rainer 1986, p. 34; Meyer 1975, p. 59 and Vellekoop 1967, pp. 103-4.
63 Lib. III, cap. 4,3 (ed. Lindsay 1966, I).
64 Hopper 1938, p. 41.
65 PL 175, 22A-B. Dating of Hugh of St. Victor follows ODCC, p. 674.
66 Meyer 1975, p. 117.
67 *Epistola* 23 (PL 30, 214C). The word *per* is missing in many Dardanus Mss.
68 Raban Maurus, *De universo*, Lib. XVIII, cap. 4 (PL 111, 498A) and *Commentarium in librum I Paralipomenon* (PL 109, 346C); Walafrid Strabo?, *Glossa Ordinaria*, Lib. I Paralipomenon, cap. 15 (PL 113, 652A). The text of Raban Maurus is based on Isidore's *Etymologiae*, Lib. III, cap. 22,7.
69 Postscript to *Fides Sancti Athanasii Episcopi* (ed. Sehrt-Starck 1955, III, 3, p. 1117, l. 8-10).
70 Von Naredi-Rainer 1986, p. 39; Meyer 1975, p. 73.
71 *Selectorum Psalmorum expositio* (PL 172, 271D).
72 Giesel 1978, p. 131.
73 Seebass (1970, p. 564) on the *cithara*: "Ihre D-Form bezieht sich auf David, den sie heiligenden Träger, wobei der Anlass und Ursprung dieser Assoziation

wohl die der Musiktheorie bekannte 'cithara in modum Δ (oder D) litterae' ist."

74 Giesel 1978, p. 147.

75 Vellekoop 1967, p. 103.

76 Walafrid Strabo?, *Glossa Ordinaria*, Lib. I Paralipomenon, cap. 15 (PL 113, 652A). The explanation *decalogum legis* is also used by Isidore of Seville, *Etymologiae*, Lib. II, cap. 22,8 (ed. Lindsay 1966, I); pseudo-Jerome, *Epistola* 23 (PL 30, 215B); Raban Maurus, *Commentarium in librum I Paralipomenon* (PL 109, 346B) and *De universo*, Lib. XVIII, cap. 4 (PL 111, 498C); Remigius of Auxerre, *Enarrationes in Psalmos*, Praeambula (PL 131, 147D); Rupert of Deutz, *De trinitate et operibus ejus*: In libros Regum, Lib. I (PL 167, 1096D) and *Prologus Ruperti in librum Psalmorum*, cap. 3 (PL 167, 1181A); Gerhoh of Reichersberg, *Commentarius aureus in Psalmos*, Ps. 1 (PL 193, 629B); Honorius of Autun, *Selectorum Psalmorum expositio* (PL 172, 271A); Jerome of Moravia, *Tractatus de musica*, cap. 4 (GS I, p. 9b).

77 *De Psalmorum libro exegesis*, Praefatio altera (PL 93, 481C). The formulation *decem praeceptorum* is also found in Bartholomaeus Anglicus, *De proprietatibus rerum*, cap. 142 (ed. Müller 1909, pp. 252-3) and Johannes Aegidius of Zamora, *Ars musica*, cap. 17 (ed. Robert-Tissot 1974, p. 118). This explanation differs from the conventional one in which the *cithara* is explained as the symbol indicating the agreement between the Old and New Testament, as given by Raban Maurus, *Commentarium in librum I Paralipomenon*, cap. 15 (PL 109, 346C-D), pseudo-Jerome, *Epistola* 23 (PL 30, 214C-D) and Walafrid Strabo?, *Glossa Ordinaria*, Lib. I Paralipomenon, cap. 15 (PL 113, 652A).

78 *Lib. I Paralipomenon*, cap. 15 (PL 113, 652A).

79 (*Exegetica*, In Psalmos) PG 10, 716D-17A. Giesel 1978, pp. 151-3. Dating follows ODCC, pp. 652-3.

80 Eusebius of Caesarea, (*Commentaria in Psalmos*) (PG 23, 66A).

81 Hilary of Poitiers, *Prologus in librum Psalmorum* (PL 9, 237B-C). Dating follows ODCC, p. 649.

82 CCL 97, pp. 11-2. Similar wording in pseudo-Bede, *Interpretatio psalterii artis cantilenae, vel specierum singularum, vel nominum quae commemorantur in Psalmis* (PL 93, 1099-1101A); Raban Maurus, *Commentarium in librum I Paralipomenon*, cap. 15 (PL 109, 346); Walafrid Strabo?, *Glossa Ordinaria*, Lib. I Paralipomenon, cap. 15 (PL 113, 651D-2A); Remigius of Auxerre, *Enarrationes in Psalmos*, Praeambula (PL 131, 138B-C); Bruno of Würzburg, *Expositio Psalmorum, canticorum, orationis Dominicae et symbolorum, Prolegomena*, cap. 4 (PL 142, 44B).

83 Lib. III, cap. 22,7 (ed. Lindsay 1966, I). Similar wording is used in Raban Maurus, *De universo*, Lib. XVIII, cap. 4 (PL 111, 498B-C); Jerome of Moravia, *Tractatus de musica*, cap. 4 (GS I, p. 9b); Johannes Aegidius of Zamora, *Ars musica*, cap. 17 (ed. Robert-Tissot 1974, p. 118).

84 *Selectorum Psalmorum expositio* (PL 172, 271D). See also Remigius of Auxerre, *Enarrationes in Psalmos*, Praeambula (PL 131, 147C).

85 Cassiodorus, *Expositio Psalmorum*, Praefatio, cap. 4 (CCL 97, p. 12). Similar wording is found in Remigius of Auxerre, *Enarrationes in Psalmos*, Praeambula (PL 131, 138C) and Bruno of Würzburg, *Expositio Psalmorum, canticorum, orationis Dominicae et symbolorum*, Prolegomena, cap. 4 (PL 142, 44B). Gerhoh of Reichersberg uses a different formulation in *Commentarius aureus in Psalmos* (PL 193, 629B). See Giesel 1978, pp. 157-9.
86 Esmeijer 1978, p. 118.
87 The symbolic meanings are examined in detail by Esmeijer 1978, pp. 118-23. The prototype of the visual-exegetical scheme of the *psalterium decachordum* is found in the *Psalterium decem chordarum* and the *Liber Figurarum* of Joachim of Fiore (c. 1130-1202). See Esmeijer 1978, p. 123 and Obrist 1988.
88 Esmeijer 1978, p. 121.
89 Pickering 1970, pp. 285-307.
90 *Ruodlieb* epigram 11 (the text is printed in Chapter 3.2), and the *Paralipomenon* text in a copy of the 'Hortus' manuscript in Paris (see note 91).
91 Text based on Green 1979, Reconstruction No. 202, with interpolations from the Ms. Paris, BN., nouv. acq. fr. 6045, f. 59r.
92 Ed. Hildebrandt 1982, p. 221.
93 McKinnon 1965a, p. 244: "Medieval men are prone to traditionalism but not archeologism, and they have no scruples about incorporating contemporary elements into their allegory."

CHAPTER 4

1 The conclusions of Haseloff were taken over by Ragusa 1966, pp. 141-59 and Brown 1983, p. 41 footnote 18.
2 Steger 1961; Rensch 1964; Seebass 1973b; Owens 1990.
3 Steger 1961, p. 2.
4 Rensch 1964, pp. 109-28.
5 Foster 1977, pp. 12-39. Brown (1983) bases his exposition of musical instruments in the initials of Psalms 1 and 80 on Foster's study.
6 Leroquais 1940-1, pp. XLIV-LI.
7 There are a number of surviving medieval Psalters from the thirteenth century with more or less complete illustrations of all one-hundred and fifty Psalms; for example the Mss. Cambridge, University Libr., Ee.IV.24; London, BL., Harley 2895; Manchester, Rylands Libr., 22; Paris, Bibl. Ste.-Geneviève, 56; Paris, BN., lat. 10435; Paris, BN., lat. 11560.
8 Leroquais 1940-1, p. LIV.
9 There is a similarity between the title illuminations in the Byzantine Psalters and the B initials in western Psalters with regard to their treatment of the *Origo* theme. As has been said in connection with the B initial, its theme is not a direct parallel but a reduction of the thematic material of the frontispieces in western European Psalters.

The Byzantine and Hebrew system of Psalm arrangement is discussed by Steger 1961, pp. 147-8.

10 Goldschmidt 1895, pp. 2-3; Haseloff 1938, p. 6; Leroquais 1940-1, pp. LI-LXII.

11 Leroquais 1940-1, p. XIX.

12 The numbering of the Psalms corresponds with that of the Vulgate (=*Liber Psalmorum iuxta Septuaginta Emendatus*). It is assumed that the division of Psalms into two groups, one for Matins and one for Vespers, probably stems from the time when the office consisted of two chief elements: the early Christian morning and evening services (LW [2], 2324-9). The points at which the Psalms were divided for use in the Matins and Vespers (Psalms 1 and 109) recall an old principle of Psalter division (Kahsnitz 1979, p. 126). According to Kahsnitz this liturgical division in two became intertwined with the liturgical division in eight and the formal division in three. However, the liturgical division into two is not intended to split the Psalter into two independent parts. In this way, it differs from the Byzantine kathismata.

13 Figure based on Leroquais 1934, p. XIX. (LW [2], 2327-8).

14 There is no need to repeat the development of the systems for making the divisional arrangement here. Detailed expositions on this subject can be found in Goldschmidt 1895, pp. 1-9; Haseloff 1938, p. 21 and 60; Nordenfalk 1939; Kahsnitz 1979, pp. 115-41 and LW [2], 2324-9.

15 See Haseloff 1938, p. 14 and 22; Nordenfalk 1939, p. 108; Pächt 1985, pp. 82-9.

16 Here we are concerned with "Illustrationen historischen Inhalts in symbolischer-übertragener Beziehung zum Text" (Haseloff 1938, p. 9).

17 Haseloff 1938, p. 62.

18 See Suckale-Redlefsen 1972, pp. 26-31.

19 Peter Lombard, *Commentarium in Psalmos*, Praefatio (PL 191, 60B).

20 Honorius of Autun, *Expositio in Psalmos selectos*, Primus psalmus de incarnatione Christi (PL 172, 274C). See Bruno of Würzburg, *Expositio Psalmorum*, Ps. 1 (PL 142, 49A).

21 Honorius of Autun, *Expositio in Psalmos selectos* (PL 172, 274D). Also Cassiodorus, *Expositio Psalmorum*, Ps. 1 (CCL 97, pp. 30-1) and Bruno of Würzburg, *Expositio Psalmorum*, Ps. 1 (PL 142, 49B-50A).

22 Augustine, *Enarratio in Psalmum* 1 (CCL 38, p. 276).

23 Steger 1961; Seebass 1973b; Kahsnitz 1979.

24 See the Mss. London, BL., Add. 44874, f. 7v (David with harp; surrounding him in four medallions: a cymbala player, two fiddlers, a player of a wind instrument); Melk, Stiftsbibl., 1, f. 12r (David depicted four times: with a harp, fiddle, hurdy-gurdy and a psaltery); Oxford, Bodleian Libr., Laud. Misc. 752, f. 263v (David with psaltery, a harpist, a horn player, a cymbala player and a figure with hand cymbals); Paris, Bibl. Mazarine, 36, f. 214r (David with harp, fiddles, a psaltery, cymbala and a double flute). In connection with the theme of David and his co-psalmists in the B initials of double Psalters — these Psalters include both the *Psalterium Gallicanum* and the *Psalterium iuxta Hebraeos* of Jerome — see Heiman 1965, p. 95.

25 See the Mss. Bamberg, Staatsbibl., 48, f. 10r (David with lyre, a fiddler and a harpist); Brussels, KB., 9961-2, f. 14r (David with harp, two fiddlers); Brussels, KB., 10730, f. 153r; Brussels, KB., 14682, f. 22v (David with harp, fiddler); Douai, Bibl. Municipale, 233, f. 2r (David with harp, fiddler, horn player); London, BL., Lansdowne 383, f. 15v (a fiddler, a harpist and a monster with a drum — neither the fiddler nor the harpist can be identified as David); London, Society of Antiquaries, 59, f. 38v (in medallions: David with harp, two fiddlers, a psaltery and hurdy-gurdy); New York, Pierpont Morgan Libr., 756, f. 11r (David with harp, a fiddler and a drummer); New York, Pierpont Morgan Libr., 791, f. 170r (David with harp, three fiddlers, a horn player); Oxford, Bodleian Libr., Canon. Pat. lat. 217, f. 3r (David depicted twice: as harpist and as fiddler); Paris, BN., nouv. acq. lat. 1392, f. 20r (David with harp and a fiddler); Princeton, University Libr., Garrett 28, f. 209r.
In several fourteenth-century manuscripts the *Origo* theme has been re-positioned in a miniature above the initial: New York, Metropolitan Museum, Cloisters, 69.86, f. 15r (David with harp, a psaltery player and a fiddler); Rome, Bibl. Vaticana, Urb. lat. 603, f. 13r (David with harp, a performer on the psaltery and a fiddler).
Recent studies of the fiddle interpret the bow and strings of the instrument as representing the symbolic link between the earthly and heavenly (Ravenel 1985, p. 105). This could be a reason why the fiddle is often depicted together with the harp of David. However, I know of no conclusive evidence for this proposition.

26 Also in the Ms. Paris, BN., lat. 11539-42, f. 26v. Sometimes the harp is also depicted with other unplayed stringed instruments, as in the two fourteenth-century miniatures in the Mss. Paris, Bibl. de l'Arsenal, 5212, f. 378r (rebec, psaltery and three singing figures) and Paris, BN., fr. 962, f. 17r (rebec, psaltery).

27 See the Mss. Abbéville, Bibl. de la Ville, 3, f. 7r; Avranches, Bibl. de la Ville, 3, f. 3r; Baltimore, Walters Art Gallery, 115, f. 13r; Brussels, KB., 10521, f. 265r; Cambridge, Fitzwilliam Museum, McClean 15, f. 176v; Cambridge, Fitzwilliam Museum, McClean 44, f. 1r; Cambridge, Trinity College, B.5.26, f. 1r; Durham, Cathedral Libr., A.II.4, f. 65r; Frankfurt, Stadtbibl., Batt. 150, f. 8r; Graz, Universitätsbibl., II.204, f. 1r; Herdringen, Schlossbibl., Psalter, n.s.m., f. 6r; Hildesheim, St.-Godehard-Bibl., Psalter, n.s.m., p. 73; Holkam, Leicester coll., 26, f. 7r; London, BL., Add. 24686, f. 11r; London, BL., Add. 28681, f. 18r; London, BL., Add. 42130, f. 13r; London, BL., Add. 44949, f. 39r; London, BL., Egerton 2867, f. 244v; London, BL., Royal 1.B.XII, f. 178r; Manchester, Rylands Libr., 117, f. 9r; New York, Public Libr., 4, f. 193r; Oxford, All Souls College, 7, f. 7r; Oxford, Bodleian Libr., Auct. D.3.2., f. 195r; Oxford, Bodleian Libr., Auct. D.3.5, f. 111r; Oxford, Bodleian Libr., Laud. Lat. 87, f. 215r; Oxford, Bodleian Libr., Lyell empt. 4, f. 8v; Oxford, Jesus College, D.40, f. 8r; Paris, Bibl. Ste.-Geneviève, 1181, f. 177r; Paris, BN., lat. 15, f. 216v; Paris, BN., lat. 1029A, f. 10r; Paris, BN., lat. 14397, f. 166r; Paris, BN., lat. 15467, f. 258r; Princeton, Museum of Art, 28-12, f. 5v;

Princeton, University Libr., Garrett 29, f. 345r; Princeton, University Libr., Garrett 34, f. 7r; Princeton, University Libr., Garrett 35, f. 14r; San Marino, Huntington Libr., E.L. 9.H.17, f. 42r; San Marino, Huntington Libr., H.M. 26061, f. 166r.

28 Also in the Mss. Amiens, Bibl. de la Ville, 21, f. 219r; Amiens, Bibl. de la Ville, 124, f. 7v; Arras, Bibl. de la Ville, 88, f. 1r; Arras, Bibl. de la Ville, 561, f. 122v; Baltimore, Walters Art Gallery, 45, f. 16r; Brussels, KB., IV.10, f. 13v; Brussels, KB., 14682, f. 22v; Cambrai, Bibl. Municipale, 102-3, f. 232r; Cambrai, Bibl. Municipale, 102-3, f. 1r; Cambridge, Magdalena College, 7, f. 8v; Cleveland, Museum of Art, 53.145, w.f.; Florence, Bibl. Laurenziana, Plut. XV.11, f. 275r; Frankfurt, Kunstgewerbemuseum, L.M. 20, f. 74r; London, BL., Add. 21926, f. 26r; London, BL., Royal 2.B.II, f. 7r; London, BL., Yates Thompson 15, f. 20r; London, BL., Yates Thompson 18, f. 9r; London, BL., Yates Thompson 22, f. 161v; London, Soane Museum, 9, f. 132r; Lyons, Gillet coll., Psalter, n.s.m., f. 7r; Maihingen, Bibl. Wallerstein, I.2.qu.24, f. 15v; Malvern, Dyson Perrins coll., 34, f. 7r; Manchester, Rylands Libr., 117, f. 9r; Munich, Bayerische Staatsbibl., Clm. 3900, f. 8r; New York, Pierpont Morgan Libr., 97, f. 24v; Oxford, Bodl. Libr., Auct. D.2.2, f. 8r; Oxford, Bodl. Libr., Auct. D.4.2, f. 15v; Oxford, Bodl. Libr., Douce 5,6, f. 18r; Oxford, Bodl. Libr., Douce 24, f. 7v; Padua, Bibl. Seminario, 353, f. 23r; Paris, BN., lat. 1075, f. 19r; Paris, BN., lat. 11534-5, f. 17v; Paris, BN., lat. 11539-42, f. 26v; Paris, BN., lat. 16260, f. 263v; Paris, BN., lat. 16272, f. 1v; Paris, nouv. acq., lat. 3104, f. 27r; Princeton, University Libr., Garrett 28, f. 209r; Rouen, Bibl. Publique, 3106, f. 22r; San Marino, Huntington Libr., H.M. 1050, f. 5v; Tournai, Bibl. de la cathédrale Notre-Dame, Psalter, n.s.m., f. 7r; Venice, Bibl. Marciana, lat. I.77 (2397), f. 27r; Verdun, Bibl. Municipale, 107, f. 1r; Vienna, Österreichische Nationalbibl., 1139, f. 166r; Würzburg, Universitätsbibl., Mp. theologica in quarto 70, f. 1r.
In some fourteenth-century manuscripts there is a miniature with the same theme above the initial B: London, BL., Yates Thompson 20, f. 381r; London, BL., Yates Thompson 22, f. 161v; New York, Metropolitan Museum, Cloisters, 69.86, f. 15r.

29 For example the Mss. Cambrai, Bibl. Municipale, 102-3, f. 232r; Oxford, Bodleian Libr., Douce 24, f. 7v. In the illustration in the Ms. Arras, Bibl. de la Ville, 561, f. 122v the themes have changed positions.

30 See Chapter 2.2.2, especially Table 1.

31 London, BL., Add. 15452, f. 182r and Moulins, Musée Municipale, Bible, n.s.m., f. 215r; Oxford, Bodleian Libr., Auct. E. infra 1-2, f. 2r. In the Ms. Malvern, Dyson Perrins coll., 119, f. 105v the writing figure seems more like a monk than King David.

32 Berlin, Kupferstichkabinett, 78.A.8, f. 14v; Berlin, Staatsbibl. Preussischer Kulturbesitz, theol. lat. fol. 379, f. 232v; Dresden, Arnhold coll., Psalter, n.s.m., f. 12v (the lower half of the initial shows three crowned David?-figures, one of whom is holding a harp and another a lyre-like instrument); Hereford, Cathedral Libr., O.3.XV, f. 43r; Kassel, Landesbibl., theologica in quarto 8,

f. 251r; Munich, Bayerische Staatsbibl., Clm. 23094, f. 7v; Rome, Bibl. Vaticana, Pal. lat. 26, f. 13r.
King David with the harp is represented as part of the *Stirps Jesse* in the Ms. Douai, Bibl. Municipale, 171, f. 1r; Krivoklát, 'Castle Libr.', I.b.23, f. 14r; London, BL., Add. 38116, f. 14v; London, Lambeth Palace Libr., 233, f. 15r; New York, Pierpont Morgan Libr., 43, f. 27v; New York, Public Libr., Spencer 2, f. 15r; Oxford, Bodl. Libr, Lat. Liturg. d.42, f. 20r.

33 Cf. Mark 1:10, Luke 3:22, John 1:32.

34 See also the Ms. Engelberg, Stiftsbibl., 113, f. 11r. In the Ms. Oxford, Bodl. Libr., Laud. Misc. 752, a large bird, probably a dove, is depicted in the initial B on f. 236v in a medallion on King David's right. The dove points with its head in David's direction.

35 Liverpool, Public Library, 12004, f. 12r; London, BL., Add. 17392, f. 1r.

36 Gerhoh of Reichersberg, *Commentarium in Psalmos*, Ps. 26 (PL 193, 1173D).

37 Cambridge, Fitzwilliam Museum, Psalter, n.s.m., f. 29r; Oxford, New College, 322, f. 28r; Paris, Bibl. Ste.-Geneviève, 56, f. 2v.

38 See Gerhoh of Reichersberg, *Commentarium in Psalmos* (PL 193, 1176C/D).

39 Haseloff 1938, p. 24.

40 Pseudo-Bede, *In Psalmorum librum exegesis*, In psalmum 38 (PL 93, 687C). See Stegmüller, 2, No. 1665.

41 Cassiodorus, *Expositio Psalmorum*, Ps. 38 (CCL 97, p. 354); Gerhoh of Reichersberg, *Commentarium in Psalmos*, Ps. 38 (PL 193, 1375C).

42 Cambridge, University Libr., Ee.IV.24, f. 13r; Chantilly, Musée Condé, 9 (1695), f. 72r. According to Haseloff 1938, p. 35, there is no connection between the illustration and the Psalm text.
The theme of the initial illumination in f. 9r in the Psalter Heiligenkreuz, Stiftsbibl., 66, is difficult to explain: unattached objects — a fiddle and bow, a lyre and a horn — are placed next to David, who is playing the harp. No connection can be shown with the *Origo* text since there are no co-psalmists represented.

43 Honorius of Autun, *Expositio in Psalmos selectos*, Prologus in Psalmum 51 (PL 172, 290D-291A).

44 The Mss. Cambridge, Fitzwilliam Museum, McClean 43; Florence, Bibl. Riccardiana, 435; Oxford, Bodleian Libr., Douce 5,6. Also the manuscript from England, viz. London, BL., Add. 21926.

45 Haseloff 1938, p. 17.

46 Ibid., p. 63; Nordenfalk 1939, p. 111.

47 Haseloff 1938, p. 64.

48 Gerhoh of Reichersberg, *Commentarium in Psalmos*, Ps. 68 (PL 194, 268B).

49 Haseloff 1938, p. 17

50 London, BL., Arundel 157, f. 71v; London, BL., Lansdowne 431, f. 64v.

51 It is noteworthy that a fiddle is added to the instrumentarium in E initials from England. This is the case, for example, in the Mss. Cambridge, Trinity College, B.11.4, f. 96r; London, BL., Arundel 157, f. 71v and London, BL., Lansdowne 431, f. 64v (harp, trumpet, psaltery, fiddle); Evreux, Bibl.

Municipale, 4, f. 135r and London, BL., Add. 16975, f. 86r (harp, psaltery, fiddle); London, BL., Add. 21926, f. 115v (organ, harp, psaltery); London, BL., Add. 49622, f. 107v (harp, psaltery, fiddle, tambourine); Paris, BN., lat. 1023, f. 36v (harp, psaltery).

52 Van Schaik 1989.

53 For example in the Ms. Oxford, Bodleian Libr., Douce 366, f. 109r; Paris, BN., nouv. acq. lat. 1392, f. 113v.

54 The Mss. London, BL., Harley 5102, f. 77v; Paris, BN., lat. 11, f. 181v; Paris, BN., lat. 11934, f. 246r; Paris, BN., lat. 13260, f. 19v; Paris, BN., lat. 14284, f. 19r; Paris, BN., lat. 16260, f. 279r.

55 In the Mss. London, BL., Royal 1.D.I, f. 246v; London, BL., Royal 2.B.II, f. 88v and New York, Pierpont Morgan Libr., 102, f. 84r, the instrument is placed next to or behind the throne on which David is seated. In other Mss., such as Paris, Bibl. Ste.-Geneviève, 2690, f. 99r and Zagreb, 'National and University Libr.', MR 159, f. 246r, the harp is depicted near David.

56 Giesel 1978, pp. 150-9.

57 E.g. Cassiodorus, *Expositio Psalmorum*, Ps. 80 (CCL 98, p. 750) and pseudo-Bede, *In Psalterium librum exegesis*, Ps. 80 (PL 93, 921B).

58 Peter Lombard, *Expositio Psalmorum*, Ps. 80 (PL 142, 308A) and Gerhoh of Reichersberg, *Commentarium in Psalmos*, Ps. 80 (PL 194, 499A).

59 CCL 98, p. 751,

60 Haseloff 1938, pp. 100-1 and pp. 105-19.

61 See relevant parts in Foster 1977, p. 32: footnote 41.

62 Kassel, Landesbibl., theologica in quarto 8, f. 266v.

63 PL 142, 355B. The explanation of the words from verse 1 of the Psalm as a reference to (the coming of) Christ is also found in Jerome, *Tractatus in Psalmos*, De psalmo 97 (CCL 78, p. 161); Cassiodorus, *Expositio Psalmorum*, Ps. 97 (CCL 98, p. 876); Bruno of Cologne, *Expositio in Psalmum* 97 (PL 152, 1152D); Peter Lombard, *Commentarium in Psalmos*, Ps. 97 (PL 191, 889C/D) and Gerhoh of Reichersberg, *Commentarium in Psalmos*, Ps. 97 (PL 194, 590C-D).

64 Cf. Haseloff 1938, p. 18.

65 Haseloff 1938, p. 64.

66 Pseudo-Bede, *In Psalterium librum exegesis*, Ps. 97 (PL 93, 990D). See also Cassiodorus, *Expositio Psalmorum*, Ps. 97 (CCL 98, p. 876).

67 Jerome, *Tractatus in Psalmos*, De psalmo 97 (CCL 78, p. 93); Bruno of Cologne, *Expositio in Psalmos*, Ps. 97 (PL 152, 1153D-4A).

68 Cassiodorus, *Expositio Psalmorum*, Ps. 97 (CCL 98, pp. 878-9).

69 Bruno of Segni, *Expositio in Psalmos*, Ps. 97 (PL 164, 1073D-4A).

70 Haseloff 1938, especially p. 12, 18 and 45; Nordenfalk 1939, p. 10.

71 Cassiodorus, *Expositio Psalmorum*, Ps. 109 (CCL 98, pp. 1006-7); pseudo-Bede, *In Psalterium librum exegesis*, Ps. 109 (PL 93, 1035C); Bruno of Segni, *Expositio in Psalmos*, Ps. 109 (PL 164, 1125B-6C); Gerhoh of Reichersberg, *Commentarium in Psalmos*, Ps. 109 (PL 194, 693B-4D).

CHAPTER 5

1 Hammerstein 1974, p. 63; Mâle 1953, p. 340; Randall 1966, pp. 3-8.
2 Aubert 1929, p. 3; Randall 1966, pp. 8-20.
3 Klingender 1971, p. 328.
4 Adolf 1950, p. 49; Mâle 1953, p. 340; Debidour 1961, pp. 385-6; Rensch 1964, pp. 150-2; Vitale-Brovarone 1978, pp. 121-9; Vogel 1978, II, p. 482; Okken-Mück 1981, pp. 170-88; Jullian 1987, p. 38; Garnier 1988.
5 Hammerstein 1974, p. 67. Hammerstein is not the first to suggest such an explanation; several earlier studies included statements in this direction: Adolf 1950, p. 52, Rensch 1964, p. 151 and Wehrhahn-Stauch 1968, p. 683.
6 Adolf 1950, p. 52; Randall 1957, p. 104; Rensch 1964, pp. 150-1 and p. 214.
7 Vogel 1973, pp. 351-4, ills. 118, 120 and 125. Cf. Adolf 1950, p. 50.
8 Adolf 1950, p. 49; Gandillac-Jeauneau 1968, p. 487; Hammerstein 1974, p. 73.
9 Ed. Perry 1975, p. 390: Appendix Perottina, 14! The substance of this fable is written in the Aesop tradition; however, there is no known fable from this author dealing with an ass and a musical instrument. Possibly Phaedrus worked from older material (Perry 1952, p. lxxxvi). The title *Asinus ad lyram* is attributed to Perotti.
10 Perry 1975, pp. xcvii-xcviii.
11 — Ονος λύρας in Greek writings (here printed in Latin translation): Aelian, *De natura animalium* (LCL X, pp. 322-4); Apostolius (CPG II, centuria XII, p. 563, No. 82 and footnote, also CPG II, centuria XII, p. 566, No. 91a and footnote); Clement of Alexandria, *Stromata* (PG 8, 689A); Diogenianus (CPG I, centuria VII, p. 291, No. 33, especially the footnote); Eustathius of Thessalonica, *Commentarii ad Homeri Odysseam*, 373 (ed. Stallbaum 1825, p. 304); Gregory of Cyprus (CPG I, centuria III, p. 370, No. 29 and CPG II, Cod. mosq. centuria IV, p. 126, No. 66); Lucian, *Adversus indoctum* (ed. Macleod, II, p. 122, l. 28) and *De Mercede conductis* (ed. Macleod, II, p. 226, l. 24-5); Macarius (CPG II, centuria VI, p. 193, nos. 38 and 39); Menander, fragment (ed. Allinson 1959, p. 408, l. 18) and fragment (ed. Allinson 1959, p. 460, l. 527K); Photius, fragment (LCL, [without number] p. 460, l. 3); *Suidae Lexicon*, No. 391 (ed. Adler 1967).
The ὄνος λύρας references in Latin texts are quoted in the text.
— *(An) onos liras*. One reference that is not cited in the text is the *Liber iocalis*, ll. 530-1 (Lehmann 1938, p. 56).
— *Asinus ad lyram*. References which are not quoted in the text are the *Vita Heinrici IV Imperatoris*, 8 (MGH, XII, p. 277) and the *Epistola* 165 of Petrus Cellensis (PL 202, 608C).
12 See note 11, i.e. the sources which follow "Ονος λύρας in Greek writings", with the exception of those mentioned in note 13.
13 See Adler 1967, p. 542, No. 391; Macarius (CPG II, centuria VI, p. 193, No. 38) and Apostolius (CPG II, centuria XII, p. 566, No. 91a).
14 Okken-Mück 1981.

15 Nonius Marcellus, *De compendiosa doctrina*, Lib. I, cap. 1-3 (ed. Lindsay 1964, I).

16 Ed. Lindsay 1964, I, p. 71. Okken-Mück 1981, p. 171, footnote 552: "(Zählung nach der Ausg. von Jos. Mercerus, Paris 1583:) S. 49, Zeile 33 — S. 50, Zeile 1. (Im Zitat sind die Akzente der zitierten Edition weggelassen.) Der kritische Nonius-Apparat verzeichnet keine mittelalterlichen Glossen zum Zitat; vgl. S. XIX: Archetypus-Nennung. Vgl. zur Konjekturalkritik: [Vahlen 1974,] S. 8. Kritischer Text: [Bücheler 1963,] S. 298 [...]. Vgl. noch: Der Kleine Pauly. Lexikon der Antike. (...) hrsg. von Konrat Ziegler und Walther Sontheimer. Bd 4. Munich 1972. Sp. 153: Nonius Marcellus, röm. Grammatiker aus Thubursicum Numidarum (Sukh Arras) in Afrika, lebte nach dem 2. und vor dem 5. Jahrhundert."
See further the *Satiricon* of Gaius Titus Petronius (ed. Bücheler 1963, p. 321, No. 543) and the *Noctes Atticae* of Aulus Gellius, Lib. III, cap. 16,13 (ed. Marshall 1968, I, p. 156). Nonius, who knew the title *Testamentum* of the satires (ed. Lindsay 1964, p. 767, No. 478, l. 13), only mentions the first three satires; the fourth, which includes the figure of speech, is missing.

17 Op. cit. Okken-Mück 1981, pp. 170-1.

18 *Epistola ad Marcellam* XXVII (CSEL 54, p. 224, l. 4); see Lambert 1969, pp. 482-6 for an account of this letter. The excerpts in question are in the Öffentliche Bibl. der Universität Basel: B.X.22, f. 248 (CIX)vb, and A.IV.20, f. 115r-42r.

19 *Epistola ad Vigilantium* LXI (CSEL 54, p. 581, l. 6-7) with the written forms: *asino lyra* and *asino lira*.

20 *De nuptiis Philologiae et Mercurii*, Lib. VIII, cap. 807 (ed. Dick 1969, p. 426, l. 9-10). See also Chapter 1, note 14 on the date of the writing.

21 Okken-Mück 1981, p. 173, footnote 560: "Vgl. Martianus Capella: Variantenapparat." See note 20.

22 Ed. Lutz 1939, p. 167, l. 30-2.

23 Ed. Lutz 1965, p. 243, l. 1-5. Okken-Mück 1981, p. 174, footnote 562: "Remigius übernahm nach mittelalterlicher Gelehrtenart den Kommentar des Johannes; aber auch den Martianus-Capella-Kommentar des Dunchad=des Martin von Laon hat Remigius in herkömmlicher Weise ausgewertet. Heute lässt sich nicht mehr bestimmen, wieviel Remigius dem letzteren Kommentar zur ὄνος λύρας-Stelle entnommen hat; die diesbezügliche Partie des Kommentars ist ja verlorengegangen. — Vgl. dazu [Lutz 1944,] S. XIII."

24 Okken-Mück 1981, p. 174, footnote 563: "Die Kommentare des Johannes Scottus und des Dunchad (=Martin von Laon) sind beide jeweils nur in einer Handschrift überliefert. Den Erfolg hatte erst der Erbe: Der Kommentar des Remigius ist in über 70 Hss überliefert; die Mehrzahl dieser Handschriften wurde während des 10., 11. und 12. Jhs geschrieben. — Vgl. dazu: [Lutz 1962,] S. 5-6: Über den Gelehrtenruhm des Remigius; S. 17: Über die von Remigius ausgewerteten Kommentare des Johannes und des Dunchad; S. 40: Über die Überlieferung. — Vgl. auch: Wessner: Martianus Capella. In: Paulys Real-Encyclopädie: Anm. 553. Bd. 14. Sp. 2003-2016, bes. Sp. 2012-2014: Über

die Wirkung des Martianus Capella und seines Kommentators Remigius von Auxerre."

25 *Consolatio*, Lib. 1, Prosa IV (CCL 94, I, p. 6). Shanzer (1986) makes plausible the idea that Boethius could still quote Varro's Satires and that the Greek figure of speech is quoted directly by Boethius from a work of Varro which is now lost.

26 Ed. Sehrt-Starck 1933, I, 1, p. 25, l. 16-20. Frakes 1987, p. 29: footnote 14 sums up the commentaries which may have been available to Notker. Okken-Mück 1981, p. 175, footnote 565 on the edition of Sehrt-Starck: "Zeilen 16-20, mit einem Eingriff in den kritischen Text: Die editorische 'Besserung' *An onos* wird rückgängig gemacht; im Zitat erscheint wieder das handschriftlich überlieferte *Ananos*, ohne Morphemgrenze und mit falschem 'a'."

27 Adolf (1950, p. 51) tried to explain the written form *ananos* by proposing that Notker Labeo did not find the passage *ananos lyras* important — "apt to encourage his students' love of profanity". On the other hand Okken-Mück 1981, p. 176, footnote 566 proposes: "Vgl. [Naumann 1913,] S. 34-59: Die Zusammenstellung des von Notker aus R und X verwendeten Apparates (Naumann bezeichnet mit R den Kommentar des Remigius, mit X den Kommentar des Anonymus.) — Vgl. ebda bes. S. 37: 23,7 *i. expers lyrae* R. (Also: Naumann gibt keine Entsprechung im Kommentar des Anonymus an, somit auch keine Glosse, die von Remigius hätte verwertet werden können!) — Auf S. 74 eröffnet Naumann allerdings wieder die Möglichkeit, dass des Remigius Fehler zustandekam durch Ausschreiben des vom Anonymus verfassten Kommentars: "Das Missverständnis der griechischen Stellen kommt mindestens schon auf R und X; 23,7 ἂν ὄνος λύρας gänzlich falsch als 'expers lirae' (...)."

Vgl. dazu auch: [Courcelle 1967,] S. 244: Courcelle bestätigt des Remigius Autorschaft; S. 259-263: Remigius schreibt den vom Anonymus verfassten Consolatio-Kommentar aus; S. 264: der Anonymus kann sehr wohl im Kloster St. Gallen zuhause gewesen sein; S. 270f: Notker hat die Consolatio-Kommentare des Remigius und des Anonymus in einer von ihren zahlreichen Kompilationen benutzt; vorzugsweise hat Notker sich an Remigius gehalten; S. 271: Der Consolatio-Kommentar des Remigius war ständiger Begleiter der Consolatio-Lektüre im 10. und 11. Jahrhundert; S. 254-259: Datierung des Consolatio-Kommentars des Remigius, und zugleich des Martianus-Capella-Kommentars des Remigius: Zeitspanne 902-908."

28 Ed. Silk 1935, p. 32, l. 14-9. Okken-Mück 1981, p. 177, footnote 568: "Vgl. [Silk 1935,] S. XVI-XVIII: Über die Griechischkenntnisse des Kommentators; bes. S. XVIII: "It appears to be reasonable to conclude that the commentator, whether or not he was an expert Grecian, was able to consult Greek patristic writers in the original (...)." — Vgl. auch ebda S. XXIII-XXVI: Remigius schrieb den Kommentar aus, ihm lag ein jetzt verschollenes Exemplar des Kommentars vor; S. L-LIII: Zur Überlieferung; bes. S. L-LI: "The greater part of the commentary is preserved in only one manuscript, MS Digby 174 of the Bodleian Library. MS latin 15104 of the Bibliothèque Nationale contains a part

of the commentary on Book III of the 'Consolatio' and most of that on Book V. MS 78.19 of the Laurenziana in Florence contains considerable portions of the text in the form of scholia accompanying the text of the 'Consolatio'." — Der kritisch edierte Text hat also im ὄνος λύρας-Passus nur die eine Handschrift Digby 174 zur Grundlage. In dieser Handschrift erscheint anstelle der beiden griechischen Wörter ὄνος λύρας der Wortlaut *onos lucis* (vgl. [Silk 1935,] S. 32 unter dem Strich im Apparat.) Die vom Hrsgr vorgenommene Einsetzung der griechischen Wörter dürfte eine wohlbegründete Wiederherstellung sein: Der Kommentator konnte mit griechischen Wörtern etwas Rechtes anfangen; der Kommentar setzt offenbar einen Consolatio-Text mit heiler ὄνος λύρας-Stelle voraus; also dürfte der Kommentator in seiner eigenen Niederschrift noch korrekt ΟΝΟΣ ΛΥΡΑΣ geschrieben haben. — Übrigens: Der Hrsgr erblickt im Kommentator keinen Geringeren als Johannes Scottus Eriugena, oder statt seiner immerhin einen loyalen Schüler des grossen Meisters: Vgl. dazu S. XXVII-L."

29 Okken-Mück 1981, pp. 173-7.

30 Vitale-Brovarone 1978, p. 124.

31 According to Ms. Florence, Bibl. Laurenziana, Plut. 78, 19, f. 6r; dating from Courcelle 1967, p. 411.

32 Okken-Mück 1981, p. 178.

33 Op. cit. Vitale-Brovarone 1978, p. 125: *In Boethius cum triplici commento*. The pseudo-Thomas Aquinas manuscripts are all given a fourteenth- or fifteenth-century dating (Courcelle 1967, pp. 414-5). The Dominican Nicolas Triveth uses similar wording in his 'Consolatio' commentary; see the quotation Vitale-Brovarone 1978, p. 125 from the Ms. Paris, BN., lat. 6404, f. 1r. Courcelle (1967, pp. 412-3) also gives this Ms. a fourteenth- or fifteenth-century dating.

34 Based on the Ms. Troyes, Bibl. Municipale, 898 (text edition Schroth 1976, p. 122); dating follows Schroth 1976, pp. 28-9.

35 Based on the Ms. Erfurt, in-f. 358 (op. cit. Schroth 1976, p. 104); dating follows Schroth 1976, pp. 86-7.

36 Ed. Skeat 1954, p. 8.

37 *Cronica Boemorum* (MGH, Scriptores IX, p. 125). See Okken-Mück 1981, p. 179, footnote 571.

38 Op. cit. Delisle 1880, p. 206. In the twelfth century an ass and a lyre are mentioned in a bestiarium ascribed to the cleric Hugh of Fouilloy (Folieto). The text in which a number of the characteristics of the ass are described, also mentions that 'he took delight in the lyre'; see *De bestiis et aliis rebus*, Lib. IV, cap. 1 (PL 177, 137D). Pseudo-Hugh of St.-Victor is usually named as author of the manuscript (Stegmüller, 3, No. 3787). Rudolf Goy (1976, pp. 491-2, No. 242) ascribes authorship of *De bestiis* to Hugh of Fouilloy.

39 GS I, p. 247a. See Bernhard 1979, p. 37.

40 Ed. McLaughlin 1956, p. 285. Migne (PL 178, 306B) counts this as the eighth letter.

41 Ed. McLaughlin 1956, p. 289. Migne (PL 178, 310A) reports the figure of speech in Greek: αλλὄνος λύρας. This text variant is not present in the McLaughlin edition. McLaughlin comments mistakenly on the passage in footnote 88 op p. 289: "The initial letters *an* may be from the Greek ean." The figure of speech is also sometimes used in a religious sense by Sicardus (1160-1215), bishop of Cremona, in a moralising allegory entitled *Mitrale, sive De officiis ecclesiasticis summa*, Lib. III, cap. 4 (PL 213, 118B).
42 Ed. Wright 1965, p. 22; published in accordance with the manuscript London, BL., Cotton Nero A.V. The text is based on the *Compotus* of Helpericus of St.-Gall and a certain Gerlandus from the eleventh century; See p. X.
43 Ed. Raynaud de Lage 1966, I; on the dating see pp. XXVI-XXX. Regarding French literature a comic interpolation in the French novel *Floire et Blancheflor* should also be mentioned. This is dated between the second half of the twelfth and the end of the thirteenth century (Leclanche 1980, p. 11 and Okken-Mück 1981, footnote 575). This interpolation describes how the magician conjures up the illusion that oxen fly through the air and asses play the harp (ed. Leclanche 1980, ll. 811-2).
44 Ed. Robinson 1957, p. 397.
45 Ed. MacCracken 1934, p. 480.
46 See Vitale-Brovarone 1978 on the tradition of the figure of speech in Italian literature after 1400. The use of the figure of speech in English literature is traced by Whiting 1968, p. 16, No. A227 and Okken-Mück 1981, pp. 170-88 reports its history in German literature.
47 Greene 1931, p. 534.
48 Vogel 1973, p. 312.
49 *De natura animalium*, Lib. X, cap. 28 (LCL 448, pp. 322-4).
50 PG 26, 920A. Other examples by Vogel 1973, pp. 262-6.
51 Hammerstein 1974, p. 65.
52 Raban Maurus, *Allegoriae in Sacram Scripturam* (PL 112, 868A): *Asina, Synagoga, ut in Evangelio: "Invenietis asinam alligatam* [Matthew 21:1-2]," *id est, videbitis plebem Judaicam peccatorum funibus constrictam*. See by the same author, *Commentaria in Paralipomena*, Lib. II, cap. 27 (PL 109, 405A). See further Peter Damian (1007-72), *Sermo* 7 (PL 144, 544C); Rupert of Deutz, *De trinitate et operibus ejus in librum Judicum*, cap. 5 (PL 167, 1028B): *Ascensores asinarum populus Israel dicitur*.
The idea is also widespread outside religious literature. We read, for example, in a Latin source for the bestiarium (1119-35) by Philippe de Thaon: *Et asinus quem laniat / Judeos significat* (ed. Walberg 1970, p. ciii).
53 See Green 1979, Commentary, ill. 234; the source reference is in Commentary No. 212.
54 Text based on Green 1979, Commentary No. 212 and Reconstruction No. 212.
55 *Allegoriae in Sacram Scripturam* (PL 112, 867D).
56 Vetter 1908, p. 357, l. 34-p. 358, l. 4.
57 Ed. Schönbach 1964, p. 357, l. 34-41; see also p. 89, l. 15.
58 Ibid., p. 16, l. 11-6.

59 Ed. Ehrismann, III, p. 273.
60 Götting 1932; De Vries 1981, p. 29, H.5.b.
61 Hammerstein 1974, p. 74.
62 Ibid.
63 See also Brioude, capital in the church of St.-Julien; cathedral of Chartres, ledge figure on the south side of the bell tower; Nantes, capital in the cathedral of St.-Pierre.
64 Hammerstein 1974, ills. 93e and 125. Instead of an ass, a goat is depicted with a harp on the capital in Notre-Dame in Beaune; cf. Hammerstein 1974, ill. 73. See further Klingender 1971, ill. 232; Vogel 1973, ills. 130, 132, 139 and 140; Garnier 1988.
65 Hammerstein 1974, ills. 72, 101, 125, 133 and 134.
66 Ibid., p. 65.
67 The ass with the harp has an unusual place in the ceiling painting of the abbey church in Peterborough. The scene symbolizes *luxuria*. See Nordström 1955, p. 246.
68 Hammerstein 1974, p. 75.
69 Vogel 1978, p. 637 states in this connection: "Hammersteins Deutung ist für mich jedoch ein Musterbeispiel für jene Art von Auslegung, die auf ein bestimmtes Ergebnis hinauswill und dafür die Einzelheiten presst."
70 Ed. Caratzas 1977, p. 152: "[...] finally the Synagogue, her face veiled, her feet bare, holding in one hand the sacrificial knife, in the other the paschal victim the figurative sense of which she misunderstood, and a tablet which proclaims her shameful blindness."
71 Dating follows Dolezalek 1972: "Torino BN, D.V.19." See Montel 1980, No. 88.
72 This is the case with the depictions in Alnay-de-Saintonge; Arlanza; Brioude;-Bruyères; Cosne; Cunault; Decize; Estella; La Plaisance-surGartempe; London, BL., Lansdowne 420, f. 12v; Meillers; Milan; Nantes; St.-Benoît-sur-Loire; St.-Nectaire; Otranto; Turin. Due to damage to the sculptures in Chartres and Nevers it is impossible to be sure if the ass is playing the harp.

EXCURSION

1 Van Schaik 1990, pp. 99-123.
2 PL 194, 499D-500A. Gerhoh's divisions agree roughly with those of Cassiodorus in his *Expositio Psalmorum* (CCL 98, p. 750). Cassiodorus distinguishes six instead of seven *symphoniae*.
3 PL 194, 500B.
4 *Expositio in Psalmos*, Ps. 150 (PL 152, 1420C).
5 See Sachs 1984, pp. 459-75 and Sachs 1970; Smits van Waesberghe 1951b, 1969, pp. 32-4 and 1953, pp. 156-85; Hoffmann-Axthelm 1981, pp. 9-90; McKinnon-Anderson 1984a, pp. 532-3.

Hammerstein 1952, pp. 204-18 ascribes the harp, bells and the organ with an ordering role when they are depicted together with King David. However he ignores the specific *mensura* terminology and fails to connect the concept of *ordo* with the initial illustrations in Psalms 1, 80 and 97.

6 This method of working is extensively described by the eleventh-/ twelfth-century German monk Theophilus in his writing *De diversis artibus*, cap. 85: *De campanis fundendis*. The chapters *De mensura cymbalorum* (cap. 86) and *Item de cymbalis musicis* (cap. 87) deal with the weights of wax. They are all present in the text edition of Dodwell 1961, pp. 150-9. Freise (1985, pp. 357-62) makes it believable that Theophilus was a pen name for the monk Roger of Helmarshausen. He brought out a literary version of his engineering handbook, at the latest in c. 1125, shortly before his death. Prior to this (soon after 1100?) it was probably nothing more than a bundle of notes.

7 According to Sachs (1984, pp. 468-9), taking an organ pipe with the length L and diameter d, the length of a pipe giving a sound a whole tone lower (9:8) can be calculated by using the formula: L + 1/8L (+ 1/8d).

8 Foster 1977, p. 37.

9 GS I, pp. 265b-6a.

10 See for example Price 1984. On p. 186 he remarks: "By the twelfth century ensemble music with *cymbala* was more organized, as Honorius of Autun, a Benedictine writer on the arts, makes evident in a description of a religious service." This statement is based on a passage from *De animae exsilio et patria* (PL 172, 1244D): [...] *organa fistulis, citharae fidibus concrepant, cymbala pulsu tinniunt*. Price translates this passage as follows: "The organ sounds together with flutes, cythars and lutes, and the cymbala bells chime out as they are struck." I think it would be more accurate to translate the Latin text with: "Organs produce sound by means of pipes, cythars by means of strings, and the cymbals sound when they are struck." In the quotation of Honorius the wind, stringed and percussion instruments represent the sacred *ordo*. This is completely in keeping with the character of the text, which tries to give an account of the place of music in the medieval fields of learning.

11 Concerning the *cymbala* see the detailed exposition by Van Schaik 1989.

APPENDICES

OVERVIEW OF SOURCES OF VISUAL MATERIAL

These appendices bring together the data on the sources of the visual material referred to in Chapters two to five. Only sources which are mentioned as (supportive) evidence in the text or in the notes have been included. All appendices follow the same plan. The sources are arranged according to technique (sculpture, illuminated manuscripts, etc.). The present place at which the source is kept, the dating and, as far as is known, the place of origin are given. Specifications such as "Bible I" and "Bible II" in connection with manuscripts indicate the first, respectively the second, section of a composite signature. If there is no reference to a secondary source for the data of a depiction, then this is taken from The Index of Christian Art of the Department of Art History of the Rijksuniversiteit in Utrecht.

APPENDIX I — THE HARP AND DAVID

ILLUMINATED MANUSCRIPTS

Amiens, Bibliothèque de la Ville, 124, f. 7v (B-Psalm 1).
— Psalter. Late 13th century.
Arras, Bibliothèque de la Ville, 88, f. 1r (B-Psalm 1).
— Psalter. 14th century.
Arras, Bibliothèque de la Ville, 561, f. 122v (B-Psalm 1).
— Bible. 13th century.
Avranches, Bibliothèque de la Ville, 3, f. 3r (B-Psalm 1).
— Bible. 13th century.
Avranches, Bibliothèque de la Ville, 76, f. 1v (frontispiece of Psalm commentary).
— *Enarrationes in Psalmos* of Augustine. France, mid-11th century.
Bamberg, Staatsbibliothek, Lit. 5 (olim Ed.V,9), f. 2v (frontispiece of Troper).
— Troper and Tonary. Reichenau?, 1001-2. See Seebass 1973b, p. 175, Bildband Pl. 76.
Belvoir Castle, Library, Duke of Rutland Psalter, n.s.m., f. 98r (C-Psalm 97).
— England?, c. 1250.
Berlin, Staatsbibliothek Preussischer Kulturbesitz, theol. lat. fol. 358, f. 1v (frontispiece of Psalter).
— Werdener Psalter. Werden, 1040-50.

Berlin, Staatsbibliothek Preussischer Kulturbesitz, theol. lat. 379, f. 232v (B-Psalm 1).
— Bible. C. 1240.
Boulogne-sur-Mer, Bibliothèque de la Ville, 5, f. 177r (B-Psalm 1).
— Bible. St.-Vaast, second half of 13th century.
Bourges, Bibliothèque Municipale, 3, f. 255v (B-Psalm 1).
— Bible. 12th century.
Brussels, Koninklijke Bibliotheek, 9391, f. 4r (miniature of Psalm 1).
— Book of Hours. Northern France, first half of 14th century.
Cambrai, Bibliothèque Municipale, 102-3, f. 232r (B-Psalm 1).
— Book of Hours I. St.-Sèpulcre de Cambrai, 1295-6.
Cambridge, Corpus Christi College, 53, f. 19r (B-Psalm 1).
— Psalter. Early 14th century.
Cambridge, Fitzwilliam Museum, 13, f. 7r (B-Psalm 1).
— Psalter. 13th century.
Cambridge, Fitzwilliam Museum, 330, No. 6 (B-Psalm 1).
— Psalter. C. 1240.
Cambridge, Gonville and Caius College, 350/567, f. 159r (B-Psalm 1).
— Bible. Oxford, c. 1230-40.
Cambridge, Magdalena College, 7, f. 8v (B-Psalm 1).
— Psalter. Second half of 13th century.
Cambridge, University Library, Ee.IV.24, f. 13r (D-Psalm 38).
— Psalter. Paris, c. 1270.
Chantilly, Musée Condé, 9 (1695), f. 72r (D-Psalm 38).
— Psalter of Queen Ingeborg. Northern France (Anchin?), c. 1210.
Coblenz, Landeshauptarchiv, Abt. 710, Nr. 110, f. 153v (frontispiece of Psalter).
— Unfinished Bible. 11th-12th century. See Seebass 1973b, p. 177.
Copenhagen, Kongelige Bibliotek, 2, f. 120r (B-Psalm 1).
— Bible. First half of 13th century.
Dijon, Bibliothèque Municipale, 14, f. 13v (frontispiece of Psalter).
— Bible of Etienne Harding, abbot of Cîteaux. Cîteaux, c. 1109.
Dresden, Arnhold collection, Psalter, n.s.m., f. 12v (B-Psalm 1).
— Psalter. C. 1250.
Evreux, Bibliothèque Municipale, 4, f. 135r (E-Psalm 80).
— Miniatures. 13th century.
Florence, Biblioteca Laurenziana, Plut. XV.11, f. 275r (B-Psalm 1).
— Bible. Early 13th century.
Frankfurt, Kunstgewerbemuseum, L.M. 20, f. 74r (B-Psalm 1).
— Psalter. C. 1265.
Geneva, Bibliothèque Universitaire, fr. 2, f. 213r (B-Psalm 1).
— Bible. 14th century.
Glasgow, University Library, Hunter 229, f. 21v (frontispiece of Psalter).
— Hunterian Psalter. Northern England, 12th century.
Den Haag, Koninklijke Bibliotheek, 76.E.11, f. 2r (B-Psalm 1).
— Psalter. 13th century.

Heiligenkreuz, Stiftbibliothek, 8, f. 3r (B-Psalm 1).
— Psalter. 13th century.
Herdringen, Schlossbibliothek, Psalter, n.s.m., f. 6r (B-Psalm 1).
— Psalter. England, c. 1290.
Hereford, Cathedral Library, O.3.XV, f. 43r (B-Psalm 1).
— Psalter. Late 12th-early 13th century.
Kassel, Landesbibliothek, theologica in quarto 8, f. 251r (B-Psalm 1).
— Bible. Paris?, early 13th century.
London, British Library, Add. 16975, f. 86r (E-Psalm 80).
— Psalter. England, 13th century.
London, British Library, Add. 21926, f. 26r (B-Psalm 1), f. 115v (E-Psalm 80).
— Psalter. Late 13th century.
London, British Library, Add. 38116, f. 14v (B-Psalm 1, *Stirps Jesse*).
— Psalter. Late 13th century.
London, British Library, Add. 42130, f. 13r (B-Psalm 1).
— Luttrell Psalter, c. 1340.
London, British Library, Add. 44874, f. 37v (D-Psalm 26), f. 115r (E-Psalm 80).
— Evesham Psalter. England?, 13th century.
London, British Library, Add. 44949, f. 39r (B-Psalm 1).
— Psalter. 14th century.
London, British Library, Add. 47674, f. 1r (B-Psalm 1).
— Psalter. Late 12th-early 13th century.
London, British Library, Add. 49622, f. 8r (B-Psalm 1).
— Psalter. Early 14th century.
London, British Library, Add. 54179, f. 76v (E-Psalm 80)
— Psalter. 13th century.
London, British Library, Arundel 83, f. 55v (margin ill. of Psalm 80).
— Psalter. Eastern England, first half of 14th century.
London, British Library, Cotton Tiberius C.VI, f. 10r (frontispiece of Psalter) and 30v (*Origo* ill.).
— Psalter. Winchester (School), 1041-66. See Seebass 1973b, p. 178, Bildband Pl. 117 and 119.
London, British Library, Egerton 1139, f. 23v (B-Psalm 1).
— Psalter of Queen Melisande of Jerusalem. Jerusalem, 12th century.
London, British Library, Egerton 2867, f. 244v (B-Psalm 1).
— Bible. 13th century.
London, British Library, Harley 2839-40, f. 285v (B-Psalm 1).
— Bible I. 13th century.
London, British Library, Harley 5102, f. 77v (E-Psalm 80).
— Psalter. East Midlands, c. 1220.
London, British Library, Lansdowne 431, f. 64v (E-Psalm 80).
— Psalter. Eastern England, 1220-30?
London, British Library, Royal 1.B.XII, f. 178r (B-Psalm 1).
— Bible. 1254.

London, British Library, Royal 2.A.XXII, f. 15r (B-Psalm 1).
— Psalter. Westminster, late 12th century.
London, British Library, Royal 2.B.VII, f. 85r (B-Psalm 1).
— Queen Mary Psalter. England, early 14th century.
London, British Library, Yates Thompson 14, f. 7r (B-Psalm 1).
— Psalter. St.-Omer, first half of 14th century.
London, British Library, Yates Thompson 18, f. 9r (B-Psalm 1).
— Psalter. C. 1300.
London, Beatty collection, 32, f. 1r (frontispiece).
— Psalter and Psalm commentary of Peter Lombard. Southern Germany, 12th century. See Millar 1927, p. 109-11; Steger 1961, Denkmal 53a.
London, Beatty collection, 50, f. 144r (B-Psalm 1).
— Bible. 13th century.
London, Lambeth Palace Library, 563, f. 20r (B-Psalm 1).
— Psalter. St.-Neots, c. 1220.
London, Soane Museum, 9, f. 132r (B-Psalm 1).
— Bible. First half of 13th century.
Lyons, Gillet collection, Psalter, n.s.m., f. 7r (B-Psalm 1).
— Psalter. Tours, 14th century.
Manchester, Rylands Library, 117, f. 9r (B-Psalm 1).
— Psalter, Book of Hours. 13th century.
Munich, Bayerische Staatsbibliothek, Clm. 835, f. 31r (B-Psalm 1).
— Psalter. 12th-13th century.
Munich, Bayerische Staatsbibliothek, Clm. 2599, f. 96v (Pythagoras as a musician).
— Compilation of manuscripts. 13th century.
New York, Pierpont Morgan Library, 43, f. 27v (B-Psalm 1).
— Huntingfield Psalter. Oxford, c. 1200.
New York, Pierpont Morgan Library, 97, f. 24v (B-Psalm 1).
— Psalter. Flanders?, 13th century.
New York, Pierpont Morgan Library, 102, f. 84r (E-Psalm 80).
— Psalter. England, c. 1270-1300.
New York, Pierpont Morgan Library, Glazier 42, f. 167v (Q-Psalm 51).
— Bible. 13th century.
New York, Public Library, Spencer 2, f. 15r (B-Psalm 1).
— Psalter. First half of 14th century.
Oxford, All Souls College, 7, f. 7r (B-Psalm 1).
— Psalter. Early 14th century.
Oxford, Bodleian Library, Auctarium D.2.2, f. 8r (B-Psalm 1).
— Psalter. Canterbury, 14th century.
Oxford, Bodleian Library, Auctarium D.3.2, f. 195r (B-Psalm 1).
— Bible. England, 13th century.
Oxford, Bodleian Library, Auctarium D.4.2, f. 15v (B-Psalm 1).
— Psalter. Netherlands, 13th-14th century.
Oxford, Bodleian Library, Auctarium E.infra 1-2, f. 2r (B-Psalm 1).
— Bible II, with double Psalter. England, c.1185. See Heimann 1965, p. 95.

Oxford, Bodleian Library, Bodley 284, f. 1r (B-Psalm 1).
— Psalter. Oxford, c. 1210-20?
Oxford, Bodleian Library, Bodley 842, f. 66v (drawing of a *cithara*).
— *Breviarium regulare musica* of Willelmus. England, c. 1400.
Oxford, Bodleian Library, Canon. Pat. lat. 217, f. 3r (B-Psalm 1).
— Psalm commentary of Peter Lombard. Late 12th century.
Oxford, Bodleian Library, Douce 50, p. 265 (E-Psalm 80).
— Psalter. England, 13th century.
Oxford, Bodleian Library, Laud. Lat. 87, f. 215r (B-Psalm 1).
— Bible. 13th century.
Oxford, Bodleian Library, Laud. Misc. 752, f. 236v (B-Psalm 1).
— Bible. 12th century.
Oxford, Bodleian Library, Liturgical 407, f. 77v (D-Psalm 52).
— Psalter. England, early 13th century.
Oxford, Bodleian Library, Lyell empt. 4, f. 8v (B-Psalm 1).
— Psalter. Early 14th century.
Oxford, New College, 322, f. 28r (D-Psalm 26).
— Psalter. Oxford, c. 1240-50.
Paris, Bibliothèque Ste.-Geneviève, 8-10, f. 194r (B-Psalm 1).
— Bible II. 12th century.
Paris, Bibliothèque Ste.-Geneviève, 56, f. 2v (B-Psalm 1).
— Psalm commentary of Peter Lombard. France, late 12th century.
Paris, Bibliothèque Ste.-Geneviève, 2690, f. 99r (E-Psalm 80).
— Psalter. Paris, c. 1250.
Paris, Bibliothèque Nationale, lat. 1, f. 215v, 216r (text and ill. of the *Origo Psalmorum*).
— Vivian Bible (Bible of Charles the Bold). School of Tours, c. 850. See Seebass 1973b, p. 181.
Paris, Bibliothèque Nationale, lat. 40, f. 199v (B-Psalm 1).
— Bible. 13th century.
Paris, Bibliothèque Nationale, lat. 1029A, f. 10r (B-Psalm 1).
— Book of Hours. St.-Maur or Verdun, 13th-14th century.
Paris, Bibliothèque Nationale, lat. 1152, f. 1v, 2r-2v (text and ill. of the *Origo Psalmorum*).
— Psalter of Charles the Bold. St.-Denis, 842-869. See Seebass 1973b, p. 182.
Philadelphia, Free Library, Lewis 185, f. 77v (Q-Psalm 51).
— Psalter. 13th century.
Pommersfelden, Graf von Schönbornsche Schlossbibliothek, 334 (olim 2777), f. 148v (*Origo* ill.).
— Bible. Second half of 11th century. See Seebass 1973b, p. 184, Bildband Pl. 102.
Princeton, University Library, Garrett 28, f. 209r (B-Psalm 1).
— Psalter. 13th century.

Rome, Biblioteca San Paolo fuori le mura, Bible of Callisto, n.s.m., f. 147v, 169r (text and ill. of the *Origo Psalmorum*).
— Bible of Callisto. Reims (St.-Denis?) or School of Corbie, c. 870-5. See Seebass 1973b, p. 185, Bildband Pl. 99.

Rome, Biblioteca Vaticana, lat. 83, f. 12v (*Origo* ill.).
— Psalter and Hymnary of Ambrose. Northern Italy: Milan or vicinity (Bobbio?), last quarter of 10th century. See Steger 1961, Denkmal 19, Pl. 9.

Rouen, Bibliothèque Publique, 3106, f. 22r (B-Psalm 1).
— Psalter. 13th century.

St.-Paul im Lavanttal, Kathedral-Archiv, XXV.2.19, f. 18r (margin ill. of Psalm 1).
— Psalter. 13th century.

Turin, Biblioteca Nazionale Universitaria, D.V.19, f. 50r (Arbor Iuris).
— *Petri Exceptiones legum Romanorum*. Southern France, early 13th century. See Montel 1980, No. 88.

Utrecht, Bibliotheek der Rijksuniversiteit, 32, f. 91v (ill. of Psalm 151).
— Utrechts Psalter. Hautvillers near Reims, c. 820-40.

Verdun, Bibliothèque Municipale, 107, f. 1r (B-Psalm 1).
— Book of Hours. Verdun, early 14th century.

Vienna, Österreichische Nationalbibliothek, 1139, f. 166r (B-Psalm 1).
— Bible. Second half of 13th century.

Zagreb, 'National and University Library', MR 159, f. 232r (B-Psalm 1), f. 246r (E-Psalm 80).
— Bible. Northern France, 14th century.

STAINED GLASS

Mancetter, Church, depiction of the *Stirps Jesse*, window (east side).
— 14th century.

Merevale, Church of Mary the Virgin, depiction of the *Stirps Jesse*, window (east side).
— 14th century.

TEXTILES

Lyons, Musée Histoire des Tissus, vestment (orphrey?, embroidery), No. 1187, depiction of the *Stirps Jesse*.
— 14th century.

APPENDIX II — THE DELTA HARP

A. DELTA HARPS

ILLUMINATED MANUSCRIPTS

Bamberg, Staatsbibliothek, Lit. 5 (olim Ed.V,9), f. 2v (frontispiece of Troper: Musical praise in the Old and New Convenant?).
— Troper, Tonary. Reichenau?, 1001-2. See Seebass 1973b, p. 175, Bildband Pl. 76.

Dresden, Sächsische Landesbibliothek, Oc. 50, f. 11v (24 Elders).
— Revelation of St. John. France (probable Metz), first half of 14th century. See Bruck 1906, ill. 109, No. 52.

Paris, Bibliothèque Nationale, lat. 1, f. 215v (frontispiece of Psalter), f. 216r (initial P).
— Vivian Bible (Bible of Charles the Bold). School of Tours, c. 850. See Seebass 1973b, p. 181.

Piacenza, Biblioteca Capitolare, 65, f. 262v (classification of musical instruments according to the *De institutione musica* of Boethius).
— Manuscript compilation. Italy, 12th century. See Seebass 1973b, p. 184, Bildband Pl. 42.

Rome, Biblioteca San Paolo fuori le mura, Bible of Callisto, n.s.m., f. 147v (frontispiece of the *Origo Psalmorum*).
— Bible of Callisto. Reims (St.-Denis?) or the School of Corbie, c. 870-5. See Seebass 1973b, p. 185, Bildband Pl. 99.

Rome, Biblioteca Vaticana, lat. 83, f. 12v (frontispiece of Psalter).
— Psalter and Hymnary of Ambrose. Northern Italy: Milan or vicinity (Bobbio?), last quarter of 10th century. See Steger 1961, Denkmal 19, Pl. 9.

St.-Gall, Stiftsbibliothek, 21, p. 5 (ill. of Psalter).
— Psalter. St.-Gall, 12th century. See Seebass 1973b, p. 186, Bildband Pl. 108.

St.-Gall, Stiftsbibliothek, 23, p. 12 (ill. of Psalter).
— Folchard Psalter. St.-Gall, c. 865. See Seebass 1973b, p. 186, Bildband Pl. 77.

SCULPTURE

Poitiers, Cathedral, console on the southern side of the nave.
— 12th century. See Hammerstein 1962, ill. 52.

B. SCHEMATIC REPRESENTATIONS OF INSTRUMENTS RESEMBLING DELTA HARPS

MANUSCRIPTS

London, British Library, Cotton Tiberius C.VI, f. 16v (ill. to the Dardanus passage).
— Psalter. Winchester (school), 1041-66. See Seebass 1973b, p. 178, Bildband Pl. 117 and 119.

London, Beatty collection, 32, f.1r (frontispiece Psalter).
— Psalter and Psalm commentary of Peter Lombard. Southern Germany, 12th century. See Millar 1927, p. 109-11; Steger 1961, Denkmal 53a.

Munich, Bayerische Staatsbibliothek, Clm. 14523, f. 51v, 52r (ills. to the Dardanus passages).
— Manuscript compilation with Dardanus letter. Freising, 10th century. See Seebass 1973b, p. 181.

Oxford, Balliol College, 173a, f. 76r and 76v (ills. to the Dardanus passages).
— Dardanus letter. Early 12th century. See Page 1977, Pl. 11.

Paris, Bibliothèque Nationale, lat. 7211, f. 150v (ills. to the Dardanus passages).
— Compilation of musical theoretical treatises. Southern France, 11th-12th century. See Hammerstein 1959, p. 120b, No. 1.

Turin, Biblioteca Nazionale Universitaria, D.III.19, f. 34r (ills. to the book *De musica* of Isidore of Seville).
— *Etymologiae*. 10th century. See Seebass 1973b, p. 187.

APPENDIX III — THE HARP IN THE PSALM INITIALS

ILLUMINATED MANUSCRIPTS

Abbéville, Bibliothèque de la Ville, 3, f. 7r (B-Psalm 1).
— Psalter. Abbaye de Valoires, 14th century.
Amiens, Bibliothèque de la Ville, 21, f. 219r (B-Psalm 1).
— Bible. Early 13th century.
Amiens, Bibliothèque de la Ville, 124, f. 7v (B-Psalm 1).
— Psalter. Late 13th century.
Arras, Bibliothèque de la Ville, 88, f. 1r (B-Psalm 1).
— Psalter. 14th century.
Arras, Bibliothèque de la Ville, 561, f. 122v (B-Psalm 1).
— Bible. 13th century.
Avranches, Bibliothèque de la Ville, 3, f. 3r (B-Psalm 1).
— Bible. 13th century.
Baltimore, Walters Art Gallery, 45, f. 16r (B-Psalm 1).
— Psalter. Late 13th century. See Randall 1960, fig. 1.
Baltimore, Walters Art Gallery, 115, f. 13r (B-Psalm 1).
— Psalter. C. 1310.
Bamberg, Staatsbibliothek, 48, f. 10r (B-Psalm 1).
— Bible. Early 13th century.
Belvoir Castle, Library, Duke of Rutland Psalter, n.s.m., f. 8v (B-Psalm 1), f. 98r (C-Psalm 97).
— England?, c. 1250.
Berlin, Staatsbibliothek Preussischer Kulturbesitz, theol. lat. fol. 379, f.232v (B-Psalm 1).
— Bible. C. 1240.
Berlin, Kupferstichkabinett, 78.A.8, f. 14v (B-Psalm 1).
— Psalter. First half of 13th century.
Boulogne-sur-Mer, Bibliothèque de la Ville, 5, f. 177r (B-Psalm 1).
— Bible. St.-Vaast, second half of 13th century.
Bourges, Bibliothèque Municipale, 3, f. 255v (B-Psalm 1).
— Bible. 12th century.
Brussels, Koninklijke Bibliotheek, IV.10, f. 13v (B-Psalm 1).
— Psalter. 13th century.
Brussels, Koninklijke Bibliotheek, 9391, f. 48v (miniature of Psalm 80).
— Book of Hours. North-France, first half of 14th century.
Brussels, Koninklijke Bibliotheek, 9961-2, f. 14r (B-Psalm 1).
— Peterborough Psalter. England, 1300-18.
Brussels, Koninklijke Bibliotheek, 10521, f. 265r (B-Psalm 1).
— Bible. Second half of 13th century.

Brussels, Koninklijke Bibliotheek, 10730, f. 153r (B-Psalm 1).
— Bible. 13th century.
Brussels, Koninklijke Bibliotheek, 14682, f. 22v (B-Psalm 1).
— Psalter. 13th century.
Cambrai, Bibliothèque Municipale, 102-3, f. 232r (B-Psalm 1).
— Book of Hours I. St.-Sépulcre de Cambrai, 1295-6.
Cambrai, Bibliothèque Municipale, 102-3, f. 1r (B-Psalm 1).
— Book of Hours II. St.-Sépulcre de Cambrai, 13th-14th century.
Cambridge, Corpus Christi College, 3-4, f. 13r (B-Psalm 1).
— Bible II. Dover, 12th century.
Cambridge, Corpus Christi College, 53, f. 19r (B-Psalm 1).
— Psalter, Chronicles, Bestiary. Early 14th century.
Cambridge, Emmanuel College, 252 (3.3.21), f. 12v (B-Psalm 1).
— Psalter. London, c. 1220-30. See Morgan 1982, cat. 52.
Cambridge, Fitzwilliam Museum, Psalter, n.s.m., f. 29r (D-Psalm 26).
— Psalter. Second half of 14th century.
Cambridge, Fitzwilliam Museum, 2-1954, f. 1r (B-Psalm 1).
— Psalter. 13th century.
Cambridge, Fitzwilliam Museum, 13, f. 7r (B-Psalm 1).
— Psalter. 13th century.
Cambridge, Fitzwilliam Museum, 330, No. 6 (B-Psalm 1).
— Psalter. C. 1240.
Cambridge, Fitzwilliam Museum, McClean 15, f. 176v (B-Psalm 1).
— Bible. C. 1300.
Cambridge, Fitzwilliam Museum, McClean 44, f. 1r (B-Psalm 1).
— Psalter. Second half of 13th century.
Cambridge, Gonville and Caius College, 350/567, f. 159r (B-Psalm 1).
— Bible. Oxford, c. 1230-40.
Cambridge, St.-John's College, D.6, f. 31v (B-Psalm 1), f. 75r (D-Psalm 52).
— Psalter, Book of Hours. England, 13th century.
Cambridge, St.-John's College, K.30, f. 86r (D-Psalm 101).
— Psalter. North Midlands, c. 1190-1200? See Morgan 1982, cat. 15, ill. 55.
Cambridge, Magdalena College, 7, f. 8v (B-Psalm 1).
— Psalter. Second half of 13th century.
Cambridge, Trinity College, B.5.26, f. 1r (B-Psalm 1).
— *Enarrationes in Psalmos* of Augustine. Canterbury, 1070- 1100. See Kahsnitz 1979, ill. 243.
Cambridge, Trinity College, B.11.4, f. 96r (E-Psalm 80).
— Psalter. England?, mid-12th century.
Cambridge, University Library, Ee.IV.24, f. 13r (D-Psalm 38).
— Psalter. Paris, c. 1270.
Chantilly, Musée Condé, 9 (1695), f. 72r (D-Psalm 38), f. 127r (C-Psalm 97).
— Psalter of Queen Ingeborg. Northern France (Anchin?), c. 1210.

Cleveland, Museum of Art, 53.145, n.s.m. (B-Psalm 1).
— Vellum from a Psalter. Bruges, 13th century.
Copenhagen, Kongelige Bibliotek, 2, f. 120r (B-Psalm 1).
— Bible. First half of 13th century.
Dijon, Bibliothèque Communale, 2, f. 278v (D-Psalm 109).
— Bible. 11th-12th century.
Douai, Bibliothèque Municipale, 9, f. 1v (B-Psalm 1).
— Psalter. Anchin, first half of 12th century.
Douai, Bibliothèque Municipale, 23, f. 3v (B-Psalm 1).
— Genesis, Psalter. 12th century.
Douai, Bibliothèque Municipale, 171, f. 1r (B-Psalm 1).
— Psalter. Early 14th century.
Douai, Bibliothèque Municipale, 233, f. 2r (B-Psalm 1).
— *Breviarium in Psalmos* of pseudo-Jerome. Late 12th century.
Douai, Bibliothèque Municipale, 250, f. 2v (B-Psalm 1).
— *Enarrationes in Psalmos* of Augustine. 12th century.
Dresden, Arnhold collection, Psalter, n.s.m., f. 12v (B-Psalm 1).
— Psalter. C. 1250.
Dublin, Trinity College, 53, f. 151r (B-Psalm 1).
— New Testament and double Psalter. Winchcombe, 12th century. See Heimann 1965, p. 93.
Durham, Cathedral Library, A.II.4, f. 65r (B-Psalm 1).
— Carilef Bibel. Normandy?, late 11th century.
Edinburgh, National Library of Scotland, 10000 (Olim 3141), f. 7r (B-Psalm 1), f. 85v (C-Psalm 97).
— Iona Psalter. Oxford, c. 1210. See Morgan 1982, cat. 29.
Engelberg, Stiftsbibliothek, 113, f. 11r (B-Psalm 1).
— Psalter. Engelberg, mid-13th century.
Evreux, Bibliothèque Municipale, 4, f. 135r (E-Psalm 80).
— Miniatures. 13th century.
Florence, Biblioteca Laurenziana, Edili 125-6, f. 12v (B-Psalm 1).
— Bible II. 11th-12th century.
Florence, Biblioteca Laurenziana, Plut. XV.11, f. 275r (B-Psalm 1).
— Bible. Early 13th century.
Florence, Biblioteca Riccardiana, 323, f. 14v (B-Psalm 1).
— Psalter. 13th century.
Frankfurt, Stadtbibliothek, Batt. 150, f. 8r (B-Psalm 1).
— Book of Hours. C. 1300.
Frankfurt, Kunstgewerbemuseum, L.M. 20, f. 74r (B-Psalm 1).
— Psalter. C. 1265.
Geneva, Bibliothèque Universitaire, fr. 2, f. 213r (B-Psalm 1).
— Bible. 14th century.
Graz, Universitätsbibliothek, II.204, f. 1r (B-Psalm 1).
— Psalter. 13th century.

The Hague, Koninklijke Bibliotheek, 76.E.11, f. 2r (B-Psalm 1).
— Psalter. 13th century.
The Hague, Koninklijke Bibliotheek, 76.F.13, f. 29r (B-Psalm 1).
— Psalter. Fécamp, c. 1180-1200.
Hamburg, Staatsbibliothek, In. Scr. 83, f. 82v (E-Psalm 80).
— Psalter. Germany?, mid-13th century.
Heiligenkreuz, Stiftsbibliothek, 8, f. 3r (B-Psalm 1).
— Psalter. 13th century.
Heiligenkreuz, Stiftsbibliothek, 66, f. 9r (D-Psalm 38), f. 65r (E-Psalm 80).
— Psalter. Heiligenkreuz, 13th century.
Herdringen, Schlossbibliothek, Psalter, n.s.m., f. 6r (B-Psalm 1).
— Psalter. England, c. 1290.
Hereford, Cathedral Library, O.3.XV, f. 43r (B-Psalm 1).
— Psalter. 12th-13th century.
Hildesheim, St.-Godehard-Bibliothek, Psalter, n.s.m., p. 73 (B-Psalm 1).
— Albani Psalter. St.-Albans, early 12th century.
Holkam, Leicester collection, 26, f. 7r (B-Psalm 1).
— Psalter. Second half of 14th century.
Imola, Biblioteca Communale, 100, f. 11r (B-Psalm 1).
— Psalter. Early 13th century.
Kassel, Landesbibliothek, theologica in quarto 8, f. 251r (B-Psalm 1), f. 257r (D-Psalm 38), f. 264r (E-Psalm 80), f. 266v (C-Psalm 97).
— Bible. Paris?, early 13th century.
Krivoklát, 'Castle Library', I.b.23, f. 14r (B-Psalm 1).
— Psalter. Second half of 13th century.
Leiden, Universiteitsbibliotheek, B.P.f.76 A, f. 30v (B-Psalm 1).
— Psalter. Northern England, c. 1190-1200. See Morgan 1982, cat. 14, ill. 49.
Leningrad, 'Public Library', Lat. Q.V.I.67, f. 7r (B-Psalm 1).
— Psalter. 13th century.
Liverpool, Public Library, 12004, f. 12r (B-Psalm 1).
— Psalter. First half of 13th century.
London, British Library, Add. 15452, f. 182r (B-Psalm 1).
— Bible. Early 13th century.
London, British Library, Add. 16975, f. 25r (B-Psalm 1), f. 86r (E-Psalm 80).
— Psalter. England, 13th century.
London, British Library, Add. 17392, f. 1r (B-Psalm 1).
— Psalter. 12th century.
London, British Library, Add. 21926, f. 26r (B-Psalm 1), f. 115v (E-Psalm 80).
— Psalter. Late 13th century.
London, British Library, Add. 24686, f. 11r (B-Psalm 1).
— Tension Psalter. 1284.
London, British Library, Add. 28681, f. 18r (B-Psalm 1).
— Psalter. Second half of 13th century.

London, British Library, Add. 38116, f. 14v (B-Psalm 1).
— Psalter. Late 13th century.
London, British Library, Add. 42130, f. 13r (B-Psalm 1), f. 174v (C-Psalm 97).
— Luttrell Psalter, c. 1340.
London, British Library, Add. 44874, f. 7v (B-Psalm 1), f. 37v (D-Psalm 26), f. 115r (E-Psalm 80).
— Evesham Psalter. England?, 13th century.
London, British Library, Add. 44949, f. 39r (B-Psalm 1).
— Psalter. 14th century.
London, British Library, Add. 47674, f. 1r (B-Psalm 1).
— Psalter. Late 12th-early 13th century.
London, British Library, Add. 49622, f. 8r (B-Psalm 1), f. 107v (E-Psalm 80).
— Psalter. Early 14th century.
London, British Library, Add. 50000, f. 83r (Q-Psalm 51).
— Psalter. Second half of 13th century.
London, British Library, Add. 54179, f. 76v (E-Psalm 80).
— Psalter. 13th century.
London, British Library, Arundel 60, f. 13r (B-Psalm 1).
— Psalter of New Minster. England, 1060-80. See Kahsnitz 1979, ill. 121.
London, British Library, Arundel 157, f. 71v (E-Psalm 80).
— Psalter. England, c. 1190-1200.
London, British Library, Cotton Vespasian A.I., f. 1v (B-Psalm 1).
— Psalter of Augustine. Peterborough, c. 1220? See Morgan 1982, cat. 46, ill. 154.
London, British Library, Egerton 1139, f. 23v (B-Psalm 1).
— Psalter of Queen Melisande of Jerusalem. Jerusalem, 12th century.
London, British Library, Egerton 2867, f. 244v (B-Psalm 1).
— Bible. 13th century.
London, British Library, Egerton 3277, f. 46v (S-Psalm 68).
— Psalter, Book of Hours. 14th century.
London, British Library, Harley 2839-40, f. 285v (B-Psalm 1).
— Bible I. 13th century.
London, British Library, Harley 5102, f. 77v (E-Psalm 80).
— Psalter. East Midlands, c. 1220.
London, British Library, Lansdowne 383, f. 15v (B-Psalm 1).
— Psalter. Shaftesbury Abbey, mid-12th century.
London, British Library, Lansdowne 420, f. 12v (B-Psalm 1).
— Psalter. C. 1220-30.
London, British Library, Lansdowne 431, f. 11r (B-Psalm 1), f. 64v (E-Psalm 80).
— Psalter. Eastern England, c. 1220-30?
London, British Library, Royal 1.B.XII, f. 178r (B-Psalm 1).
— Bible. 1254.
London, British Library, Royal 1.D.I, f. 232r (B-Psalm 1), f. 246v (E-Psalm 80).
— Bible. C. 1250.

London, British Library, Royal 1.E.IX, f. 151r (E-Psalm 80).
— Bible of Richard II. Late 14th century.
London, British Library, Royal 2.A.XXII, f. 15r (B-Psalm 1).
— Psalter. Westminster, late 12th century.
London, British Library, Royal 2.B.II, f. 7r (B-Psalm 1), f. 88v (E-Psalm 80).
— Psalter. England, 13th century.
London, British Library, Royal 2.B.VII, f. 85r (B-Psalm 1).
— Queen Mary Psalter. England, early 14th century.
London, British Library, Yates Thompson 14, f. 7r (B-Psalm 1).
— Psalter. St.-Omer, first half of 14th century.
London, British Library, Yates Thompson 15, f. 20r (B-Psalm 1).
— Psalter, Book of Hours. Late 13th-early 14th century.
London, British Library, Yates Thompson 18, f. 9r (B-Psalm 1), f. 104r (E-Psalm 80).
— Psalter. C. 1300.
London, British Library, Yates Thompson 20, f. 381r (B-Psalm 1).
— Bible. 14th century.
London, British Library, Yates Thompson 22, f. 161v (B-Psalm 1).
— Bible. Second half of 13th century.
London, Beatty collection, 50, f. 144r (B-Psalm 1).
— Bible. 13th century.
London, Lambeth Palace Library, 233, f. 15r (B-Psalm 1).
— Psalter. C. 1313-20.
London, Lambeth Palace Library, 563, f. 20r (B-Psalm 1).
— Psalter. St.-Neots, c. 1220.
London, Soane Museum, 9, f. 132r (B-Psalm 1).
— Bible. First half of 13th century.
London, Society of Antiquaries, 59, f. 38v (B-Psalm 1).
— Psalter of Robert de Lindesey. Before 1222.
Longleat, Collection of the Marquess of Bath, II, f. 7r (B-Psalm 1).
— Psalter. 14th century.
Lyons, Gillet collection, Psalter, n.s.m., f. 7r (B-Psalm 1).
— Psalter. Tours, 14th century.
Madrid, Biblioteca Nacional, 6422, f. 7r (B-Psalm 1).
— Psalter. 13th century.
Madrid, Museo Lazaro Galdiano, 15289, f. 176v (B-Psalm 1).
— Bible. First half of 13th century.
Maihingen, Bibliothek Wallerstein, I.2.qu.19, f. 12r (B-Psalm 1).
— Psalter. Early 13th century.
Maihingen, Bibliothek Wallerstein, I.2.qu.24, f. 15v (B-Psalm 1).
— Psalter. Second half of 13th century.
Malvern, Dyson Perrins collection, 34, f. 7r (B-Psalm 1).
— Psalter, Book of Hours. Early 14th century.
Malvern, Dyson Perrins collection, 119, f. 105v (B-Psalm 1).
— Bible. Second half of 12th century.

Manchester, Rylands Library, 117, f. 9r (B-Psalm 1).
— Psalter, Book of Hours. 13th century.
Melk, Stiftsbibliothek, 1, f. 12r (B-Psalm 1).
— Psalter. France, c. 1270-80.
Moulins, Musée Municipale, Bible, n.s.m., f. 215r (B-Psalm 1).
— Bible. Souvigny, 12th century.
Munich, Bayerische Staatsbibliothek, Clm. 835, f. 31r (B-Psalm 1).
— Psalter. 12th-13th century.
Munich, Bayerische Staatsbibliothek, Clm. 3900, f. 8r (B-Psalm 1).
— Psalter. Second half of 13th century.
Munich, Bayerische Staatsbibliothek, Clm. 15909, f. 8r (B-Psalm 1).
— Psalter. Mid-13th century.
Munich, Bayerische Staatsbibliothek, Clm. 16137, f. 7r (B-Psalm 1).
— Psalter. First half of 13th century.
Munich, Bayerische Staatsbibliothek, Clm. 23094, f. 7v (B-Psalm 1).
— Psalter. 13th century.
New York, Metropolitan Museum, Cloisters, 69.86, f. 15r (miniature of Psalm 1).
— Psalter, Book of Hours. First half of 14th century.
New York, Pierpont Morgan Library, 43, f. 27v (B-Psalm 1).
— Huntingfield Psalter. Oxford, c. 1200.
New York, Pierpont Morgan Library, 97, f. 24v (B-Psalm 1).
— Psalter. Flanders?, 13th century.
New York, Pierpont Morgan Library, 102, f. 84r (E-Psalm 80).
— Psalter. England, c. 1270-1300.
New York, Pierpont Morgan Library, 730, f. 20r (B-Psalm 1).
— Psalter, Book of Hours. Arras or Cambrai, late 13th century.
New York, Pierpont Morgan Library, 756, f. 11r (B-Psalm 1).
— Psalter. Canterbury?, late 13th century.
New York, Pierpont Morgan Library, 791, f. 170r (B-Psalm 1).
— Bible with double Psalter. England, early 13th century. See Heimann 1965, p. 95.
New York, Pierpont Morgan Library, Glazier 25, f. 5v (B-Psalm 1).
— Psalter. London, c. 1220-30? See Morgan 1982, cat. 50.
New York, Pierpont Morgan Library, Glazier 42, f. 167v (Q-Psalm 51).
— Bible. 13th century.
New York, Public Library, 4, f. 193r (B-Psalm 1).
— Bible. Second half of 13th century.
New York, Public Library, Spencer 2, f. 15r (B-Psalm 1).
— Psalter. First half of 14th century.
Oxford, All Souls College, 7, f. 7r (B-Psalm 1).
— Psalter. Early 14th century.
Oxford, Bodleian Library, Ashmole 1525, f. 79r (C-Psalm 97).
— Psalter. C. 1290.
Oxford, Bodleian Library, Auctarium D.2.2., f. 8r (B-Psalm 1).
— Psalter. Canterbury, 14th century.

Oxford, Bodleian Library, Auctarium D.3.2., f. 195r (B-Psalm 1).
— Bible. England, 13th century.
Oxford, Bodleian Library, Auctarium D.3.5., f. 111r (B-Psalm 1).
— Bible. England?, mid-13th century.
Oxford, Bodleian Library, Auctarium D.4.2., f. 15v (B-Psalm 1).
— Psalter. The Netherlands, 13th-14th century.
Oxford, Bodleian Library, Auctarium E.infra 1-2, f. 2r (B-Psalm 1).
— Bible II, with double Psalter. England, c. 1180-90. See Heimann 1965, p. 95.
Oxford, Bodleian Library, Bodley 284, f. 1r (B-Psalm 1).
— Psalter. Oxford, c. 1210-20?
Oxford, Bodleian Library, Canon. Pat. lat. 217, f. 3r (B-Psalm 1).
— Psalm commentary of Peter Lombard. Late 12th century.
Oxford, Bodleian Library, Douce 5,6, f. 18r (B-Psalm 1).
— Psalter. Flanders, 14th century.
Oxford, Bodleian Library, Douce 24, f. 7v (B-Psalm 1).
— Psalter. Northern France?, c. 1300.
Oxford, Bodleian Library, Douce 50, p. 265 (E-Psalm 80).
— Psalter. England, 13th century.
Oxford, Bodleian Library, Douce 131, f. 68v (E-Psalm 80).
— Psalter. England?, 14th century.
Oxford, Bodleian Library, Douce 366, f. 10r (B-Psalm 1), f. 109r (E-Psalm 80).
— Psalter. England, late 13th-early 14th century.
Oxford, Bodleian Library, Land. Lat. 87, f. 215r (B-Psalm 1).
— Bible. 13th century.
Oxford, Bodleian Library, Laud. Misc. 752, f. 236v (B-Psalm 1).
— Bible. 12th century.
Oxford, Bodleian Library, Lat. Bibl. e. 7, f. 176v (B-Psalm 1).
— Bible and selected masses. Oxford, c. 1234-40. See Morgan 1982, cat. 69.
Oxford, Bodleian Library, Lat. Liturgical d.42, f. 20r (B-Psalm 1).
— Book of Hours. First half of 14th century.
Oxford, Bodleian Library, Liturgical 407, f. 9v (B-Psalm 1), f. 77v (D-Psalm 52).
— Psalter. England, early 13th century.
Oxford, Bodleian Library, Lyell empt. 4, f. 8v (B-Psalm 1).
— Psalter. Early 14th century.
Oxford, Jesus College, D.40, f. 8r (B-Psalm 1).
— Psalter. 14th century.
Oxford, New College, 322, f. 28r (D-Psalm 26).
— Psalter. Oxford, c. 1240-50.
Padua, Biblioteca Seminario, 353, f. 23r (B-Psalm 1).
— Psalter. 13th century.
Paris, Bibliothèque de l'Arsenal, 5212, f. 378r (miniature of Psalm 1).
— Bible. Late 14th century.

Paris, Bibliothèque Ste.-Geneviève, 8-10, f. 194r (B-Psalm 1).
— Bible II. 12th century.
Paris, Bibliothèque Ste.-Geneviève, 56, f. 2v (B-Psalm 1).
— Psalm commentary of Peter Lombard. France, late 12th century.
Paris, Bibliothèque Ste.-Geneviève, 1181, f. 177r (B-Psalm 1).
— Bible. France, second half of 13th century.
Paris, Bibliothèque Ste.-Geneviève, 2690, f. 7r (B-Psalm 1), f. 99r (E-Psalm 80).
— Psalter. Paris, c. 1250.
Paris, Bibliothèque Mazarine, 36, f. 214r (B-Psalm 1).
— Bible. Late 12th-early 13th century.
Paris, Bibliothèque Nationale, fr. 962, f. 17r (miniature of Psalm 1).
— Psalter. Paris, second half of 14th century.
Paris, Bibliothèque Nationale, fr. 13091, f. 31r (B-Psalm 1), f. 85r (D-Psalm 38).
— Psalter of the Duke of Berry. Late 14th century.
Paris, Bibliothèque Nationale, lat. 15, f. 216v (B-Psalm 1).
— Bible. First half of 13th century.
Paris, Bibliothèque Nationale, lat. 1023, f. 36v (E-Psalm 80).
— Book of Hours of Philip the Fair. Before 1296.
Paris, Bibliothèque Nationale, lat. 1029A, f. 10r (B-Psalm 1).
— Book of Hours. St.-Maur or Verdun, 13th-14th century.
Paris, Bibliothèque Nationale, lat. 1073A, f. 17r (B-Psalm 1).
— Psalter, Book of Hours. Paris, 1220-30.
Paris, Bibliothèque Nationale, lat. 1075, f. 19r (B-Psalm 1).
— Psalter. France, c. 1250. See Haseloff 1938, Pl. 16.
Paris, Bibliothèque Nationale, lat. 1076, f. 7r (B-Psalm 1).
— Psalter. Northern France, second half of 13th century.
Paris, Bibliothèque Nationale, lat. 1987, f. 217v (D-Psalm 1).
— *Enarrationes in Psalmos* of Augustine. 11th-12th century.
Paris, Bibliothèque Nationale, lat. 10428, f. 165r (B-Psalm 1).
— Bible. 13th century.
Paris, Bibliothèque Nationale, lat. 11534-5, f. 17v (B-Psalm 1).
— Bible II. Late 12th century.
Paris, Bibliothèque Nationale, lat. 11539-42, f. 26v (B-Psalm 1).
— Bible II. 13th century.
Paris, Bibliothèque Nationale, lat. 11560, f. 26r (C-Psalm 97).
— Bible moralisée. First half of 13th century.
Paris, Bibliothèque Nationale, lat. 14397, f. 166r (B-Psalm 1).
— Bible. First half of 13th century.
Paris, Bibliothèque Nationale, lat. 15467, f. 258r (B-Psalm 1).
— Bible. 1270.
Paris, Bibliothèque Nationale, lat. 16260, f. 263v (B-Psalm 1).
— Bible. Second half of 13th century.
Paris, Bibliothèque Nationale, lat. 16272, f. 1v (B-Psalm 1).
— Psalter. Paris, second half of 13th century.

Paris, Bibliothèque Nationale, nouv. acq. lat. 1392, f. 20r (B-Psalm 1), f. 113v (E-Psalm 80).
— Psalter. Paris, first half of 13th century.

Paris, Bibliothèque Nationale, nouv. acq. lat. 3104, f. 27r (B-Psalm 1).
— Psalter, Book of Hours. Second half of 13th century.

Philadelphia, Free Library, Lewis 185, f. 77v (Q-Psalm 51).
— Psalter. 13th century.

Princeton, Museum of Art, 28-12, f. 5v (B-Psalm 1).
— Psalter. 13th century.

Princeton, University Library, Garrett 28, f. 209r (B-Psalm 1).
— Bible. 13th century.

Princeton, University Library, Garrett 29, f. 345r (B-Psalm 1).
— Bible. C. 1300.

Princeton, University Library, Garrett 34, f. 7r (B-Psalm 1).
— Psalter. 13th century.

Princeton, University Library, Garrett 35, f. 14r (B-Psalm 1).
— Psalter. C. 1300.

Rome, Biblioteca Vaticana, Pal. lat. 26, f. 13r (B-Psalm 1).
— Psalter. Germany?, mid-13th century.

Rome, Biblioteca Vaticana, Urb. lat. 603, f. 13r (B-Psalm 1).
— Book of Hours. First half of 14th century.

Rouen, Bibliothèque Publique, 3106, f. 22r (B-Psalm 1).
— Psalter. 13th century.

San Marino, Huntington Library, E.L.9.H.17, f. 42r (B-Psalm 1).
— Psalter. First half of 14th century.

San Marino, Huntington Library, H.M. 1050, f. 5v (B-Psalm 1).
— Psalter. C. 1300.

San Marino, Huntington Library, H.M. 26061, f. 166r (B-Psalm 1).
— Bible with selected masses. C. 1240. See Morgan 1982, cat. 77.

St.-Blasien, *De cantu et musica sacra*, II, of Martin Gerbert, Pl. 24, fig. 9; Pl. 25, fig. 10; Pl. 29, fig. 9; Pl. 30, fig. 10 (ills. to the Dardanus passages).
— (Drawings according to a codex from the second half of the 12th century; destroyed by fire in 1768). Gerbert 1774.

St.-Florian, Stiftsbibliothek, XI.6, f. 144v (B-Psalm 1).
— Old Testament. Early 14th century.

St.-Gall, Stiftsbibliothek, 402, f. 15r (*sic!*) (B-Psalm 1).
— Book of Hours. First half of 13th century.

St.-Paul im Lavanttal, Kathedral-Archiv, XXV.2.19, f. 18r (margin ill. opposite B-Psalm 1).
— Psalter. 13th century.

Sarnen, Kollegium-Bibliothek, 37, f. 7r (B-Psalm 1).
— Psalter. Engelberg, 12th-13th century.

Schaffhausen, Stadtbibliothek, Generalia 5, f. 11r (B-Psalm 1).
— Psalter. First half of 13th century.

Tournai, Bibliothèque de la cathédrale Notre-Dame, Psalter, n.s.m., f. 7r (B-Psalm 1).
— Psalter. 14th century.
Troyes, Bibliothèque Municipale, 92, f. 2r (B-Psalm 1).
— Psalm commentary of Peter Lombard. Second half of 12th century.
Venice, Biblioteca Marciana, lat. I.77 (2397), f. 27r (B-Psalm 1).
— Psalter. 12th-13th century.
Verdun, Bibliothèque Municipale, 107, f. 1r (B-Psalm 1).
— Book of Hours. Verdun, early 14th century.
Vienna, Österreichische Nationalbibliothek, 1139, f. 166r (B-Psalm 1).
— Bible. Second half of 13th century.
Vienna, Österreichische Nationalbibliothek, 1826*, f. 7r (B-Psalm 1), f. 85v (C-Psalm 97).
— Psalter. Second half of 14th century.
Vienna, Österreichische Nationalbibliothek, 1898, f. 14v (B-Psalm 1).
— Psalter. C. 1300.
Würzburg, Universitätsbibliothek, Mp. theologica in quarto 70, f. 1r (B-Psalm 1).
— Psalter. Mid-13th century.
Zagreb, 'National and University Library', MR 159, f. 246r (E-Psalm 80).
— Bible. Northern France, 14th century.
Zurich, Zentralbibliothek, Rheinau 85, f. 7r (B-Psalm 1).
— Psalter. 1253.
Zurich, Zentralbibliothek, Rheinau 167, f. 10r (B-Psalm 1).
— Psalter. 1227-41.

APPENDIX IV - THE ASS WITH THE HARP

FRESCO

Arlanza, Church of San Pedro (fresco).
— Spain, c. 1220. See Randall 1960, p. 26, ill. 26.

ILLUMINATED MANUSCRIPTS

Glasgow, University Library, Hunter 229, f. 68r (E-Psalm 67).
— Hunterian Psalter. Northern England, 12th century.
London, British Library, Harley 5102, f. 13v (D-Psalm 17).
— Psalter. East Midlands, c. 1220. See Klingender 1971, p. 399.
London, British Library, Lansdowne 420, f. 12v (B-Psalm 1).
— Psalter. London, c. 1220-30. See Klingender 1971, p. 400, ill. 232.
Munich, Bayerische Staatsbibliothek, gall. 16, f. 8r (miniature at the bottom of the Beatus page).
— Psalter of Queen Isabella of England. After 1308.
Paris, Bibliothèque Nationale, lat. 8959 Flavius Josephus, f. 101v (initial Q).
— France, late 12th century. See Vogel 1973, ill. 146.
Turin, Biblioteca Nazionale Universitaria, D.V.19, f. 50r, (Arbor Iuris).
— *Petri Exceptiones legum Romanorum*. Southern France, early 13th century. See Montel 1980, No. 88.

MOSAIC

Otranto, Cathedral Maria Annunziata (floor mosaic).
— Italy, 1163-6. See Hammerstein 1974, p. 74, ill. 68.

PAINTING

Peterborough, Abbey church (ceiling painting).
— England, 1236-7. See Nordström 1955, p. 246.
Tudela, Cathedral Collegiata (ceiling painting).
— Spain, 12th century. See Stauder 1969, p. 31.

SCULPTURE

Alnay-de-Saintonge, Church of St.-Pierre-de-la-Tour (sculpture on the south portal of the transept).
— France, after 1160. See Debidour 1961, ill. 278; Stauder 1969, ill. 2; Vogel 1973, p. 356, ill. 126.
Brioude, Church of St.-Julien (capital).
— France, 12th century. See Debidour 1961, p. 385, ill. 366.
Bruyères, Church, sculpture on the roof ridge of the south wall.
— France, 12th century. See Von Glasenapp [No year given], ill. 29.
Chartres, Cathedral (sculpture on the ridge of the southern side of the bell tower).
— France, 13th century. See Stauder 1969, ill. 1; Hammerstein 1974, p. 74, ill. 95.
Cosne, Church of St.-Aignan (sculpture on the front portal).
— France, 12th century? See Mâle 1953, p. 340.
Cunault, Church of Notre-Dame (remainder of a sculpture on a capital in the nave).
— France, c. 1175. See Stauder 1969, p. 25.
Decize, Church of St.-Aré (capital on the left column in the north portal).
— France, 12th century? See Debidour 1961, p. 385.
Estella, Palacio de los Reyes (capital).
— Spain, 12th century. See Vogel 1973, p. 355, ill. 127.
Fleury-la-Montagne, Church (sculpture on a capital in the west portal).
— France, late 11th-early 12th century. See Debidour 1961, p. 385.
La Plaisance-sur-Gartempe, Church (capital).
— France, 11th-12th century. See Weir-Jerman 1986, p. 55, Pl. 26.
Meillers, Church of St.-Julien (capital in the west portal).
— France, 12th century. See Vogel 1973, p. 356, ill. 128; Mâle 1953, p. 340, ill. 366.
Milan, Church of San Ambrogio (sculpture on the marble pulpit).
— Italy, first half of 12th century? See Klingender 1971, p. 289.
Nantes, Cathedral of St.-Pierre (capital from the cathedral), kept in the Musée Archéologique Thomas Dobrée.
— France, 12th century. See Mâle 1953, ill. 241.
Nevers, Church of St.-Sauveur (capital), kept in the Musée Archéologique "Lapidaire" in Nevers.
— France, 12th century. See Dupont 1976, ill. 3.
St.-Benoît-sur-Loire, Abbey church (sculpture on the front portal).
— France, 12th century. See Mâle 1953, p. 340 and Hammerstein 1974, ill. 96.
St.-Nectaire, Church of St.-Nectaire (capital).
— France, 12th century. See Rochias 1910, ill. 20.

St.-Parize-le-Chatel, Church (capital in the crypt).
— France, late 11th century. See Debidour 1960, ill. 363; Stauder 1969, p. 25.

Tudela, Cathedral Collegiata (sculpture in the west portal).
— Spain, 12th century. See Stauder 1969, p. 31.

ABBREVIATIONS

AfMw	Archiv für Musikwissenschaft
Bibl.	biblioteca/bibliotheek/Bibliothek/bibliothèque. Cf.: Libr.
BL.	British Library
BN.	Bibliothèque Nationale
cat.	catalogue
CCL	Corpus Christianorum, Series Latina
coll.	collection
CPG	E. Leutsch (ed.), *Corpus Paroemiographorum Graecorum*. 3 vols. (Göttingen 1839) R/Hildesheim 1958-61.
CSEL	*Corpus Scriptorum Ecclesiasticorum Latinorum*, editum consilio et impensis Academiae litterarum Caesareae Vindobonensis, Vienna 1867-.
CSM	Corpus Scriptorum de Musica.
ed.	edited/edition/editor(s)
f.	folio
GEW	H. Friske, *Griechisches Etymologisches Wörterbuch*. Heidelberg 1960.
Gl	Steinmeyer-Sievers, *Die althochdeutschen Glossen*, 5 vols. Berlin 1879-1922.
GS	Martin Gerbert, *Scriptores ecclesiastici de musica sacra*, 3 vols. St.-Blasien 1784.
ill(s).	illumination(s)/illustration(s)
JAMS	Journal of the American Musicological Society
KB.	Koninklijke Bibliotheek
LCL	The Loeb Classical Library
LdM	Lexikon des Mittelalters. Munich [etc.] 1977-.
Libr.	Library
LW	*Liturgisch Woordenboek*, [2 vols.] L. Brinkhoff, G. Laudy, A. Verheul and Th. Vismans (ed.). Roermond [etc.] 1958-68.
MGH	Monumenta Germaniae Historica
MS	Medieval Studies
Ms(s).	Manuscript(s)
n.s.m.	no shelf mark
ODCC	*The Oxford Dictionary of the Christian Church*, F. Cross and E. Livingstone (ed.). Oxford (1957) 2/1985.
PG	J.-P. Migne (ed.), *Patrologiae cursus completus*. Series Graeca. Paris 1857-.
PL	J.-P. Migne (ed.), *Patrologiae cursus completus*. Series Latina. Paris 1844-.
Pl.	Plate
R/	Reprint
TVNM	Tijdschrift van de Vereniging voor Nederlandse Muziekgeschiedenis
w.f.	without foliation

BIBLIOGRAPHY

Adkins 1963: Cecile Adkins, *The theory and practice of the monochord.* (Ph. D. diss., State University of Iowa) Ann Arbor 1963.

Adler 1967: Ada Adler (ed.), *Suidae Lexicon*, 3. Stuttgart (1933) R/1967. (Lexicographi Graeci 1.)

Adolf 1950: Helen Adolf, *The ass and the harp*. -In: Speculum 25 (1950), pp. 49-57.

Allinson 1959: Francis Allinson (ed.), *Menander: The principal fragments.* London 1959.

Angelis: V. de Angelis, *Papiae elementarium*, I-III. Milan 1977-80. (Testi e documenti per lo studio dell'Antichità 58.)

Aubert 1929: Marcel Aubert, *La Sculpture Française.* Florence 1929.

Avernary 1961: Hanoch Avernary, *Hieronymus' Epistel über die Musikinstrumente und ihre altöstlichen Quellen.* -In: Anuario Musical 16 (1961), pp. 55-80.

Bandmann 1960: Günther Bandmann, *Melancholie und Musik: ikonographische Studien.* Cologne 1960. (Wissenschaftliche Abhandlungen der Arbeitsgemeinschaft für Forschung des Landes Nordrhein-Westfalen 12.)

Barker 1984: Andrew Barker (ed.), *Greek musical writings,* 1: The musician and his art. Cambridge [etc.] 1984. (Cambridge Readings in the Literature of Music.)

Bernhard 1979: Michael Bernhard, *Studien zur Epistola de armonica institutione des Regino von Prüm.* Munich 1979. (Bayerische Akademie der Wissenschaften — Veröffentlichungen der Musikhistorischen Kommission 5.)

Bischoff 1928: Bernhard Bischoff, *Nachträge zu den altdeutschen Glossen.* -In: Beiträge zur Geschichte der deutschen Sprache und Literatur 52 (1928), pp. 153-68.

Blaise 1975: Albert Blaise, *Lexicon Latinitatis Medii Aevi.* Turnhout 1975.

Borchling 1897: Conrad Borchling, *Der jüngere Titurel und sein Verhältnis zu Wolfram von Eschenbach.* Göttingen 1897.

Bower 1967: Calvin Bower, *Boethius' The principals of music, an introduction, translation and commentary.* (Ph. D. Diss., George Peabody College for Teachers) Ann Arbor 1967.

Brown 1983: Howard Mayer Brown, *The Trecento harp.* -In: Studies in the performance of late medieval music, ed. by Stanley Boorman. Cambridge 1983, pp. 35-73.

Bruck 1906: Robert Bruck, *Die Malereien in den Handschriften des Königreiches Sachsen.* Dresden 1906.

Bücheler 1963: Franciscus Bücheler, *Petronii Saturae.* Adiectae sunt Varronis et Senecae Saturae similisque reliquae. Berne [etc.] 8/1963.

Du Cange: Charles du Fresne Sieur du Cange, *Glossarium Mediae et Infimae Latinitatis.* 10 vols. [No place given] (1883-7) R/Graz 1954.

Caratzas 1977: Aristide Caratzas (ed.), *Herrad of Landsberg: Hortus Deliciarum (Garden of Delights).* Commentary and Notes A. Straub and G. Keller. New York 1977.

Carter 1980: Henry Carter, *A Dictionary of Middle English musical terms.* (Bloomington 1961) R/Millwood 1980.

Courcelle 1967: Pierre Courcelle, *La consolation de philosophie dans la tradition littéraire: antécédents et postérité de Boèce.* Paris 1967.

Crocock 1985: C. Crocock (ed.), *The Ruodlieb.* Warminster 1985.

Van Dale 1984a: *Van Dale Groot woordenboek der Nederlandse taal.* 3 vols. Utrecht [etc.] 11/1984.

— 1984b: *Van Dale Groot woordenboek van hedendaags Nederlands.* Utrecht [etc.] 1984.

Daniélou 1957: J. Daniélou, *David.* -In: Reallexikon für Antike und Christentum 3 (Stuttgart 1957), 594-603.

Debidour 1961: Victor-Henry Debidour, *Le bestiaire sculpté du Moyen Age en France.* Paris 1961.

Deferrari-Campbell 1932: Roy Deferrari, James Campbell, *A concordance of Prudentius.* Cambridge, Mass. 1932. (The Medieval Academy of America 9.)

Dekkers 1961: Eligius Dekkers, *Clavis patrum Latinorum* qua in novum Corpus Christianorum edendum optimas quasque scriptorum recensiones a Tertulliano ad Bedam commode recludit Eligius Dekkers, opera usus qua rem praeparavit et iuvit Aemilius Gaar. Editio altera aucta et emendata. Steenbrugge 1961. (Sacris erudiri 3.)

Delisle 1880: Léopold Delisle, *Mélanges de Paléographie et de Bibliographie.* Paris 1880.

Dick 1969: Adolfus Dick (ed.), *Martianus Capella.* Addenda adiecit Jean Préaux. Editio stereotypa correctior editionis anni MCMXXV. (Leiden 1925) R/Stuttgart 1969.

Diefenbach 1968: Lorenz Diefenbach, *Glossarium Latino-Germanicum Mediae et Infimae Aetatis.* (Frankfurt a.M. 1857) R/Darmstadt 1968.

Dodwell 1961: Charles Dodwell, *Theophilus Presbyter: The various arts.* London 1961.

Dolezalek 1972: Gero Dolezalek, *Verzeichnis der Handschriften zum römischen Recht bis 1600,* 2. Frankfurt a.M. 1972.

Droysen 1969: Dagmar Droysen, *Zum Problem der Klassifizierung von Harfen darstellungen in der Buchmalerei des frühen und hohen Mittelalters.* -In: Jahrbuch des Staatlichen Instituts für Musikforschung Preussischer Kulturbesitz 1968. Berlin 1969, pp. 87-98.

Dupont 1976: Jean Dupont, *Nivernais Bourbonnais Roman.* Paris 1976.

Ehrismann: Gustav Ehrismann (ed.), *Der Renner von Hugo von Trimberg.* 4 vols. Tübingen 1908-12. (Bibliothek des Litterarischen Vereins in Stuttgart 247, 248, 252 and 256.)

— 1915: Gustav Ehrismann, (ed.), *Rudolfs von Ems Weltchronik.* Aus der Wernigeroder Handschrift. Berlin 1915. (Deutsche Texte des Mittelalters 20.)

— 1943: Gustav Ehrismann, *Rudolf von Ems.* -In: Verfasserlexikon 3 (Berlin 1943), 1121-6.

Ellsworth 1984: Oliver Ellsworth, *The Berkeley Manuscript.* A new critical text and translation. Lincoln 1984.

Esmeijer 1978: Anna Esmeijer, *Divina Quaternitas.* A preliminary study in the method and application of visual exegesis. Assen 1978.

Ford 1966: Gordon Ford (ed.), *The Ruodlieb.* Leiden 1966.

Forstner 1961: Dorothea Forstner, *Die Welt der Symbole.* Innsbruck 1961.

Foster 1977: Genette Foster, *The iconology of musical instruments and musical performance in thirteenth-century French manuscript illuminations.* (Ph. D. diss., City University of New York) Ann Arbor 1977.

Frakes 1987: Jerold Frakes, *Griechisches im frühmittelalterlichen St. Gallen.* Ein methodologischer Beitrag zu Notker Labeos Griechischkenntnissen. -In: Zeitschrift für deutsche Philologie 106 (1987), pp. 25-45.

Frede 1981: Hermann Frede, *Kirchenschriftsteller: Verzeichnis und Sigel.* 3., neubearbeitete und erweiterte Auflage des "Verzeichnis der Sigel für Kirchenschriftsteller" von Bonifatius Fischer. Freiburg 1981. (Vetus Latina 1/1.)

Freise 1985: Eckhard Freise, *Zur Person des Theophilus und seiner monastischen Umwelt.* -In: Ornamenta Ecclesiae. Kunst und Künstler der Romanik. Katalog zur Ausstellung des Schnütgen-Museums in der Josef-Haubrich-Kunsthalle, 1. Herausgegeben von Anton Legner. Cologne 1985, pp. 357-62.

Friedlein 1966: Godofredus Friedlein (ed.), *Anicii Manlii Torquati Severini Boetii De institutione arithmetica libri duo, De institutione musica libri quinque.* (Leipzig 1867) R/Frankfurt a.M. 1966.

Gandillac-Jeauneau 1968: Maurice de Gandillac, Eduard Jeauneau, *Entretiens sur la Renaissance du 12e siècle.* Paris [etc.] 1968.

Garnier 1988: François Garnier, *L'âne à la lyre.* Sottisier d'iconographie médiévale. Paris 1988.

Gerbert 1774: Martin Gerbert(us), *De cantu et musica sacra* a prima ecclesiae aetate usque ad praesens tempus. 2 vols. St.-Blasien 1774.

Giesel 1978: Helmut Giesel, *Studien zur Symbolik der Musikinstrumente im Schrifttum der alten und mittelalterlichen Kirche* (von den Anfängen bis zum 13. Jahrhundert). Regensburg 1978. (Kölner Beiträge zur Musikforschung 94.)

Von Glasenapp: Franzgeorg von Glasenapp, *Varia/Rara/Curiosa.* Bildnachweise einer Auswahl von Musikdarstellungen aus dem Mittelalter. [No place and year given.]

Goldschmidt 1895: Adolph Goldschmidt, *Der Albanipsalter in Hildesheim und seine Beziehung zur symbolischen Kirchenskulptur des XII. Jahrhunderts.* Berlin 1895.

Götting 1932: Franz Götting, *Der Renner Hugos von Trimberg.* Studien zur mittelalterlichen Ethik in nachhöfischer Zeit. Münster 1932. (Forschungen zur Deutschen Sprache und Dichtung 1.)

Goy 1976: Rudolf Goy, *Die Überlieferung der Werke Hugos von St. Viktor.* Ein Beitrag zur Kommunikationsgeschichte des Mittelalters. Stuttgart 1976. (Monographien zur Geschichte des Mittelalters 14.)

Graff 1827: Eberhard Graff (ed.), *Diutiska*, 2. Stuttgart/Tübingen 1827.
— 1963: Eberhard Graff, *Althochdeutscher Sprachschatz oder Wörterbuch der alt hochdeutschen Sprache.* 7 vols. (Berlin 1834-46) R/Hildesheim 1963.
Green 1979: Rosalie Green (ed.), *Herrad of Hohenbourg: Hortus Deliciarum.* Commentary and Reconstruction. London [etc.] 1979. (Studies of the Warburg Institute 36.)
Greene 1931: Henry Greene, *The song of the ass.* -In: Speculum 6 (1931), pp. 534-40.
Gressmann 1905: Hugo Gressmann, *Musik und Musikinstrumente im alten Testament.* -In: Religionsgeschichtliche Versuche und Vorarbeiten, II. Band, 1. Heft, herausgegeben von Albrecht Dieterich und Richard Wünsch. Giessen 1905.
Grimm 1984: Jacob and Wilhelm Grimm, *Deutsches Wörterbuch.* 33 vols. (Leipzig 1854-1951) R/Munich 1984.
Gushee 1975: Lawrence Gushee, *Aureliani Reomensis Musica Disciplina.* [No place given] 1975. (CSM 21.)
Gutbrod 1965: Jürgen Gutbrod, *Die Initiale in Handschriften des achten bis dreizehnten Jahrhunderts.* Stuttgart 1965.
Hammerstein 1952: Reinhold Hammerstein, *Die Musik am Freiburger Münster.* Ein Beitrag zur musikalischen Ikonographie. -In: AfMw 9 (1952), pp. 204-18.
— 1959: Reinhold Hammerstein, *Instrumenta Hieronymi.* -In: AfMw 16 (1959), pp. 117-34.
— 1962: Reinhold Hammerstein, *Die Musik der Engel.* Untersuchungen zur Musikanschauung des Mittelalters. Berne [etc.] 1962.
— 1974: Reinhold Hammerstein, *Diabolus in musica.* Munich 1974. (Neue Heidelberger Studien zur Musikwissenschaft 6.)
Haseloff 1938: Günther Haseloff, *Die Psalterillustration im 13. Jahrhundert. Studien zur Geschichte der Buchmalerei in England, Frankreich und den Niederlanden.* Kiel 1938.
Heimann 1965: Adelheid Heimann, *A twelfth-century manuscript from Winchcombe and its illustrations. Dublin, Trinity College, Ms. 53.* -In: Journal of the Warburg and Courtauld Institutes 28 (1965), pp. 93-109.
Heinsius 1968: Maria Heinsius, *Der Paradiesgarten von Herrad von Landsberg.* Ein Zeugnis mittelalterlicher Kultur- und Geistesgeschichte im Elsass. Colmar [etc.] 1968.
Heinz-Mohr 1971: Gerd Heinz-Mohr, *Lexikon der Symbole.* Bilder und Zeichen der christlichen Kunst. Düsseldorf 1971.
Helm 1907: Karl Helm (ed.), *Heinrich von Hesler: Apokalypse*; aus der Danziger Handschrift. Berlin 1907. (Deutsche Texte des Mittelalters 8.)
Hermann 1957: A. Hermann, *Dardanus.* -In: Reallexikon für Antike und Christentum 3 (Stuttgart 1957), 593-4.
Herzog 1969: Reinhart Herzog, *Martianus Capella.* -In: Der Kleine Pauly. Lexikon der Antike 3 (Stuttgart/Munich 1969), 1054-6.
Heyse 1969: Elisabeth Heyse, *Hrabanus Maurus' Enzyklopädie "De rerum naturis".* Untersuchungen zu den Quellen und zur Methode der Kompilation.

Munich 1969. (Münchener Beiträge zur Mediävistik und Renaissance-Forschung.)

Hickmann 1953: Hans Hickmann, *Les harpes de l'Égypte pharaonique.* Essai d'une nouvelle classification. -In: Extrait de l'Institut d'Égypte 35 (1952-3), pp. 309-68.

Hildebrandt 1974: Reiner Hildebrandt (ed.), *Summarium Heinrici,* 1, Textkritische Ausgabe der ersten Fassung, Buch I-X. Berlin 1974. (Quellen und Forschungen zur Sprach- und Kulturgeschichte der Germanischen Völker, Neue Folge 61 (185).)

— 1982: Reiner Hildebrandt (ed.), *Summarium Heinrici,* 2, Textkritische Ausgabe der zweiten Fassung, Buch I-VI sowie des Buches XI in Kurz- und Langfassung. Berlin 1982. (Quellen und Forschungen zur Sprach- und Kulturgeschichte der Germanischen Völker, Neue Folge 78 (202).)

— 1986: Reiner Hildebrandt (reviewer), Wegstein, *Studien zum 'Summarium Heinrici'.* -In: Anzeiger für deutsches Altertum 97 (1986), pp. 120-9.

Hoffmann-Axthelm 1981: Dagmar Hoffmann-Axthelm, *Instrumentensymbolik und Aufführungspraxis.* Zum Verhältnis von Symbolik und Realität in der mittelalterlichen Musikanschauung. -In: Basler Jahrbuch für historische Musikpraxis 4, 1980. Winterthur 1981, pp. 9-90.

Hoffmann von Fallersleben 1968: August Hoffmann von Fallersleben, *Horae Belgicae* 5-8. (Hannover 2/1856) R/Amsterdam 1968.

Holthausen 1930: F. Holthausen, *Wortdeutungen.* -In: Indogermanische Forschungen — Zeitschrift für Indogermanistik und allgemeine Sprachwissenschaft 48 (1930), pp. 254-67.

— 1934: F. Holthausen, *Gotisches Etymologisches Wörterbuch.* Heidelberg 1934. (Germanische Bibliothek IV.Reihe / 8.Band.)

Hopper 1938: Vincent Hopper, *Medieval number symbolism: its sources, meaning, and influence on thought and expression.* New York 1938.

Huschenbett 1978: Dietrich Huschenbett, *Albrecht, Dichter des Jüngeren Titurel.* -In: Verfasserlexikon 1 (Berlin [etc.] 2/1978), 158-73.

Jullian 1987: Martine Jullian, *L'image de la musique dans la sculpture romane en France.* -In: Cahiers de civilisation médiévale Xe-XIIe siècles, 30e Année 1 (1987), pp. 33-44.

Kahsnitz 1979: Rainer Kahsnitz, *Der Werdener Psalter in Berlin: Ms. theol. lat. fol. 358.* Eine Untersuchung zu Problemen mittelalterlicher Psalterillustration. Düsseldorf 1979. (Beiträge zu den Bau- und Kunstdenkmälern im Rheinland 24.)

Kalusche 1986: Bernd Kalusche, *Harfenbedeutungen.* Ideale, ästhetische und reale Funktionen eines Musikinstruments in der abendländischen Kunst — Eine Bedeutungsgeschichte. Frankfurt a.M. [etc.] 1986. (Europäische Hochschulschriften Reihe 28 Kunstgeschichte, Band 69.)

Karg-Gasterstädt 1955: E. Karg-Gasterstädt, *Notker Labeo.* -In: Verfasserlexikon 5 (Berlin 1955), 775-90.

Kessler 1977: Herbert Kessler, *The illustrated bibles from Tours.* Princeton 1977. (Studies in manuscript illumination 7.)

Klein 1966: E. Klein, *A Comprehensive etymological dictionary of the English language,* 1. Amsterdam 1966.

Klingender 1971: Francis Klingender, *Animals in art and thought.* London 1971.

Kluge 1967: Friedrich Kluge, *Etymologisches Wörterbuch der Deutschen Sprache.* 20. Auflage bearbeitet von Walther Mitzka. Berlin 1967.

Knapp 1977: Fritz Knapp (ed.), *Ruodlieb.* Mittellateinisch und Deutsch. Stuttgart 1977. (Reclams Universal-Bibliothek 9846.)

Kneif 1963: Tibor Kneif, *Zur Entstehung der musikalischen Mediävistik.* (Diss.) Göttingen 1963.

Köhler 1958: Wilhelm Köhler, *Die karolingischen Miniaturen,* 2: Die Hofschule Karls des Grossen. Berlin 1958.

Körting 1907: Gustav Körting, *Lateinisch-romanisches Wörterbuch.* Paderborn 1907.

Kortekaas 1984: G. Kortekaas (ed.), *Historia Apollonii Regis Tyri.* Groningen 1984. (Mediaevalia Groningana, Fasciculus III.)

Kuhn 1981: Hugo Kuhn, *Gottfried von Strassburg.* -In: Verfasserlexikon 3 (Berlin [etc.] 2/1981), 153-68.

Lambert 1969: Bernard Lambert: *Bibliotheca Hieronymiana Manuscripta,* IB. La tradition manuscrite des oeuvres de Saint Jérôme. Steenbrugge 1969. (Instrumenta Patristica 4.)

— 1970: Bernard Lambert, *Bibliotheca Hieronymiana Manuscripta,* IIIA. La tradition manuscrite des oeuvres de Saint Jérôme. Steenbrugge 1970. (Instrumenta Patristica 4.)

Langosch 1943: Karl Langosch, *Ruodlieb.* -In: Verfasserlexikon 3 (Berlin 1943), 1137-47.

Latham: Ronald Latham, *Dictionary of medieval Latin from British sources.* London 1975-.

— 1980: Ronald Latham, *Revised Medieval Latin Word-List from British and Irish Sources.* London (1965) R/1980.

Leclanche 1980: Jean-Luc Leclanche, *Floire et Blancheflor.* Le conte de Floire et Blancheflor. [No place given] 1980. (Les classiques français du Moyen Age 105.)

Lehmann 1938: Paul Lehmann: *Mitteilungen aus Handschriften*, 5. Munich 1938. (Sitzungsberichte der Bayerischen Akademie der Wissenschaften zu München. Philosophisch-historische Abteilung Jahrgang 1938, Heft 4.)

Leitzmann 1965: Albert Leitzmann (ed.), *Wolfram von Eschenbach*: *Parzival.* 3 Hefte. Tübingen 1961-5. (Altdeutsche Textbibliothek 12-4.)

Lenaz 1975: Luciano Lenaz (ed.), *Martiani Capellae De nuptiis Philologiae et Mercurii liber secundus.* Padua 1975.

Leroquais 1934: Victor Leroquais, *Les bréviaires manuscrits des bibliothèques publiques de France*, 1. Paris (1834) R1934.

— 1940-1: Victor Leroquais, *Les psautiers manuscrits latins des bibliothèques publiques de France.* 2 vols. Mâcon 1940-1.

Lexer 1970: Matthias Lexer (ed.), *Mittelhochdeutsches Handwörterbuch.* 3 vols. (Leipzig 1869-78) R/Stuttgart 1970.

Lexicon Aegidii Forcellini: *Totius latinitatis lexicon.* Opera et studio Aegidii Forecellini lucubratum. 10 vols. Prati 1858-87.

Lindsay 1964: Wallace Lindsay (ed.), *Nonius Marcellus*: *De compendiosa doctrina*; libros XX Onionsianis copiis usus edidit W. M. Lindsay, I, Lib. I-III. (Leipzig 1903) R/Hildesheim 1964.

— 1966: Wallace Lindsay (ed.), *Isidori Hispalensis Episcopi Etymologiarum sive Originum libri XX.* Recognovit brevique adnotatione critica instruxit W. M. Lindsay. 2 vols. Oxford (1911) R/1966.

Lutz 1939: Cora Lutz (ed.), *Johannis Scotti Annotationes in Marcianum.* Cambridge, Mass. 1939. (The Medieval Academy of America Publications 34.)

— 1944: Cora Lutz (ed.), *Dunchad*: *Glossae in Martianum.* Lancaster [etc.] 1944. (Philological Monographs published by the American Philological Association 12.)

— 1962: Cora Lutz (ed.), *Remigii Autissiodorensis Commentum in Martianum Capellam,* Libri I-II. Leiden 1962.

— 1965: Cora Lutz (ed.), *Remigii Autissiodorensis Commentum in Martianum Capellam,* Libri III-IX. Leiden 1965.

Maas-Snyder 1989: Martha Maas, Jane Snyder, *Stringed Instruments of Ancient Greece*. New Haven [etc.] 1989.

MacCracken 1934: H. MacCracken (ed.), *The minor poems of John Lydgate,* 2: Secular Poems. London 1934.

Macleod: M. Macleod, *Luciani Opera.* 3 vols. Oxford 1972-80.

Mâle 1953: Emile Mâle, *L'art religieux du XIIe siècle.* Paris 1953.

Malone 1962: Kemp Malone (ed.), *Widsith.* Copenhagen 1962.

Marshall 1968: P. Marshall (ed.), *Aulus Gellius*: *Noctes Atticae.* 2 vols. Oxford 1968. (Scriptorum Classicorum Bibliotheca Oxoniensis.)

Martin 1900-3: Ernst Martin (ed.), *Wolframs von Eschenbach Parzival und Titurel.* 2 vols: 1 Text, 2 Kommentar. Halle a.S. 1900 and 1903. (Germanistische Handbibliothek IX, 1-2).

Masser 1981: Achim Masser, *Heinrich von Hesler.* -In: Verfasserlexikon 3 (Berlin [etc.] 2/1981), 749-55.

McKinnon 1965a: James McKinnon, *The Church Fathers and musical instruments.* (Ph. D. diss., Colombia University) Ann Arbor 1965.

— 1965b: James McKinnon, *The meaning of patristic polemic against musical instruments.* -In: Current Musicology 1 (1965), pp. 69-82.

— 1968: James McKinnon, *Musical instruments in medieval psalm commentaries and psalters.* -In: JAMS 21 (1968), pp. 3-20.

— 1984: James McKinnon, *Trigonon.* -In: The New Grove Dictionary of Musical Instruments 3 (London [etc.] 1984), pp. 626-7.

— 1987: James McKinnon, *Music in early Christian literature.* Cambridge 1987. (Cambridge Readings in the Literature of Music.)

McKinnon-Anderson 1984a: James McKinnon, Robert Anderson, *Cymbalum.* - In: The New Grove Dictionary of Musical Instruments 1 (London [etc.] 1984), pp. 532-3.

McKinnon-Remnant 1984b: James McKinnon, Mary Remnant, *Psaltery.* -In: The New Grove Dictionary of Musical Instruments 3 (London [etc.] 1984), pp. 151-5.

McLaughlin 1956: T. McLaughlin, *Abelard's rule for religious women.* -In: Mediaeval Studies 18 (1956), pp. 241-92.

Meringer 1904: Rudolf Meringer, *Wörter und Sachen.* -In: Indogermanische Forschungen. Zeitschrift für Indogermanische Sprach- und Altertumskunde 16 (1904), pp. 101-96.

Meyer 1975: Heinz Meyer, *Die Zahlenallegorese im Mittelalter: Methode und Gebrauch.* Munich 1975. (Münstersche Mittelalter-Schriften 25.)

Migne 1890: M. Migne, *Lexicon manuale ad scriptores mediae et infimae latinitatis.* Paris 1890.

Millar 1927: Eric Millar, *The library of A. Chester Beatty.* A descriptive catalogue of the western manuscripts by Eric George Millar, 1. Oxford 1927.

— 1952: Eric Millar, *A thirteenth-century York Psalter.* A manuscript written and illustrated in the diocese of York about A.D. 1250 described by Eric George Millar. Oxford 1952.

Montel 1980: Costanza Montel, *I manoscritti latini dal VII alla metà del XIII secolo.* I manoscritti miniati della Biblioteca Nazionale di Torino 1. Turin 1980.

Morgan 1982: Nigel Morgan, *Early Gothic manuscripts* [1]. A survey of manuscripts illuminated in the British Isles, 4. Oxford 1982.

Müller 1909: Hermann Müller (ed.), *Der Musiktraktat in dem Werke des Bartholomaeus Anglicus De proprietatibus rerum.* -In: Riemann-Festschrift — Gesammelte Studien. Leipzig 1909, pp. 241-55.

Münxelhaus 1976: Barbara Münxelhaus, *Pythagoras musicus.* Zur Rezeption der pythagoreischen Musiktheorie als quadrivialer Wissenschaft im lateinischen Mittelalter. Bonn [etc.] 1976. (Band 19 der Orpheus-Schriftenreihe zu Grundfragen der Musik.)

Mynors 1963: R. Mynors (ed.), *Cassiodori Senatoris Institutiones.* Oxford (1937) R/1963.

Von Naredi-Rainer 1986: Paul von Naredi-Rainer, *Architektur und Harmonie.* Zahl, Mass und Proportion in der abendländischen Baukunst. Cologne (1982) 3/1986.

Naumann 1913: H. Naumann, *Notkers Boethius.* Strassburg 1913.

Nickel 1976: Gerhard Nickel (ed.), *Beowulf und die kleineren Denkmäler der alt englischen Heldensage Waldere und Finnsburg.* 3 vols. Heidelberg 1976.

Niermeyer 1976: Jan Niermeyer, *Mediae Latinitatis Lexicon Minus.* Leiden 1976.

Nordenfalk 1939: Carl Nordenfalk, *Insulare und kontinentale Psalterillustrationen aus dem XIII. Jahrhundert.* -In: Acta Archaeologica 10, Fasc. 1-3 (1939), pp. 107-20.

Nordström 1955: Folke Nordström, *Peterborough, Lincoln, and the science of Robert Grosseteste: A study in 13th century architecture and iconography.* -In: The Art Bulletin 27/4 (1955), pp. 241-72.

Obrist 1988: Barbara Obrist, *La figure géométrique dans l'oeuvre de Joachim de Flore.* -In: Cahiers de civilisation médiévale Xe-XIIe siècles 31 (1988), pp. 297-321.

Ochsenbein 1981: Peter Ochsenbein, *Heinrich von Neustadt.* -In: Verfasserlexikon 3 (Berlin [etc.] 2/1981), 838-45.

Okken 1983: Lambertus Okken, *Die Glasspiegel in der deutschsprachigen Literatur um 1200.* -In: Janus. Revue internationale de l'histoire des sciences, de la médecine, de la pharmacie et de la technique, 70 (1983), pp. 55-96.

Okken-Mück 1981: Lambertus Okken, Hans-Dieter Mück, *Die satirischen Lieder Oswalds von Wolkenstein wider die Bauern.* Exkurs III. Göppingen 1981, pp. 170-88. (Göppinger Arbeiten zur Germanistik 316.)

Onions 1967: Charles Onions (ed.), *The Oxford Dictionary of English etymology.* Oxford (1966) R/1967.

Owens 1990: Margareth Boyer Owens, *The Image of King David in Prayer in Fifteenth-Century Books of Hours.* -In: Imago Musicae — International Yearbook of Musical Iconography 6, 1989. Lucca 1990, pp. 22-38.

Pächt 1985: Otto Pächt, *Buchmalerei des Mittelalters.* Eine Einführung. Munich (1984) 2/1985.

Page 1977: Christopher Page, *Biblical instruments in medieval manuscript illustration.* -In: Early Music 5 (1977), pp. 299-309.

— 1981: Christopher Page, Anglo-Saxon Hearpan: *Their terminology, technique, tuning and repertory of verse 850-1066.* (Unpublished Ph. D. diss., University of York — Centre for Medieval Studies). Boston Spa 1981.

— 1983: Christopher Page, *The medieval Organistrum and Symphonia,* 2: Terminology. -In: The Galpin Society Journal 36 (1983), pp. 71-87.

— 1987: Christopher Page, *Voices and instruments of the Middle Ages.* Instrumental practice and songs in France 1100-1300. London [etc.] 1987.

Palisca 1978: Claude Palisca (ed.), *Hucbald, Guido, and John on music.* Three medieval treatises. Translated by Warren Babb. Edited with introduction by Claude V. Palisca. New Haven [etc.] 1978. (Music Theory Translation Series 3.)

Papias 1966: *Papias Vocabulista.* (Venice 1496) R/Turin 1966.

Perry 1952: Ben Perry (ed.), *Aesopica.* Urbana 1952. (Fabulae Latinae 542.)

— 1975: Ben Perry (ed.), *Babrius and Phaedrus.* London (1965) R/1975. (LCL 436.)

Persson 1891: Per Persson, *Studien zur Lehre von der Wurzelerweiterung und Wurzelvariation.* -In: Upsala Universitets Årsskrift. Uppsala 1891, pp. 1-280.

— 1912: Per Persson, *Beiträge zur Indogermanischen Wortforschung.* 2 vols. Uppsala 1912.

Pickering 1970: Frederick P. Pickering, *Literature and art in the Middle Ages.* London [etc.] 1970, pp. 285-307.

Pietzsch 1929: Gerhard Pietzsch, *Die Klassifikation der Musik von Boetius bis Ugolino von Orvieto.* Halle 1929. (Studien zur Geschichte der Musiktheorie im Mittelalter 1.)

Pokorny 1959: Julius Pokorny, *Indogermanisches Etymologisches Wörterbuch,* 1. Berne [etc.] 1959.

Price 1984: Percival Price, *Bells and man.* Oxford (1983) R/1984.

Priebsch 1909: Robert Priebsch (ed.), *Die heilige Regel für ein vollkommenes Leben.* Eine Cisterzienserarbeit des XIII. Jahrhunderts, aus der Handschrift Additional 9048 des British Museum. Berlin 1909. (Deutsche Texte des Mittelalters 16.)

Ragusa 1966: Isa Ragusa, *A Gothic psalter in Princeton: Garrett MS. 35.* (Ph. D. diss., New York University) [No place given] 1966, pp. 141-59.

Randall 1957: Lilian Randall, *Exempla as a source of Gothic marginal illumination.* -In: Art Bulletin 39 (1957), pp. 97-104.

— 1966: Lilian Randall, *Images in the margins of Gothic manuscripts,* London [etc.] 1966.

Randall 1960: Richard Randall, *A cloisters bestiary.* New York 1960.

Ranke 1969: Friedrich Ranke (ed.), *Gottfried von Strassburg: Tristan und Isold.* Dublin [etc.] (1930) 14/1969.

Ravenel 1985: Bernard Ravenel, *Rebec und Fiedel*: Ikonographie und Spielweise. -In: Basler Jahrbuch für historische Musikpraxis 8, 1984. Winterthur 1985, pp. 105-30.

Raynaud de Lage 1966: Guy Raynaud de Lage (ed.), *Le Roman de Thèbes,* 1. Paris 1966.

Reaney 1966: Gilbert Reaney (ed.), *Willelmus: Breviarium regulare musicae.* [No place given] 1966. (CSM 12.)

Rensch 1964: Rosalyn Rensch, *Symbolism and form of the harp in western European manuscript illuminations of the ninth to the sixteenth century.* (Ph. D. diss., University of Winconsin — Madison) Ann Arbor 1964.

Riedel 1959: Herbert Riedel, *Musik und Musikerlebnis in der erzählenden deutschen Dichtung.* Bonn 1959. (Abhandlungen zur Kunst-, Musik- und Literaturwissenschaft 12.)

Rietschel 1965: Christian Rietschel, *Sinnzeichen des Glaubens.* Kassel 1965.

Robert-Tissot 1974: Michel Robert-Tissot (ed.), *Johannes Aegidius de Zamora: Ars musica.* [No place given] 1974. (CSM 20.)

Robinson 1957: F. Robinson, *The works of Geoffrey Chaucer.* London 2/1957.

Rochias 1910: G. Rochias, *Les chapiteaux de l'église de Saint-Nectaire.* Caen 1910.

Sachs 1940: Curt Sachs, *The history of musical instruments.* New York 1940.

— 1964: Curt Sachs, *Real-Lexikon der Musikinstrumente.* Zugleich ein Polyglossar für das gesamte Instrumentengebiet. London 1964.

Sachs 1970: Klaus-Jürgen Sachs, *Mensura fistularum.* Die Mensurierung der Orgelpfeifen im Mittelalter, 1. Stuttgart 1970. (Schriftenreihe der Walcker-Stiftung für Orgelwissenschaftliche Forschung 1.)

— 1984: Klaus-Jürgen Sachs, *Die Rolle der Mensura von Monochord, Orgelpfeifen und Glocken in der mittelalterlichen Ars Musica.* -In: Mensura, Mass, Zahl, Zahlensymbolik im Mittelalter, 2. Halbband. Berlin 1984, pp. 459-75. (Miscellanea Mediaevalia 16/2.)

Van Schaik 1983: Martin van Schaik, *Muziekinstrumenten en instrumentenkombinaties in de Duitse literatuur (ca. 800-1350).* Utrecht 1983. (Scripta Musicologica Ultrajectina 7.)

— 1985: Martin van Schaik, *Appendix Musik* — Musik, Aufführungspraxis und Instrumente im Tristan-Roman Gottfrieds von Strassburg. -In: Lambertus Okken, Kommentar zum Tristan-Roman Gottfrieds von Strassburg, 2. Amsterdam 1985, pp. 163-224. (Amsterdamer Publikationen zur Sprache und Literatur 58.)

— 1989: Martin van Schaik, *The Cymbala in Psalm 80 Initials: A Symbolic Interpretation.* -In: Imago Musicae — International Yearbook of Musical Iconography 5, 1988. Basel [etc.] 1989, pp. 23-40.

— 1990: Martin van Schaik, *Boethius, De institutione musica* and *Regino van Prüm, Epistola*. -In: L. Grijp, P. Scheepers (ed.), Van Aristoxenos tot Stockhausen 1: Van Oudheid tot Renaissance. Groningen 1990, pp. 99-123 and pp. 151-158.

— 1991: Martin van Schaik, *Die gesellschaftliche Funktion der Harfe in der deutschen Literatur des Mittelalters*. -In: H. Rosenzweig (ed.), Historische Harfen — Historical Harps. Beiträge zur Theorie und Praxis historischer Harfen. (Schola Cantorum Basiliensis) Dornach 1991, pp. 9-23.

— 1992: *The harp bag in the Middle Ages*. [This article will be published in: Proceedings of the International Historical Harp Symposium Utrecht 1992.]

Schönbach 1964: Anton Schönbach, *Altdeutsche Predigten.* 3 vols. (Graz 1886-91) R/Darmstadt 1964.

Schroth 1976: Rolf Schroth, *Eine altfranzösische Übersetzung der 'consolatio philosophiae' des Boethius (Handschrift Troyes Nr. 898).* Edition und Kommentar. Berne [etc.] 1976. (Europäische Hochschulschriften, Reihe XIII, 36.)

Schweikle 1983: Günther Schweikle, *Hugo von Trimberg.* -In: Verfasserlexikon 4 (Berlin [etc.] 2/1983), 268-82.

Seebass: Tilman Seebass, *Idee und Status der Harfe im europäischen Mittelalter.* (Unpublished paper.)

— 1970: Tilman Seebass, *Etwas über die sakrale und profane Bedeutung der Musikinstrumente im Mittelalter.* -In: Bericht über den internationalen Musikwissenschaftlichen Kongress. Bonn 1970, pp. 564-70.

— 1973a: Tilman Seebass, *Die Bedeutung des Utrechter Psalters für die Musikgeschichte.* -In: J.H.A. Engelbregt, Tilman Seebass, Kunst- en muziekhistorische bijdragen tot de bestudering van het Utrechts Psalterium. Utrecht 1973, pp. 35-48.

— 1973b: Tilman Seebass, *Musikdarstellung und Psalterillustration im früheren Mittelalter.* Studien ausgehend von einer Ikonologie der Handschrift Paris Bibliothèque Nationale Fonds Latin 1118. Text- und Bildband. Berne 1973.

Sehrt-Starck 1933: Edward Sehrt, Taylor Starck (ed.), *Notkers des Deutschen Werke,* Band 1, Heft 1: Boethius De Consolatione Philosophiae I und II. Halle a. S. 1933. (Altdeutsche Textbibliothek 32.)

— 1955: Edward Sehrt, Taylor Starck (ed.), *Notker des Deutschen Werke,* Band 3, Teil 3: Der Psalter CI-CL nebst cantica und katechetischen Stücken. Halle a. S. 1955. (Altdeutsche Textbibliothek 43.)

Seiler 1882: Friedrich Seiler, *Ruodlieb, der älteste Roman des Mittelalters, nebst Epigrammen, mit Einleitung, Anmerkungen und Glossar.* Halle a. S. 1882.

Sendrey 1970: Alfred Sendrey, *Musik in Alt-Israel.* Leipzig 1970.

Shanzer 1986: Danuta Shanzer, *The late antique tradition of Varro's Onos Lyras.* -In: Rheinisches Museum für Philologie, Neue Folge 129 (1986), pp. 272-85.

Silk 1935: Edmund Silk (ed.), *Saeculi noni auctoris in Boetii Consolationem Philosophiae commentarius.* Rome 1935. (Papers and Monographs of the American Academy in Rome 9.)

Singer 1906: S. Singer (ed.), *Heinrichs von Neustadt "Apollonius von Tyrland" nach der Gothaer Handschrift.* Berlin 1906. (Deutsche Texte des Mittelalters 7.)

Skeat 1954: Walter Skeat (ed.), *The complete works of Geoffrey Chaucer. Boethius and Troilus.* London (1900) R/1954.

Smits van Waesberghe 1951a: Joseph Smits van Waesberghe (ed.), *Aribonis De Musica.* Rome 1951. (CSM 2.)

— 1951b: Joseph Smits van Waesberghe, *Cymbala* - Bells in the Middle Ages. Rome 1951. (Musicological Studies and Documents 1.)

— 1953: Joseph Smits van Waesberghe, *De musico-paedagogico et theoretico Guidone Aretino eiusque vita et moribus.* Florence 1953.

— 1955: Joseph Smits van Waesberghe (ed.), *Guidonis Aretini Micrologus.* [No place given] 1955. (CSM 4.)

— 1969: Joseph Smits van Waesberghe, *Musikerziehung.* Lehre und Theorie der Musik im Mittelalter. Leipzig 1969. (Musikgeschichte in Bildern III, 3.)

Sperber 1912: Hans Sperber, *Deutsch Harfe und seine Verwandten.* -In: Wörter und Sachen — Kulturhistorische Zeitschrift für Sprach- und Sachforschung 3 (1912), pp. 68-77.

Stallbaum 1825: G. Stallbaum, *Commentarii ad Momoeri Odysseam,* I. Leipzig 1825.

Starck 1978: Taylor Starck, *Althochdeutsches Glossenwörterbuch.* Heidelberg 1978.

Starck-Wells 1972: Taylor Starck, J. Wells (ed.), *Althochdeutsches Glossenwörterbuch.* Heidelberg 1972-.

Stauder 1969: Wilhelm Stauder, *Asinus ad lyram.* -In: H. Osthoff zu seinem siebzigsten Geburtstag. Tutzing 1969, pp. 25-32.

Steger 1961: Hugo Steger, *David Rex et Propheta.* König David als vorbildliche Verkörperung des Herrschers und Dichters im Mittelalter, nach Bilddarstellungen des achten bis zwölften Jahrhunderts. Nuremberg 1961. (Erlanger Beiträge zur Sprach- und Kunstwissenschaft 6.)

— 1971: Hugo Steger, *Philologia Musica.* Sprachzeichen, Bild und Sache im literarisch-musikalischen Leben des Mittelalters: Lire, Harpfe, Rotte und Fidel. Munich 1971. (Münstersche Mittelalter-Schriften 2.)

Stegmüller: Fridericus Stegmüller (ed.), *Repertorium Biblicum Medii Aevi.* 11 vols. Madrid 1950-80.

Steinmeyer-Sievers: Elias Steinmeyer and Eduard Sievers, *Die althochdeutschen Glossen.* 5 vols. Berlin 1879-1922.

Stubbs 1965: William Stubbs (ed.), *Memorials of St. Dunstan.* Archbishop of Canterbury. London (1874) R/1965. (Rerum Britannicarum Medii Aevi Scriptores (Rolls Series) 63.)

Suckale-Redlefsen 1972: Gude Suckale-Redlefsen, *Die Bilderzyklen zum Davidleben.* Von den Anfängen bis zum Ende des 11. Jahrhunderts. (Diss.) Munich 1972.

Swarzenski 1936: Hanns Swarzenski, *Die lateinischen illuminierten Handschriften des XIII. Jahrhunderts in den Ländern an Rhein, Main und Donau.* 2 vols. Berlin 1936.

Timmers 1985: J. Timmers, *Christelijke symboliek en iconografie.* Weesp (1978) R/1985.

Torp 1909: A. Torp, *Wortschatz der Germanischen Spracheinheit.* Göttingen 1909.

Vahlen 1974: Johannes Vahlen, *In Marci Terentii Varronis Saturarum Menippearum reliquias coniectanea.* (Leipzig 1858) R/Hildesheim [etc.] 1974.

Vellekoop 1967: Kees Vellekoop, *Zusammenhänge zwischen Text und Zahl in der Kompositionsart Jacob Obrechts.* -In: TVNM 20/3 (1967), pp. 97-119.

— 1984: Kees Vellekoop, *Die Orgel von Winchester: Wirklichkeit oder Symbol?* -In: Basler Jahrbuch für historische Musikpraxis 8, 1984. Winterthur 1985, pp. 183-96.

Vellekoop-Van Schaik 1988: Kees Vellekoop, Martin van Schaik, *Muziek tussen extase en 'offer in de geest'.* -In: R. Stuip, C. Vellekoop (ed.), Culturen in contact. Botsing en integratie in de Middeleeuwen. Utrecht 1988, pp. 66-88. (Utrechtse Bijdragen tot de Mediëvistiek 8.)

Vetter 1908: Ferdinand Vetter (ed.), *Die Predigten Taulers*; aus der Engelberger und Freiburger Handschrift sowie aus Schmidts Abschriften der ehemaligen Strassburger Handschriften. Berlin 1908. (Deutsche Texte des Mittelalters 11.)

Vitale-Brovarone 1978: Alessandro Vitale-Brovarone, *The asinus citharaedus in the literary and iconographic tradition of the Middle Ages.* -In: Marche Romane 28 — Epopée animale, fable et fabliau, Mediaevalia 78 (1978), pp. 121-9.

Vogel 1973: Martin Vogel, *Onos Lyras.* 2 vols. Düsseldorf 1973. (Band 13 und 14 der Orpheus-Schriftenreihe zu Grundfragen der Musik.)

— 1978: Martin Vogel, *Chiron.* 2 vols. Bonn 1978. (Band 25 und 26 der Orpheus-Schriftenreihe zu Grundfragen der Musik.)

Vollmann 1985: Konrad Vollmann (ed.), *Ruodlieb.* Faksimile-Ausgabe des Codex Latinus Monacensis 19486 der Bayerischen Staatsbibliothek München und der Fragmente von St. Florian, Band II, Erster Teil: Kritischer Text. Wiesbaden 1985.

Vorreiter 1977: Leopold Vorreiter, *Harfen Westeuropas im Mittelalter.* -In: Archiv für Musikorganologie, Heft 1 (Munich 1977), pp. 44-67.

De Vries 1981: Ad de Vries, *Dictionary of symbols and imagery.* Amsterdam (1974) R/1981.

De Vries 1977: Jan de Vries, *Altnordisches etymologisches Wörterbuch.* Leiden 3/1977.

Vulgata 1969: *Biblia Sacra iuxta Vulgatam Versionem.* Recensuit et brevi apparatu instruxit Robertus Weber. 2 vols. Stuttgart 1969.

Walberg 1970: Emmanuel Walberg, *Le Bestiaire.* Texte critique. Geneva 1970.

Watson 1934: Arthur Watson, *The early iconography of the tree of Jesse.* London 1934.

Wehrhahn-Stauch 1968: L. Wehrhahn-Stauch, *Esel, Wildesel.* -In: Lexikon der Christlichen Ikonographie 1 (Basel 1968), pp. 681-4.

Weir-Jerman 1986: Anthony Weir, James Jerman, *Images of lust.* Sexual carvings on mediaeval churches. London 1986.
Whiting 1968: Bartlett Whiting, *Proverbs, sentences and proverbial phrases from English writings mainly before 1500.* Cambridge, Mass. 1968.
Wildhagen 1964: Karl Wildhagen (ed.), *Der Cambridger Psalter.* (Hamburg 1910) R/Darmstadt 1964.
Wimmer 1966: Otto Wimmer, *Die Attribute der Heiligen.* Innsbruck 1966.
Wirtz 1974: Wilhelmina Wirtz, *Floire et Blancheflor nach der Pariser Handschrift 375 (A) mit Glossar neu herausgegeben.* (Frankfurt 1937) R/Hildesheim 1974.
Wolf 1964: Werner Wolf (ed.), *Albrechts von Scharfenberg Jüngerer Titurel,* II, 1 (Strophe 1958-3236). Berlin 1964. (Deutsche Texte des Mittelalters 55.)
Wright 1965: Thomas Wright (ed.), *Livre des Créatures (Liber de Creaturis).* -In: Popular treatises on science written during the Middle Ages in Anglo-Saxon, Anglo-Norman, and English. London (1841) R/1965.
Zahlten 1979: Johannes Zahlten, *Creatio Mundi.* Darstellungen der sechs Schöpfungstage und naturwissenschaftliches Weltbild im Mittelalter. Stuttgart 1979. (Stuttgarter Beiträge zur Geschichte und Politik 13.)
Zeydel 1959a: Edwin Zeydel, *Die elf Epigramme der Münchener Ruodlieb-handschrift.* -In: Deutsche Vierteljahrschrift für Literaturwissenschaft und Geistesgeschichte 33 (1959), pp. 257-68.
— 1959b: Edwin Zeydel, *Ruodlieb.* The earliest courtly novel. Introduction, text, translation, commentary and textual notes. Chapel Hill 1959. (University of North Carolina Studies in the Germanic Languages and Literature 23.)
Zingel 1957: Hans Zingel, *Die Harfe als Symbol und allegorisches Attribut.* -In: Die Musikforschung 10 (1957), pp. 39-48.
— 1968: Hans Zingel, *König Davids Harfe in der abendländischen Kunst.* King David's harp as represented in European art. Cologne 1968.
Zupitza 1896: Ernst Zupitza, *Die Germanischen Gutturale.* -In: Schriften zur Germanischen Philologie, Heft 8 (1896), pp. 1-260.

LIST OF ILLUSTRATIONS

1 *Hortus deliciarum* of Herrad of Hohenburg, f. 32r, *Musica* within thc "Artes Liberales" (detail). (Hohenburg, second half of 12th century; destroyed by fire in 1870.) Copied from the original. — Photograph: after Green 1979, Reconstruction No. 33.

2 St.-Blasien, *De cantu et musica sacra*, II, by Martin Gerbert, Pl. 32, Fig. 19, *Cythara anglica* and other instruments. (Drawing after a codex from the second half of the 12th century; destroyed by fire in 1768.) — Photograph: after Gerbert 1774.

3 London, British Library, Sloane 3983, f. 13r, armed man with musical instruments (detail). Astrological tract. The Netherlands? (early 14th century). — Photograph: British Library.

4 Oxford, Bodleian Library, Bodley 842, f. 66v, drawing of a *cithara* in the *Breviarium regulare musicae* of Willelmus. England (c. 1400). — Photograph: Bodleian Library.

5 London, British Library, Additional 44874, f. 37v, initial D of Psalm 26. Evesham Psalter. England? (13th century). — Photograph: British Library.

6 Rome, Biblioteca Vaticana, lat. 83, f. 12v, frontispiece. Psalter and Hymnary of Ambrose. Milan or vicinity (last quarter of 10th century). — Photograph: after Steger 1961, Tafel 9.

7 Oxford, Bodleian Library, Liturgical 407, f. 77v, initial D of Psalm 52. Psalter. England (early 13th century). — Photograph: Bodleian Library.

8 New York, Pierpont Morgan Library, 102, f. 84r, initial E of Psalm 80. Psalter. England (c. 1270-1300). — Photograph: Pierpont Morgan Library.

9 New York, Pierpont Morgan Library, 43, f. 27v, initial B of Psalm 1. Huntingfield Psalter. Oxford (c. 1200). — Photograph: Pierpont Morgan Library.

10 Paris, Bibliothèque Nationale, lat. 1, f. 215v, frontispiece of Psalter. Vivian Bible. Tours (c. 850). — Photograph: Bibliothèque Nationale.

11 Coblenz, Landeshauptarchiv, Abt. 710, No. 110, f. 153v, frontispiece of Psalter. Incomplete Bible (11th-12th century). — Photograph: after Seebass 1973b, Bildband Pl. 80.

12 Herdringen, Schlossbibliothek, Psalter (private property), n.s.m., f. 6r, initial B of Psalm 1. England (c. 1290). — Photograph: Schloss Herdringen.

13 Drawing of a gothic harp with vertically placed tuning-pegs. — Author's drawing.

14 Drawing of a gothic harp with horizontally placed tuning-pegs. — Author's drawing.

15 Glasgow, University Library, Hunter 229, f. 21v, frontispiece of Psalter (detail). Hunterian Psalter. Northern England (12th century). — Photograph: University Library.

16 Avranches, Bibliothèque de la Ville, 76, f. 1v, frontispiece, (detail). *Enarrationes in Psalmos* of Augustinus. France (mid-11th century). — Photograph: Bibliothèque de la Ville.

17 Moissac, Abbey church of St.-Pierre, capital (c. 1100). — Photograph: after Steger 1971, ill. 24.

18 Toulouse, Musée des Augustins, No. 473, capital from the convent of Ste.-Marie-la-Daurade. (Late 11th century). — Photograph: Bildarchiv Foto Marburg, No. 32817.

19 Munich, Bayerische Staatsbibliothek, Clm. 14523, f. 51v, 52r, Dardanus passages with ills. Freising (10th century). — Photograph: Bayerische Staatsbibliothek.

20 Turin, Biblioteca Nazionale Universitaria, D.III.19, f. 34r, ills. for the book *De musica* of Isidore of Seville. *Etymologiae*. (10th century). — Photograph: Biblioteca Nazionale Universitaria.

21 St.-Blasien, *De cantu et musica sacra*, II, by Martin Gerbert, Pl. 25, fig. 10, Dardanus passages with ills. (After a codex from the second half of the 12th century; destroyed by fire in 1768.) — Photograph: after Gerbert 1774.

22 St.-Blasien, *De cantu et musica sacra*, II, of Martin Gerbert, Pl. 29, Fig. 9, Dardanus passages with ills. (After a codex from the second half of the 12th century; destroyed by fire in 1768.) — Photograph: after Gerbert 1774.

23 London, Beatty collection, 32, f. 1r, frontispiece of Psalter. Psalm commentary of Peter Lombard. Southern Germany (12th century). — Photograph: after Millar 1927, I, Pl. 83.

24 *Hortus Deliciarum* of Herrad of Hohenburg, f. 59r, David with a *psalterium decachordum*. (Hohenburg, second half of 12th century; destroyed by fire in 1870.) Copied from the original. — Photograph: after Green 1979, Reconstruction No. 81.

25 Paris, Bibliothèque Nationale, lat. 1, f. 216r, initial P. Vivian Bible. Tours (c. 850). — Photograph: Bibliothèque Nationale.

26 Berlin, Kupferstichkabinett, 78.A.8, f. 14v, initial B of Psalm 1. Psalter. (first half of 13th century). — Photograph: Kupferstichkabinett.

27 Boulogne-sur-Mer, Bibliothèque de la Ville, 5, f. 177r, initial B of Psalm 1. Bible. St.-Vaast (second half of 13th century). — Photograph: Bibliothèque de la Ville.

28 Paris, Bibliothèque Nationale, lat. 1073A, f. 17r, initial B of Psalm 1. Psalter, Book of Hours. Paris (1220-30). — Photograph: Bibliothèque Nationale.

29 Munich, Bayerische Staatsbibliothek, Clm. 16137, f. 7r, initial B of Psalm 1. Psalter. (13th century). — Photograph: after Swarzenski 1936, ill. 720.

30 London, British Library, Additional 44874, f. 7v, initial B of Psalm 1. Evesham Psalter. England? (13th century). — Photograph: British Library.

31 Munich, Bayerische Staatsbibliothek, Clm. 15909, f. 8r, initial B of Psalm 1. Psalter. (Mid-13th century). — Photograph: after Swarzenski 1936, ill. 515.

32 Oxford, Bodleian Library, Bodley 284, f. 1r, initial B of Psalm 1. Psalter. Oxford (c. 1210-20?). — Photograph: after Morgan 1982, ill. 110.

33 Oxford, New College, 322, f. 28r, initial D of Psalm 26. Psalter. Oxford (c. 1240-50). — Photograph: after Morgan 1982, ill. 249.

34 Kassel, Landesbibliothek, theologica in quarto 8, f. 257r, initial D of Psalm 38. Bible. Paris? (early 13th century). — Photograph: Gesamthochschul-Bibliothek.

35 New York, Pierpont Morgan Library, Glazier 42, f. 167v, initial Q of Psalm 51. Bible. (13th century). — Photograph: Pierpont Morgan Library.

36 London, British Library, Additional 50000, f. 83r, initial Q of Psalm 51. Psalter. (second half of 13th century). — Photograph: British Library.

37 Cambridge, St.-John's College, D.6, f. 75r, initial D of Psalm 52. Psalter, Book of Hours. England (13th century). — Photograph: Cambridge, University Library.

38 London, British Library, Egerton 3277, f. 46v, initial S of Psalm 68. Psalter, Book of Hours. (14th century). — Photograph: British Library.

39 Heiligenkreuz, Stiftsbibliothek, 66, f. 65r, initial E of Psalm 80. Psalter (13th century). — Photograph: Österreichische Nationalbibliothek.

40 Oxford, Bodleian Library, Douce 131, f. 68v, initial E of Psalm 80. Psalter. England? (14th century). — Photograph: Bodleian Library.

41 Brussels, Koninklijke Bibliotheek, 9391, f. 48v, miniature above the initial E. Book of Hours. Northern France (first half of 14th century). — Photograph: Koninklijke Bibliotheek.

42 Edinburgh, National Library of Scotland, 10000, f. 85v, initial C of Psalm 97. Iona Psalter. Oxford (c. 1210). — Photograph: after Morgan 1982, ill. 98.

43 Cambridge, St.-John's College, K.30, f. 86r, initial D of Psalm 101. Psalter. North Midlands (c. 1190-1200?) — Photograph: after Morgan 1982, ill. 55.

44 Paris, Bibliothèque Nationale, lat. 1987, f. 217v, initial D of Psalm 109. *Enarrationes in Psalmos* of Augustine. (11th-12th century). — Photograph: Bibliothèque Nationale.

45 *Hortus Deliciarum* of Herrad of Hohenburg, f. 150r, the crucifixion of Christ. (Hohenburg, second half of 12th century; destroyed by fire in 1870.) Copied from the original. — Photograph: after Green 1979, Commentary ill. 234.

46 Alnay-de-Saintonge, church of St.-Pierre-de-la-Tour, sculpture on the southern portal of the transept (after 1160). — Photograph: Bildarchiv Foto Marburg, No. 32350.

47 Chartres, cathedral, figure on ledge on south side of the bell-tower (13th century). — Photograph: Bildarchiv Foto Marburg, No. 35415.

48 Munich, Bayerische Staatsbibliothek, gall. 16, f. 8r, miniature at the bottom of the Beatus page of the Psalter of Queen Isabella of England (after 1308). — Photograph: Bayerische Staatsbibliothek.

49 London, British Library, Lansdowne 420, f. 12v, initial B of Psalm 1 (c. 1220-30). — Photograph: British Library.

50 Meillers, church of St.-Julien, sculpture on the capital of the west portal (12th century). — Photograph: Bildarchiv Foto Marburg, No. 40114.

51 Turin, Biblioteca Nazionale Universitaria, D.V.19, f. 50r, Arbor Iuris. Southern France (early 13th century). — Photograph: Biblioteca Nazionale Universitaria.

52 Oxford, Bodleian Library, Douce 50, p. 265, initial E of Psalm 80. Psalter. England (second half of 13th century). — Photograph: Bodleian Library.

ACKNOWLEDGEMENTS

The following bodies gave their kind permission for the publication of illustrations:
Bayerische Staatsbibliothek, Munich; Biblioteca Apostolica Vaticana, Rome; Biblioteca Nazionale Universitaria, Turin; Bibliothèque de la Ville, Avranches; Bibliothèque de la Ville, Boulogne-sur-Mer; Bibliothèque Nationale, Paris; Bildarchiv Foto Marburg, Marburg; Bodleian Library, Oxford; British Library, London; Gesamthochschul-Bibliothek, Kassel; Koninklijke Bibliotheek, Brussels; Kupferstichkabinett, Berlin; Landeshauptarchiv, Coblenz; New College, Oxford; Stiftsbibliothek, Heiligenkreuz; The Pierpont Morgan Library, New York; Trustees of the National Library of Scotland, Edinburgh; University Library Cambridge; University Library Glasgow; Westfälisches Archivamt, Münster.

ILLUSTRATIONS

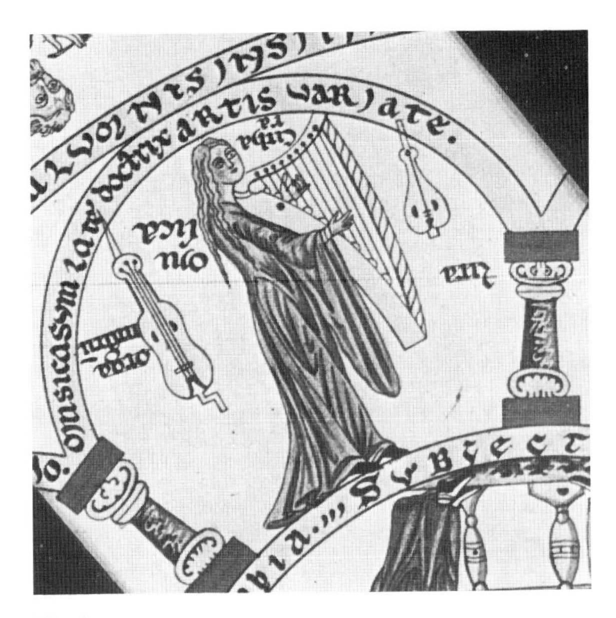

Ill. 1

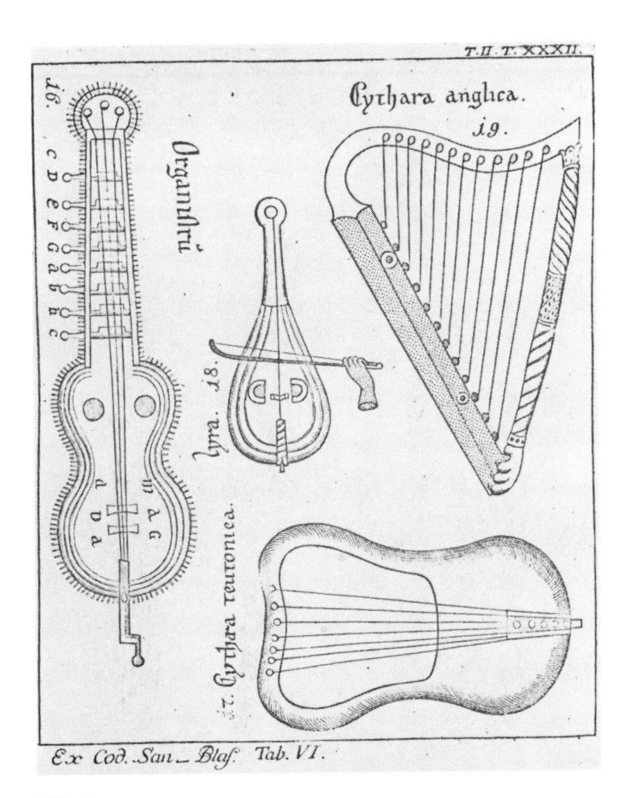
T.II. T. XXXII.
Cythara anglica.
19.
Organistrũ
16.
Lyra. 18.
17. Cythara teutonica.
Ex Cod. San_Blas. Tab. VI.

Ill. 2

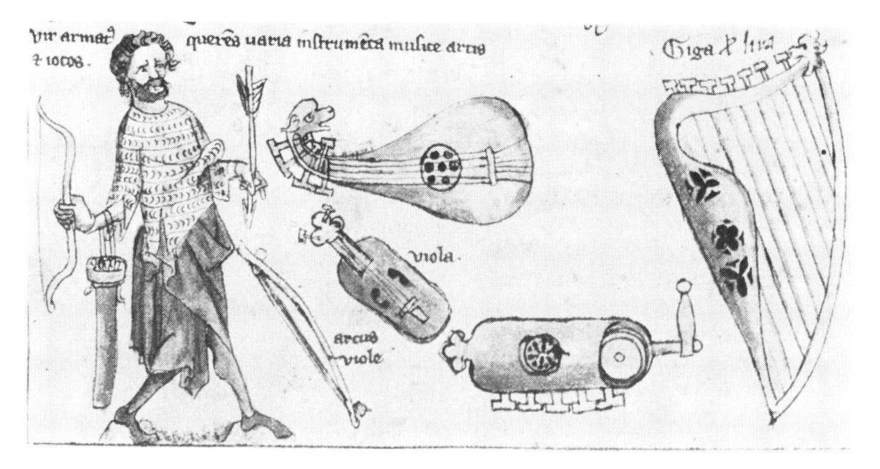

Ill. 3

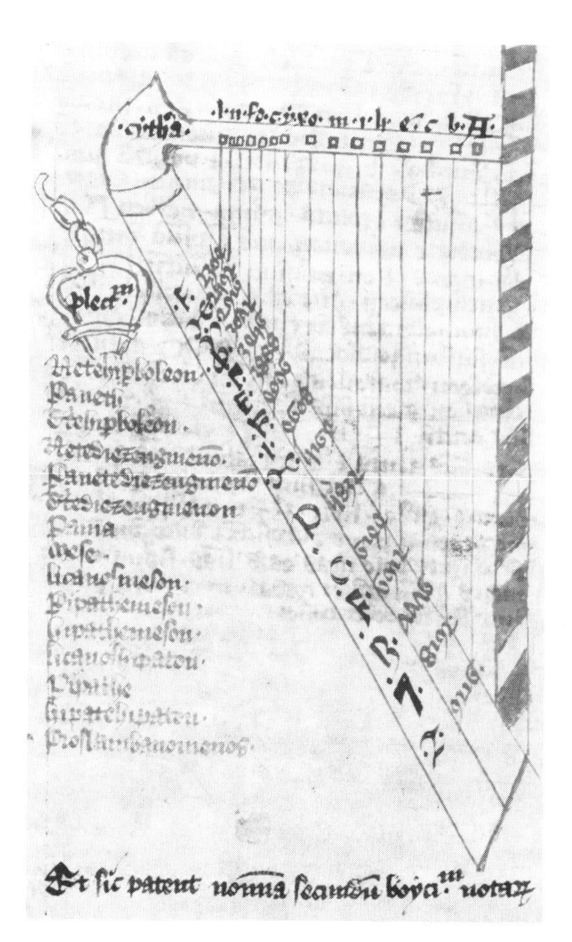

Ill. 4

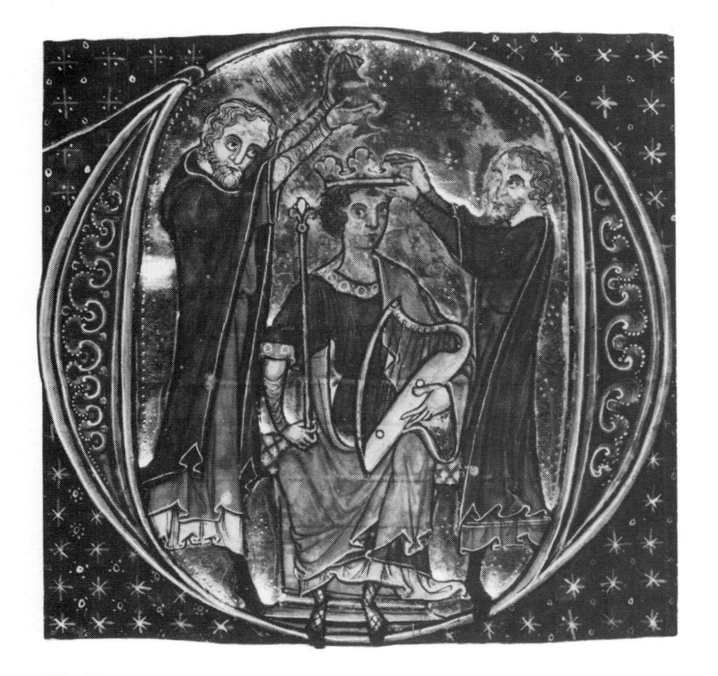

Ill. 5

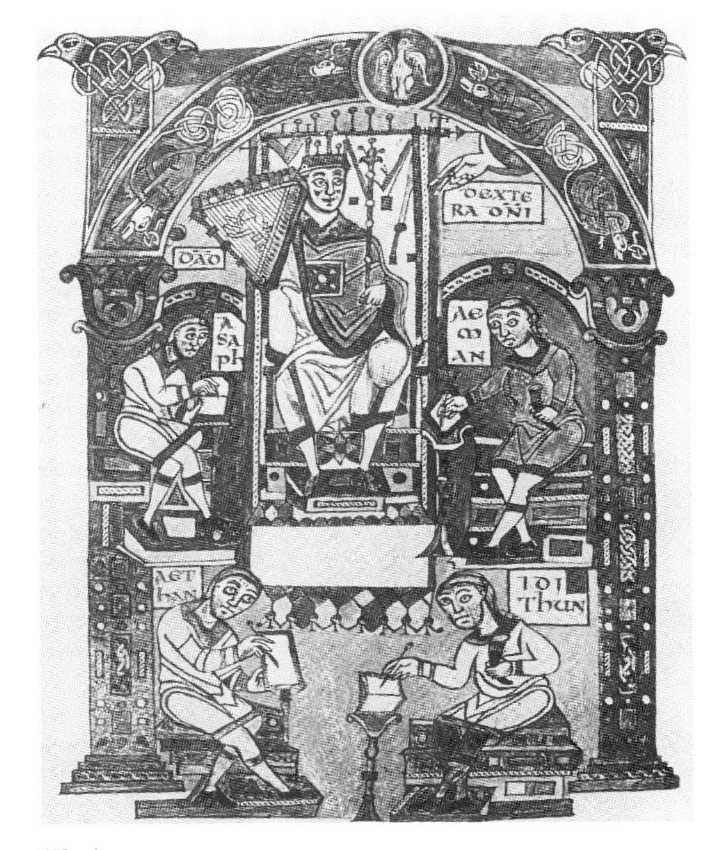

Ill. 6

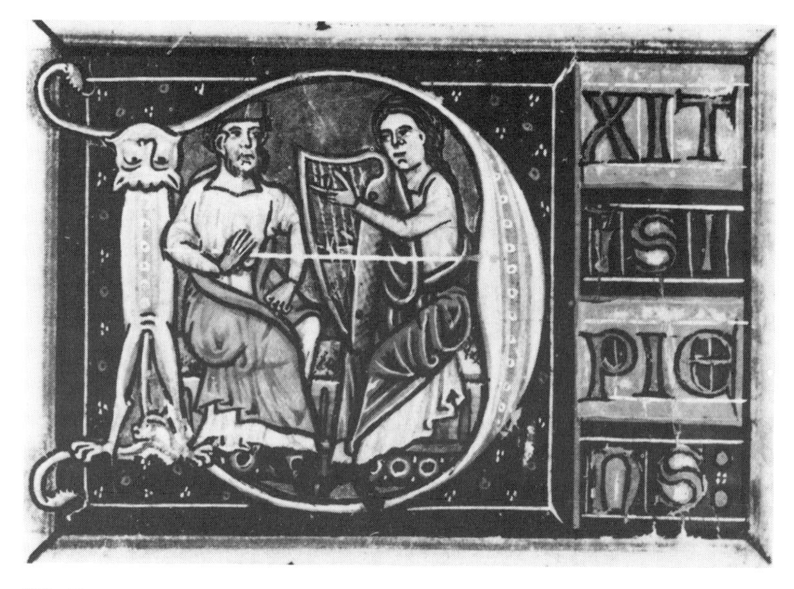

Ill. 7

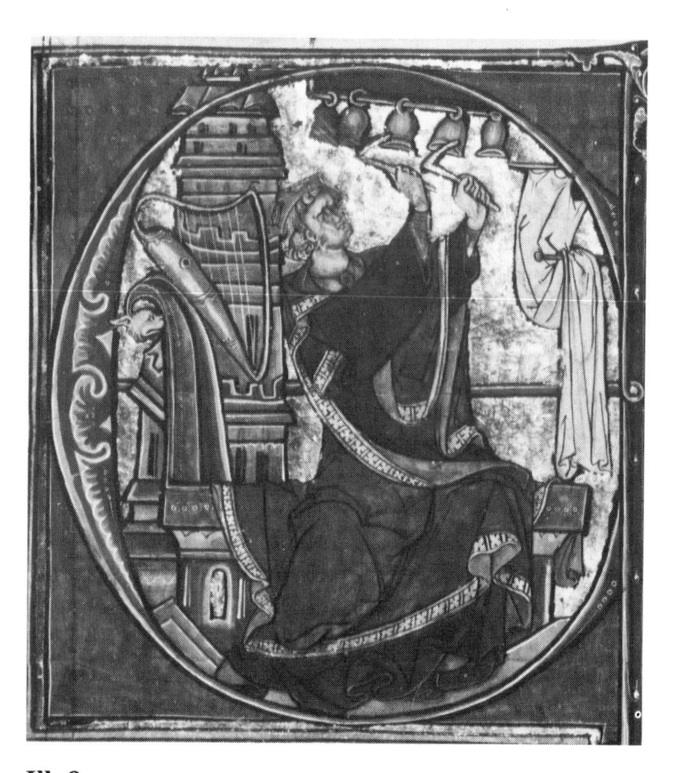

Ill. 8

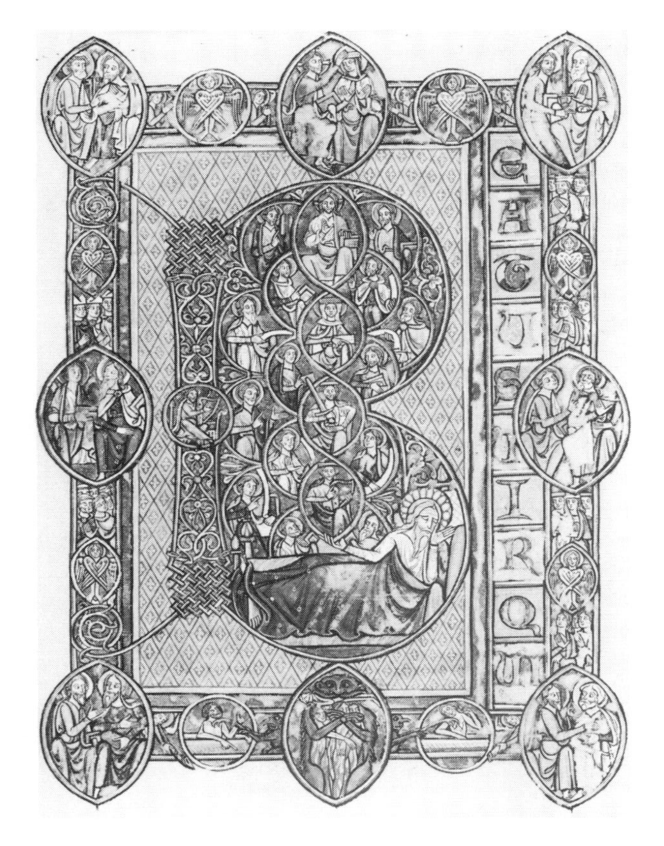

Ill. 9

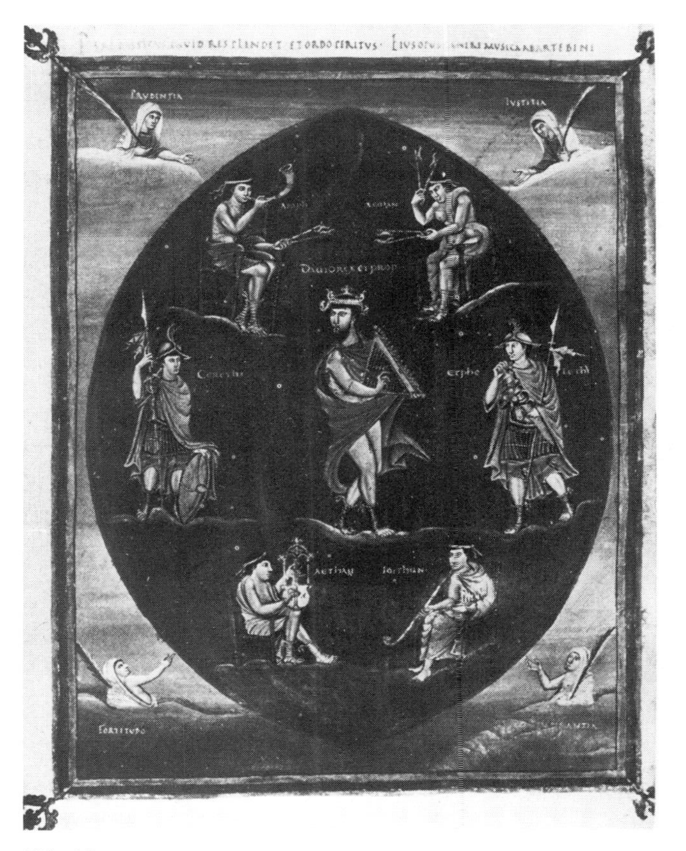

Ill. 10

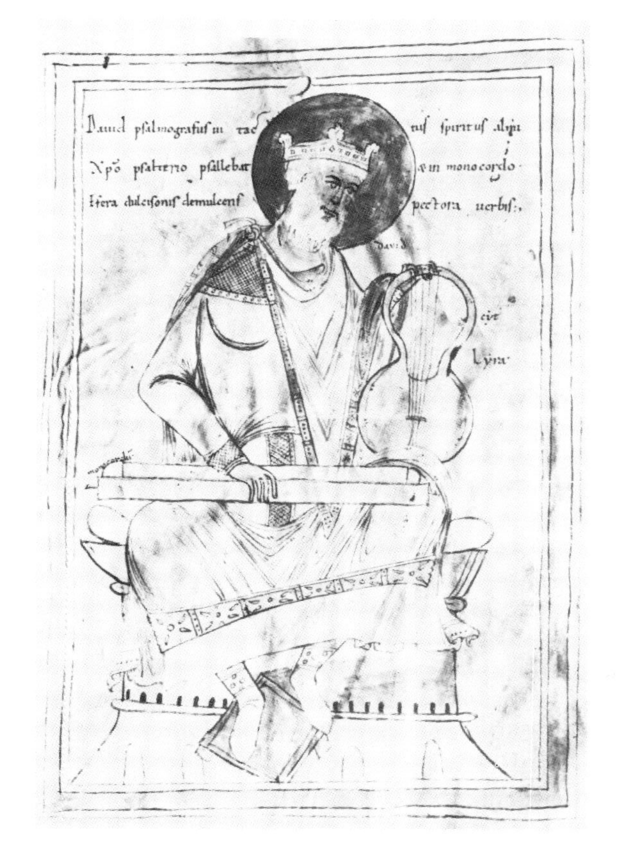

Ill. 11

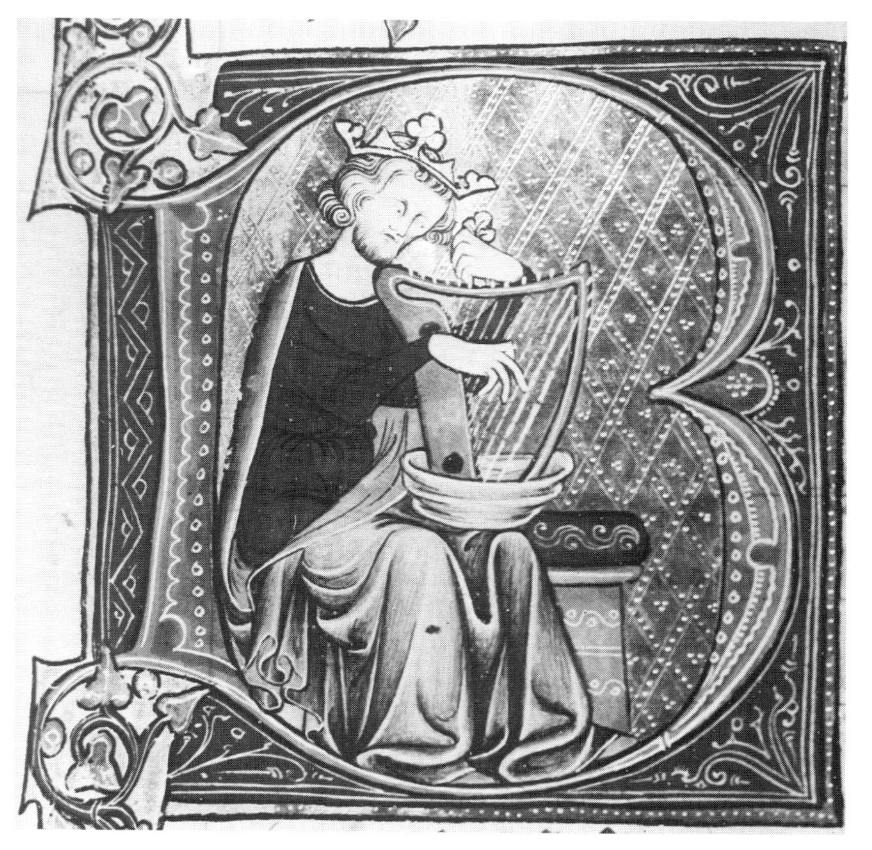

Ill. 12

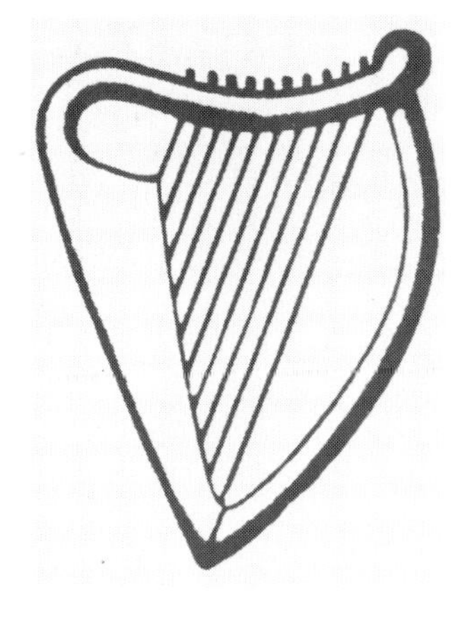

Ill. 13

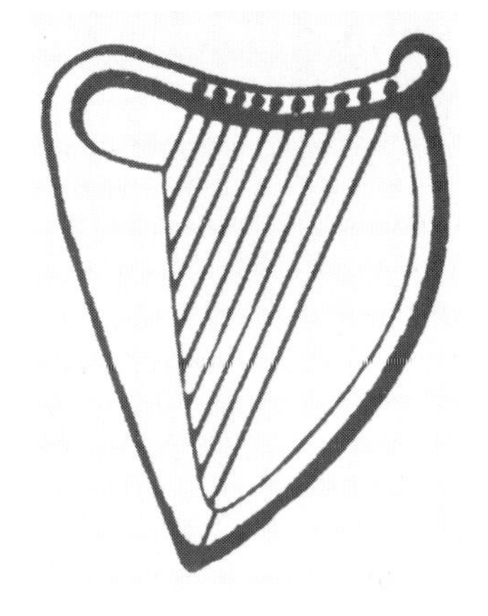

Ill. 14

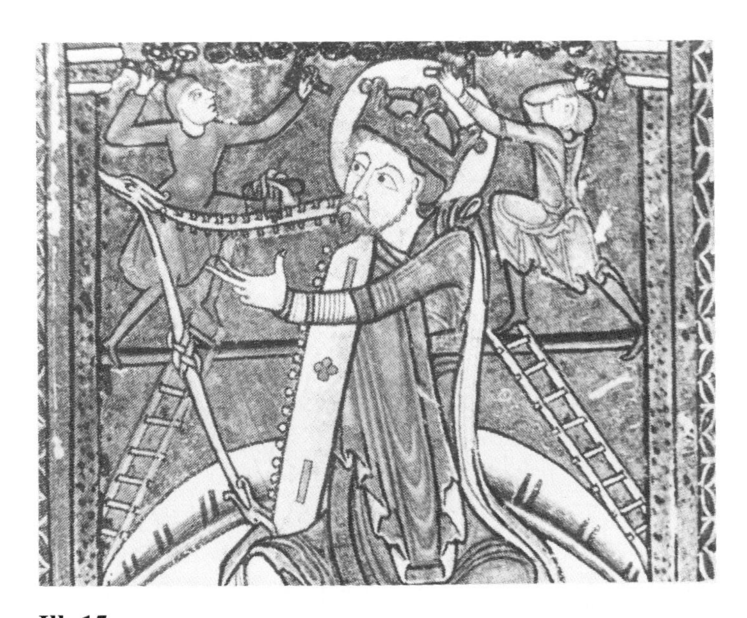

Ill. 15

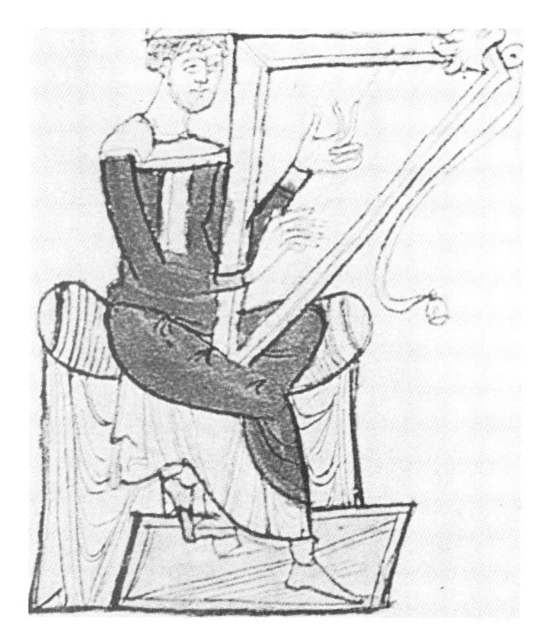

Ill. 16

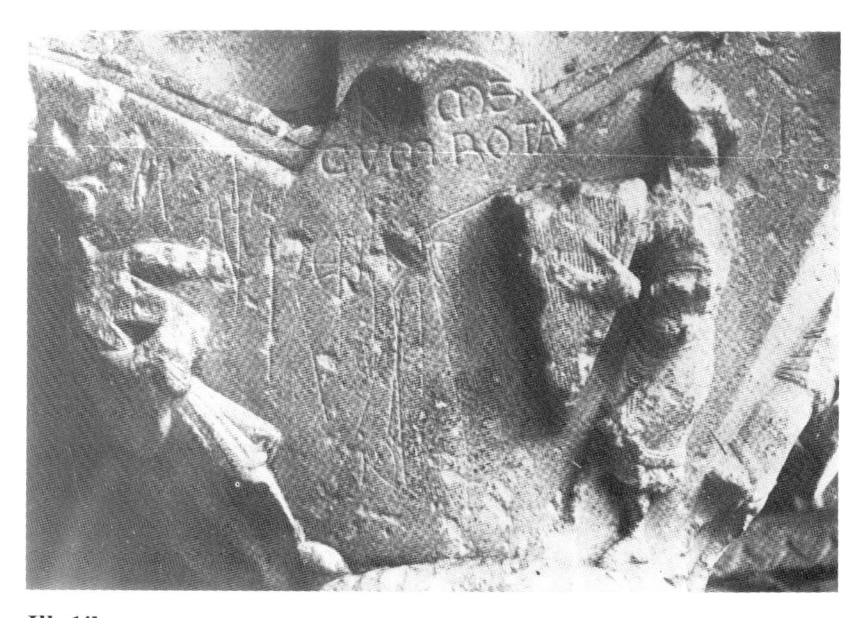

Ill. 17

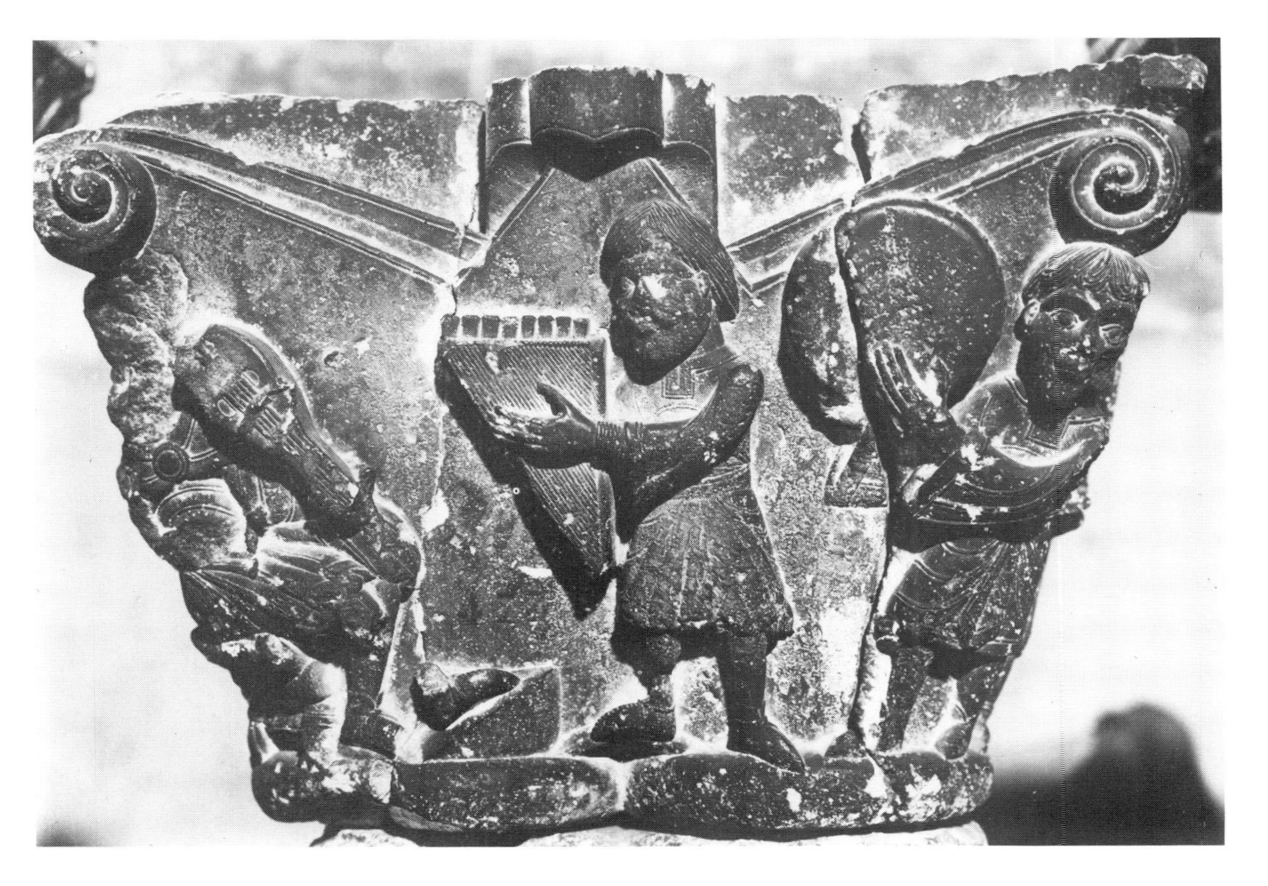

Ill. 18

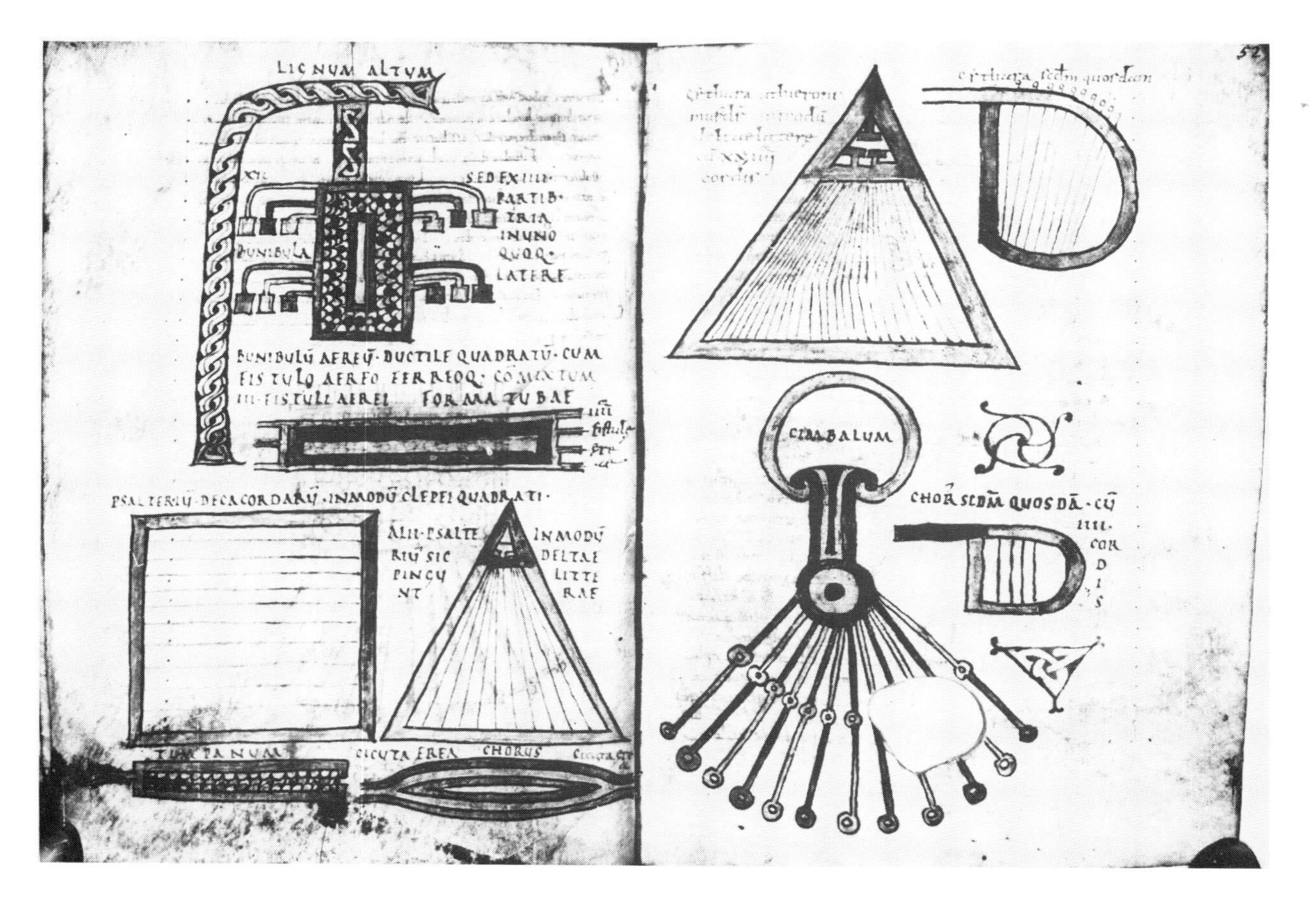

Ill. 19

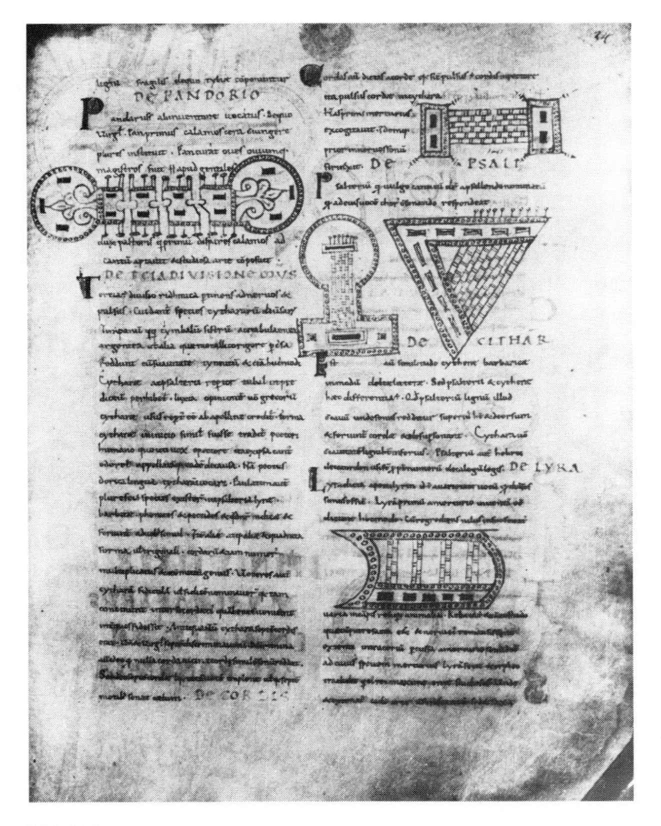
DE PANDORIO
DE PSALT
DE CITHAR
DE LYRA

Ill. 20

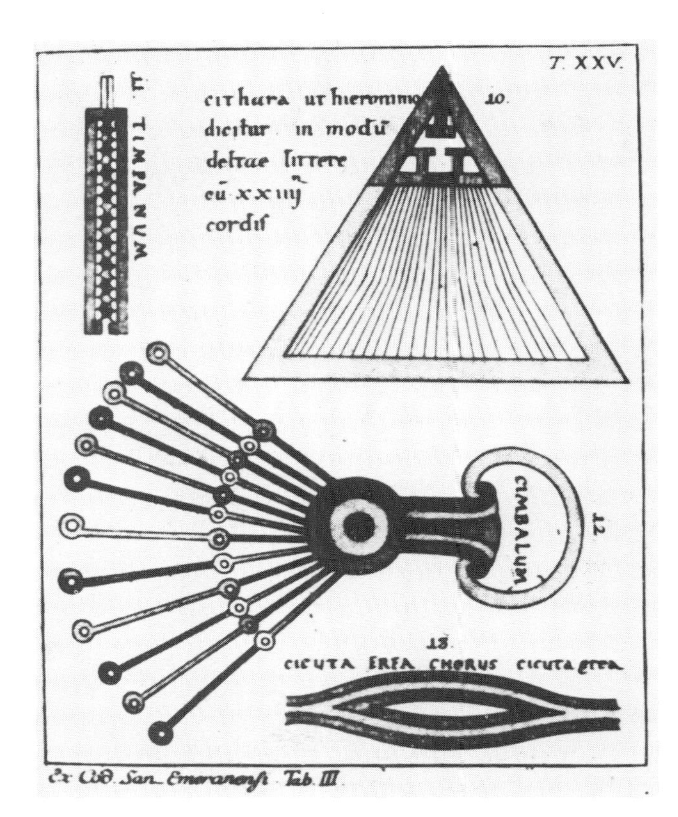
T. XXV.
10.
cithara ut hieronimo
dicitur in modū
deltae littere
cū xxiiij
cordis
11. TIMPANUM
12.
CIMBALUM
13.
CICUTA ERFA CHORUS CICUTA greca
Ex Cod. San. Emeranensi Tab. III.

Ill. 21

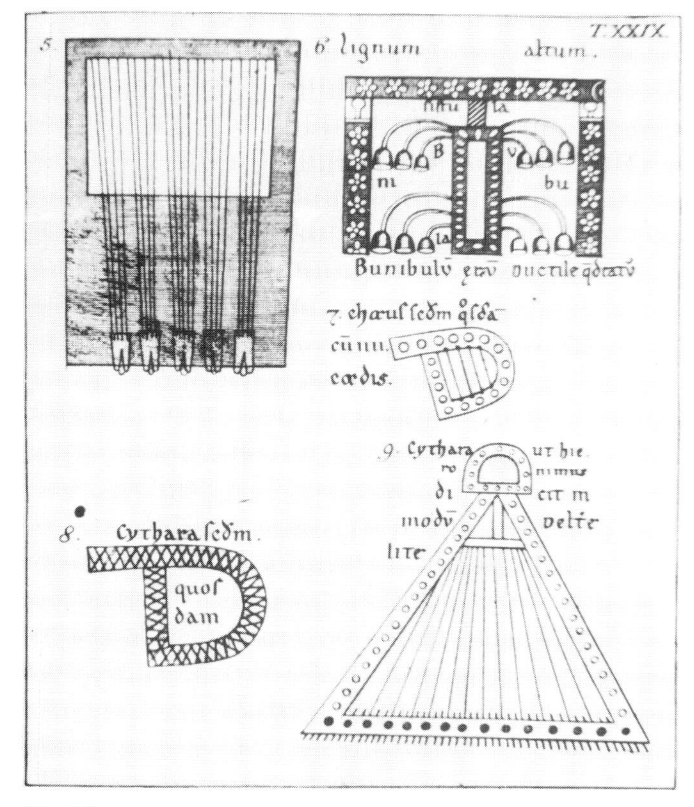
5.
6. lignum altum.
T. XXIX
8. Cythara sedm.
quos
dam
9. Cythara

Ill. 22

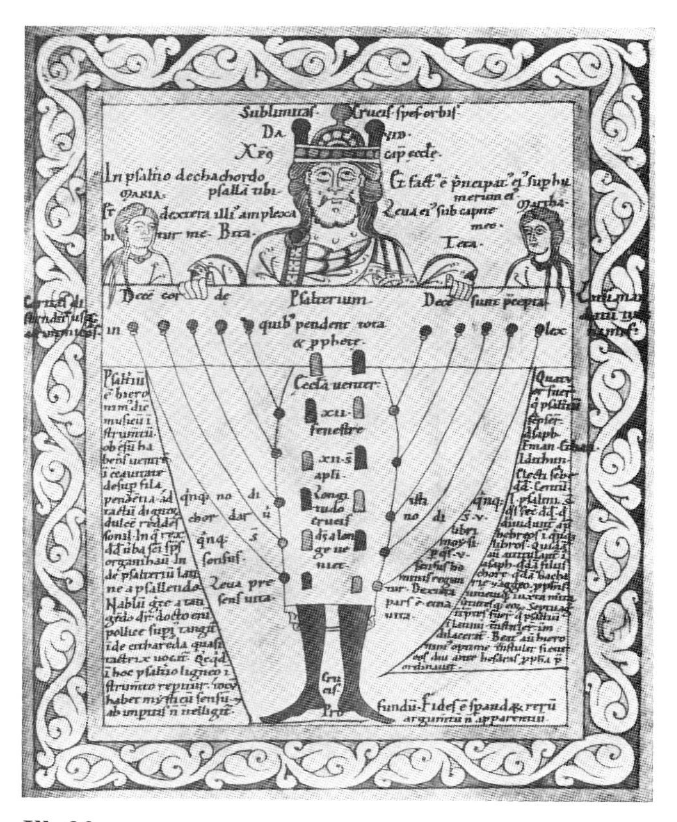
Psalterium.

Ill. 23

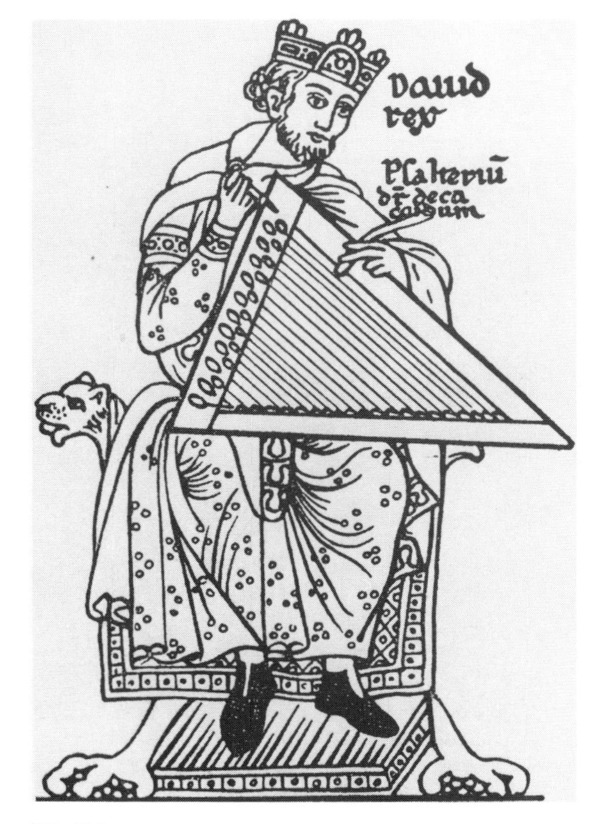

Ill. 24

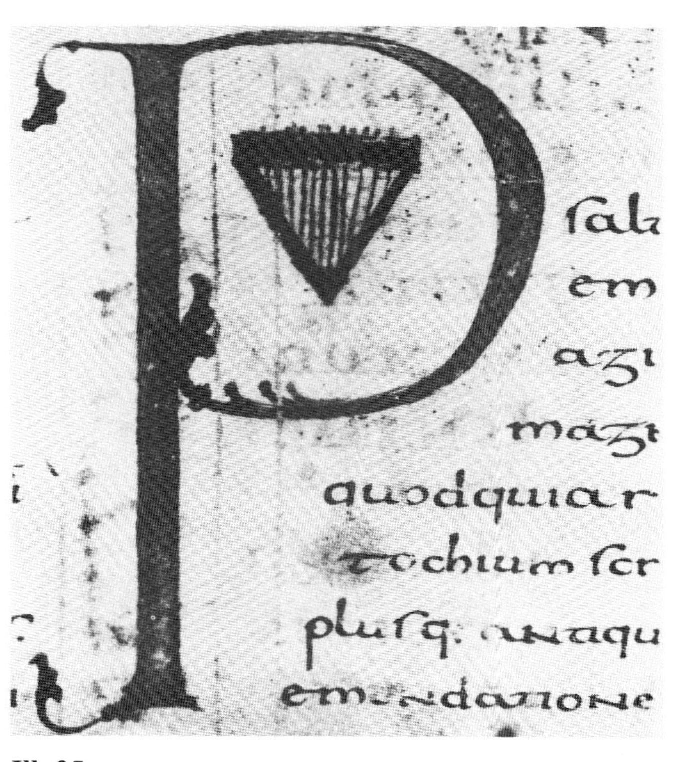

Ill. 25

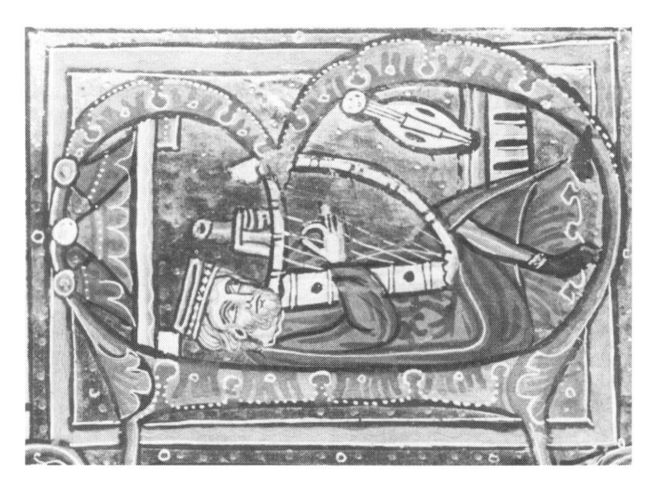

Ill. 27

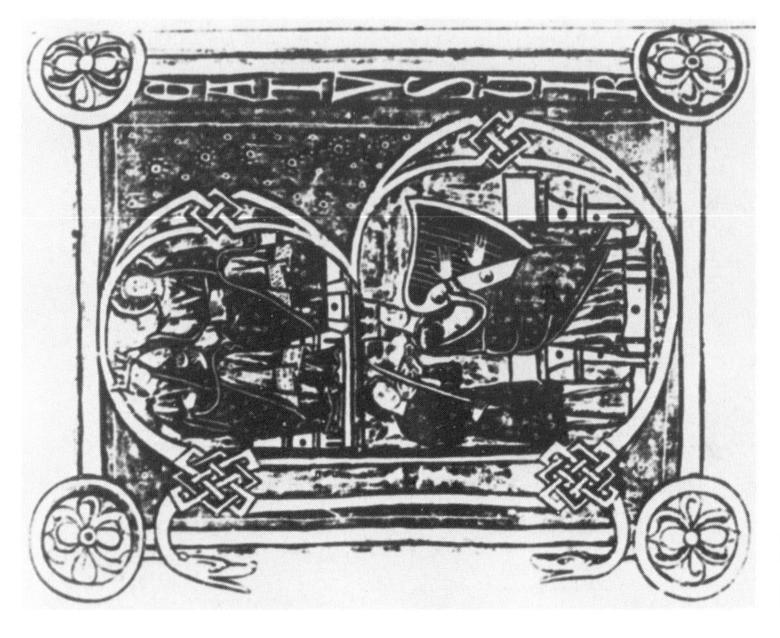

Ill. 26

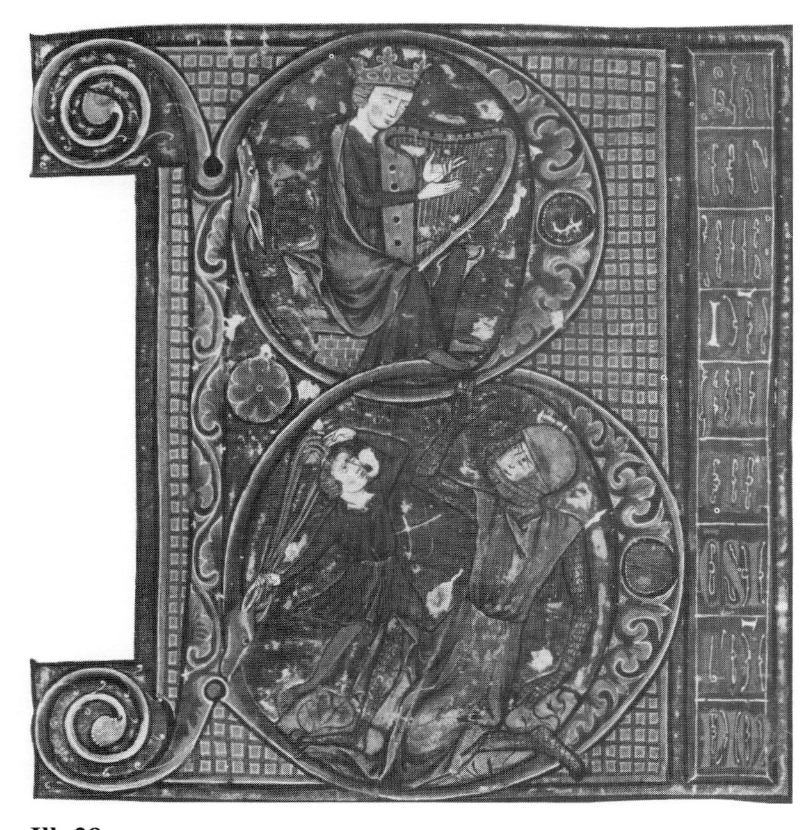

Ill. 28

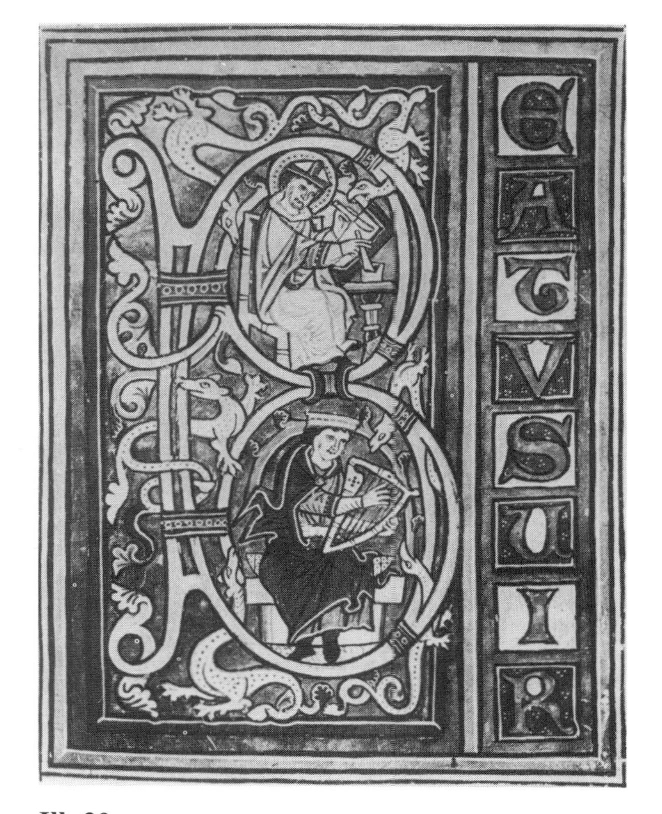

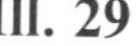

Ill. 29

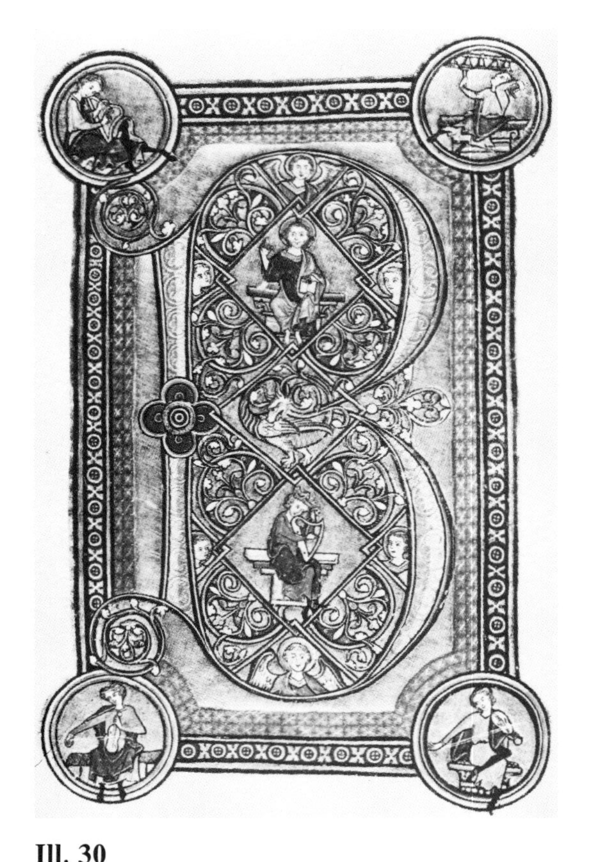

Ill. 30

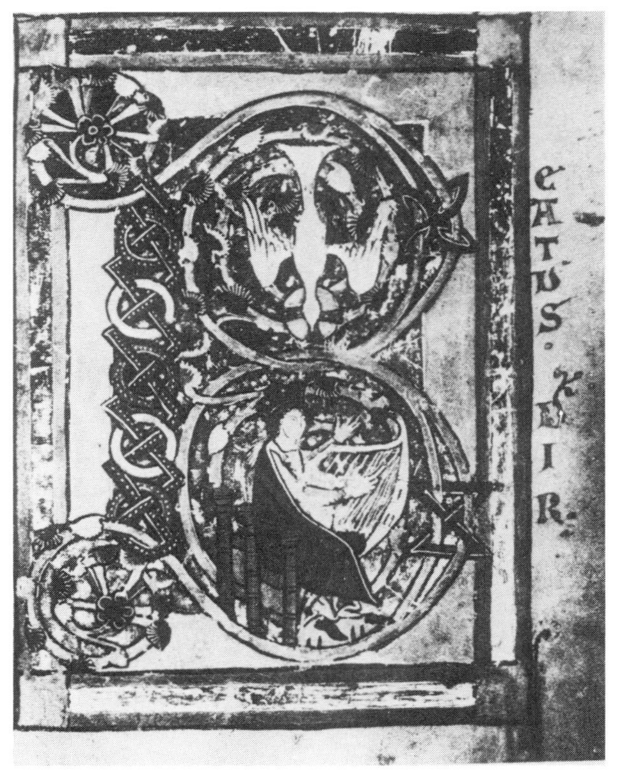

Ill. 31

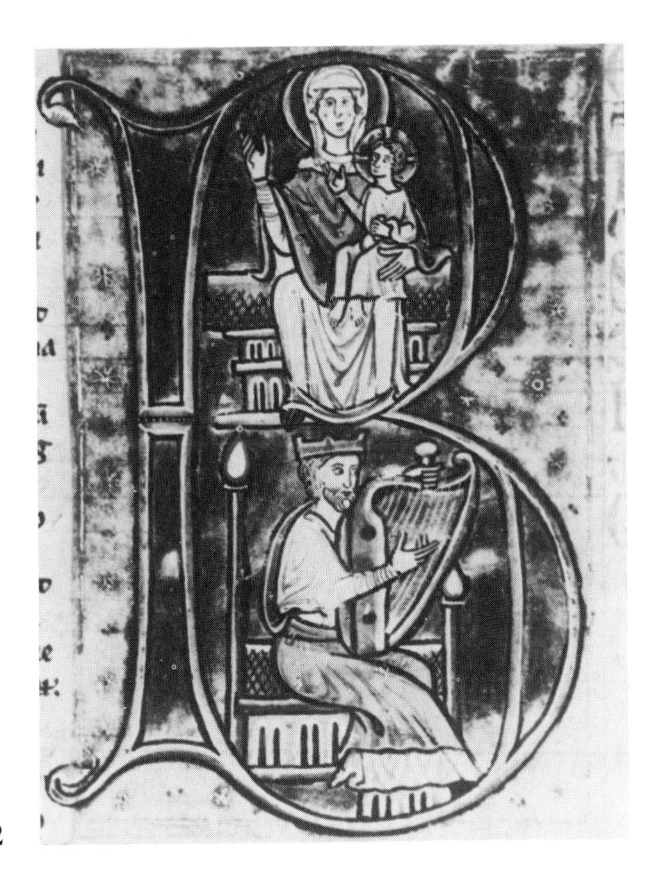

Ill. 32

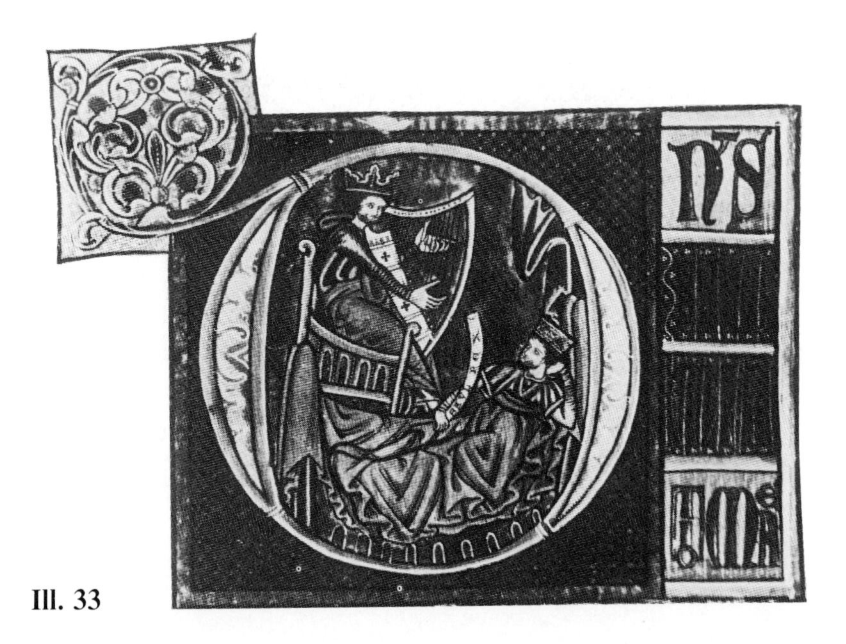

Ill. 33

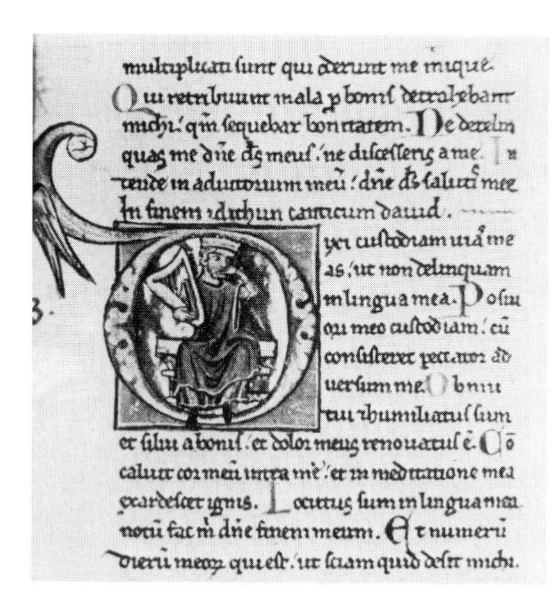

Ill. 34

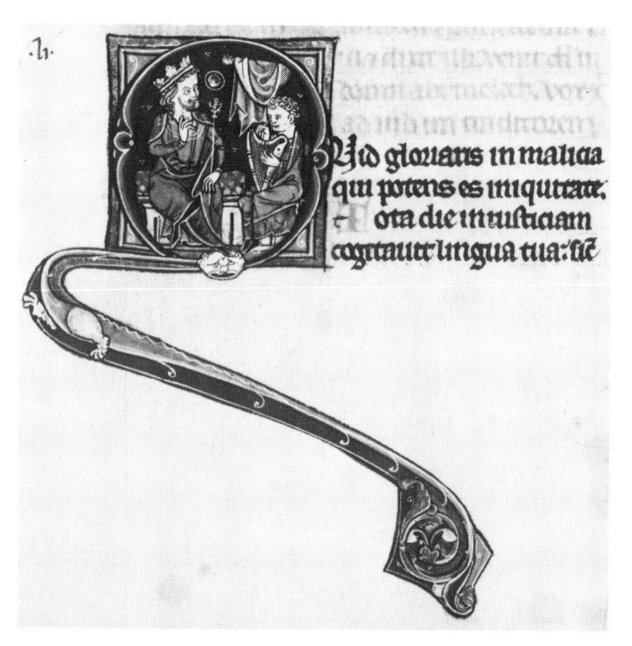

Ill. 35

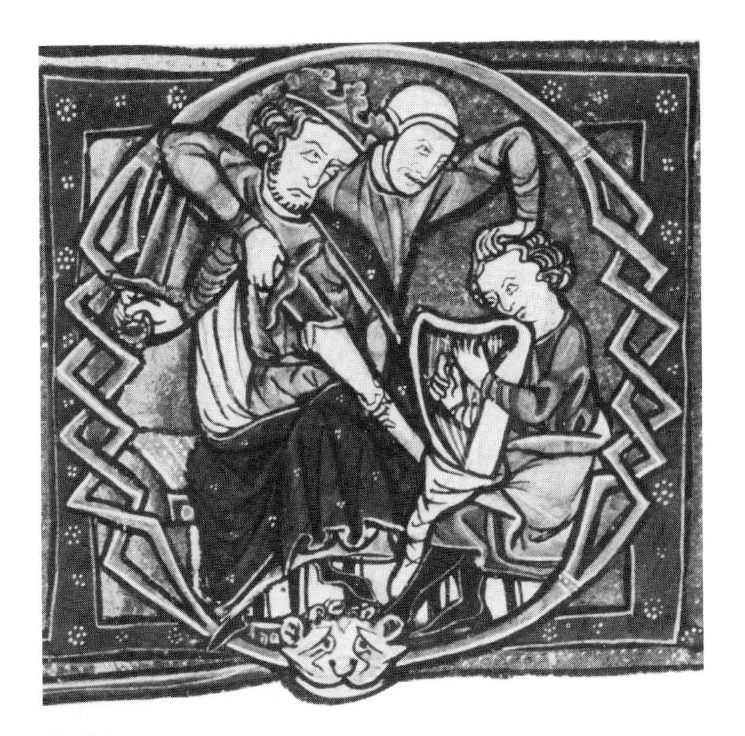

Ill. 36

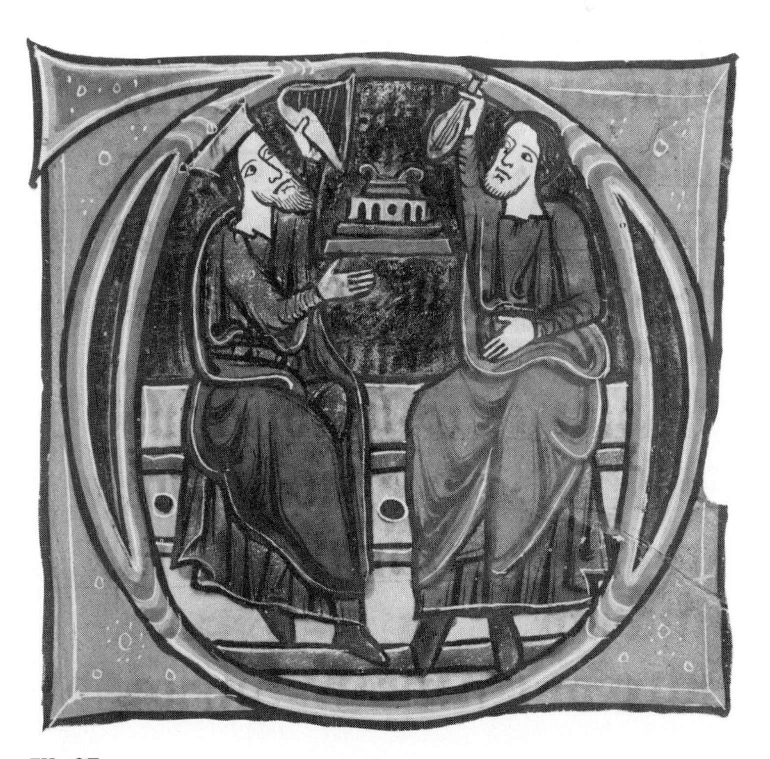

Ill. 37

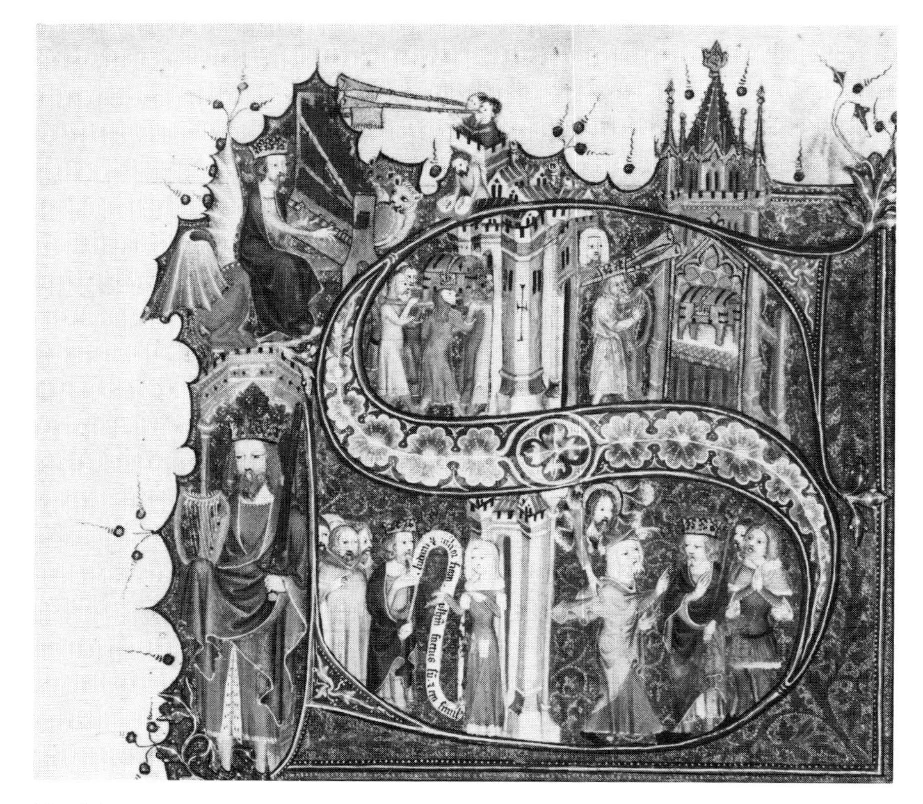

Ill. 38

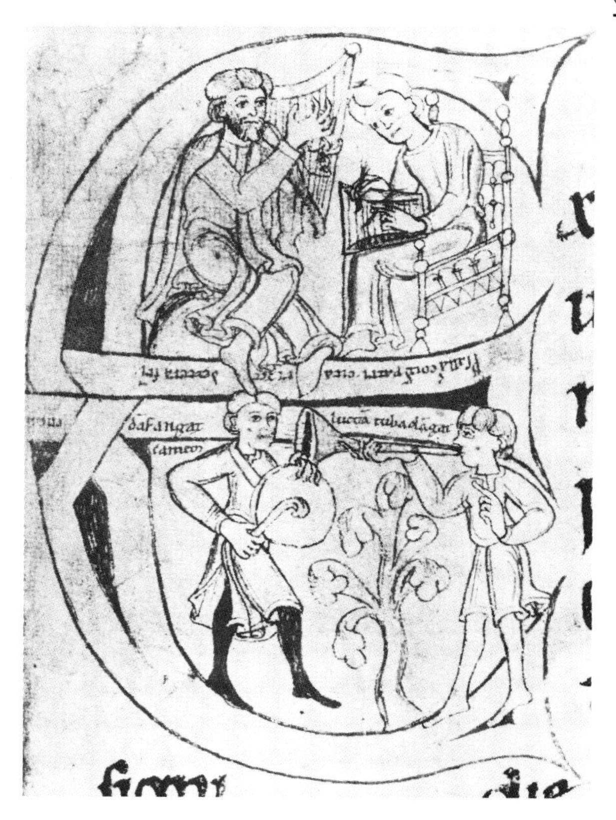

Ill. 39

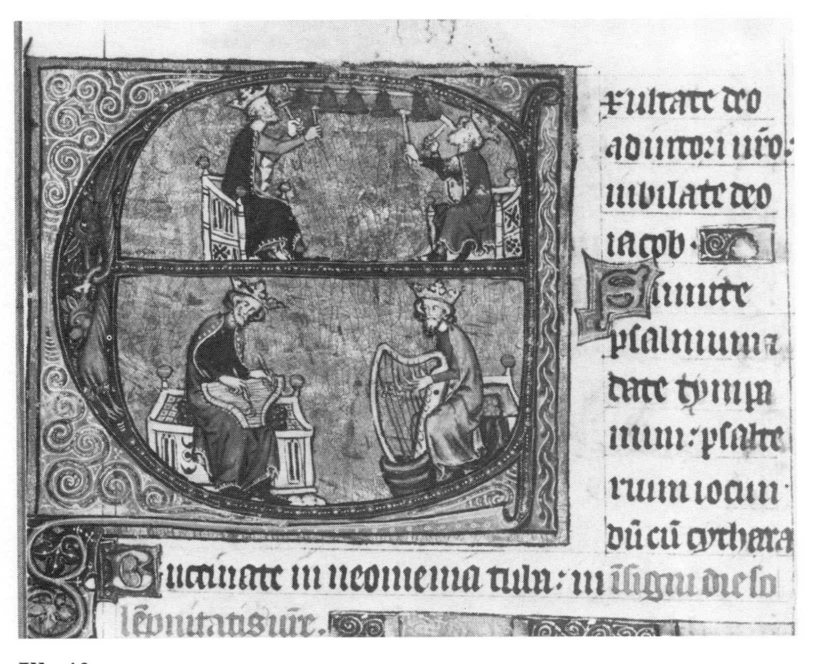

xultate deo
adiutori nro:
iubilate deo
iacob·
Sumite
psalmum
date tympa
num: psalte
rium iocun
dū cū cythara
Buccinate in neomenia tuba: in insigni die so
lempnitatis uře.

Ill. 40

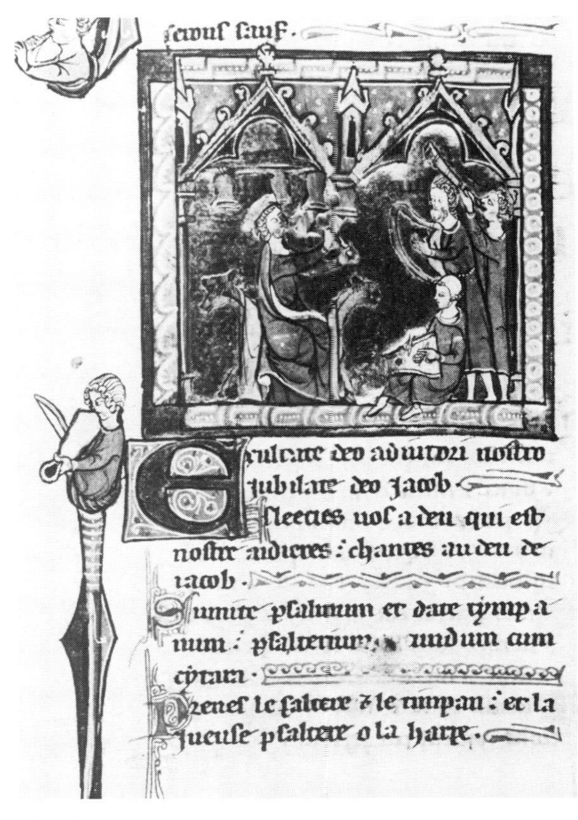

xultate deo adiutori nostro
iubilate deo Jacob·
sleecies vos a deu qui est
nostre aidieres: chantes au deu de
iacob·
Sumite psalmum et date tympa
num: psalterium iocundum cum
cytara·
Prenes le salteire & le timpan: et la
Jueuse psaltere o la harpe·

Ill. 41

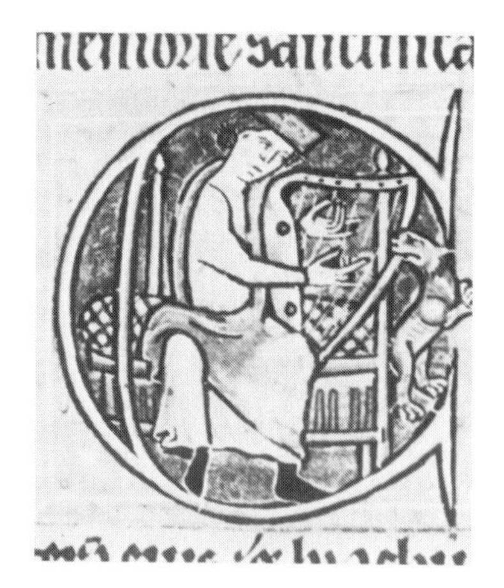

Ill. 42

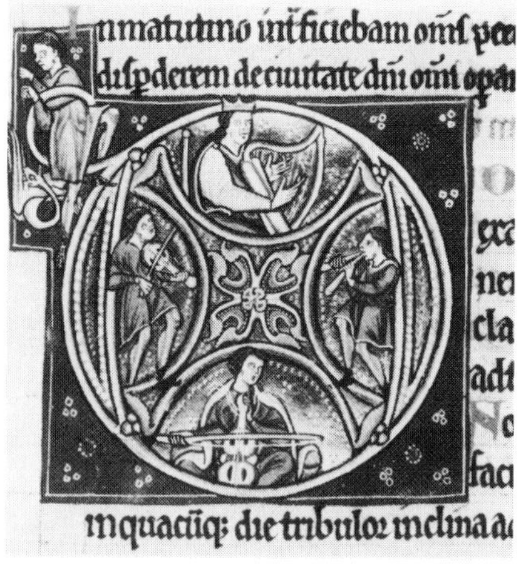

Ill. 43

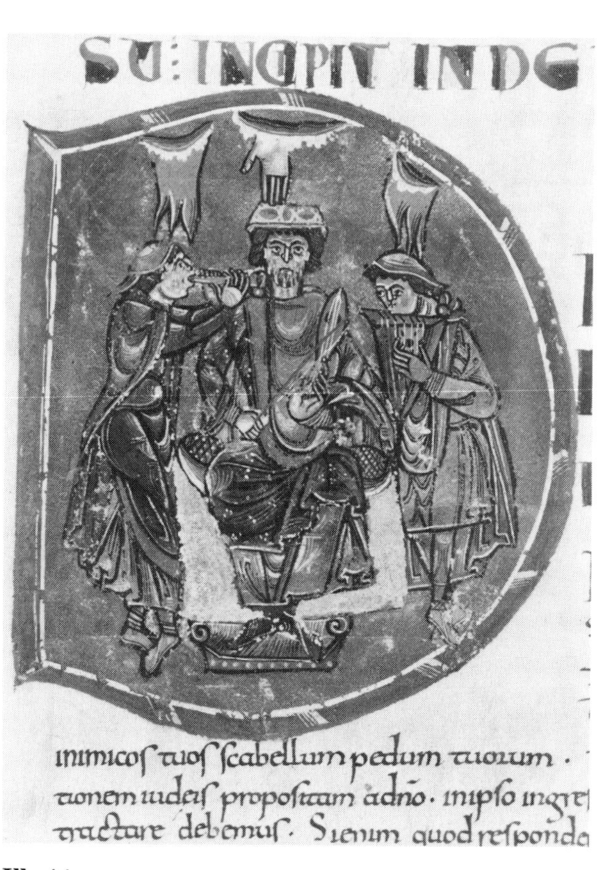

Ill. 44

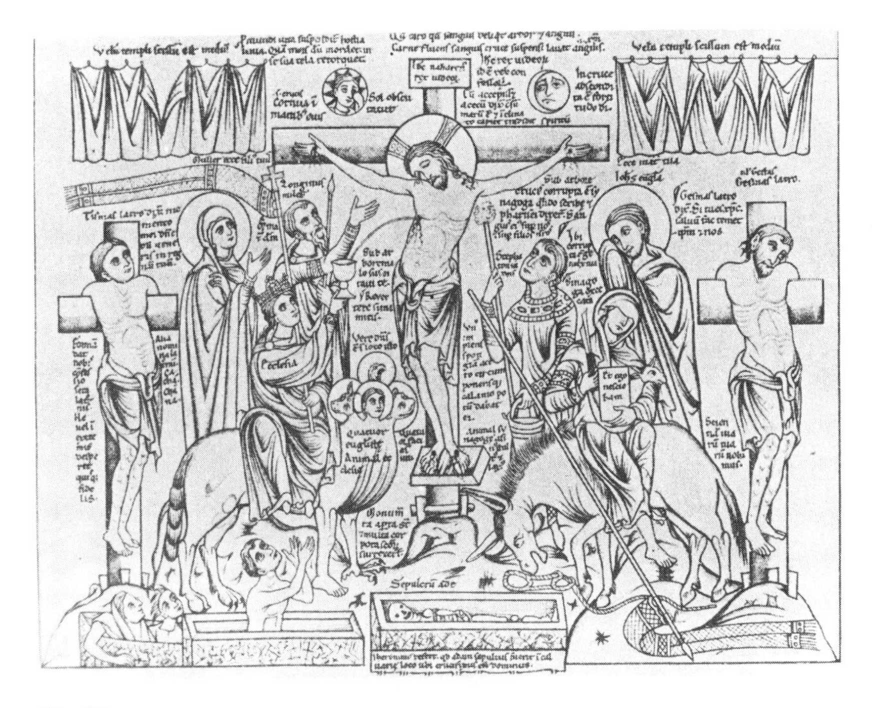

Ill. 45

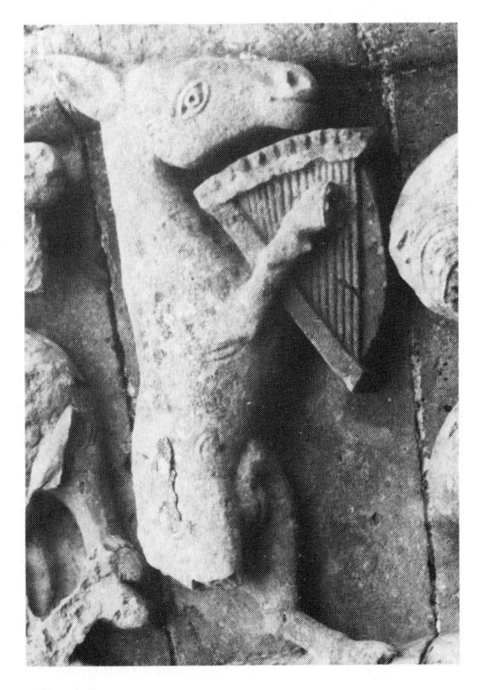

Ill. 46

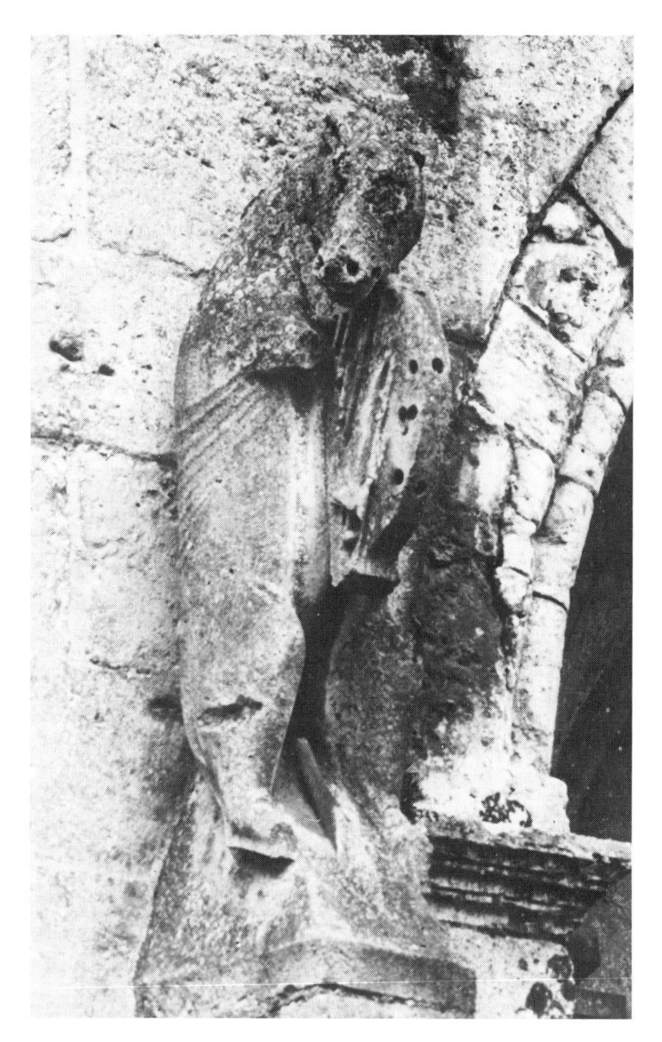

Ill. 47

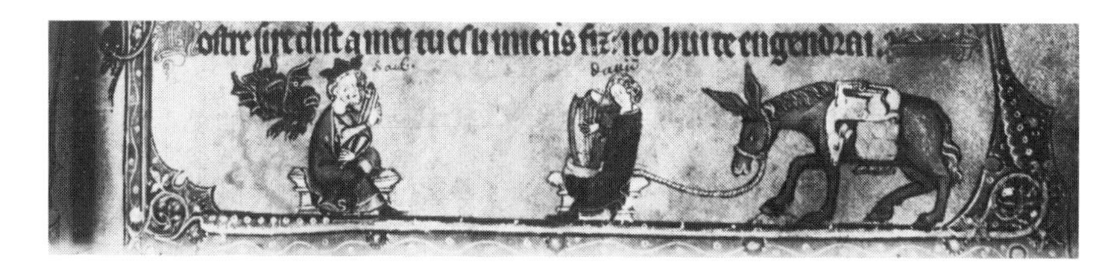

Ill. 48

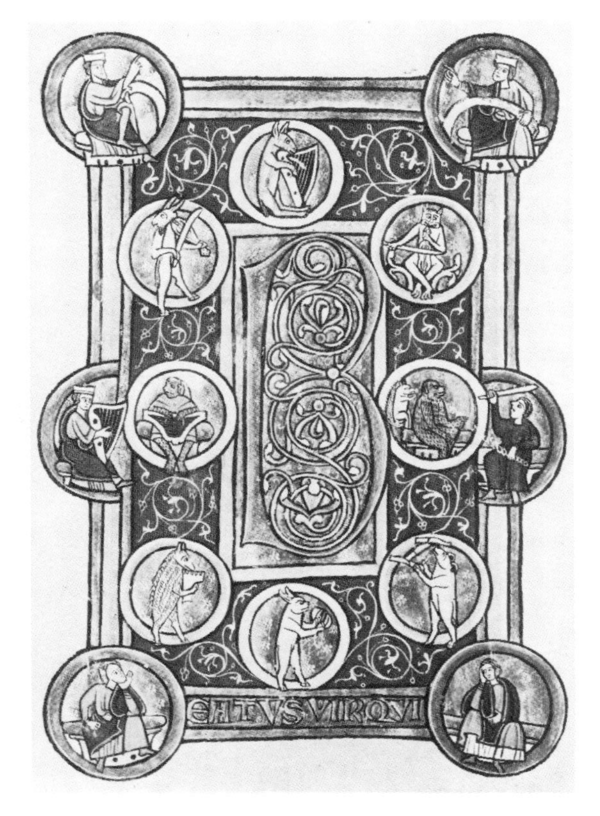

Ill. 49

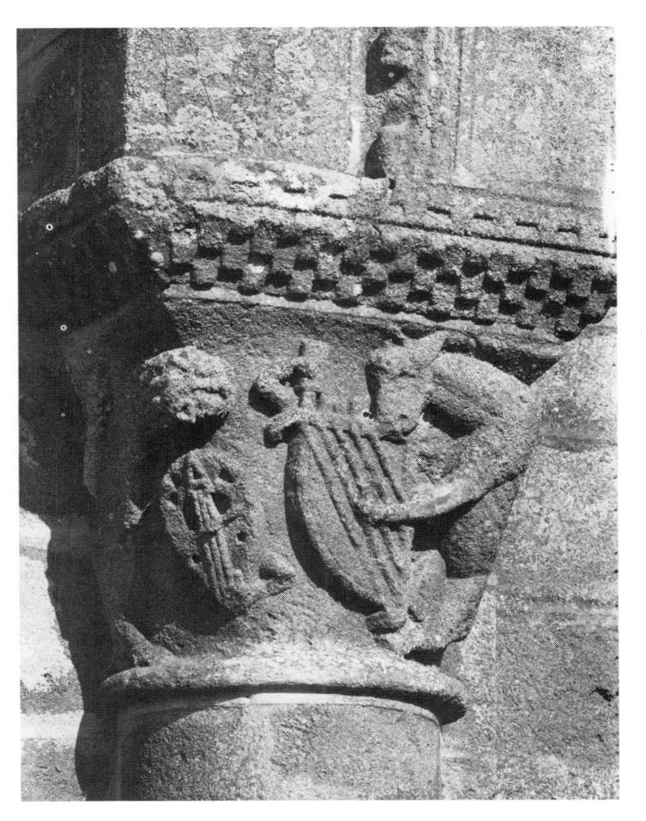

Ill. 50

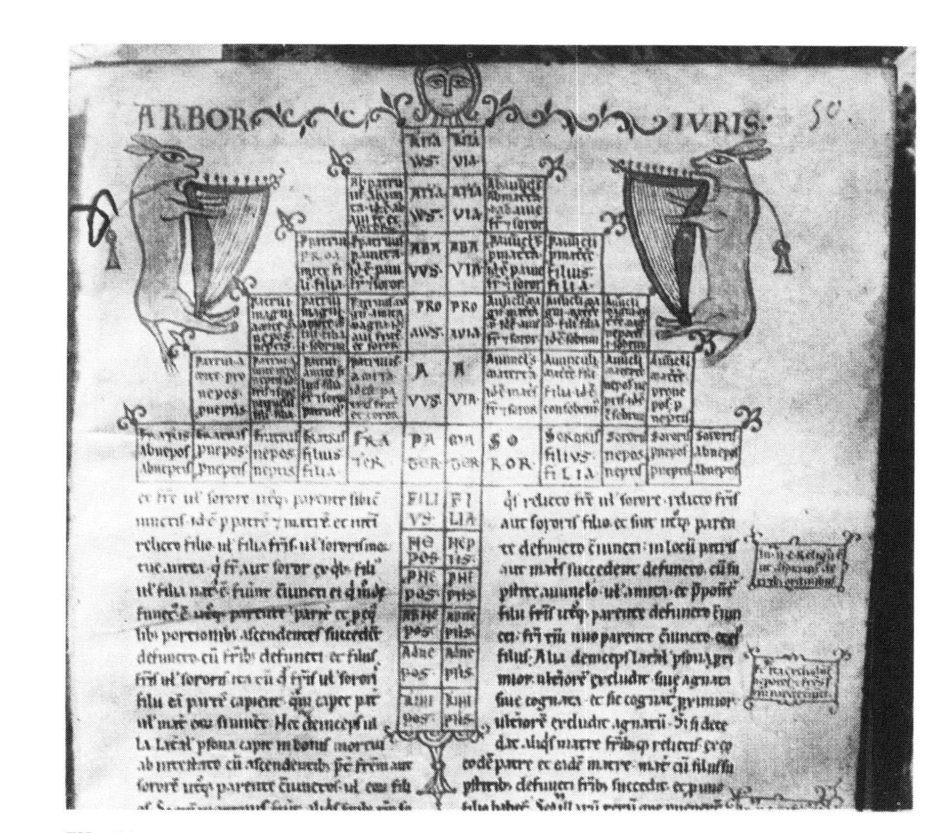

Ill. 51

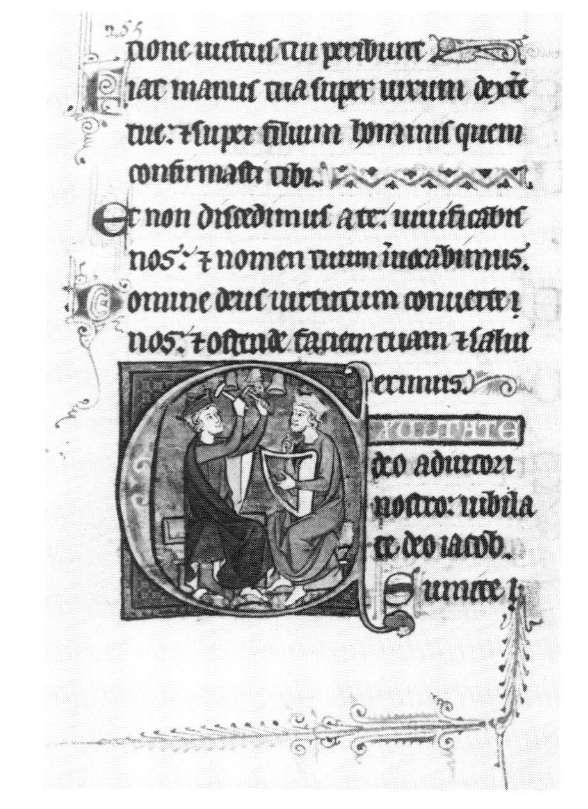

Ill. 52

INDEX

Abraham, 127
ADOLF, Helen, 116
Aelian, 127
Ahimelech, 104, 105
Albrecht, 33
Ambrose, 49
Anfortas, 33
arbor consanguinitatis, 133
Ark of the Covenant, 106
arpa, 18
Arpi (tribe), 18, 19, 36
Artes liberales, 32
Asaph, 48, 86
Asclepiades, 41
asinus ad lyram, 122, 124
ass, 127; (harp-playing) 116, 125, 128-9, 130-135; (lyre-playing) 117-24, 126, 135
Athanasius of Alexandria, 127
Augustine, 56, 98
Aurelianus of Réôme, 41, 45
bagpipes, 28
Bartholomaeus Anglicus, 56, 66, 72, 73, 74
bells, 107, 137, 138, 140
Bêne, 33
Benedict, (Rule of), 124
Bible moralisée, 110
BISCHOFF, Bernhard, 28
Boethius, 35, 41, 44, 46, 88, 121, 122, 123, 125, 136
Brian Boru-harp, 56
BROWN, Howard Mayer, 13
Bruno of Cologne, 137
Bruno of Segni, 112
Bruno of Würzburg 66, 71, 73, 111
Cain, 45
canticum novum, 111, 139
Cassiodorus, 41, 66, 70, 71, 72, 73, 82, 83, 84, 90, 103, 109, 112, 113
Cerethi, 48
Chaucer, Geoffrey, 123, 125
chelys, 24, 25, 27
CHESTER BEATTY, A., 84
Christ, 42, 43, 49, 79, 80, 84, 85, 90, 98, 104, 105, 106, 112, 113, 114, 127, 129; (Child) 101, 110, 111, 132, 133, 135; (*Corpus Christi*) 51, 82, 85, 88, 90; (Logos) 47, 50, 58, 100, 108, 113, 114-5, 138
Cicero, 44
cithara, 9, 16, 21, 22, 24, 25, 26, 27, 28, 32, 34, 35, 36, 37, 40, 42, 46, 48, 51, 55, 56, 62, 63, 64, 106, 107, 109, 111, 112, 133, 134, 136, 138, 139; (*barbarica*) 20, 65, 66, 68, 69, 72, 74; (delta shaped) 64, 65, 67, 68, 72, 73, 74, 75, 76, 77, 78, 79, 81, 82, 83, 84, 85, 86
citharista, 27
citre, 22
clavus, 55, 56
Clement of Alexandria, 41
column, 16, 17, 52
Complines, 93
concordia discors, 84
cornea, 48, 111
Cosmas of Prague, 123
cosmology, 47, 50
Criseyde, 125
crotta, 19, 28
crwth, 20, 49
cymbala, 43, 48, 51, 107, 108, 109, 136, 137, 138, 141
cynerum, 68, 72

cynira, 48, 49
cythara, 26, 36, 108
Cythara anglica, 32, 33
Cythara teutonica, 32, 33
Dardanus, 64, 65, 71, 74, 75, 79, 81, 85, 87, 88
David (King) 9, 11, 34, 37, 38, 40-8, 50, 51, 52, 57, 58, 59-61, 64, 70, 75, 80, 84-6, 88, 90, 92, 95, 102-5, 106-12, 116, 129-30, 132-5, 137, 138, 139, 140; (*figura* of Christ) 58, 84, 98, 100, 101, 108, 112, 132, 138; (*princeps musicus*) 99; (*propheta*) 97; (*rex*) 39, 86
David cycles, 96, 97
dekas, 77, 80
DIEFENBACH, Lorenz, 23, 24, 27
divisio instrumentorum, 136
Doeg, 104, 105
DROYSEN, Dagmar, 12
drum, 28
Duke of Rutland, 111
Ecclesia, 127, 133
Elders, 81, 90
Epiphany, 127
ESMEIJER, Anna, 62
Ethan, 48, 86
Eusebius of Caesarea, 82
evangelists, 49
exachordum, 27
fiddle, 36, 49, 113
flatus, 137
forepillar, 16
FOSTER, Genette, 12, 13,
Gabriel,
Gâwân, 33
gematria, 79
Gerbert, Martin, 32, 33, 65, 75
Gerhoh of Reichersberg 71, 73, 102, 103, 106, 109, 136, 137, 139
GIESEL, Helmut, 10, 63, 80
giga, 36
gîge, 20
God, 47, 49, 50, 78, 83, 90, 104, 106, 110, 113, 136, 137, 138, 139, 140, 141, 117, 127, 129, 134
Goliath, 38, 98, 99, 100, 104
Gottfried of Strassburg, 22, 53
Gôwerzîn, 33
Guido of Arezzo, 27, 40
HAMMERSTEIN, Reinhold, 38, 64, 116, 129, 131-2
harp, (attribute) 38, 39, 43, 58, 97, 101, 109; (delta harp) 49, 62, 63, 85, 86, 90; (English harp) 33; (etymology) 16, 20, 21, 22, 23, 25, 37; (neck) 51, 52, 53, 54, 55, 58; (quadrangular) 64; (Romanesque) 32; (strings) 16, 17, 26, 45, 50, 51, 53, 54, 56, 58, 88, 133, 134; (symbol) 9, 10, 14, 39, 58, 97, 109, 112, 137; (triangular) 48, 55; (tuning) 50, 51, 52, 53, 55, 99, 108, 113, 114, 133
harpa, 16, 17, 18, 19, 20, 21, 22, 23, 24, 25, 27, 28, 35, 36, 37, 68
**harpa*, 17, 18
harpfa, 21, 86
harpha (herphe), 26, 86
harppō* (harppōn*), 17, 18
harp-cither, 28
harp-psaltery, 17, 22, 70, 105, 113, 130-1, 133
hearp(an), 20, 22
HASELOFF, Günther, 91, 92, 105, 111
Heinrich of Hesler, 54
Heinrich of Neustadt, 20
Heinricus, 23, 26, 29, 31, 68, 71
Heloise, 124
Heman, 48, 86
Herod, 20
Herrad of Hohenburg, 32, 73, 127
Herrad of Landsberg, see Herrad of Hohenburg
hexachord (*hexachordum*), 27
Hilary of Poitiers, 82
HILDEBRANDT, Reiner, 26, 29, 31
Hippolytus, 49, 81, 82

historia, 110, 111
Holy Scriptures, 10, 11, 33, 43, 63, 64, 65, 69, 75, 77, 78, 79, 92, 95, 109, 112, 124
Holy Spirit, 41
Homer, 19
Honorius of Autun, 71, 73, 79, 80, 83, 98, 104
horn, 48, 111
Hugh of St. Victor, 78
Hugh of Trimberg, 9, 42, 128, 129
hurdy-gurdy, 28, 32, 36
ignorantia, 124, 129
Index of Christian Art, 11, 15
intentione, 137
Isaac, 127
Isabella of England (Queen), 131
Isidore of Seville, 20, 23, 25, 26, 27, 29, 31, 35, 41, 45, 66, 68, 69, 72, 73, 78, 82, 83, 88
Isolde, 22
Jacob, 107, 132
Jeduthan, 48, 86
Jerome, 62, 70, 71, 72, 74, 80, 119, 124, 127
Jerome of Moravia, 68, 73
Jesse, 132; see also *Stirps Jesse*
Jesus, 127
Johannes Aegidius of Zamora, 35, 41, 56, 66, 68, 72, 73, 74
Johannes Tauler, 128
John Lydgate, 126
John Scottus Eriugena, 120
Jonah, 106
Joseph, 127
Jubal, 45
KALUSCHE, Bernd, 13
kathismata, 93
**ker(b)*, 17, 18, 36
kinnor, 65, 66, 68
kinnyra, 67, 68
kithara, 26, 27, 65, 67, 68, 69, 74, 82
KLINGENDER, Francis, 116
**korbā*, 17, 18
**korbhnā*, 17, 18
Last Judgement, 111
laudatorium, 62, 66, 68, 70
Lauds, 93
Laurentius, 30
Levi, 48
Linus of Thebes, 35
lira, 32, 36, 121
liturgy, (Gallican) 93; (Roman) 93
lyra, 9, 16, 19, 20, 21, 32, 35, 50, 67, 117-25, 130, 135
lyra-harpa, 24
lyre, 20, 24, 28, 35, 41, 46, 49, 68, 117, 119-24, 131, 134
Macrobius, 44
macrocosmos, 41, 44, 50, 51, 58, 114, 138
Majestas Domini, 49
mandola, 35, 36
Marcus Terentius Varro, see Varro
Martianus Capella, 18, 19, 119, 120, 121, 122
Mary, 43, 101, 127
Matins, 93
McKINNON, James, 70
mensura, 58, 108, 136, 138, 139; (*diametri*) 139, 140
MERINGER, Rudolf, 17
Michael of Meaux, 55, 56
microcosmos, 39, 41, 42, 58, 113, 114-115, 132
Milo of St.-Amand, 20
monochord, 35, 46, 50, 138
Moses, 44, 45
musa, 25
musica mundana, 139
nabla(th), 65, 66, 67, 69
nablon, 65, 69
nablum, 65, 66, 68, 69, 70, 72
nagel, 53, 54
nebel, 62, 66, 67, 69, 70, 72, 80, 90
Nicetas of Remesiana, 42
Nicomachus of Gerasa, 44
Nonius, 118, 119
Notker Teutonicus, 21, 22, 66, 73, 76, 79, 121
numerical symbolism, 77-81;

(number 3) 78-79; (number 4) 79-80; (number 10) 80-81; (number 24) 81
numerus, 138, 139, 140
Office, 92
OKKEN, Lambertus, 118, 119, 122, 123
ὄνος λύρας, 14, 116, 117, 118, 119, 121, 122, 123, 130, 134, 135
ordo, (divine) 51, 114, 136, 140, 141
organ, 46, 51, 137, 138, 141
organistrum, 32
organon, 69
organum, 65, 66, 67, 68, 69, 136, 138, 139
Origo Psalmorum, 48, 69
Orpheus, 41
PAGE, Christopher, 13, 55, 56
Pandarus, 125
Papias, 18, 25, 36
Paul, 129
peg arm, 16, 17, 51, 74
percussio, 137
percussion instruments, 138
Perotti, Niccolo, 117
Peter Abelard, 124
Peter Comestor, 45
Peter Lombard, 76, 84, 97, 109
Phaedrus, 117, 118
Phelethi, 48
Philippe de Thaon, 125
Philo of Alexandria, 40, 58
Philosophia, 122
PICKERING, Frederick, 12, 62, 85
Plato, 40, 58
plectron, 68
plectrum, 26, 31, 53, 55, 56, 57
POKORNY, Julius, 57
pondus 138, 139
prefiguration, 58, 90, 109, 110, 112, 114, 115
Prudentius, Aurelius Clemens, 23, 24, 25, 27, 29, 30, 31
Psalter plan, 93, 94
psaltērion, 67, 69, 70, 82, 90
psalterium, (instrument) 9, 16, 20, 21, 22, 27, 46, 48, 51, 62, 63, 64, 65, 66, 67, 68, 69, 72, 74, 107, 109; (book) 92; (delta shaped) 70, 73, 74, 75, 76, 77, 78, 79, 81, 82, 83, 84, 85, 86, 90, 113; (*psalterium decachordum*) 68, 69, 80, 84, 86
psaltery, 35, 48, 50, 106, 108; (triangular) 46, 62, 64
pseudo-Bede, 48, 49, 66, 71, 72, 73, 81
pseudo-Jerome, 64, 66, 73
pseudo-Odo, 140
pseudo-Thomas Aquinas, 123
pulsu, 137
Pythagoras, 44, 45, 46, 58, 139
Pythagorean (teaching) 40; (theory of numbers) 77, 78; (proportions) 50, 138
Raban Maurus, 64, 66, 68, 72, 73, 74, 79, 127
RANDALL, Richard, 116
rattle, 29
Regino of Prüm, 21, 25, 44, 124
Remigius of Auxerre, 18, 19, 65, 66, 71, 73, 83, 120, 121, 122
RENSCH, Rosalyn, 12, 20, 62, 116
RIEDEL, Herbert, 34
Romanus, 30
rot(t)a, 28, 46, 64, 66, 68, 69, 70
rotte, 20, 46, 68
Rudolf of Ems, 34
Rupert of Deutz, 73, 76
saltyre, 22
sambiût, 20
sambuca, 25, 27
sambykē, 25
Samuel, 101
Saul (King), 34, 37, 40, 41, 42, 58, 95, 102, 103, 104, 105, 109, 110, 112, 132
SEEBASS, Tilman, 12, 13, 46
seitenspil, 42
Sekundille, 33
SENDREY, Alfred, 69

SIEVERS, Eduard, 23, 28
significatio, 11
singing, 19, 21, 31, 41, 43, 47, 64, 86, 112; (clerics) 51, 108, 109, 111, 127, 137, 139, 141
sistrum, 28, 29
Solomon, 43, 102, 103
sound box, 16, 17, 51, 56, 76
sound chest, 26, 68, 82
spiritus, 137
STARCK, Taylor, 23
STEGER, Hugo, 11, 12, 13, 39, 62, 63, 92
STEINMEYER, Elias, 23, 28
Stirps Jesse, 43, 61, 100; see also Jesse
stringed instruments, 138
strings, (delta shaped instruments) 75, 76, 77, 78, 81, 82, 83, 89, 90; (harp-psaltery) 130; see also harp strings
symphonia, 28, 136
Synagogue, 127, 132, 133
swalwe, 33, 34
Tauler, see Johannes Tauler
ten commandments, 81, 112
tensibilia, 21
testudo, 24, 27
tetraktys, 77, 80
tetramorph, 127
trigōnon, 70
Trinity, 62, 63, 78, 79, 85, 90, 113; (of instruments) 140
tripartition, (of instruments) 138
Tristan, 53, 54
Troilus, 125
trumpet, 48, 107, 108, 111, 112
tuba, 107, 108, 111
Tubal(-cain), 45, 46
tuning, (key) 31, 50, 51, 52, 54, 55, 56, 57, 59; (peg) 51, 52, 53, 54, 55, 56, 57, 58, 74, 75, 82; (pin) 51, 54, 55, 57; see also harp tuning
tympanum, 28, 107, 108
Varro, Marcus Terentius 118, 119
Venantius Fortunatus, 19
Vespers, 93
videl, 20
VITALE-BROVARONE, Alessandro, 122
VORREITER, Leopold, 12, 62
Walafrid Strabo, 66, 73, 74
WELLS, J., 23
Willelmus, 36, 56
William of Aragon, 123
wind instruments, 138
wirbel, 54
Wolfram of Eschenbach, 33
wrast, 57
wreistel, 57
wrest, 57
ZINGEL, Hans, 12, 13, 38